Y0-ABP-986

The Garland Library of War and Peace

The Garland Library of War and Peace

Under the General Editorship of

Non-Violent Coercion

A Study in Methods of Social Pressure

by

Clarence Marsh Case

with a new introduction
for the Garland Edition by

A. Paul Hare

Garland Publishing, Inc., New York & London
1972

Library of Congress Cataloging in Publication Data

Case, Clarence Marsh, 1874-1946.
Non-violent coercion.

(The Garland library of war and peace)
Includes bibliographical references.
1. Nonviolence. I. Title. II. Series.
HM278.C36 1972 301.6'32 71-147615
ISBN 0-8240-0372-1

Printed in the United States of America

Editor's Preface

Non-Violent Coercion *has two contexts: the systematic study of nonviolent action, which is the context from which A. Paul Hare writes the introduction for this edition, and the sociological career of Clarence Marsh Case.*[1]

Born in Indianapolis, Indiana, in 1874 (he died in 1946), Case earned his B.A. at Earlham College in 1905, his M.A. at Brown University in 1908, studied at Harvard Graduate School in 1908-09, and earned his Ph.D. at the University of Wisconsin in 1915. Before completing his work at Earlham he had been a teacher and principal in public schools, and during much of his educational program he served as a minister, to a Friends meeting in Indiana and to a private school in Rhode Island. Throughout his long academic career he attempted to fuse the concern with values which he had manifested in ministry and teaching with the scientific approach to social behavior which he explored in his studies.

From 1910-17 he was professor and head of the department of social sciences at Penn College, Oskaloosa, Iowa; from 1917-23 associate professor of sociology at the State University of Iowa; and subsequently he made his academic home at the University of Southern California where he was professor of sociology. During the course of his career he was associate editor of the Journal of Applied Sociology *and a member of the advisory board of the* American Journal of Sociology. *He was recognized as a stimulating and brilliant teacher, and his last book, a collection of selected essays, was arranged for by his students and colleagues.*

His major writings include: Non-Violent Coercion *(1923),* Outlines of Introductory Sociology *(1924),* Social Progress and Human Progress *(1931), and* Essays in Social Values *(1944). A complete list of his published writings is appended to the* Essays.

In some respects Clarence Marsh Case is a transitional figure in the development of sociology. He was preoccupied with historical development, the evolution of society in a qualitative sense, and in this regard he picked up the problems occupying the generation of his teachers – that of William Graham Sumner and Herbert Spencer, of Lester Frank Ward and Edward A. Ross. But he was interested also in the mechanics of social change, in social processes that would attract modern attention. His somewhat drawn-out education and the early responsibility for teaching a broad range of social sciences gave him a breadth of view that he wrote into his introductory text of 1924. It was an exhaustive book of readings representing contemporaneous views of the range and methodology of social sciences, the nature of social phenomena, social evolution and processes, and specific social problems. He was interested in specific social issues and in sociological theory. And he tried to relate the two by investigating the development of social attitudes, that is to say, of values which are corollated with behavioral patterns.

Case introduced the concept of "culture" in order to relate social processes to values: "social values themselves are defined as those things in the natural or social environment which have acquired a meaning *for the members of the group, by serving as actual or possible objects for their activities, i.e., their* attitudes." [2] *Thus, social values, expressed through* culture *constituted a distinct field of phenomena for Case. They were not merely judgments such as a philosopher might make; they were facts, elements of the social process, and if one could identify the mechanics of their formation and operation one might be able to create an integrative theory for the social sciences, a sort of gestalt sociology.*[3]

Case pursued this line of thought theoretically, and he tried to construct a range and hierarchy of social attitudes which could provide an index of growing social maturity.[4] *He was trying to relate historical and abstract analysis, social theory and social issues, objective and subjective evidence. An essential part of this task and an illustration of its terms was his attempt to relate conflict and cooperation.*

Before Sarajevo and after Pearl Harbor, Case declared against war and for creative peacemaking. But he did not make the mistake of separating the two. In remarks delivered the year after Non-Violent

Coercion *was published he complained that conflict and cooperation usually had been discussed "by sociologists with rather exclusive emphasis on one or the other of its aspects."*[5] *In large measure, he said, this had resulted from a distorted application of Darwinian evolution to social development. Warfare often was explained as a natural process, when it was not positively justified in this light. Drawing especially upon the work of Prince Kropotkin, Charles Ellwood, E.A. Ross, Jacques Novicow, and Charles H. Cooley, Case argued that this was a wrong interpretation of evolutionary competition, that it overlooked the essential element of cooperation in all human ventures (including war), and that in any case war had "completely changed its character since 1914. . . . it has become so destructive that none of the things that were said about war before that time would hold true concerning the institution in its new aspects."*[6]

The error was not merely in overlooking the importance of cooperative association, but in separating it from competition, Gregg said. Gandhi's noncooperation movement confirmed his own analysis that "a vast deal of our harmonious existence is in forms of . . . antagonistic cooperation. . . ."[7] *War and injustice could be eliminated only by the application of both noncooperation and cooperation. The essential problem of human progress, Case concluded, is not to eliminate hostility but, rather, to lift it from its brutal and violent forms toward rational and ethical means. The appropriate social object is not perfect harmony but rather controlled conflict:*

> *The way, then, to maintain social life upon a basis of disagreement and conflict is to provide more and different forms of expression and a wider range of action, so that the individual may choose his own associates and alliances, and through these alliances, or in person, come into conflict and struggle with other persons and groups, opposing vigorously but not destructively; or, in other words, lift conflict from the merely physical to the social, rational, and ethical levels. It is only under such circumstances that society can function on the highest level of potentiality.*[8]

Case's Non-Violent Coercion *is a classic work not only because it is the first systematic approach to the field, but also because it is thoroughly grounded in his own developing social theory.*

Charles Chatfield
Wittenberg University

PREFACE

NOTES

[1] *A. Paul Hare is professor and chairman, Department of Sociology and Anthropology, Haverford College, and co-editor with Herbert H. Blumberg of* Nonviolent Direct Action; American Cases: Social-Psychological Analyses *(Washington: Corpus Books, 1968). He has been a visiting professor at several African universities, is the author and co-editor of studies in small group research, and is editor of* Sociological Inquiry.

[2] Outlines of Introductory Sociology *(New York: Harcourt, Brace & Co., 1924), p. xxx.*

[3] *See Case, "Toward Gestalt Sociology,"* Sociology and Social Research, *XV (September-October, 1930), pp. 3-27, reprinted in his* Essays in Social Values, *ed., Emory S. Bogardus (Los Angeles: University of Southern California, 1944 [reprinted in 1967 by Books for Libraries Press, Inc., Freeport, N.Y.]), pp. 105-19.*

[4] *See especially Case, "The Social Infant on the Road,"* Sociology and Social Research, *XXIII (September-October, 1938), pp. 3-17; "The Social Infant on the Road,"* ibid., *XXIII (May-June, 1939), pp. 403-30; and "A Tentative Social Age Trend Chart," all printed in the* Essays.

[5] *"Conflict and Cooperation in Social Progress," remarks at the California State Conference for Social Work, May, 1924, in* ibid., *p. 55.*

[6] Ibid., *p. 57.*

[7] Ibid., *p. 59.*

[8] Ibid., *p. 58.*

Introduction

Case began his study of Non-Violent Coercion *before World War I as a graduate student. Then after completing a thesis on the subject, he added to his account with new materials, especially about the characteristics of conscientious objectors, which only became available after the war. Thus his book is valuable in three ways: (a) he gives a history of the groups and individuals who had professed pacifism and advocated nonviolence up to the time of the World War, (b) he reflects the public concerns about the efficacy of nonviolent action which were current at this time, and (c) he brings to bear on the subject the social-psychological theory and observation of his day. On the last point we should note that sociology did not develop a large body of quantitative research until World War II. Even by the 1970s sociologists were just developing theories in the detail necessary to explain more fully the phenomenon which concerned Case. Thus Case's primary method of documentation, through historical example and case study, was the major method available to him at the time. The early history of the peace sects and the peace movement has not changed. The facts in the examples remain as they were for that period. As perhaps the first academic treatment of the subject of nonviolence, Case's work continues to be a landmark in the area. For the student of nonviolence who wishes to approach the subject from a social or psychological perspective, the book on* Non-Violent Coercion *would be a good place to begin.*

Throughout the text it is clear that Case's sympathy lies with the nonviolent actor. He wants the reader to know that nonviolence has worked in the past, that it will work in the future, and that some of the negative things said about nonviolence and its proponents are not true. As a social scientist, he wants to present his case in as objective a manner as possible. He dramatizes his major theme in the title of the book, Non-Violent Coercion, *hoping to shock the reader to attention by the juxtaposition of these two words. He suspects that the general public believes that the word nonviolence is associated with running away from conflict or at best resisting in a very passive way. He wishes to make it clear that nonviolent action in its ideal form, as it was currently being practiced by Gandhi in India, required an aggressive stance and that it was designed to force people to turn from error toward truth.*

After an introductory chapter, Case devotes the following six chapters to a historical account of the role of nonviolence in the major religions and philosophies of the world and of the activities of the major peace sects. This serves to legitimate the (then) present-day practice of nonviolent action by demonstrating that it has been valued by all major religions and practiced in various forms by some of the traditional peace churches (Brethren, Mennonites, Quakers, and others) for some hundreds of years. Case sees a special connection between nonviolence and the Christian tradition when he cautions that one might miss the "great central truth of the history of passive resistance. That central fact is the personality of Jesus" (p. 47).

In the next four chapters, Case attempts to counteract the stereotype that passive resisters are cowards or sissies by presenting data on the physical, social, and psychological characteristics of conscientious objectors in World War I. From studies conducted by military doctors, he demonstrates that conscientious objectors did not differ in physical traits from other army recruits, but were on the average of higher intelligence, with the exception of objectors who were classed as "alien enemies" who were of lower intelligence. In sum, Case observes that the C.O.s reacted as they did not because of any particular set of psychological characteristics, but because they were "convinced exponents of a group ideal and tradition" (p. 193). Thus here, and in his later work, Case stresses the importance of values in determining social behavior. The major determinants of the pacifist position are "essentially cultural."

The final section of the book is devoted to examples of the contemporary use of nonviolence as an instrument of social change. Examples are drawn from confrontations between individuals, between individuals and the state, and from groups involved in nonviolent revolution. In the last category Case recounts the satyagrahas of Gandhi in some detail.

Case's other work

Case does not continue his analysis of nonviolent coercion in any of his later works although traces of his continuing interest appear in various forms. His next book, Outlines of Introductory Sociology: A Textbook of Readings in Social Science *(1924), is a collection of articles on all aspects of sociology, designed to be used in connection with an introductory sociology course. There is no special section on nonviolence; however in his chapter on "Group expansion" he uses as examples the "enlargement of a peace-group through social evolution" and an account of pre-League of Nations attempts to form a league to enforce peace. Also in his selection of readings on "race problems" he includes a lecture by Gandhi on "race friction in South Africa."*

In Social Process and Human Progress *(1931), where we might expect him to promote nonviolence as a method of social change, there is no reference to nonviolence in the index. Further, there is only one reference to Gandhi. In a chapter on "Social diffusion and social progress" Case notes that Gandhi and his followers were against a machine-dominated form of civilization.*

Case's last book, Essays in Social Values *(1944), is a collection of his papers edited by Emory Bogardus. Included is the text of a talk he gave at a conference on social work in 1924 on the topic "Conflict and cooperation in social progress." There are passing references to Gandhi's noncooperation movement as an example of a nonviolent solution to the problem of conflicting interests. The references are of necessity brief and do not seem to develop the theme beyond the statement in his book on* Non-Violent Coercion *which had been published only a year earlier.*

Of more interest is the first essay in the volume, which had not previously been published, describing "A tentative social age trend chart." Case had been working on the concept of "social age" since 1928. He wanted to distinguish "social age" from "developmental age" which had been well documented by child psychologists. As an example he notes that "the 'grabbing' attitude so characteristic of both the chronological and the social infant, when generalized into group practice or policy, produces such societal imbecilities as aggressive international warfare, or the socially senseless growth of vastly swollen fortunes in the national life" (p. 10). His "social age trend chart" includes 25 behavior traits, ordered from the most infantile to the most adult. A person using the chart notes the presence or absence of each trait at three levels of awareness (1:

Awareness of the presence of others, 2: Awareness of the pleasure of others, and 3: Awareness of the welfare of others). Within each level of awareness there are 11 group settings, ranging from small groups such as the family and play group, to large groups such as the nation and internation. In all, the matrix has 825 cells. The list of behavior traits begins, at the infantile end with mess-making, grabbing, and squalling, and continues through traits such as "dialoguing" which show more awareness of others and more responsiveness to their needs. At the top of the list are traits which are very similar to those required by Gandhi of his followers:

16. *Honest dealing (acting openly and dependably)*

17. *Truthtelling (speaking openly and dependably)*

18. *Fair Playing (seeking no advantage denied to opponents)*

19. *Peace Preserving (includes law observance, and more)*

20. *Altro-Leading (leading others for their benefit)*

21. *Social Opposing (pronouncing any act bad,*

not because the speaker dislikes it, but because it can be shown to be injurious to society)

22. *Ethical Opposing (hostility toward principles rather than persons)*

23. *Nonconforming (refusing to yield to group dictation)*

24. *Conscientious Objecting (refusing, for conscience' sake, to obey the group will, but accepting punishment for so refusing without complaint)*

25. *Peacemaking (more creative than peace preserving; it fosters good will by doing justice)*

Thus Case ends his academic career as it began, with a strong commitment to nonviolence, not just as a tactic, but as a way of life, a standard against which to judge the social development of individuals and societies.

Professor Martin H. Neumeyer, a former colleague of Professor Case at the University of Southern California, recalls the year he lived in Professor Case's house while Professor Case was on sabbatical leave. One day while re-reading Non-Violent Coercion, *using Professor Case's own copy, Professor Neumeyer discovered a letter from Dr. Edward A. Ross. Dr. Ross had been in Gandhi's home in India and had browsed in Gandhi's library while waiting for an interview. He discovered that Professor Case's book had been used extensively and was marked with notations. Dr. Ross concluded that outside of the Bible,* Non-Violent Coercion *was the most frequently used book in Gandhi's library.*

A. Paul Hare
Haverford College

NON-VIOLENT COERCION

NON-VIOLENT COERCION

A Study in Methods of Social Pressure

BY

CLARENCE MARSH CASE

Associate Professor of Sociology,
The State University of Iowa

NEW YORK AND LONDON

THE CENTURY CO.

1923

PRINTED IN U. S. A.

PREFACE

The interest of the present writer in the problem of this book is of long standing, but it dates in a special sense from the summer preceding the World War, when Professor Edward A. Ross suggested to the undersigned, then a graduate student at the University of Wisconsin, a study of the Social Psychology of Passive Resistance. The suggestion was adopted, and resulted in a dissertation which included several chapters of the present work.

In the meantime the World War had begun in Europe, and later spread to America, introducing, in its course and consequences, new and startling aspects of this very ancient yet perennial problem. These events of recent history were so challenging that I was unable to dismiss the subject, but continued my investigations from year to year until the original study has expanded into the present volume, and in so doing has undergone a decided transformation in both scope and emphasis.

I am thus indebted to Professor Ross for calling my attention to the need for a serious sociological analysis of this problem, and I have been favoured with his counsel and encouragement at many turns in the road. I count it an honor to acknowledge the benefits received from his enthusiastic support and extraordinary grasp of sociological subjects, but I must myself shoulder responsibility for the point of view and method of treatment which characterize the work as it is now presented to the reader.

In its present form, the study reflects a two fold evolution, the one having taken place in the progress of objective events in the world of affairs, the other in the changing point of view brought about in my own thought by the study of those facts. The requirements of space have rendered unavoidable an inadequate presentation of the materials at several points, while one whole aspect of the subject, namely, the problem of war and peace in their wider international bearings, I have had to reserve entirely for treatment elsewhere.

Credit to various authors and correspondents is given through foot-notes in the usual manner, but there remains a debt which is not fully met in that way. I have been favored with willing and valued assistance, in the form of correspondence or personal conference, from leading members of the historic peace sects in Canada, Australia, Great Britain, and the United States; from prominent conscientious objectors; from Chinese, Korean, and Indian students in several universities; from army officers and psychologists; and from religious and social workers of the Young Men's Christian Association and other organizations; also from many of my university colleagues and personal friends.

CLARENCE MARSH CASE

CONTENTS

CONTENTS

INTRODUCTION

For centuries men slew their foes by jabbing holes in them—a slow and laborious process which they wearied of long before the enemy had been disposed of. The coming of gun-powder enabled one by pressing a trigger to throw a pellet of lead through the foeman at a considerable distance. Then arrived the machine-gun, which with the turning of a crank will hail deadly missiles upon the enemy. The crown of lethal efficiency, however, is the peppering of your enemy from the air with noiseless, invisible death. In the war-after-the-next the two belligerents almost simultaneously will launch over the enemy territory a huge fleet of aëroplanes dropping containers of poison gas. After having done a workmanlike job, each fleet will return home to find its people blotted out. The crews of the air fleets will be the sole survivors of the first offensive. Thereafter they will never complain of lack of elbow-room in their own country.

Governments, with machine-guns and bombing aëroplanes in stock, will not restrict themselves to muskets when they confront insurgents. So the frightful weapons which nations forge for one another are bound to be wielded against disobedient minorities. More and more armed resistance to government is becoming an invitation to massacre. Naturally those who feel themselves wronged are casting about for some less suicidal means of vindicating their supposed rights. Hence, the old-fashioned method of passive resistance, practised for ages on a small scale by petty groups, is coming into favor.

INTRODUCTION

Disobedience without violence wins, *if it wins,* not so much by touching the conscience of the masters as by exciting the sympathy of disinterested onlookers. The spectacle of men suffering for a principle *and not hitting back* is a moving one. It obliges the power holders to condescend to explain, to justify themselves. The weak get a change of venue from the will of the stronger to the court of public opinion, perhaps of world opinion.

This is the more important because in our time the number of spectators to appeal to has been enormously increased. Thanks to wireless and print and radio, every intelligent member of the human race can be brought to notice and comment on any big struggle between strong and weak in any part of the globe; so that the method of *non-violent coercion,* which this book sets forth, may have a future no man yet dreams of.

EDWARD ALSWORTH ROSS.

NON-VIOLENT COERCION

CHAPTER I

NATURE AND SCOPE OF THE PROBLEM

THE reader, observing our title-page, may wonder at the incongruity of the terms there found in company. If it be a marvel to see the lion and the lamb lie down together, how much more dubious to behold them hooked into the same yoke and bending their necks in unison to the work of social pressure, under such thin verbal disguises as "non-violence" and "coercion"! Yet this extraordinary combination is not the outcome of a preconceived notion, but represents a working arrangement, to which the writer came naturally during the course of a prolonged effort to find separately the working efficiency of these two principles of human conduct, neither of which was found to function rightly alone.

The phrase "passive resistant" calls to mind with the average reader the image of certain peculiar people who refuse to fight, yet cannot be hired to run away. Known in earlier times as "non-resistants" and "passive resistants," in the years preceding the World War they came to be merged under the wider and more popular term "pacifist," always disagreeable in sound, and fated soon to take on an equally odious meaning. As the emotional tension incident to a state of war increased, the still more highly colored epithet "slacker" became current among the people. At the same time government officials, having need of more exact and dispassionate phraseology, introduced the term "conscientious objector" to designate more exactly one phase of the movement. This apt phrase seems to have been coined by General Smuts, in South Africa, long before the World War.[1]

In the present work the phrase "not-violent resistance" is used as a more explicit synonym for the older term "passive resistance," and the two expressions will be used throughout these pages as interchangeable terms. "Non-resistance," on the other hand, is used to convey very nearly the same meaning, but is such a self-contradictory term that it will be avoided except where an extremely negative and submissive attitude is under discussion. In so far as "slackers" are concerned, it will very soon appear that those really deserving that odious name belong to a moral and social genus falling outside the scope of this study.

As understood in this investigation, non-violent resistance is a principle of social action that has had a long and stormy history in the Western world, and during recent months it has shaken the *Orient* to its foundations, especially in India.

The war itself, along with the significant events just mentioned, has raised the problem of non-violent coercion to a position of extraordinary importance for human progress. In all the history of mankind, as everybody knows, nothing approaching the recent holocaust of violence was ever seen before. Physical might upon the grandest scale has now played its part on the world-stage. It saved the freedom-loving nations from arrogant dominion, it overturned the thrones of ancient, oppressive, and insolent autocracies, but left the problem of salvaging civilization itself to an impoverished and demoralized world. It thus

[1] See "Speeches and Writings of M. K. Gandhi," Madras, 1919; p. 126.

becomes even more evident that the shortcomings of violence are inherent, deep-rooted, and incurable; that it is as impotent to build enduring welfare as it is mighty for the destruction of those evil growths that obstruct the pathway of the positive good.

At this juncture there are those who urge that the most fruitful principle of social action is complete *non*-resistance—the extreme negation and antithesis of warlike force. Thus one heard, during the earlier months of the war, about a so-called "martyr-nation" as the one thing supremely needed to point the true way for the world to follow. In support of this idea an array of examples, purporting to demonstrate the efficacy of entire non-resistance, was brought forth from the mid-Victorian literature of the peace movement and the fancy of certain Utopian writers. But these anecdotes will be found to cover no more than the question of personal retaliation, leaving the tremendous problem of inter-group conflicts virtually untouched.

In such discussions one beholds the logical confusion wrought by the attempt to treat a highly complex problem precisely as if it were a very simple one. Of course the question of war or peace is just as simple as the Golden Rule and the Sermon on the Mount, in the last analysis, but when we attempt to apply it specifically to concrete situations in the world of sinful men, many of whom are not actuated by unswerving good will, the problem becomes enormously complicated. Buddha, Jesus, the Apostle Paul, and others are ranged in hostile array, or even quoted against themselves, because there are really three questions wrapped up in this seemingly simple one.

The three are distinct, but closely related. For example, if one may not justly defend himself against a foul personal assault, does the same principle of conduct likewise forbid him to become a participant in the resistance of his social group against criminal disturbers of its safety and peace? This involves questions about the moral legitimacy of the magistrates and the constabulary which have occupied a large place in the history of passive, i. e., non-violent, resistance. Beyond this looms the stupendous problem of the aggressive and defensive activities of national groups. This is, of course, the yet unsolved problem of war and militarism—questions upon whose solution the progress of man on this planet depends. Summing up, we have then these three problems: (1) that of individual resistance, or personal retaliation; (2) that of intra-group resistance, or criminal justice; (3) that of inter-group resistance, which means international wars.

More specifically stated, some of the questions now to be considered are: What have been the *social antecedents and the significance* of the individuals, and especially the groups, that have stood for the principles of non-violence? What inborn or acquired traits underlie it? What social heritages, attitudes, and conditions foster it? By what specific processes does it modify the behavior of the social groups, such as sects, neighborhoods, or nations, within which it appears? More specifically, in just what ways has the practice and preaching of passive resistance modified the ideas, feelings, and actions of men as members of society, and what impress has it made upon public opinion, political and social institutions, and governmental policy? What light does it shed upon the relative value of persuasion, non-violent coercion, and violence, for the resistance of aggression, or the accomplishing of desired social ends? Finally, what logical and moral relation exists between passive resistance, as usually known, and non-violent coercion as described in our later chapters?

These considerations possess tremendous importance for the present-day discussion of "preparedness" and related questions, because there is a marked tendency for peace advocates to assume that what is true of *personal* non-resistance is likewise true of group non-resistance, which does not necessarily follow. The result is that many true friends of peace are hanging back from the movement to enforce peace by means of world organization. This failure to rally to such a worthy cause is due, apparently, to their fear of the word "enforce," and this fear, in turn, is rooted in the erroneous opinion, held by such friends of peace, that Christian non-resistance requires the rejection of physical force under all circumstances in human affairs. Or, to put the same thing in another way, they seem to believe that the physical coercion exerted by an international fleet would be a case of *war,* which, as the writer holds, is not true, it being simply an extension of the *police* principle, i. e., the use of public force against the private violence of lawless nations.

The consequence of this philosophy of absolute non-resistance is to place its advocates in an almost purely negative position in practice. Since they oppose all armament and every form of coercion they must take the negative on every definite proposition along the line of "preparedness." On the other hand, they do not support heartily, if at all, the league to enforce peace. Their misconceived doctrine of *non*-resistance allows them no positive program whatever beyond the making of non-enforceable agreements between nations. Aside from such measures, which would be invaluable under world organization and a world police force, but which seem, in the light of recent European practice, distressingly futile otherwise, they can offer the nation nothing but submission to an invader, trusting to the hope that his insolence would be virtually disarmed by unresisting meekness. The laws of group psychology operate squarely against the success of such an experiment, even if there were the slightest prospect of the experiment's being tried in the present stage of human development. The truth seems to be that the spirit of peace, like most good things, will become effective only through *organization.*

It may be clear, from the above reflections, that the problem before us in this study is not a simple one, capable of being dismissed with a wave of the hand by extremists on either side. Enough has been said to indicate some of the lines of investigation along which the truth must be sought. Moreover, this is far from being an academic subject, at least since that fateful hour when the outbreak of the World War plunged the powers from their armed pacifism into a condition where militaristic activities and considerations, if not ideals, have held well-nigh unhampered sway. In this emergency the passive resistant was rudely snatched from his obscurity and given, under his new name of "conscientious objector," a significant part in the great drama. We say significant because the passive resistant, no matter how inadequate or even inglorious he may seem in his own private person, may possibly represent a new social type, prophetic of a better social order; and at any rate he embodies a unique and challenging rule of conduct which must surely have some application to collective human life.

The conscientious objectors, at the opening of the World War, fell into two groups, one of which, the religious sectarian type, was more or less familiar and quite generally trusted, even if little understood. The other was the non-religious objector, a new and problematical character in the public mind. Thus was presented a twofold problem to the military authorities, and the situation was further complicated by a third factor known as the pro-German element. The three were often confused by uninformed or reckless persons, which naturally rendered the public even less discriminating and tolerant than it might otherwise have been. Of these three types of objector, only the first-named possessed anything in the way of a historical background, and this was largely unknown to the government or even the more informed among the people at large. The chapters immediately following this are designed to afford a brief view of them in perspective, giving a picture which was not available to the general reader when the hand of destiny thrust them forth from their peaceful seclusion into the center of a world in turmoil.

In so doing we shall view the passive resistant first in the perspective of his drably picturesque history, then try to sketch his experiences during the World War, whose vast conscription net spared not even those quiet backwaters where the quaintest of the peace sectarians strove to maintain, undisturbed by an onrushing world, the pacific traditions of their ancient and simple faith.

The plan of treatment pursued is, first, to trace, in the immediately following chapters, the origins and earlier history of this extraordinary idea, and of the quaintly picturesque sects which have given to it an organized expression. Next will follow certain interpretative chapters which seek to portray the logical difficulties, psychological basis, and practical effectiveness or futility of non-violent resistance. Then the attempt will be made to distinguish the older movement from its more recent and strictly modern phase, and to show, finally, the bearing of this doctrine upon the great problems of modern democracy and social idealism, as expressed in the strike, the boycott, and non-coöperation as organized in India during the World War.

The present study is not primarily a product of the war, although it has been affected by the great conflict in many ways, which was of course inevitable. But it was begun just before the war opened in Europe. The chapters as they stand reflect a twofold process of evolution, one being that which occurred in the author's thought as the subject was pursued from stage to stage; the other representing a remarkable accumulation of objective facts and a consequent expansion in the scope of the subject, produced by the rapid progress of events since the summer of 1914.

It is to be hoped that the time is ripe for an impartial exposition of this subject. It was an inevitable accompaniment of the destructive activities and perils of the war that impassioned thinking and speaking should become the order of the day. In all such heated discussions *labeling* with highly colored epithets comes to take the place of *reasoning,* and words of exact and impartial description find themselves thrust aside, as too colorless and feeble in times when every one is grasping for terms highly charged with strongest emotion. Few, if any, of those who lived through the World War have escaped some lapses into this tar-bucket method, to which all tongues are naturally heir.

Now that the emotional unhingement necessarily entailed by the war, and the sedulous exploitation of that state of mind by selfish reactionaries, have both begun to pass away, things begin to resume their true proportions in the perspective of the passing years. Under these circumstances it may be profitable to inquire concerning the actual social value of those peculiar social attitudes variously known as non-resistance, passive resistance, pacifism, and conscientious objection, on the one hand, and the strike, boycott, and non-coöperation and other forms of coercive social pressure upon the other. Many able, but more or less partial and fragmentary, studies have been made of all these things by both their advocates and their enemies.

In the present study, we have endeavored to avoid both vilification and laudation, seeking simply to *understand* the principles and methods as they present themselves to view. In this lies the principal excuse for a book on this subject, the various aspects of which we have tried to grasp under the phrase, "non-violent coercion." Whether the conclusions here drawn are accepted or not, the reader is asked to regard the book as an honest effort to apply the scientific, inductive method in a philosophical spirit to a field of social phenomena not hitherto explored extensively in that objective, impartial way through which scientific thinking has attained to a real understanding of other fields of fact less intimately entwined with those human motives and prejudices which often blur for our eyes the true outlines of things as they are.

CHAPTER II

PHILOSOPHERS AND TEACHERS OF NON-VIOLENCE

ONE way to approach this problem is to explore the ancient and Oriental world, in order, by means of an inductive study of the available facts, to ascertain whether we are dealing with a form of personal and social reaction common to humanity, or whether it is peculiar to civilized, European, and modern men of the Christian faith, as a glance at the list of sects that have figured in history would at first suggest.

CONFUCIUS

At the time of Confucius (about 551–478 B. C.) China was in a state of disorder and political confusion brought about, apparently, by the contentions of feudalistic princes whom the feeble imperial authority could not control. Confucius himself was a statesman by nature, and a political philosopher and exponent of practical ethics merely by force of circumstances. In fact he devoted his life to an effort to realize a stable and efficient government founded on sound and just political theory, and the failure to realize this aim became, as it were, his dying lament. Thus when the end of his life drew near he declared: "No intelligent monarch arises; there is not one in the empire that will make me his master. My time has come to die."[1] Since

[1] "The Ethics of Confucius," by Tozaburo Kudo, a thesis presented to the faculty of Yale University for the degree of doctor of philosophy, 1904; p. XIX.

the philosopher had long been connected with the governments of the several Chinese provinces, going "from state to state, and from court to court, faithfully teaching the principles of the ancient sages,"[1] the passage quoted may indicate regret over the close of his own absorbing political career as well as despair for the cause of good government at large.

Confucius was nothing if not practical. Says Kudo: "He praises King Shun (2255–2205 B.C.) for attaining the Mean by getting the opinions of all his people, and by determining the Mean between their two extremes."[2] This is probably the origin of the celebrated Confucian doctrines of virtue tempered with moderation; of "jin," that elusive blend of all the virtues, illuminated by learning and circumscribed by "the rules of propriety."[3] It is benevolent, just, manly, and vigorous, and always intensely practical—just the sort of conduct and character one ought to expect from one who could endorse King Shun's unique attempt to derive the golden median of conduct by the application of statistical method![4]

But Confucianism had also its idealistic side, even if rather somber of hue. All the world knows that the Chinese sage formulated the Golden Rule in its negative form: "What you do not want done to yourself, do not do to others." But, though negative in form, it was probably

[1] Kudo, *op. cit.;* p. xix.

[2] *Ibid.;* p. 131.

[3] *Ibid.;* p. xxii.

[4] The doctrine of the Mean also figures largely in Aristotle's Ethics, but it is with him "a balance of mind." See "The Moral Philosophy of Aristotle," by Walter M. Hatch and others; p. 274. The Chinese work entitled the "Doctrine of the Mean" was, apparently, written by a grandson of Confucius. See Kudo, *op. cit.;* p. xvi. It is not meant to be implied here, however, that the Mean in the thought of Confucius was as mechanical as King Shun's above-quoted method would indicate.

intended by Confucius as a positive rule. Moreover, according to Dr. Kudo,[1] he counsels against the avenging of injuries received, and exhorts his hearers to assail their own wickedness rather than the wickedness of others. Indeed the pardoning of "small faults" is named as one of the *duties* of an officer of the government. So we may not only say, with Kudo, that "there is in general no vindictive spirit," but may even attribute to Confucius a genial spirit, and an attitude of kindly forbearance.

Nevertheless, the Reverend Master Kung[2] is not to be reckoned among the true passive resistants; neither as opposing group violence, since he names a military equipment as the third requisite of government,[3] nor as against personal retaliation, as appears most strikingly in his interesting encounter with Lao Tse, described as follows by Professor Legge:[4] "We have rejoiced in his enunciation of the golden rule; Lao Tse had advanced even beyond this in the field of morality, and said, 'Return good for evil.' Some of Confucius' school heard the maxim, and, being puzzled by it, consulted the master. He also was puzzled, formed a syllogism in his mind about it, and replied, 'What then will you return for good? Recompense injury with justice, and return good for good.'" Dr. Kudo thinks it possible that Confucius is here using the word "injury" to indicate "not trivial offenses, but serious wrongs which a man cannot tolerate without demanding justice." In the light of the teachings quoted above, this is not only possible, but probable. The same author adds that, "According to Choo He, 'justice' here means 'fair-

1 *Ibid.;* pp. 18–20.

2 The Chinese title for Confucius.

3 Kudo, *op cit.;* p. xxix.

4 "The Religions of China," by James Legge, professor of the Chinese language and literature in the University of Oxford; pp. 143–144.

ness in dealing with injury, without selfish motives"![1] Kudo thinks this has been unjustly interpreted by those who see in it merely the spirit of "eye for eye and tooth for tooth." Professor Legge, also, finds it impossible to "think that Confucius has any thought of vengeance when he used the term," but he wishes that the sage "had risen to the height of the thought that was put before him."[2]

Lao Tse

Lao Tse, the founder of Taoism, was apparently a contemporary of Confucius, although Taoism as a religious system did not exist until some time after the commencement of the Christian era, according to Professor Legge. Whether the two sages ever met or not is problematical, but the above described skirmish in the persons of their disciples brings out very forcibly the difference between their ethical systems. Lao Tse was a mystic, who finally withdrew from the world, while Confucius died in its midst.[3] The founder of Taoism drew his moral principles not, like those of Confucius, from the average opinion, practical situation, and social experience of men,[4] but by intuition, from a world of mystical contemplation, supplemented, however, by a very thoughtful observation of the processes of nature. Professor Legge describes Taoism as "the style of action . . . proceeding from a mind in a

[1] Legge, *op. cit.;* pp. 143–144.

[2] Kudo, *op. cit.;* pp. 19-20.

[3] Kudo, *op. cit.;* p. xxii.

[4] Some would deny to Confucius the title of religious teacher in any sense, but this view implies too narrow a conception of religion. Confucius really gathered together and expanded the ancient religious tenets of the Chinese race, in which ancestor worship held a prominent place. His system was of course a "moral" system, inasmuch as it was founded on the *mores* or customs, and this is what is meant by the "rules of propriety."

state of calm repose . . . without bias of partiality," and characterized by such principles that "humanity has a distinguished place in the teachings." Holding humility, as the one supreme thing, in his embrace, the sage, says Lao Tse, "is a pattern to the world. He is free from self-display, and so he shines; from self-assertion, and so he is distinguished; from boasting, and so his merit is acknowledged; from self-conceit, and his superiority is allowed. *It is because he is thus free from striving* that therefore no one can strive with him." [1] This noble ethical program is founded by Lao Tse upon a law of universal compensation, according to which "the incomplete becomes complete; the crooked becomes straight; the hollow becomes full; the worn becomes new; he who desires little gets much; he who desires much goes astray." [2]

Humility is indeed the key-note of these sayings, but it rests upon a deeper, underlying current of serenity, which finds its unfailing fountainhead in an abiding sense of harmony with the purposes and processes of the world. He who has attained this exalted level of "non-assertion," thereby "complying with Heaven," learns how to diminish daily, yet mounts to that plane where "there is nothing that he cannot achieve." "He assists," says Lao Tse, "the ten thousand things in their natural development, but he does not venture to interfere." [3]

The characteristic expression of this imperturbable placidity is highly significant for the central problem of the present essay. "He never tires," says Dr. Carus, "preaching to act non-action . . . and he assures that through non-action everything can be accomplished." This seemingly paradoxical conception impresses one even on first

[1] Legge, *op. cit.;* 220-229. Italics are the present writers.
[2] *Ibid.*
[3] "The Tao-Teh-King," Chap. lxiv, Transliteration of Dr. Carus.

acquaintance as being closely akin to the *laissez-faire* of the classical Anglo-French economists, and it is logically related to that governmental philosophy of Herbert Spencer which was aptly dubbed "administrative nihilism" by Huxley; for Lao Tse, as we are told by his translator, "requests the government not to govern, but simply to administer. Rulers should not interfere with the natural development of their people, but practise non-acting, not-meddling, non-interference, or as the French call it, *laisser faire,* so that the people shall scarcely know that they have rulers."[1]

It is hard to distinguish this principle of non-activity from the very similar philosophy of ascetic passivism which we shall frequently meet in the following history of non-resistance. With Leo Tse, however, it was no doctrine of defeat or submission, but represents a very real conquest of the spirit, and that for several reasons. In the first place, he observes that "the ten thousand things, the grass as well as the trees, are while they live tender and supple. When they die they are rigid and dry. Thus the hard and the strong are the companions of death. The tender and the delicate are the companions of life."

Twenty centuries later the Darwinian students of evolution arrived at the same truth from another angle when they perceived that it is the unadaptable, the highly specialized, forms of life that become the chosen companions of death, while it is the immature, the unspecialized, the plastic and adaptable that are the companions of life. This, which thus far has been emphasized especially with regard to organisms, and particularly to species, may prove to be equally true of social groups, traditions, and institutions, including war and the more ruthless aspects of the sovereign political state.

[1] Carus, *op cit.;* p. 19.

Lao Tse next reflects that "the world's weakest overcomes the world's hardest. Non-existence enters into the impenetrable. Thereby I comprehend of non-assertion the advantage, and of silence the lesson. There are few in the world who attain," he sagely adds, "the advantage of non-assertion."[1] This beneficent principle of non-action is not, however, pure *inactivity*. Dr. Carus finely characterizes it as "simply not acting a part; not doing things in an artificial way; it is not forcing the nature of things. . . . It is, briefly, not 'non-action,' but non-assertion."[2]

It was out of this insight into the processes of nature, and this philosophic acquiescence in the ultimate outcome of things, that the non-resistance teaching of the Taoist school of ethics was born. But, as one may easily perceive in all the sayings of its founder, and especially in the following beautiful passage, it goes beyond mere *non-resistance* or any other purely negative doctrine. It becomes willing acquiescence—nay, more than that, an *active coöperation* with the more eternal aspects of existence which strongly recalls the Christian apostle's expression, "workers together with God." In the light of his impartial devotion, like many another who has thus learned to discount the noisy strivings and contentions of men, Lao Tse is rewarded with more than common understanding of the ultimate futility of the accepted *methods* so unthinkingly employed, as the following reveals:

He who excels as a warrior is not warlike. He who excels as a fighter is not wrathful. He who excels in conquering the enemy does not strive. He who excels in employing men is lowly.

This is called the virtue of not-striving. This is called utiliz-

[1] *Ibid.*, p 19.
[2] *Ibid.;*

ing men's ability. This is called complying with heaven—since olden times the highest.[1]

If now we attempt a final estimate of the two great Chinese teachers, in order to grasp their relative importance for the purpose of the present study, it is evident, first, that *Confucius* may be taken as the typical juridical resistant of the noblest order. Scorning petty spitefulness and eschewing private vengeance, his retaliation is according to the forms of law and through the constituted authorities. Therefore he proposes to repay injury with justice. He leaves a margin for forbearance and apparently for forgiveness, but it is rather limited in scope, and he squarely repudiated Lao Tse's proposal to return good for evil. In this connection we may credit Confucius with the fact that he remained at his post in society, while Lao Tse fled into solitude, and in so doing discredited his own principles, in the eyes of all who are in search of a rule for the actual conduct of social life among men as they are.

Yet, after all is said for the doctrine of the Mean, and of "jin" as a sort of moral "reciprocity,"[2] there is something disappointing about the answer of Confucius. His teaching is purely of the earth, and it should not surprise one to find it "earthy" when placed alongside the mystical idealism of Lao Tse. The latter's teaching may be dubbed unpractical and visionary, especially by legalists like Confucius, but that is precisely the source of its value. It is the result, not of calculation, but of spiritual vision. Perhaps it was just this lack of moral vision that limited benevolence, in the thought of Confucius, to "a virtue which the superior class of men exercises in relation to in-

[1] *Ibid.;* p. 132. The passage quoted constitutes the whole of Chap. lxviii of the "Tao-Teh-King."

[2] Kudo, *op. cit.;* p. 211.

feriors," and which led him to give the impression that "he did not mean to apply this to human beings in general, but rather to his own countrymen."[1] Dr. Kudo, himself reared as a Japanese Confucianist, has given us an invaluable key to the explanation of passive resistance when he says: "Confucius could not understand the height of benevolence beyond the human relations in society. His moral ideal was not 'Be thou perfect as the Heavenly Father,' but 'the superior man.' "[2]

It is not asserted that even Lao Tse himself had attained to this high spiritual conception in all clearness, but perhaps his teaching was more universal and more actively benevolent than that of Confucius simply because it was more idealistic, more "heavenly."

But, after all, Confucius, as already remarked, faced the whole social situation. For the individual he counseled kindness and the elimination of a vengeful spirit; in the *magistrate* and *constabulary* he pointed out the proper agencies of a just redressing of injuries; and the *military* establishment he held to be an essential element of the state. What would be Lao Tse's conclusions on the last two points we can only surmise. He does not seem to have wrestled with those complex problems of political practice which have proved such irreducible stumbling-blocks to passive resistants in all succeeding ages. But on the question of the ethical quality of personal reaction toward injuries received he rose above Confucius, and clearly enunciated the power of meekness to conquer, of the true nobility of returning good for evil. The net result of the Chinese philosophy is therefore a very clear and noble statement of the doctrine of non-resistance. But its suprapersonal, or social, applications were not worked out, and

[1] *Ibid.;* p. 50.
[2] *Ibid.;* p. 21.

no organized sect, devoted to its practice, arose. It exists, moreover, almost entirely as the isolated utterances of a single philosopher, Lao Tse; but the beauty and depth of his formulation of the ethical principle can hardly be surpassed: "It is because he is thus free from striving that . . . no one can strive with him." [1]

BUDDHA

We have heard Lao Tse declare that "he who desires much goes astray," and in this expression is seen his connection with the root idea of Buddhism. The Chinese mystic lived in the sixth century B. C., but his teachings were formulated in a religious system many centuries later. Gautama, the founder of Buddhism, is assigned to the fifth century, but his teaching is itself rooted in the much more ancient Brahmanism. To trace out any possible reciprocal influence between the two teachers would involve historical and textual research entirely outside the range and powers of a study like the present one. The important point to notice is that the teachings of both had their root in a *mystical* attitude which repudiated *desire*. It is so well known that Hindu religion proceeds by suppression of the impulses and ambitions of men that no detailed proof is needed here. Resigning by an act of the will "this pleasing anxious being" even while yet in the flesh, it seeks to sink and dissolve the individual consciousness in the measureless ocean of the Absolute Totality of Things. With this absolute surrender of the Egoistic consciousness there seems to come a strange attitude of *impartiality* and lack of *bias*, which makes no exception even

[1] Legge, *op. cit.;* p. 221. Dr. Carus renders it thus: "Because he strives not, no one in the world will strive with him." *Op. cit.;* p. 131.

in favor of one's own individual fortunes.[1] In so far as this takes place, there is an actual diminishing of the real volume of life at its very fountain-head; since, as Professor Perry aptly says, "the mark of life is partiality for itself," and the very drama of universal life is "the long struggle of interest against inertia and indifference."[2] Yet along with this negative process in Buddhism there goes an expansion of mind and heart which expresses itself in a positive attitude of *love* toward all men, and sometimes of all things. This twofold experience is well shown in the story of Prince Gautama, the Buddha, i. e., the "Enlightened One."

Reared in the delicate luxury of his father's court, and long shielded from every knowledge of human misery, when finally a sudden realization of the wretchedness and woe of the world beat like a devastating flood against his heart, he fled from his own fortune into the wilderness, and "directed his steps to the blessed Bodhi-tree beneath whose shade he should accomplish his search."[3] Here, after long tarrying and meditation, he attained Buddhahood, or, in other words, became "Enlightened." The first message flowing from such an experience as this would possess an intrinsic interest in any case, but its importance for the present research is extraordinary. Says Carus:[4] "The Blessed One having attained Buddhahood pronounced this solemn utterance: '*Blissful is freedom from malice!* Blissful is absence of lust and the loss of all pride that

1 "The fifth meditation is the meditation on serenity, in which you rise above love and hate, tyranny and oppression, wealth and want, and regard your own fate with impartial calmness and perfect tranquillity." Cf. "The Gospel of Buddha According to Old Records," by Paul Carus, Chicago, 1904; p. 154.

2 "The Moral Economy," by Ralph Barton Perry; p. 10.

3 Carus, *op. cit.;* p. 29.

4 *Ibid.*

comes from the thought, "I am." I have recognized the deepest truth, which is sublime and peace-giving, but difficult to understand!' " In this remarkable revelation from out Gautama's mystical illumination, we perceive an intimate connection between a peace-loving, peace-giving, non-resistance, on the one hand, and the mystical feeling of impersonal enlargement of soul upon the other.[1] It is emphasized here because it occurs again and again in the history of passive resistance, as following chapters will show.

We thus see that Buddha's first enlightened utterance was to sound the praises of that blissful state which enjoys "*freedom from malice.*" As Warren says: "He was full of tact, and all his ways were ways of peace. . . . Anger had no place in his character . . . and it had equally none in his religio-philosophic system."[2] His good will was "without measure toward all the world, above, below, around; unstinted, unmixed with any feeling of making distinctions or showing preferences."[3] This kindliness is a continuous flow of acts, and it extends to the animal kingdom, on the part of the teachers at least, as is to be seen in the "Story of the Goose-Killing Priest."[4] A young priest, soon after his ordination, was loitering with a companion on the river's bank. As two wild geese came flying by, the youth, in a spirit of banter, wantonly hurled a potsherd and wounded the fowl, then despatched it. A company of priests came running up and carried the offender before the Teacher.

[1] For discussions of mysticism see Jones, "Studies in Mystical Religion," Chapter I, and "Spiritual Reformers in the 16th and 17th Centuries"; also Royce, "The World and the Individual," Vol. I, Chap. IV, Sec. vii.

[2] "Buddhism in Translations," by Henry Clarke Warren, p. 1; Vol. III of "Harvard Oriental Series."

[3] Carus, *op. cit.;* p. 55.

[4] Warren, *op. cit.;* p. 433.

"Is it true?" asked the Teacher, "what they say, that you have taken life?"

"Reverend Sir, it is true."

"Priest, . . . it was a very serious sin for you to take life after you had retired from the world under the dispensation of such a Buddha as I. A priest should always keep his hands and feet, and his voice under restraint." So saying, he pronounced this stanza:

"Restrained of hand, restrained of foot,
Restrained of voice, restrained in all,
Reflective, calm, content alone,
'T is he that is a priest in truth."

Again, a certain priest having been killed by a snake, the matter was reported to the Blessed One, who said:

"Surely now, O priests, that priest never suffused the four royal families of snakes with his friendliness. For if, O priests, that priest had suffused the four royal families of the snakes with his friendliness, that priest, O priests, would not have been killed by the bite of a snake." [1]

Warren characterizes this as a "sublime state of friendliness," but probably, as Aiken suggests,[2] this scrupulous regard for every form of life was the outgrowth of the Buddhist doctrine of transmigration of souls. The purpose underlying it is not absolutely unselfish. It apparently represents one of the *works* by which salvation is earned, for even Sakka, "the leader of the gods," is represented as saying:

Myself I seek to keep subdued
In interest of my future weal. [3]

Fantastic as many of the Buddhist legends and sayings

[1] *Ibid.;* p. 302.

[2] "The Dhamma of Gotama the Buddha, and the Gospel of Jesus the Christ." by Charles Francis Aiken, Boston, 1900; p. 38.

[3] Warren, *op. cit.;* p. 427.

are, there are many passages of striking beauty and deep insight. Nowhere is this more true than when we leave the doctrines of self-denial and restraint as abstract virtues, and observe how the Buddhist would react to injuries received. Aiken [1] says that the teaching of Gotama [2] on the forgiveness of injuries is clearly enunciated in the laws of Manu, which contain the earlier Brahmanistic teachings. It is there enjoined upon the ascetic that he "patiently bear hard words, let him not insult anybody; and let him not become anybody's enemy for the sake of this (perishable) body. Against an angry man let him not in return show anger, let him bless when cursed, and let him not utter speech, devoid of truth, scattered at the seven gates."

This noble teaching, thus clearly present in ancient *Brahmanism,* was made still more explicit and prominent in Buddhism. Nowhere in literature, perhaps, can be found a finer picture of the really unassailable dignity and elevation of him who benignantly endures abusive speech than in the following noble passage from Gautama's career:

"If a man foolishly does me wrong, I will return to him the protection of my ungrudging love; the more evil comes from him, the more good shall go from me; the fragrance of goodness always comes to me, and the harmful air of evil goes to him."

A foolish man learning that Buddha observed the principle of great love which commends to return good for evil, came and abused him. Buddha was silent, pitying his folly. The man having finished his abuse, Buddha asked him, saying: "Son, if a man declined to accept a present made to him, to whom would it belong?" And he answered: "In that case it would belong to the man who offered it." "My son," said Buddha, "you have railed at me, but I decline to accept your abuse, and request you

[1] *Op. cit.;* p. 40.

[2] The Southern Hindu form for Gautama.

to keep it yourself. Will it not be a source of misery to you?" (While Buddha continued in similar strain, the man stood speechless before him, when the teacher added:) "A wicked man who reproaches a virtuous one is like one who looks up and spits at heaven; the spittle soils not the heaven, but comes back and defiles his own person. The slanderer is like one who flings dust at another when the wind is contrary; the dust does but return on him who threw it. The virtuous man cannot be hurt, and the misery that the other would inflict comes back on himself." The abuser went away ashamed, but he came again and took refuge in the Buddha, the Dharma, and the Sangho.[1]

This total elimination of anger is one of the cardinal principles of the Buddhist ethics, but the teaching is marred by an appeal to a process of spurious *analysis*, For example, chiding a priest for giving way to his temper, the Master asks: "Tell me what you are angry with! Are you angry with the hair of the head, or with the hair of the body, or with the nails, etc. . . . ? For a person who has made the above analysis, there is no hold for anger, any more than there is for a grain of mustard seed on the point of an awl, or for a painting in the sky."[2] The significance of this analytical process for the explanation of passive resistance, and especially of non-resistance, will be discussed in connection with Stoicism, but its more ancient origin should be noted at this point.

It is to this problem of personal retaliation that Buddhism, which Aiken calls "one of the gentlest of religions,"[3] makes it most positive contribution. We may even regard it as the rudiments of a social psychology of passive resistance. In the first place, it should be observed that

[1] Carus, *op. cit.;* 140–146. The expression would seem to mean "took refuge in the Enlightened One, the doctrinal system, and the brotherhood of disciples."

[2] Warren, *op. cit.;* p. 159.

[3] *Op. cit.;* p. 106.

this phase of the Buddhist doctrine is founded on *empirical* study; for "the Blessed One *observed the ways of society* and noticed how much misery came from malignity and foolish offences done only to gratify vanity and self-seeking pride."[1] To this is added the further observation that "the whole world dreads violence."[1] Seeking a remedy for this dread destructive force which lurks in the bosom of society, the sage arrives at a positive principle: "By love alone can we conquer evil."[2] Then, advancing a long stride in his psychological analysis, he enunciates a *law* of *human* social interaction: "Say no harsh words to thy neighbor. *He will reply to thee in the same tone.*"[3]

In the beautiful story of Prince Dirghayu this principle is applied. King Brahmadatta, having conquered, driven into exile, and finally hunted to death King Dirgheti and his queen, lived in constant terror of the anticipated vengeance of their son, Prince Dirghayu, who had escaped. In the course of events, the prince came into the employ of the murderer of his parents, and was chosen to serve him as personal attendant. One day, while on the hunt, the tired king fell asleep with his head in the lap of the prince. The latter drew his sword to avenge his parents, when the parting words of his murdered father rang in his ears: "Not by hatred is hatred appeased. Hatred is appeased only by not-hatred." The prince stayed his hand and sheathed his sword, but when the king awoke he again brandished his sword over the latter's prostrate form, at the same time disclosing his own identity. As the king begged piteously for his life, "Dirghayu said without bitterness or ill-will, 'How can I grant you your life, O king, since my life is endangered by you? It is you, O king, who must grant me my life.'

[1] Carus, *op. cit.;* 145.
[2] Aiken, *op. cit.*, quoting Lillie.
[3] Carus, *Ibid.*

"And the king said: 'Well, my dear Dirghayu, then grant me my life, and I will grant you your life.' "[1]

When they had sworn cessation of hostility, the king asked for the interpretation of King Dirgheti's dying injunction; whereupon the prince explained the same as follows: "When he said, 'Not by hatred is hatred appeased; hatred is appeased by not-hatred,' he meant this: You have killed my father and mother, O king. If I should deprive you of life, then your partisans would deprive me of life; my partisans again would deprive those of life. Thus by hatred, hatred would not be appeased. But now, O king, you have granted me my life, and I have granted you your life, thus by not-hatred has hatred been appeased!"[2] And so, the Blessed One declares, "This is an eternal law."[3]

With this teaching on *personal* retaliation and non-resistance, the positive contribution of Buddhism to a theory of passive resistance is ended. When confronted by "Simha, the general," with a very definite query, the Teacher committed himself explicitly against the literal application of his principle to both magistracy and war. Simha said: " 'I am a soldier, O Blessed One, and am appointed by the king to enforce his laws and to wage his wars. Does the Tathagata who teaches kindness without end and compassion for all sufferers, permit the punishment of the criminal? And further does the Tathagata teach the doctrine of a complete self-surrender, so that I should suffer the evil-doer to do what he pleases and yield submission to him who threatens to take by violence what is my own? Does the Tathagata[4] teach the doctrine

[1] Carus, *op. cit.;* p. 93.

[2] *Ibid.;* pp. 93-94.

[3] *Ibid.;* p. 87.

[4] I. e., the Perfect One.

that all strife, including such warfare as is waged for a righteous cause, should be forbidden?"

The reply of Buddha is equally definite, and is contained in a very elevated passage, but it will best serve the present purpose to condense it considerably, yet following very closely the language of the "Translations."[1] Point by point, the answer is:

> He who deserves punishment must be punished, and this conflicts in no way with the injunction concerning universal love and kindness. The criminal is not punished through the ill-will of the judges, but on account of his own evil-doing. The evil-doer's own acts have brought upon him the injury that the executor of the law inflicts, and the magistrate, in punishing, shall not harbor hatred in his breast.
>
> All warfare is lamentable, but the Tathagata does not teach that those who go to war in a righteous cause, after having exhausted all means to preserve the peace, are blameworthy. He must be blamed who is the cause of war. The successful general is he who, moderating himself and extinguishing all hatred from his heart, lifts up his down-trodden foe and offers him peace and brotherhood. Struggle then, O general, courageously; and fight your battles vigorously, but be a soldier of truth and the Tathagata will bless you.
>
> The Tathagata teaches a complete surrender of self, but he does not teach a surrender of anything to those powers that are evil, be they men or gods or the elements of nature. Struggle there must be, for all life is a struggle of some kind. But he that struggles should look to it lest he struggle in the interest of self against truth and righteousness.

It thus appears that the Hindu philosophy, like the Chinese, does not extend the principle of non-resistance to *group-relations*. It, however, greatly elaborates the *personal* rendering of good for evil, enunciated by Lao Tse. But no *organized* movement arose to bear witness to the

[1] *Ibid.;* pp. 126–129.

doctrine. This was doubtless due to several causes. The social constitution had not advanced to that point where voluntary organization for social purposes is desired or tolerated; being purely personal, the beliefs outlined above caused no embarrassment to the political authorities, hence persecutions did not arise to weld together those who held non-resistance beliefs; and, finally, the sects of India have always been ascetic and individualistic rather than ethical and social. Oman devotes the equivalent of four or five chapters to his discussion of "Hindu Ascetic Sects and their Subdivisions." His account yields no trace of any *organized movement* for passive resistance. In another connection, after describing the motives that support the terrible self-mortifications practised by these ascetics, he concludes that "it is as clear as day that these motives have no conscious or unconscious relation to ethics."[1] This we may accept with reference to *social* ethics at least.

ZOROASTER

Zoroastrianism, like Buddhism and Confucianism, arises in the mists of antiquity. Miraculous power and preservation from harm are ascribed in the Pahlavi texts[2] to the child Zaratust. His "*compassionate* disposition" is emphasized, and illustrated by his kindness and mercy toward those in distress, both men[3] and beasts.[4] But no

[1] "The Mystics, Ascetics, and Saints of India," John Campbell Oman; pp. 291 ff.

[2] Translated by E. W. West in "Marvels of Zoroastrianism," being Vol. XLVII of "Sacred Books of the East."

[3] *Ibid.;* p. 152.

[4] *Ibid.;* p. 153.

trace of non-resistance to hostile aggression appears. On the contrary, a quaint legend records his contest with Duresrobo, one of the "Karaps, or priests of those times."[1] The latter said, " 'I will utterly destroy thee.' . . . Zaratust spoke interruptingly thus: 'With complete mindfulness I will look upon thee with both eyes, and will utterly destroy thee.' And, for a long time, they constantly looked, one at the other, with unshrinking gaze." Duresrobo, finally cowed, rode away, but "when he had gone a little way, he fell off the horse, through severe distress and died."[2] This naïve account is interesting because it shows that the Zoroastrian ideal of character was capable of a very vigorous resistance, albeit by quite unconventional methods.

It is the more worth while to note, as above, the *negative* contribution of Zoroastrianism to the present sketch, because we find that a historian of its modern representatives, the Parsees of India,[3] has found it necessary to say that "there is no objection whatever to a Parsi embracing the profession of a soldier on religious grounds, as has been erroneously supposed by some European writers." He then shows at some length that it is because of certain economic conditions that the Parsees have been, before the time when he wrote,[4] almost without a representative in the English army of India, and that no non-resistance principle or lack of fighting spirit can account for their seeming aversion to a military career. These, and the preceding considerations, would seem to eliminate Zoroastrianism from the list of passive resistance systems.

[1] *Ibid.;* p. x.
[2] *Ibid.;* pp. 150-151.
[3] Dosabhai Framji Karaka, "History of the Parsis"; Vol. I, p. 101.
[4] In 1905.

MOHAMMED

The religion of Mohammed is at the farthest remove from the principle now under consideration. It was at the head of a victorious army that the prophet forced the adhesion of the Arab chiefs. Known as the religion of the sword, it has been the scourge and terror of nations, as might well be expected of a faith which teaches that those who die fighting for the sacred cause shall enjoy the delights of paradise, "content with their past endeavors."[1]

That these "endeavors" are expected to be far from pacifistic is shown by the fact that there are pages in the Koran that fairly ring with "calls to battle," as appears in the following:

> Prescribed for you is fighting, but it is hateful to you. Yet peradventure ye hate a thing that is good for you. . . . God knows, and ye,—ye do not know! . . . Fight then in God's way . . . with those who fight with you, but transgress not. . . . Kill them wherever ye find them, . . . for all sacred things demand retaliation, and whoso transgresses against you, transgress against him like as he transgressed against you. . . . But if they desist, then, verily, God is forgiving and merciful . . . let there be no hostility save against the unjust. [For] whoso kills a soul, unless it be for another soul or for violence in the land, it is as though he had killed men altogether.[2]

THE STOICS

The martial spirit of the Greeks and the Romans would forbid us to expect to find in their reigning philosophy any doctrine of passive resistance. Plato assigns to the warrior class a place of honor in his picture of the ideal state,[3] they being only second to the philosophers. More-

1 Robinson, "An Introduction to the History of Western Europe"; p. 70.

2 See "Selections from the Qur'an" (Koran); in *Ideas That Have Influenced Civilization,"* by Oliver J. Thatcher; Vol. IV.

3 See "The Republic" of Plato.

over, it will be recalled that Socrates, in his criticism of music, values most highly the strains of courage and temperance. "I want to have one warlike, which will sound the word or note which a brave man utters in the hour of danger and stern resolve, or when his cause is failing, and he is going to wounds or death . . . and another to be used by him in times of peace and freedom of action. . . . These two strains I ask you to leave."[1] Socrates thus makes provision for war and for a specialized warrior class, in his social division of labor. Nevertheless, Socrates himself pursued the tactics of a typical passive resistant, inasmuch as he spent his life resisting, solely by intellectual and moral means, the traditional beliefs and institutions of his day, and when condemned to drink the poison hemlock he scorned either to resist by violence or to flee into exile. In his noble defense[2] he enunciated many of the cardinal truths that underlie the policy of passive resistance. Referring to his accusers, he says, "Meletus and Anytus will not injure me; they cannot; for it is not in the nature of things that a bad man should injure a better than himself. I do not deny that he may, perhaps, kill him, or drive him into exile, or deprive him of civil rights; and he may imagine, and others may imagine, that he is doing him a great injury: but I do not agree with him."[3]

Aristotle, in the "Nicomachean Ethics,"[4] proposes to regulate rather than eliminate "the temper," holding that "the man who is deficient in a proper feeling of anger is a kind of impassive person, and his mental state [may be

[1] "The Republic"; Book III. Quoted by Perry in "The Moral Economy"; p. 203.

[2] See the "Apology" of Plato.

[3] *Ibid.;* Section 31.

[4] Translated by Walter M. Hatch and others in "The Moral Philosophy of Aristotle." Page references are to this work.

classed as] impassivity." Nevertheless, he adds, "we incline to regard the excess of anger as more widely opposed to the virtuous ideal than its defect. Excess is more generally prevalent; it is more characteristic of human nature to avenge oneself rather than to forgive. Again, in the intercourse of life, ill-tempered men are worse than the easy-going.[1] In the case of an act of wrong; to suffer the wrong is to fall short of the due proportion, while to commit the wrong is to go beyond it.[2] Still it is a worse evil to do a wrong than to suffer one.[3] But he is far from counting anger an evil in itself as do the Taoists, Buddhists, and Stoics; for Aristotle concludes that "a state of mind in virtue of which, when we are angry, we are angry only against persons, and on occasions when our anger is right and shown in a proper manner, and justified by all the circumstances"—that such a state of mind is "equable, and in harmony with its surroundings," and "praiseworthy."[4]

On the whole, the attitude of Greek thought would support a vigorous use of force on the part of the individual, the constabulary, and the state in its military capacity, provided all these forms of resistance are tempered by law and justice.

It is in Stoicism alone that there appears any clear note of passive resistance philosophy among the Greeks and Romans. Therefore it is of considerable significance to note that the Greco-Roman system of thought by that name was founded and developed, in the main, by representatives or descendants of "the Hellenistic mixed races of the Orient."[5] The prevalence in both Oriental and

1 *Ibid.;* p. 225.
2 *Ibid.;* p. 275.
3 *Ibid.;* p. 298.
4 *Ibid.;* p. 225.
5 Windelband, "A History of Philosophy"; p. 162.

Stoic philosophy of the habit of pseudo-analysis, as a support for passivity, has already been noted. The following passage from the Roman Stoa might have been uttered, without the change of a syllable, on the banks of the Ganges: "What is the body? It is a complex of skin, bones, hair, blood, and other nastiness." "Just consider sensibly what the body is," says the Stoic. "Put it upon the dissecting-table, or regard it as it will be in the charnel-house, and see how all your false opinions, your vices, will wither up at once."[1]

Bigg has pointed out very convincingly the essential fallacy and weakness of this logical process. "It leaves out the one thing which is important, the relation of flesh to emotion, and of both to intelligence; in a word it leaves out the living personality. And therefore it really leaves out morality, at any rate it deprives morality of any reasonable basis. For what true fellowship can there be in a world of thinking corpses?"[2]

But the above criticism might easily be taken so radically as to do injustice to Stoicism. Windelband[3] has shown that the Stoic possessed the high ideal of a universal society in which "gods and men together form one great rational living structure, in which every individual is a necessary member." But it must be admitted that this was a very "high-flying idealism," which failed to coincide with any existing national state.[4] Yet a vigorous sense of duty led the Stoic to recognize his obligations as a citizen of the actual world, sadly devitalized and emaciated

[1] Quoted by Charles Bigg in his Introduction to "The Meditations of Marcus Aurelius Antoninus, translated by John Jackson." See pp. 40–41.

[2] *Ibid.*

[3] *Op. cit.;* pp. 173-176.

[4] With Cicero, "the Stoic universal state" . . . takes on the outlines of the "Roman Empire." Windelband; p. 177.

though it appeared in the light of his drastic analysis. We find that Seneca urged the duty of coöperation with the state, not only in seeking the honorable offices, but in performing the humblest duties of the citizens.[1] Epictetus exclaims: "'What then! (some one will say), do you philosophers teach us a contempt of kings?' By no means. Which of us teaches any one to contend with them about things of which they have the command?"[2] And again he is very explicit: "Let no wise man estrange himself from the government of the state; for it is both wicked to withdraw from being useful to the needy, and cowardly to give way to the worthless. For it is foolish to choose rather to be governed ill than to govern well."[3]

The tone of this last passage, however, illustrates the truth of Windelband's statement that, in the Stoic's view, "the wise man, in the self-sufficiency of his virtue, needs the state as little as he needs any other society."[4] But, rather than submit to be *mis*ruled by non-virtuous fools, we see that Epictetus urges upon the wise and virtuous the duty of ruling themselves, and assisting others to do so. Thus, while Roman Stoicism preached for the individual a negative and decidedly passive attitude, as we shall see, it formulated no doctrine of non-resistance, as applied to constabulary or military affairs. Its non-resistance, like that of Lao Tse and Gautama, was distinctly *personal,* applying only to the relations of man to man in private life.

As formulated by Epictetus and Marcus Aurelius, the one a poor, old, crippled slave, the other an idolized em-

[1] "The Creed of Lucius Annæus Seneca," by Virginia Beauchamp; p. 30.

[2] "The Works of Epictetus," translated by Thomas Wentworth Higginson; Vol. I, p. 97.

[3] *Ibid.;* Vol. II, p. 274.

[4] *Op. cit.;* p. 173.

peror on the throne of the world, the ethics of Stoicism is transcendently noble, yet tinged with incurable sadness. It is easy to see how a poor slave, whose crippled body an outrageous fortune had reduced to bondage, should find a refuge for his unconquerable spirit in the denial of the essential worth of all the things held dear by a world of masters. But it would be easy to ascribe too much importance to these outward circumstances of Epictetus's life. For even Marcus Aurelius, whom fortune had so prodigally favored that he had to admonish himself to "take heed lest the purple stain the soul," pictures life and duty in precisely similar perspective and proportions.

Epictetus [1] emphasizes in numberless ways the thought that man's estimates and emotions are the essence of his misfortunes. To one who groans, "I have lost my coat," the answer is "Ay, because you had a coat." "Has your neighbor indeed stolen your goods? What then, are you a piece of furniture?" It is the *view* we take of these things that affronts us, and not the outward happening. "When, therefore, any one provokes you, be assured that it is your own opinion which provokes you." The lordly *will* is thus made the master of life, and, enthroning it in this way, Epictetus actually practised what he taught, and went to exile, fetters, and death, "smiling, and cheerful, and serene." But it is a victory won by a sweeping relinquishment of territory. Since one is to become unconquerable by entering into no combat in which it is not in his power to conquer,[2] the range of his striving is limited, in the last analysis, to mastering his own subjective states. Discounting, as external to the rational self and therefore insignificant, wealth, reputation, wife, friends, children,—in short, all that other men have by

[1] Higginson, *op. cit.*
[2] *Ibid.;* Vol. II, p. 223.

universal assent agreed to call good,—the Stoic, says Epictetus, should "contemplate death, change, torture, exile."[1] It is thus that the kindly, yet proud-spirited, philosopher-slave made his last stand. It is the Fabian strategy of victory through planful and dignified retreat, applied to the moral life. This is one of those traits that have rendered passive resistants so baffling to oppressors of all ages. They leave the violent and bloody man to batter down laboriously the empty fortresses from which the soul has quietly withdrawn. Hence Bigg rightly says that Stoicism "is indeed a theory of tyrannicide."[2] It leaves the would-be oppressor to defeat his own ends by an impotent beating of the air.

But even Stoic endurance has its limits, and so Epictetus reminds his disciples to "remember the principal thing—that the door is open." That door is suicide, and here we note another striking similarity between the Stoic and Buddhist philosophies. Both tended to end in self-destruction, in voluntary abandonment of the dismantled wreck of personal existence. Buddha had to exhort his priests, whose good qualities were such a cause of welfare to men, to endure the flesh for the sake of the unenlightened. Thus "the Blessed One . . . out of compassion for men, laid down this precept: 'Priests, let no one destroy himself, and whosoever would destroy himself, let him be dealt with according to law.'" So now we find Epictetus taking comfort in the thought that through that same door of self-destruction he might enter at need "an abode open to all, and put off my last garment, this poor body of mine; beyond this no one has any power over me." The last clause indicates clearly that it is really a

[1] *Ibid.;* p. 114.

[2] Introduction to Jackson's "Meditations of Marcus Aurelius"; p. 47.

phase of *resistance,* the last bitter paradox of complete non-resistance—"but if you stay, do not complain."[1]

The thought of Epictetus, as has been shown, dwells much on what we may call the *impersonal* assaults of fortune, although the question of the proper reaction toward *personal* affronts is not neglected. Marcus Aurelius, however, develops this aspect more fully. In his "Meditations," rightly called one of the fairest flowers of pagan thought, he reminds himself that "earthly existence yields but one harvest, holiness of character and altruism of action." Condensing and combining various passages in his "Meditations," and others from the writings of Epictetus, we obtain the following principles of passive resistance, applying to cases "when thy neighbor sins against thee":

(1) One's first reflection, says Marcus Aurelius, should be: "With what conception of Good and Evil did he commit this sin? When this is clear to thee, astonishment and anger will give place to pity." Or, as Epictetus puts it, "You will meekly bear" with the reviler, for "you will say upon every occasion, 'It seemed so to him.' "

(2) Next one should reflect, with Epictetus, upon his own human nature and its appropriate expression. "If you are considering yourself a wolf, then . . . bite again." But, examining yourself as a man, notice your equipment. "See what faculties you have brought into the world with you. Are they fitted for ferocity? for revenge?"

(3) Passing from bodily equipment to moral constitution, before going to the attack "remember," continues Epictetus, "to say first to yourself that you are constituted gentle, and that by doing nothing violent, you will live without the need of repentance, and irreproachable."

(4) Advancing, now, with Marcus Aurelius, to more

[1] Higginson, *op. cit.;* p. 80.

positive principles: "Reflect that kindness is invincible, provided only it be genuine"; then, in utmost good will, and carefully avoiding every trace of irony, self-righteousness, or rebuke, meekly admonish the sinner, and "do thy utmost by persuasion" to show him the irrationality of his action and its harmful effects on his own life.

(5) Now, continues Marcus Aurelius, "Should one interpose with main force, take refuge in equanimity and tranquillity, and turn this obstacle into an occasion for the exercise of another virtue."

(6) Finally, says Marcus Aurelius, one should solace himself with the following reflections: "First, thy goal was not the impossible, [but] simply the putting forth of such an effort. And this end thou hast attained." Second, remember always "that indignation is not a form of courage . . . but that meekness and gentleness are more human . . . more manly, and it is he who possesses these that has strength, nerve, and bravery." Third, "the nearer patience is to dispassionateness, by so much is it nearer strength." Pain and anger are "characteristic of weakness. . . . For their victims have both received their wounds and both succumbed."

This Stoic program of non-resistance is probably the most completely detailed formulation to be found anywhere, but it should be noticed that it is applied only to personal reaction toward *personal* affronts. It is not extended to deny the right of the *magistrate* and the warring *state* to the use of violence; although Bigg says of Marcus Aurelius, "So absolute is his notion of tolerance that he will not allow a place even for indignation . . .[1] and it is

[1] Bigg's statement is not strong enough. Even *surprise* is deprecated. Marcus Aurelius says that "for a man to exhibit *surprise* if the universe produce some result, which its nature is to produce, is a piece of folly no less disgraceful than to be lost in amazement at the perversity of the fig-tree in bearing figs." Jackson, *op. cit.;* p. 145.

not easy to see how he would justify even legal punishment."[1]

One seems to be facing a startling paradox when it is remembered that those benignant thoughts were penned by a *Roman emperor,* in his tent *at the front with the legions,* during the eagerly snatched intervals of a life of activity devoted to the service of the most gigantic organization of coercion known to history, the Roman Empire. Yet Bigg probably states the real position of the true Marcus Aurelius on the matter of public coercion, for he was certainly a tragic figure, whose worldly greatness and authority were all thrust upon him. The bitter self-contradiction of his career must be left for notice in a later discussion.

JESUS OF NAZARETH

The story of Jesus of Nazareth affords, beyond comparison, a demonstration of the conquering power, in the long run, of passive resistance. It is not the purpose to discuss his teachings or his example at this stage. Inasmuch as Christianity was a *sect* during its early centuries, and became a world religion simultaneously with its abandonment of passive resistance principles, its exposition will be reserved for the next chapter. The discussion must then deal with the continued existence of Jesus as an Ideal, or Spiritual Presence, dominating all the succeeding centuries, than which there is no more unquestionable and significant fact in the history of humanity. At this stage, however, we must consider him simply as the human founder of a historical religion, thus pursuing the logical order demanded by the present sketch.

The three Stoics just considered have already carried us

[1] *Op. cit.;* p. 44.

over into the beginning of the Christian era. Seneca was born about four years before Jesus, and died in the year 65 A. D. The hard fate of the slave philosopher, Epictetus, has left the dates of both his birth and death undetermined, but he is supposed to have lived between the years 60 and 120 A. D. Marcus Aurelius was born 121 A. D., and died in 180 A. D. Thus the three together span, almost without overlapping, the first two Christian centuries. In their writings the pagan philosophy utters its last and noblest word, for the purposes of this study at least. There is no evidence that the teachings of the three Romans were especially influenced by their contemporaries, Jesus and his early disciples. On the other hand, it is impossible to account for the teachings of Jesus by seeking their roots in contemporary or earlier thought, except in so far as it may be said to represent the culmination of Judaism. There is a striking resemblance to Buddhism as regards returning good for evil, but the exceedingly slight structure of evidence reared by those who would trace the doctrines of Jesus to a Palestinian Buddhism has been destroyed by Aiken in a scholarly dissertation.[1] In that study he shows that the few parallels which actually exist "have their fitting explanation in the principle that the human mind, working in similar circumstances, will give birth to similar thoughts."

Turning to the religious history of his own people, some very interesting considerations arise concerning the indigenous nature of Jesus' teachings on non-resistance. To be sure, the idea of passive suffering, as a means of moral and social reconstruction, is as clear as crystal in the writings of the Hebrew prophets, especially Isaiah:[2] "He

[1] "The Dhamma of Gotama the Buddha and the Gospel of Jesus Christ: A Critical Inquiry into the Alleged Relations of Buddhism with Primitive Christianity," by Charles Francis Aiken; cf. p. 267.

[2] Critical considerations concerning the exact authorship of Bibli-

was oppressed, yet when he was afflicted he opened not his mouth; As a lamb that is led to the slaughter, and as a sheep that before its shearers is dumb, so he opened not his mouth."

Leopold says that "the founders of ancient Hindu religions who preceded Gautama owed their prestige to their record of suffering, patience, and solitude, just as Gautama himself won over his first disciples by the same means, as well as that irresistible spell, 'the bell which is hung in heaven.' "[1] But the humility, meekness, and sufferings of Jesus did not produce any such effect upon the mind of the Jewish people. So far as their attitude is concerned, the prophecy was literally fulfilled: "He was despised, and rejected of men. . . . And we esteemed him not."[2] The commonly accepted explanation of this well-known fact is that there existed in the social mind of the Jewish people a conception of the Messiah and his mission which was utterly violated by the career of Jesus. This is doubtless the true explanation, but it is very significant for the purposes of the present study to observe that the Jewish ideal pictured a conquering *military* hero, while they saw in Jesus only a smitten and despised non-resistant. It is not desired to exaggerate this aspect, but it certainly is important for racial and social psychology.

The situation was really anomalous. Jesus was a son of their own race, fulfilling the description of an ideal, non-resisting, vicariously suffering, national leader,—an ideal which had been set forth in the nation's most distinctive literature,—yet "as one from whom men hide their

cal passages or Buddhist texts have slight significance for social psychology. The existence of the writings in the literature of the race or the period is the essential fact.

1 "Prestige: a Psychological Study of Social Estimates," by Lewis Leopold; p. 264.

2 Isaiah; Chap. liii.

face he was despised."[1] The question arises: Was the Hebrew temperament especially incompatible with non-resistance, and had it never really responded to the ideal of "the suffering servant of Jehovah"?[2]

We know that throughout their entire history the ancient Hebrews were never lacking in warlike qualities, and that the later Jews put up more than one desperate resistance against overwhelming odds. On the other hand, the idea of passive suffering was limited to a few prophets, and in their system it figured as a divine rather than a human attribute.

At the time of Jesus there existed an ascetic communistic sect, the Essenes, who seem indeed to have held some non-resistance principles. But they were very few in number and their peace principles seem to have been simply that non-resistant, passive attitude which usually accompanies religious communism.[3] When contrasted with the revolutionary activities of the warlike Zealots, the Pharisees also appear to play the rôle of genuine passive resistants. That is to say, as Professor Shaler Mathews has shown,[4] the Pharisees were economically comfortable and socially honored, so that they reacted against the Roman domination with non-physical means, contenting themselves with writing eschatological and apocalyptical Utopias. The less comfortable and less articulate masses took to the sword, in the hope of more quickly ushering in Messiah's reign, and perished with the sword. But this policy of the Pharisees, as the Jewish literary class, can hardly be called

[1] Isaiah; Chap. liii.

[2] *Ibid.*

[3] See the history of such sects in Hinds, "American Communistic Communities." For Essenes, see "Encyclopedia of Religion and Ethics," Hastings.

[4] "The Messianic Hope in the New Testament." See especially Chap. iii.

passive resistance. It was simply acquiescence, proceeding from selfish considerations, and not from any true peace principle. So we may conclude that the Jewish race had not, up to the time of Jesus, developed any affinity for a non-resistance philosophy, and they do not seem to have shown the slightest trace of it during all their subsequent history of cruel oppression. No other race in modern times has had so much occasion [1] to enunciate a doctrine that condemns coercion and violence, and none has shown less inclination to do so.

1 Some writers assume that non-resistance is a doctrine of political oppression and despair. On this theory it should, contrary to the fact, be especially characteristic of the Jews. According to Professor Duff ("The Theology and Ethics of the Hebrews"), the prophecy of Isaiah quoted above was written by one who was a captive slave in Babylon, and indeed the title of his fifth chapter, "The Four Songs of the Suffering Slave," suggests that the assumed connection between passive resistance and political despair may actually hold in this case, which is the only instance of passive resistance in theory or practice in the history of this race, so far as the writer is aware.

CHAPTER III

NON-VIOLENCE IN THE CHRISTIAN TRADITION

IT has been seen that the net result of the non-Christian teaching on passive resistance amounted simply to the personal applications of the doctrine as treated by isolated teachers and philosophers. When confronted with the social problems that logically grow out of it, they uniformly refused to extend the application of the principle.

The question now becomes: What did Jesus teach, by precept or example, on personal retaliation, magistracy, and war? Briefly put, the answer is that his doctrine is quite full and very explicit on personal revenge and forgiveness, uncertain as to the state, and not given at all on the subject of war. An extensive array of quotations is not required in order to show that Jesus forbade a vindictive and retaliatory spirit, or that he inculcated a loving attitude that forgives "seventy times seven," and returns "good for evil." The transforming power of the spirit of "peace on earth, good will toward men," which heralded the advent of Christ in the Gospel accounts, and which breathes in his dying words on the cross, was never more beautifully set forth than in the words of Julia Ward Howe:

> In the beauty of the lilies Christ was born across the sea,
> With a glory in his bosom that transfigures you and me.

Yet those lines were penned as part of a "*Battle Hymn,*" and were sung by hosts of men marching to the terrible shock of a fratricidal war. Moreover, the moral agitation which precipitated that war was led by two fearless champions who stood squarely and explicitly upon the principle of passive resistance—John Greenleaf Whittier and William Lloyd Garrison. This slight digression may be permitted here as a foretaste of the difficult contradictions that beset every turn of the subject now before us.

The important consideration just here is to notice that this transfiguring power dwelt in the *bosom* of Jesus; that is to say, it was the essential and characteristic emanation and atmosphere of his life. One might spend his days collecting texts and tracing out the story of the followers of Christ down to the present hour, and yet miss the great central truth of the history of passive resistance. That central fact is the personality of Jesus. If one were to overlook Jesus of Nazareth as the one supreme exemplar of the victorious power of passive resistance, his case would be precisely analogous to that of the early students of nature, who had great difficulty in detecting the *atmosphere* simply because of its universal presence and its equal and never-failing pressure. Such is the spiritual atmosphere and moral pressure exerted by Jesus Christ in the Western World.

The question of participation in government hardly existed in Jesus' day. It was simply a question of submission. The Roman government stands in the background of the Gospel narrative as a given fact in a world which is distorted on its institutional side by reason of the sinful selfishness of individual lives. Jesus devoted himself to opening up in the personal experience of men streams of motive which, it was assumed, would reform social institutions by regenerating the individual life. He neither condemned nor endorsed the state as an institution. But in saying, "Render unto Cæsar the things that are Cæsar's, and unto God the things that are God's," he recognized a certain claim on the part of the actually existing government. This claim expediency taught him to recognize so long as it did not encroach on the domain of conscience; but the claims of God are supreme. There is also the saying, addressed to Pilate, "Thou couldest have no power . . . except it were given thee from above." Professor Mathews [1] quotes these passages, with the pointed remark that "any man who attempts to erect a theory of politics upon two such statements will need considerable imagination, and deserves small credence."

But we may not consider that this sums up all the teaching of Christianity concerning the state. The doctrines of the Apostle Paul formed from the very beginning an integral part of the Christian message, and he is more full and explicit on this point. To him is due the theory that the civil power is ordained of God; that the magistrate bears the sword by divine commission, and that he punishes evil-doers as the representative of God. Christians are to be obedient to rulers and to support them with their prayers. The influence of these doctrines on subsequent history will appear in connection with the various sects. Particularly important in this connection is the teaching of the apostle against the use of civil courts by Christians, who were instructed to adjust their own disputes. Professor Mathews concludes that Paul's attitude was "not . . . that of coöperation with the state, but that of submission to its requirements. In fact, he does not, apparently, think that the state is a matter in which the Christian has any particular share." [2] The clue to the apostle's

[1] "The Messianic Hope in the New Testament"; p. 311.
[2] *Ibid.;* p. 313.

teaching, as the same author[1] has pointed out with great fulness in the work quoted, lies in the belief of Paul and the early disciples that the present world lay in irremediable wickedness, and that Christians are to abide in it as mere sojourners who expect the immediate coming of Christ and the end of all temporal affairs. From that day to this there have never been lacking whole communities of men and women to hold and practise that view of life.

On the subject of *war*, neither Jesus nor any of his disciples has left direct testimony, yet the feeling that warfare is incompatible with Christianity is so nearly universal as to amount almost to a world view. Even those who practise and defend such things seem to realize, more or less keenly, the incongruity which unites the cross and the sword.

The truth would seem to be that Jesus and the writers of the New Testament left, not a *doctrine* to circumscribe, but an *ideal* to *leaven,* the moral and social life of mankind. This may be seen in the case of slavery and democracy, as well as of war. The apostle Paul exhorted Christian disciples to abide content and obedient in the status of slavery, and he returned the slave Onesimus to his master with a letter which remains to us to-day. Yet in that very letter he dealt a death-blow to human slavery when he said that, inasmuch as the runaway had been converted to Christ, the master, who was also a Christian, "should have him forever; no longer as a servant, but more than a servant, a brother beloved." The two things were not compatible, and the conscience of humanity finally wiped out the contradiction. So the Southern apologists were entirely correct in their defense of slavery by the letter of Scripture, while Whittier was still more right when he condemned

[1] See also "The Ethical Approach to the Social Question" and "Jesus Christ and the Social Question," by Francis G. Peabody.

their exegetical efforts as a wresting of the holy writings.[1]

In the same way the *letter* of the Christian Scriptures sustains autocratic government and inculcates passive submission to tyranny. Yet the *spirit* of Christianity, embodied in the same writings and eluding the mere text-collector, lies at the very heart of the demand for genuine democracy.[2] The same may be said of the movement for the larger emancipation of woman. A reactionary might easily marshal against it an array of Scripture passages, but the simple truth that a Christian view of life means a common human level for both sexes would remain unshaken. Finally, the case of war is precisely the same. The functionaries of institutional religion are never lacking to consecrate and sanctify, though hardly with New Testament words, the arms of those who fight in any cause, while silently the leaven of the faith they profess is rendering warfare unendurable to enlightened men. Many learned writers and eminent statesmen have in recent years advocated the extension of the peace-group by some form of international union, so that the peace which has excluded strife in turn from the family, the clan, the tribe, and the nation may come to embrace an *international* peace-group and finally the world. The plan is laudable in purpose, and is based on experience and sound social theory. It is mentioned here merely to say that it was clearly anticipated in the Christian principle of universal good will, by which all the nations of men were grouped into one ideal brotherhood two thousand years ago.

Regardless of its historical explanations, one fact stands out with unmistakable clearness, namely, that the early Christian church was the first peace society and the first

1 See Whittier's poems entitled "Clerical Oppressors" and "The Hunted Fugitive."

2 For a splendid exposition of the revolutionary character of Christianity, see Perry, "The Moral Economy," Chap. iv.

genuine organized expression of passive resistance in history. Perhaps it would be more accurate to call it non-resistance, rather than passive resistance. As defined in this essay, non-resistance is essentially an attitude of submission and of passive suffering, while passive resistance is a more active, and even an aggressive, attitude. It is distinguished chiefly by the fact that it rejects the use of physical force and coercion in human affairs, but it strives by all other means to overcome evil with good, particularly by political activity. Aside from this perhaps subtle but significant distinction, the two terms are used interchangeably throughout this book.

The church of the first three centuries was too thoroughly estranged from all political and social participation to permit the early Christians to be classed as passive resistants. But the earliest glimpse we may obtain of its history reveals the fact that the Christian ideal had already become that of victory through passive suffering, and personal non-resistance had already become a distinctive principle of Christian character. This is not strange when one reads in the New Testament writings, which formed their daily thoughts, that "the friendship of the world is enmity against God; therefore think it not strange concerning the fiery trial among you . . . as though a strange thing happened unto you, but inasmuch as ye are partakers of Christ's sufferings, rejoice." Yet "the Lord's servant must not strive, but be gentle towards all," bearing in mind "to be in subjection to rulers, to authorities, to be obedient . . . showing all meekness toward all men." [1]

When we couple with this meek and defenseless attitude the further position of absolute refusal to participate in even the superficial formalities of the pagan public cere-

1 James, Chap. IV, v. 4; I Peter, Chap. IV, v. 12–13; II Timothy, Chap. II, v. 24; Titus, Chap. III, v. 1–2.

monial, it is plain that the early Christians were inevitably marked for persecution and slaughter. Their unbending loyalty to Christ, and to him alone, was sure to bring them into conflict with the Roman populace, if not the Roman government.

It is well known that the Roman pantheon was very hospitable, and admitted freely the gods of all the peoples included under the sway of the empire. But the Christians, like the Jews who had preceded them in the conflict for pure monotheism, could entertain nothing but absolute abhorrence for all strange gods and their worship. Their refusal to honor the local divinities aroused the wrath of the populace, especially in the "fanatical East,"[1] while their failure to pay divine honors to the emperor often placed them before the government in the light of unpatriotic secessionists.[2] Mommsen points out that "the religion of the Roman commonwealth was, like the religions of antiquity on the whole, essentially national and in fact nothing more than the reflection of the national feeling," and similar to the religiousness met in certain extreme forms of patriotism to-day. "Accordingly, the order of Roman society demanded from the Roman citizen Roman faith and the corresponding conduct."[3] But religion was now on the decline in the Roman world, and the government was inclined to be lenient, until the marvelously aggressive missionary spirit of Christianity forced the authorities to make a stand. The high treason of the Christians was twofold in the eye of Roman law, viz, the refusal of the honors due to the gods, and the offense toward the emperor. Of the two offenses, the latter was

[1] Hardy, "Christianity and the Roman Government"; p. 121, n. 1.

[2] See Mommsen, "Der Religionsfrevel nach römischem Recht" in "Historische Zeitschrift," Vol. LXIV.

[3] *Ibid.;* p. 390.

the heavier. It was an affront to the majesty of the Roman people, and partly the ground of the popular hatred and baiting of Christians. When confessed in court, it became the legal road to martyrdom. "Under all circumstances, however, the coercion of the magistrates was directed essentially against the apostacy from national faith,"[1] and applied especially to those possessing Roman citizenship.

But, despite this legal situation, the Christians were not sought out by the government. On the contrary, the emperors, when appealed to, tried rather to check the popular clamor, and rioting against Christians was forbidden. In fact, the disorders stirred up by the persecuting activities of the populace were more displeasing to the authorities than was the obstinate conduct of a few despised sectarians, who might otherwise have been quietly ignored.[2]

In his "De Corona,"[3] Tertullian has preserved in vivid form several aspects of the situation. The bounty of the emperors was being distributed in the camp, and the soldiers, crowned with laurel, were approaching. But one of them, refusing to wear the insignia of idolatry, bore the useless garland in his hand. Tertullian pictures his heroic courage as he is "jeered at, tried, stripped, and led forth to martyrdom," under the execrations of the pagans, and the adverse judgment, possibly, of his fellow-Christians, who may consider him "headstrong and rash, and too eager to die" in thus imperiling the followers of the Christian name over "a mere matter of dress." Tertullian is filled

[1] *Ibid.;* pp. 396–397.

[2] Hardy, *op cit.;* pp. 137–138, 148–149. See also Mommsen, *op. cit.;* p. 394.

[3] "The Writings of Tertullian," in Vol. II of the "Ante Nicene Library." The essay is given in the table of contents under the title, "The Soldier's Chaplet."

with scorn for these pseudo-Christians, who "are also purposing the refusal of martyrdom" by "flight from city to city."

Although the zealous father thus deplores the presence in the church of the more prudently cautious element, the typical Christian attitude of the time was that of defenseless sheep in the midst of wolves, and it even passed over into "the hunger and the thirst for martyrdom, the ardor to render testimony, the will to imitate the Passion of Christ," which Allard [1] finds not only in the Epistle of St. Ignace to the Romans, but actually expressed in the lives of a multitude of Christians. Among various fanatic sects, this thirst for martyrdom became a "fever impossible to control," so that the church was forced to warn those who were proposing to offer themselves that the Gospel taught nothing of the kind. This occurred in the second century, and in the fourth "the disciplinary canons promulgated by Saint Pierre of Alexandria blame the laity and punish the clergy who offer themselves voluntarily to the judges." An extreme case is that of a village in Asia "whose inhabitants presented themselves *en masse* before the tribunal of the proconsul, who, astounded at their number, refused to judge them." [2] This instance shows that even non-resistance may become a matter of crowd contagion.

It was by such enthusiasm of meekness and suffering that the faith of the persecuted spread, and that Christianity arose, in three centuries, from the status of a detested and outcast sect to that of the favored religion of the Empire. This in itself represents a marvelous triumph of non-resistance principles.

The next significant fact to be noted is that when the

[1] "Dix Leçons sur le Martyre," by Paul Allard, Chap. IX, "Le temoignage des martyrs. Le valeur de ce temoignage."

[2] Tertullian, quoted by Allard, *op. cit.;* p. 325.

church won the favor of the world she abandoned simultaneously her non-resistance principles. Not only did the persecuted become the persecutor, but she who had testified, by a long line of martyrs, against war, now girded on the sword herself. But the apostacy from the doctrine of peace was never universal. The tradition arose, as we have seen, along with the Christian faith itself, and its light has never wholly waned.

In view of the almost total absence of specific teaching on war in the New Testament writings, it is interesting to note how clear and how absolutely identified with Christianity itself is the peace testimony made in the very earliest days of the church. In the essay by Tertullian quoted above, the author, in discussing the "heathen chaplet" and related questions, digresses to inquire "whether warfare is proper at all for Christians," and this digression deals, in his opinion, with the really "primary question." His conclusion is that no Christian may enter military service; and "when faith comes later, and finds any preoccupied with military service . . . there must be either an immediate abandonment of it, which has been the course with many; or all sorts of quibbling will have to be resorted to in order to avoid offending God."[1] In his quaint argument, which is put simply in the form of a question, we see two tendencies which are of the utmost significance in all the later history of passive resistance; viz., the direct appeal to Jesus of Nazareth as the answer to all arguments in favor of war, and the tendency to extend the Christian prohibition to the acts of the magistrate and officers of the law: "Shall it be held lawful to make an occupation of the sword, when the Lord proclaims that he who uses the sword shall perish by the sword? And shall the son of peace take part in battle when it does not become him even

[1] "De Corona"; Section xi.

to suc at law? And shall he apply the chain, and the prison, and the torture, and the punishment, who is not even the avenger of his own wrongs?"

Tertullian by no means stood alone among the Christian fathers in his condemnation of war and violence. A long line of eloquent writers,[1] beginning with Justin Martyr (about 114 A. D.), declared the absolute incompatibility of the Christian spirit with retaliation, either public or private. Cyprian, made Bishop of Carthage about 248 A. D., boldly refers to war as *murder* "committed wholesale";[2] while Lactantius, in the third century also, goes farther and declares it un-Christian "to accuse any one of a capital charge, because it makes no difference whether you put a man to death by word, or rather by the sword, since it is the act of putting to death itself which is prohibited."[3]

The principles thus set forth by the leaders of the church[4] they sealed with their own martyr's death; and the records indicate unnumbered instances where nameless men and women refused to avenge their wrongs even by appeal to the law, or, as soldiers, threw down their arms and suffered death rather than slay their fellow-men, saying simply and finally, "I am a Christian, and therefore I cannot fight."[5]

With the fifth century, and the temporal triumph of the church, we enter a period of about a thousand years during which the Christian policy of meekness and non-

1 See "The Primitive Christians' Estimate of War and Self-Defence," by Josiah W. Leeds, 1876.

2 *Ibid.;* p. 15.

3 *Ibid.;* p. 53.

4 Leeds gives the testimony of Justin Martyr, Athenagoras, Irenæus, Clement of Alexandria, Cyprian, Tertullian, Arnobius, Lactantius, Ignatius of Antioch, and the unknown writer of the Epistle to Diognetus.

5 See "An Inquiry into the Accordancy of War with the Principles of Christianity," by Jonathan Dymond, Philadelphia, 1835.

resistance was almost, though not totally, forgotten. The tradition was kept alive partly by the monastic orders and partly by the numerous heretical sects, during all the centuries of feudal and ecclesiastical violence. Wherever the ideal of the apostolic life revived, there non-resistance was preached and practised. Perhaps it would not be far from the truth to say that, in proportion as intimate familiarity with the New Testament writings declined, so the testimony against personal retaliation, persecution, and war became neglected. The slender stream we are now to trace will suddenly widen into a flood and separate into many lusty branches at the Reformation—precisely the time when the long-standing priestly monopoly of the Bible was broken, and the knowledge and interpretation of the Scriptures became the privilege of the common people.

In the meantime the tradition and ideal of the simple apostolic life, in so far as it was not confined to the cloisters, was cherished by a succession of heretics. They were not consciously intent upon the enunciation of any doctrine of non-resistance, but were led into it through the unconscious logic by which the mind seeks mental and moral self-consistency. In their attempt to reproduce the apostolic life, they naturally found themselves out of tune with violence, both personal and organized. It is the purpose now to mention in the barest way a few of the obscure heretics who helped to maintain the true apostolic succession of passive resistance.

The Albigenses, or Cathari, were, as the latter term indicates, the original Puritans, aiming at a recalling of the church to the pure simplicity of apostolic days. They are not so admirable as this characterization might imply, being revoltingly ascetic, and accused of immoral practices. A pronounced dualistic heresy attributed to them by the church is consistent with their semi-Oriental origin. They are supposed to have been strongly influenced by the Paulicians, or Manichees, who originated in the seventh century on the upper Euphrates, in Armenia. The dualism of the Paulicians, in turn, might possibly be traced to the ancient Parsee religion of Persia. The Paulicians were not non-resistants but quite the contrary. To the number of five thousand, they put up a terrible resistance to the Byzantine Empire, and succeeded in forming a sort of outlaw community near Tephrica, from whence they made forays into the empire. [1] Later they were placed on the Bulgarian frontier, and finally scattered. Their doctrines made their way through the Balkan countries and Italy, into northern, and later southern, France.[2] Here the theoogical tenets of the Paulicians persisted in the heresy known as Manicheeism, but their martial spirit was replaced by a modified doctrine of non-resistance. Being extreme ascetics, they had a natural affinity for non-resistance doctrine of the extreme negative type. Indeed, among their highest order, called "The Perfect," Catharism flatly repudiated the natural human instincts, and, along with the Buddhist and the Stoic, even courted death by voluntary starvation.[3] The members of this highest order "are not allowed," say Alzog,[4] "to kill any beast, reject the oath, and, for true believers, secular government and jurisdiction have no validity, as again they must not resist violence but only suffer it. Their detestation is directed in the fullest measure upon the entire condition of the Catholic

[1] See the "History of the Christian Church in the Middle Ages," by Dr. Wilhelm Moeller; pp. 27–29.

[2] See the essay by A. Luchaire on "Southern France and the Religious Opposition," in "Medieval Civilization," by Munro and Sellery.

[3] *Ibid.*

[4] "Manual of Universal Church History," by the Rev. Dr. John Alzog; p. 389.

Church, which persecutes, possesses and enjoys, instead of suffering and renouncing."

The atrocious crusade against these Albigenses was preached in 1208, after they had been long established. Moeller gives, as the year of their origin, 1162. But, if this be correct, they were preceded by other non-resistants, who spread strange doctrines in the dioceses of Liège and Arras as early as 1022, teaching, among other things, that "men must leave the world . . . *injure no one,* and practice love toward the brethren."[1] Near Cologne, in 1146, Moeller finds another sect, *Christ's Poor,* "who live apostolically without possessions, and desire not to rule but to suffer."[2] Both these are non-resistant sects, and, as will be observed, they were earlier than the Albigenses. They, along with others that could be traced, no doubt, were obscure and feeble movements. Their significance lies in the fact that they represent the occasional up-springings of a hidden, underground stream of social idealism which seeped down through the dark ages of the church, ready to burst forth in full volume when the confining strata of militant ecclesiasticism should become weakened above it.

So closely connected with the Albigenses as to be confused with them and smitten down along with them by the persecutors, were the Waldenses. They were the followers of Peter Waldo, a one-time rich merchant of Lyons, and were known also as "the Poor Men of Lyons." This is probably the most "respectable" heretical movement of the middle ages. The available evidence does not, however, make it perfectly clear that the Waldensian brotherhood should be classed as one of the distinctly non-resistant sects. The very fact that it was so respectable with the authorities and so popular with the masses raises some doubt.

[1] Moeller, *op. cit.;* pp. 383, 386.
[2] *Ibid.*

The later adherents of the sect offered armed resistance to the authorities of Savoy, in the middle of the sixteenth century,[1] and therefore cannot be regarded as thoroughgoing non-resistants. But we may perhaps safely conclude that the *early* Waldenses do represent the true non-resistance tradition, it being an essential aspect of their endeavor to revive the apostolic life. Since they probably influenced the *Humiliates* of Northern Italy in the second half of the twelfth century, according to Moeller, his characterization of the latter we may apply to the Waldenses also: "The precepts of the Sermon on the Mount gave the standard for their conception of a humble and meek life. They rejected the oath, taught the love of enemies, renunciation of revenge, and contentment."[2]

Many of these smaller sects arose and were dissipated under slight momentum; the Albigenses, though much more powerful, were virtually exterminated in two cruel crusades; while even the Waldenses fell into disfavor, endured persecution, resisted the civil power, and finally succeeded in maintaining themselves to the present day in the mountain of Dauphiné and the Piedmontese Alps.[3]

But these, and the various other groups recorded in the long history of heretical sects, may be regarded as part of a larger movement. Hartson[4] has shown how the voluntary associations of the middle ages contributed to that remarkable transformation of feudal society, with its serfs and intellectual darkness, into our modern society of democratically organized freemen and scientific enlightenment. The work of the gilds is well known, but the

[1] Moeller, *op. cit.;* pp. 429–430.

[2] *Ibid.;* p. 392.

[3] Alzog, *op. cit.;* p. 661.

[4] "A Study of Voluntary Associations, Educational and Social, in Europe during the Period from 1100 to 1700," by L. D. Hartson, in "The Pedagogical Seminary"; Vol. xviii (1911), pp. 10–29.

article mentioned shows not only the astonishing range of their activity but their intimate connection with the intellectual and religious life of the times. All of them were necessarily conducted under the auspices of religion, but their special purpose might be economic, scholastic, or religious. The point of especial importance for this sketch is that the learned and religious organizations were so closely identified that Conradi, according to Hartson, "includes the Bohemian Brethren and the Waldensians in his list of learned societies," while Hartson truly adds that the Reformation was not due solely to the work of a few great individual leaders, "but to voluntary organizations like the Bohemian Brethren and the Anabaptists." [1]

These numberless little groups of humble men and women of the middle ages prepared the soil of Europe for the great sowing, which we have now almost reached. A close student of this field has pointed out that the Anabaptists "present every appearance of having evolved from the social and religious groups which we know existed throughout Europe before them, and that, too, in the very centers where Anabaptism later flourished at its best." [2] Long before Anabaptism was heard of, those evangelical preachers, variously styled "Reformers before the Reformation," "Spiritual Reformers," etc., were "gradually leavening Central Europe with the truths of the gospel, and preparing the way for the great spiritual revolution to come." [3] They were non-resistants almost to a man; but, before taking up the broad movement which, under the vague term Anabaptism, represents the organized aspect of the tendency they inaugurated, we must notice a series of events which bridges the earlier and the later history of passive resistance.

1 "Studies in Mystical Religion," by Rufus M. Jones; p. 370.
2 *Ibid.;* p. 29.
3 Balthaser Hübmaier," by Henry C. Vedder; p. 13.

CHAPTER IV

THE BOHEMIAN BRETHREN, ANABAPTISTS, AND THE COERCIVE STATE

THE UNITAS FRATRUM [1]

WITH John Huss and the Bohemian Brethren, or Unitas Fratrum, we may date the beginning of passive resistance in its modern sense. The distinguishing feature of this modernism is its close connection with the state and with the surging forces of social and political revolution. Its modernity lies in its *public* character. Henceforth we shall see less of the monastic, ascetic, and life-denying tendency so characteristic of the Oriental, Stoic, and Christian anchorite philosophy, and more of an effort to translate negative non-resistance into a positive message of peace, and even of social reconstruction. But it would be very misleading to imply that this transformation was either sudden or complete. A great volume of purely negative passivism continued, and exists even at the present day; but the tide turned with the Bohemian movement, and the history of passive resistance becomes thereafter inseparable from the history of modern liberty. As will appear, some of the sects to be observed exhibit a vastly wider social outlook and a more positive and aggressive spirit than do others. Yet, with decided exceptions to be noted, the duty of returning good

[1] Known also as the Bohemian Brethren, the unity of the Brethren, the Unity, etc.

for evil in the personal dealings of man to man widens into the passion for spreading the kingdom of truth and social justice, by every active and aggressive means available short of physical force and violence. Passive resistants as a whole will by no means measure up to this program. It simply represents the highest point attained by the movement. Yet one thing alone is sufficient to differentiate the modern passive resistant from the primitive Christian of apostolic days. The apostles despaired completely of the present world, which was rapidly coming to naught; the passive resistant of the Reformation days has some hope that its wickedness is not irremediable, that the end of all things is not immediately at hand, and that even the kingdoms of this world may become the kingdoms of the Lord and of His Christ. This profound sense of the genuine immanence of God in the world will appear as a tremendous conviction in the spiritual reformers [1] who preceded and accompanied the Reformation, and who are the spiritual ancestors of some of the distinctive peace sects. But, as already remarked, we must turn first to the Bohemian Brethren for the transition from the medieval to the modern aspects of this principle.[2]

John Huss, the Bohemian reformer and university professor, lighted with the fires of his own martyrdom the earliest conflagrations of the Protestant Revolution. On the theological side, Huss was an enlightened but moderate

1 See "Spiritual Reformers in the 16th and 17th Centuries," by Rufus M. Jones.

2 Because of the vastness and increasing complexity of the subject, the following accounts can hardly be dignified even with the name of sketches. They are, by force of necessity, mere outlines or comments on the various topics presented. Their purpose is to touch the points which are important for the social psychology of passive resistance, as it is hoped the following chapters will demonstrate. Considerable supplementary history will appear incidentally in the later chapters.

reformer, who aimed to simplify the overgrown ecclesiasticism and corruption of Rome, and to make the Bible the central thing in the Christian life. We are interested here primarily in three things, viz., his revolutionary political teachings, his passive resistance policy, and his influence on the warlike Hussites and the peaceable Bohemian Brethren.

Huss was by intention precisely the opposite of a fomenter of violent revolution, but the conditions in Bohemia were ripe for insurrection and he unwittingly applied the torch. The fatal firebrand was John Wyclif's doctrine of "Lordship." Wyclif, the great English reformer and Bible scholar, died in 1384, but his writings had been brought to Bohemia by Bohemian students who were returning to their native land from their studies at Oxford, in England. John Huss adopted and promulgated this doctrine, so fruitful of political revolution. Wyclif had declared that "There is no unconditional and eternal heritage of secular dominion, no human title to possession can secure such; only he who stands in grace is the true lord; mortal sin disqualifies the sinner from administering God's fief."[1] Standing firmly on this doctrine, Huss resisted the traditional tyranny of the Roman Church, yet protested, along with Wyclif himself, that this did not justify violent insurrection. His teaching and his whole life breathed the gentle and forgiving spirit of a true Christian and a consistent passive resistant, but, as will appear, the consequences of his utterances flamed out beyond control.

Condemned, formally degraded from the priesthood, and cruelly reviled, in the presence of the whole ecclesiastical and feudal world in the great cathedral of Constance, Huss bore himself with an exalted dignity of meekness and love

[1] Quoted by Moeller, "History of the Christian Church in the Middle Ages"; p. 493.

that worthily honored the Master whom he strove to imitate.[1] His mantle of patient endurance for the sake of truth was to fall upon worthy successors in the persons of the Bohemian Brethren, but they were to emerge only after the terrific upheaval of the Hussite wars had subsided.

The burning of Huss (July 6, 1415) was the signal for armed revolt throughout Bohemia against the power of Rome. His countrymen carried home, as a sacred relic, the very earth wherein the stake had stood. Those who had been halting joined his followers. His personal enemies among the clergy were plundered, the archbishop was driven out of Bohemia, and the national Diet replied to the warnings of Rome in defiant threats of reprisal. This ultimatum was signed by 425 barons and knights, and was followed immediately by the organization of the Hussite League, whose members pledged themselves to open their estates to the free preaching of the Gospel, and to act together in the struggle for truth.[2] The church had for centuries claimed and exercised the right of employing physical force for the advancement of spiritual truth. The minds of men in that age of authority and spiritual darkness were not able to disenthrall themselves from the spell cast upon them by the power of tradition. They needed some sort of intellectual and moral footing for the groping forces of revolt which the wrongs of centuries, in forms economic and political as well as theological, had generated. This theoretical footing Huss had supplied in his exposition of Wyclif's "doctrine of lordship." The papal lord had by mortal sin forfeited God's fief. Allegiance to Rome and loyalty to God were sundered. All Bohemia flew to arms. Establishing themselves at Mount

[1] *Ibid.;* pp. 79–80.

[2] See the eloquent account in "The History of the Church Known as the Unitas Frartum," by Edmund De Schweinitz; Chap. viii. Bethlehem, Pa., 1885.

Tabor, the embattled peasantry, under the peerless leadership of Zizka, and inspired by their own fiery preachers, waged a terrible struggle of fifteen years against all the hosts that medieval tyranny could muster.[1] But they were finally overthrown and dispersed at Zipany in 1434.

While the Hussite insurrection is the most immediate and striking effect of the martyrdom of John Huss, it is not the most genuine and enduring. Scholars like Moeller and De Schweinitz agree in declaring that the true fruit of his testimony is to be found in the Church of the Unitas Fratrum, or Bohemian Brethren. Moeller says that after the destruction of Tabor "the scattered remnants of the Taborites combined into a religiously purified community, which renounced forcible means."[2] De Schweinitz is even more explicit in his characterization of Huss as the true prophet of passive resistance, and of the Brethren as his legitimate successors. "The reformation which he began, they, and not the Hussites, developed to its legitimate end. The martyr spirit which he manifested, they upheld. His weapons were theirs—not carnal, but the two-edged sword of the Word and the whole armor of God."[3] De Schweinitz further shows that the now ancient church of the Unity would never have arisen if Huss had not spread abroad his foundation principles. "What he taught, the Brethren reproduced in their confessions and catechisms."[4]

Hearing of the largely depopulated estate of Lititz in eastern Bohemia, they secured permission to establish there "a retreat, amidst lonely hills and mountains, where they could worship God in fellowship and peace, and a

[1] See the vivid account by MacKinnon in "A History of Modern Liberty"; Vol. I, Chap. IX.

[2] *Op. cit.;* p. 549.

[3] *Op. cit.;* p. 78.

[4] *Ibid.;* p. 102.

centre around which their associates from the country could gather."[1]

Under these romantic circumstances, the Church of the Unity of the Brethren was born in the wilderness. Here they enjoyed a few years of peace; then persecution after persecution from the national church burst upon them. They were strengthened by these fierce harryings, being led to perfect their organization, and even receiving accessions to their membership as the direct result of their steadfastness. Among these were several Waldenses from a colony near the boundaries of Austria.

As a direct result of the first persecution, representatives from the various parts of Bohemia gathered among the mountains of Reichenau, in 1464, and drew up a set of "Statutes," for the guidance of the Brethren. This venerable document, probably the oldest official utterance of all peace sects, does not set forth their views on war, but it has the following to say of magistracy: "Regarding our earthly appointed Rulers, we consider ourselves bound to show them due obedience, to follow their wise counsels, to be subject to them in all humility, to manifest loyalty, in all things, and faithfulness towards them, and to pray unto God for them."[2] This is the Pauline doctrine of passive obedience to rulers, which has figured largely in the later history of passive resistance. In a letter, 1643, to their former friend, Primate Rokycana, who had now come to acquiesce in their persecutions, their indorsement of the power of the constabulary is still more explicitly stated. "Civil power," they acknowledge, "is intended for the punishment of those who have broken the laws of society and must be coerced within proper bounds. It

1 *Ibid.;* p. 106.
2 *Ibid.*

arose in the heathen world. It is absolutely wrong to use it in matters of religion."[1] Here is an early enunciation of the principle of separation of church and state.

Through a history checkered with alternating prosperity and persecution, the Unity of the Brethren continued down to the Protestant Reformation. Its doctrinal teachings won the commendation of the great Reformers, Luther, Bucer, and Calvin. Its history becomes for a time involved in the surging movements of the revolution. Scattered from Bohemia by war and persecution, it maintained itself in Moravia, and gained a foothold in Prussia and Poland. Its later history merges with that of the Moravian Church, and, through the continuous line thus established, it exists to-day as the most ancient and venerable of all Protestant churches. But the Moravians were themselves partly a product of the Reformation, and to some passive resistance aspects of that momentous period attention must next be directed.

THE ANABAPTISTS

Those turbulent fanatics and bizarre heretics who are lumped together under the title of "Anabaptists" were long despised and maligned; and they have, in fact, much to answer for in way of fantastic theory and practice. They have been happily dubbed "the waifs of the religious world." But recent researches have revealed them in a better light, and the broad movement vaguely known as Anabaptism is seen to comprise much that was vital in religion, truly socialistic in the broadest sense, and most consonant with modern ideas of liberty of conscience. MacKinnon finds in them the only party among all the sects of the Reformation, Catholic or Protestant, who really

[1] *Ibid.;* p. 119.

believed in the rights of free conscience.[1] "Let it be remembered to their immortal glory," says he, "that, despite contempt and death, they were the pioneers of at least religious liberty as we understand it." Bax[2] has made an able study of the whole movement from the original sources. His point of view is socialistic, and brings out sympathetically the story of Anabaptism as a lower-class, communistic movement. His treatment is perhaps less penetrating on the spiritual side, but the lack has been supplied by Jones, in his profound study of the "Spiritual Reformers in the 16th and 17th Centuries," already quoted. In that work he points out that the term "Anabaptism" has been very loosely used to include "all the sixteenth-century exponents of a free, inward religion." Jones himself, however, would apply the term "Anabaptist" only to those who saw in the Gospel a new *law* to be literally obeyed; held the true church to be the visible company of such literal followers of the apostles, united under the sign of adult baptism; and denied, on Gospel grounds, the right of the magistrates to interfere with religious faith and doctrine. They held the great commandment to be love.[3] He then adopts the term "Spiritual Reformers" for another group of leaders who united in themselves harmoniously "the Mystical tendency, the Humanistic or Rational tendency, and the distinctive Faith tendency of the Reformation."[4] Among these less literally traditional and more mystical thinkers is found one, Caspar Schwenkfeld, of those who figure in the following sketches. George Fox and the English Quakers were

[1] MacKinnon, *op. cit.;* Vol. III p. 472. MacKinnon refers particularly to their successors, the English Baptists, but the statement holds for the whole Anabaptist movement.

[2] In his "Rise and Fall of the Anabaptists."

[3] *Op. cit.;* pp. 17–18.

[4] *Ibid.;* p. xv.

later and hence not included in his list, but they belong spiritually to the same group. It is not feasible to follow out closely this distinction between the mystical and traditional phases of the movement, although it is profoundly true; but some practical consequences of their unlike theology may appear in the different social rôles played by the various passive resistant sects. For the present, without attempting to differentiate between the mystical and traditional types, the general policy and career of the so-called Anabaptists must be touched upon.

As has been shown above, the germs of the movement for a more free and more personal religion were in the air at the opening of the sixteenth century, and even before that date. Various writers have traced the actual beginnings of Anabaptism to a group of enthusiasts who came together in Switzerland, at Zurich, in the year 1526. Among them were Balthasar Hubmeyer,[1] Konrad Grebel, George Blaurock, and others less prominent in later history. They rejected not only the Roman Catholic Church but also that of Luther and the other Reformers, with whom, they declared, it was "as though they were mending an old pot in which the hole only grows larger. They have smitten the vessel out of the hand of the Pope, but left the fragments therein; for a new birth of Life hath one never seen with them."[2]

At first the Anabaptist movement was allied with the reformation of Zwingli, but was soon cast out as Zwinglianism grew more prosperous and respectable. Anabaptism then threw down the gauntlet to all Protestant Europe, and its history of propagandism and persecution, of intoxicating success and heart-breaking failure, began. In this

[1] According to Vedder's account, it appears that Hübmaier was not present, but joined the group a little later.

[2] Bax, *op. cit.;* p. 3.

sketch only one phase of the movement will be followed, viz., the line of the fanatics of Münster and the final differentiation of Anabaptism into such sects as the Mennonites and others. In pursuing this course the study will be further narrowed to the vicissitudes of the conflict between the doctrines of the state and of passive resistance.

Broken up and dispersed from Zurich, the new sectarians spread throughout Southern Germany and into the Netherlands. They became especially numerous in Moravia, and converts from all parts flocked thither. The failure of the Peasant Insurrection of 1625, and the bloodthirsty revenge wreaked by the feudal and ecclesiastical overlords, had made the masses peculiarly receptive toward the teachings of the Anabaptists concerning the civil power, to which attention must now be turned.

The Anabaptists regarded the state as an institution born of the realms of darkness and designed by God as a scourge for true Christians. The Christian had no duties as a citizen except that he should be quietly submissive and endure persecution in expectation of the deliverance of God in the Day of the Lord. It might be said correctly that the Christian is not a *citizen* but simply a *subject* of the state.

But Anabaptists did not agree in all their utterances. Some of those who have been counted among them defended the scriptural legitimacy of the magistracy. Therefore we shall notice first, from a hostile, but apparently reliable witness, a summary of their political doctrines; [1]

In their propositions, says Bax, "they maintain that the preachers rely too much on the secular arm; that the attitude of the Christian toward authority should be that of submission and endurance only; that no Christian ought to take office of any kind; that secular authority has no concern with religious belief; that the Christian resists no evil; and therefore needs no law-courts nor should ever make use of the tribunals; that Christians do not kill or punish with imprisonment or the sword, but only with exclusion from the body of believers; that Christians do not resist, and hence, do not go to war."[1] On the contrary, Balthasar Hübmaier (or Hübmeyer), who, as mentioned above, is named by early chroniclers as one of the original Anabaptists, vigorously denies the charge that he was opposed to Christian magistracy.[2]

Hübmaier died a martyr's death at the stake, and the Anabaptists were driven out of Moravia. Their further history centers about the "New Jerusalem" and the brief reign of the saints, at Münster. In this strange episode was seen the metamorphosis of non-resistance into a militant crusade and political Utopia, and back again into complete non-resistance and repudiation of the state.

Bax says that "in proportion as, after the great defeat of 1525, [i. e., the Peasants' Rebellion in Germany], despair of attaining their aims by insurrectionary methods gradually settled down on the peasantry and poor handicraftsmen, the Anabaptist doctrine spread like wild-fire, attaching to itself all the elements from the earlier peasant and proletarian movements that had a similar religious coloring."[3] The theory of Bax is that non-resistance is a policy born of oppression and political despair, but it affords at most no more than a partial explanation. This Bax himself admits when he says, "The doctrine of nonresistance . . . was a natural result of the literal interpretation of many passages in the New Testament." And

[1] Bullinger, "Der Wiedertaufferen Ursprung, Furgang, Secten, Wesen," etc., translated and summarized by Bax, *op. cit.;* pp. 30–32. Bullinger's book appeared in 1531.

[2] See H. C. Vedder's "Balthaser Hübmaier; *Appendix.*

[3] *Op. cit.;* p. 27.

he mentions, as "an important feature of the movement, its strange atmosphere of Bible-reading to the exclusion of all other literature."[1] Thus it appears that, whatever may have affected the *progress* of the doctrine, its *origin*, here, as everywhere in modern times, is directly traceable to the Christian ideal and tradition.

The prophets of Anabaptism, who went wandering, like the early apostles, through the land, now began to proclaim that the Day of the Lord would soon come, to bring deliverance to his oppressed followers; and in realizing this the great center of Anabaptist activity became the city of Münster, in Westphalia.

The metamorphosis of the extreme non-resistance teaching into a militant political crusade, then back again into complete non-resistance and "political quietism,"[2] was begun by Melchior Hoffman, carried to its zenith by Jan Matthys, and brought to its conclusion by Menno Simons.

Hoffman joined the movement at Strasburg and was in most points a consistent Anabaptist, but he soon repudiated the doctrine of non-resistance in its absolute form. In its stead he set up a modified theory, in which it was maintained that the Brethren had a right to take up the sword against the godless authorities of the world, who were looked upon as "the enemies of the saints." Hoffman, however, always taught that the two-edged sword must remain in its sheath until a sign from Heaven should bid it flash forth. With him non-resistance and patient waiting were the present duty of the saints. It was under the influence of this idea of a limited and temporary non-resistance that the Anabaptist movement gained adherents in the regions adjacent to Westphalia.

At this point Jan Matthys, a Haarlem master-baker,

[1] *Ibid.;* p. 162.
[2] Bax, *op cit.;* p. 114.

appears as the new Anabaptist prophet. What was "close at hand" with Hoffman was already arrived for Matthys. What the former had held to be a vague prospect, Matthys preached as an immediate duty and a sacred task. The zeal with which the Brethren should now seize the "sword of sharpness" would be the measure of their loyalty and devotion to the cause of God. The call met with an enthusiastic response. The causes of discontent and social revolt that produced the Peasant Wars were still operating. These underlying motives for social revolution were supplied by the corruption and unseemly wealth of the church, the insatiable greed of the vampire nobles, the economic misery of the laborers held in semi-serfdom on the land, and the hard condition of the artisans in the cities, who were excluded from the growing prosperity of the new capitalistic régime by the selfish policy of the gilds and gild masters.[1] These causes, which were still actively present and most keenly felt, while the memory of their disastrous defeat of 1526 had faded somewhat away, "led," says Bax, "to the natural man reasserting himself and to renewed hopes of his being saved in this world by his own action."[2]

About this time (February, 1533), the city of Münster, in Westphalia, made a treaty of peace with its territorial overlord, who granted such favorable terms to heretics that Münster became the new center to which the discontented of every stripe flocked from all quarters. A stream of Anabaptists poured in and, under the leadership of Jan Matthys, who was later succeeded by his disciple Jan Bockelson of Leyden, eventually siezed first the established church, then the town government, and entered upon the

[1] See MacKinnon, "A History of Modern Liberty"; Vol. I, Chap. IX.

[2] *Op. cit.;* p. 114.

fulfilment of the long promised Day of the Lord. The bishop in whose see the city lay soon appeared at the head of a small army, breathing out vengeance. The Saints defended the walls during a long siege of a year or more. It is not possible or necessary to describe the fanatical extravagances and orgies that accompanied the reign of "King" Jan [1] in the New Jerusalem during those months. Picturesque as it is, it has to do with the history of antinomian fanaticism and chiliastic delusions rather than the story of passive resistance. The end of it all was the fall of the city, after a most brave and efficient defense, and the utter collapse of all the mundane hopes of the Saints.

A reaction to the original peaceable Anabaptism followed. It was seen that this doctrine of the sword of vengeance had been a delusion and a snare. Bax attributes directly to the fall of Münster that increased influence and final ascendancy of the peaceable, strictly non-resistant element, which immediately followed the catastrophe. Many Anabaptists, in Germany, Switzerland, and the Netherlands, were free from complicity in the Münster affair, and the view now destined to prevail had always been their own.

Several parties, representing various shades of the doctrine, have been distinguished in the realinement following the fall of Münster. David Georg, or Jöris, feeling the need of some concession to those who still demanded a little hope for this world, professed "to believe in the ultimate acceptance of Anabaptist teaching by the great ones of the earth, who would then voluntarily lay down their wealth and privileges, and thus the ideal of the reign of the Saints on earth would be pacifically inaugurated." [2] On the other hand were the extreme non-resistants, called

[1] Jan Bockelson, or John of Leyden.
[2] *Ibid.;* p. 327.

"Obbenites." This party "taught, as one of its leading tenets, that no other social and political conditions than those already established, were to be looked for here below, and that it was the duty of the Saints to accept them in all humility as the dispensation of God."[1] This doctrine of acquiescence was given a great impetus by the appearance of an advocate of high character and great ability, Menno Simons. His followers, the Menists of earlier writers, or modern Mennonites, took up and carried on the true non-resistance doctrine, which survived the wreck of its violent perversion at Münster, just as the Bohemian Brethren rescued the peaceable legacy of John Huss from the conflagration of the Hussite Wars.[2]

[1] *Ibid.;* p. 325.
[2] Cf. Moeller, *op. cit.*

CHAPTER V

MENNONITES AND OTHER POLITICAL NON-PARTICIPANTS

THE MENNONITES

MENNO SIMONS, the new leader of the peaceable, non-fanatical Anabaptists, of whom, as has been said, there were many, was born in 1492 in West Friesland. He was, in early life, a careless, time-serving priest of the Roman Catholic Church. The martyrdom of an Anabaptist in a neighboring town awoke him from his spiritual lethargy, and he began to study for himself the question of infant baptism. In 1535 three hundred poor fugitives from Münster were pursued to a neighboring monastery, and most of them, including his own brother, were slain. This tragic event further impressed his mind and awoke in him a strong sense of his duty to live a more profitable life in testifying to the simple truths of the Gospel. In 1536 he openly renounced the Roman Catholic Church and was baptized by Anabaptists, being ordained to the ministry by Obbe Philip, the leader of the Obbenite party mentioned above.[1]

The remainder of Menno's days were spent in disseminating the truth as understood by the non-resistant Anabaptists. He performed valiant service by his contro-

[1] See the scholarly history entitled "The Mennonites of America," by C. Henry Smith, on which this account is principally based. In this case, as elsewhere in the history, the present writer is responsible for general interpretations not otherwise credited.

versial writings and public disputations. This occurred during a brief rest from persecutions, enjoyed under the tolerant Duke Charles of Guelders in West Friesland. Soon, however, a price was set on his head and he was so persistently hounded from place to place that several persons were burned at the stake simply for giving him shelter or for printing his writings.[1]

This relentless persecution was waged against the Mennonites by the Protestant churches no less than the Roman Catholic, and the question may well be asked why there should be such a unity of hatred against a meek and non-resisting people. But their non-resistance doctrine was perhaps their worst offense. It struck at the very foundation-stone of the established state church, whether Roman Catholic, Lutheran, or Reformed. The Mennonites had a special testimony against the union of church and state, against all participation in government on the part of Christians. So distinctive is that doctrine that the whole subsequent history of the sect centers about it, as will appear more fully in connection with their later career, in Pennsylvania. It is therefore necessary to examine their statement of the non-resistant's faith. We quote from their historian, Professor Smith: "They adopted bodily the faith of the peaceful type of Anabaptists, and that was a rejection of all civil and a great deal of the prevailing ecclesiastical government as unnecessary for the Christian." They "went no further, however, in their opposition to the temporal authority than to declare that the true church and the temporal powers had nothing in common and must be entirely separate; not only must the state not interfere with the church, but *the true Christian must be entirely free from participating in civil mat-*

[1] *Ibid.;* p. 62.

ters.[1] The temporal authority must needs exist, since it was instituted of God to punish the wicked, but in that work the Christian had no hand. This position they reached from a literal interpretation of the Sermon on the Mount, where Christ taught his disciples among other things to 'love their enemies' and to 'swear not at all.' Hence their position involved opposition to the oath, holding of office, and bearing of arms.''[2]

That their teachings were regarded as a dangerous political heresy is shown by the fact that the records kept by the authorities in the heresy trials state that they were ''accused of rejecting infant baptism, and of being opposed to the oath, warfare, and the holding of office.'' Hence it is not surprising that they were assailed by the Reformed party in the Netherlands (1596) as being ''destructive of all religious and civil order.''[3] In the light of these considerations it is easier to understand why the Peace of Westphalia, 1648, failed to bring rest to the hunted Anabaptists and Mennonites.

The Mennonites were numerous in the Netherlands, Switzerland, and parts of Germany. The State Reformed Church of Switzerland persecuted them cruelly, but other states of Europe appreciated their value as citizens. So we find the States-General granting them temporary asylum, and later encouraging Frederick of Prussia, in 1710, in his desire to settle some of the Swiss Mennonites upon his unoccupied lands. A goodly number accepted the invitation, and ''were granted religious toleration and freedom from military service.''[4] They were next wanted in Russia. Catharine the Great invited them, in 1786, to

[1] Italics mine.
[2] *Op. cit.;* pp. 353–354.
[3] *Ibid.;* pp. 71 and 67.
[4] *Ibid.;* p. 79.

settle upon her waste lands in Southern Russia near the mouth of the Dnieper. She offered them free transportation, lands, religious toleration, and freedom from military service. The Prussian Government, loath to part with them, refused them passports, so that they were compelled to escape by secret flight from their too appreciative sovereign. Smith says that by 1788 about two hundred families had settled in Southern Russia.[1] Paul I, in order to encourage further immigration, granted them additional privileges, including the right of affirmation in place of the judicial oath.

So prosperous were the Mennonites in Russia that they aroused the envy of their neighbors, who begrudged them their hard-won exemptions. The same were by the czar's proclamation ordered withdrawn, gradually, within ten years. So about 1874 they were again seeking an asylum, this time in America, and were again solicited by the government to remain, with concessions. In all this is presented the remarkable spectacle of a people, declared to be dangerous to all civil order, everywhere lauded as citizens, and everywhere begged, by the "imperiled" government itself, to remain under its rule.

But in this last incident we have anticipated the later history. For the present it must suffice to note that the first emigration of this persecuted people to the New World occurred about 1663, and the place was at Plockhoy's Utopian colony on the Delaware River. The fate of this romantic Utopian enterprise, like Raleigh's lost colony at Roanoke, is wrapped in mystery. It disappeared, at least as a distinguishable Mennonite colony. The first permanent settlement of Mennonites in America was made at Germantown in 1683. Their career there is

[1] *Ibid.;* p. 324.

so intimately blended with that of the English Quakers, that the further account must be deferred for the present.[1]

THE COLLEGIANTS

A peace movement within the established churches should be mentioned at this point, inasmuch as, like one wing of the Mennonite movement, it was of Dutch origin. Smith says that the Mennonites fraternized with the *Collegiants,* who represented a movement for a creedless, spiritual worship within the various denominations. It arose in Rhynsburg, Holland, in 1619. "They evaded all controversies and tolerated all opinions not directly condemned by the Bible, and like the Mennonites they opposed oaths and war."[2]

THE MORAVIANS

The ancient Church of the Bohemian Brethren, or Unitas Fratrum, survived all the perils of persecution, reformation, and counter-reformation, and remained as a "Hidden Seed" in Bohemia and Moravia even after the visible church there had been crushed and scattered to the four winds. The beliefs and usages of the Brethren were secretly cherished in certain families, and the line of bishops was never broken. One of the latter, Jablonski, was acting as court preacher in Berlin when the time came for the revival of the "Hidden Seed"; and he, with the

[1] The method of procedure for the remainder of this chapter will be first to describe in turn the origin and foundation principles of the sects and their career in Europe, leaving their experience in America for discussion in a later chapter.

[2] *Op. cit.;* p. 69.

consent of the other surviving bishop, transferred the episcopacy to David Nitschmann, as leader of the revived Unitas Fratrum, or Moravian Church.[1]

In this remarkable revival of an ancient faith a prominent part was played by Nicholas Louis, Count Zinzendorf, scion of an Austrian house dating from the thirteenth century, whose attention was first drawn to one Christian David and his companions.

David was a young Moravian carpenter, who had recently returned from his "Wanderjahre" and a period of military service, to Moravia, having consecrated himself to the work of an evangelist. In Moravia he sought out certain of the families wherein was cherished the "Hidden Seed" of the ancient faith of the Bohemian Brethren, and with them he left the priest-ridden land of Moravia, stealing away in the darkness of night, ten persons all told. Granted an asylum by Zinzendorf, and joined later by other refugee Moravians, they revived the ancient Unitas Fratrum in the form of the modern Moravian Church.

The point of interest for this essay is, of course, the Moravian doctrine of passive resistance, but one looks in vain for a definite formal statement in Moravian publications. The Moravians make it a matter of principle to avoid any credal statement, and declare they seek to invent no new system.[2] Therefore their testimony on the problems of passive resistance is to be sought in their history. One field has already yielded rich results in our

[1] This account is based largely on "A History of the Unitas Fratrum, or Moravian Church, in the United States of America," by J. Taylor Hamilton, in "The American Church History Series"; Vol. VIII.

[2] Cf. "The Moravians and Their Faith," by Bishop Edmond de Schweinitz. Special Moravian Publication Fund Committee, Leaflet, No, 2., p. 9.

sketch of their progenitors, the Bohemian Brethren. The other must be explored in connection with their missions in America, as will be done later in this chapter. For the present it is sufficient to remark that their missionary work in the New World began in 1732, in the West Indies, and was extended to Georgia and Pennsylvania about 1735. Here their peace principles were to be severely tested.

THE SCHWENKFELDERS

The story of the Schwenkfelders is intimately connected, in its early stages, with that of Zinzendorf and the Moravians. This was more or less fortuitous, although not insignificant. But the first mention must be accorded to Caspar Schwenkfeld. From him the name is derived, and to him the Schwenkfelders look back with profoundest reverence. Like Zinzendorf he was of noble lineage, coming from Catholic parents of Silesia in Germany. He was born about 1490, and was well advanced along the road of a genuine religious reformation when Luther began his great work. Schwenkfeld, after a number of years' service in the courts of various German rulers, had turned, like Zenzendorf, from the promise of worldly honors to devote his life to the service of a spiritual kingdom. At first he and Luther worked harmoniously together, but after 1524 the latter repudiated the Silesian reformer in a fiery letter, which may be counted the opening blast of "the storm of persecution which . . . was destined, under God's providence, to blow about the heads of Schwenkfeld and his followers for more than 200 years."[1]

The passive resistance principles of the Schwenkfelders,

[1] Howard Wiegner Kriebel, "The Schwenkfelders in Pennsylvania, a Historical Sketch," in "Pennsylvania-German Society Publications," 1902; Vol. XIII, Part XII.

in so far as they are not directly drawn from the Gospels, are to be sought in the character and doctrines of their founder and in their history. While distinctly a peace sect, they have manifested their convictions by their conduct, and do not enunciate the doctrine very fully in their writings until the pressure of the American wars calls for a definite statement of policy, as will appear later.

Schwenkfeld himself was a most interesting person, whose admirable virtues and noble conduct are matched only by the lifelong abuse heaped upon his head by the intolerant dogmatists and vested ecclesiastical interests of the time.[1] As remarked in an earlier connection, he is numbered by Jones among the "Spiritual Reformers." From the opening of his powerful pen-portrait the following is taken: "Among all the Reformers of the sixteenth century who worked at the immense task of recovering, purifying, and restating the Christian Faith, no one was nobler in life and personality, and no one was more uncompromisingly dedicated to the mission of bringing into the life of the people a type of Christianity winnowed clean from the husks of superstition and tradition and grounded in ethical and spiritual reality, than was Caspar Schwenkfeld, was Silesian noble."[2]

Schwenkfeld was friendly toward the Anabaptists, but was not one of them, inasmuch as he laid so little stress upon baptism in any form. His attention was centered on the "Glory of Christ" and the deep inwardness of the religion that consists in the heart's true faith toward Him. For Schwenkfeld, says Jones, a principal sign of the transformed life is "the attainment of a joy which spreads through the inward spirit and shines on the face—a joy

[1] Kriebel, *op. cit.*, p. 6, gives a list of nineteen epithets from the armory of his calumniators, ranging all the way from plain description to the vile and venomous.

[2] Jones, *op cit.;* p. 64.

which can turn hard exile into a *Ruheschloss*, 'a castle of peace.' "[1]

This inward "castle of peace" is probably the source of the Schwenkfeldian testimony for peace and non-resistance. It is peculiarly characteristic of the Quaker type, and it is worth while to observe in passing that the source of both the Schwenkfelder and Quaker testimonies against war lies in a very deep inward spiritual experience. It was in the security of this *Ruheschloss* that Schwenkfeld relinquished all his worldly estates and castles, and wandered all his life as a voluntary exile. His peaceable good will embraced not only the Anabaptists, but also the Catholic, Lutheran and Zwinglian churches. He never sought to found a sect of his own. The sole cause of his exile was his unbending, though gentle, refusal to abate one iota of his convictions concerning the nature of the true Christian faith. His life supremely exemplifies that union of gentleness and strength which is characteristic of the passive resistant of the finest type.

The persecution of Schwenkfeld emanated principally from the rulers of church and state. "The common people could not be incited against him," and, at the time of his death in 1562, his adherents numbered at least four thousand. Among his defenders were many princes and nobles, so that nothing but the most strenuous efforts on the part of the religio-political state prevented Silesia from adopting the "Reformation by the Middle Way," as the Schwenkfeldian movement was styled.

The Schwenkfelders soon fell on evil times. Not being among the religions tolerated by the Treaty of Westphalia and other religio-political agreements, they were not permitted to maintain a congregational life, and for-

[1] *Ibid.; p.* 72.

cible baptism of their children soon began under the coercion of the state church.

The Schwenkfelders now determined on flight. Their efforts to find an asylum in Holland, near the Mennonites, were unsuccessful. In this extremity they appealed to Count Zinzendorf, and were promised a haven under his protection at Herrnhut and elsewhere. Stealing away in the night, "taking naught with them but sorrow and poverty," they left Silesia for Saxony. Here they resided, in a sort of semi-independent existence, Count Zinzendorf seeking, as "Reformer of the Schwenkfelders,"[1] to draw them into membership in the state church there.

In 1733, a change in the government of Saxony occurring, notice was given them to migrate within a year. The king of Prussia had long desired them to settle near Berlin, in order to establish the manufacture of linen there, but they still had serious objections to that plan. After the failure of several prospecting efforts in various parts of Germany, their eyes turned toward America.

Their great dread was that their poverty, which would not permit them to pay their ship passage, might require them to go as "redemptioners." In that case they would be scattered throughout the colony as bond-servants, to work out the costs of their passage. Count Zinzendorf sought to make arrangements that would avoid this calamity, with the "Trustees for Establishing the Colony of Georgia." But he was not able to complete the arrangements in time. The Schwenkfelders left singly, or in groups, as they had been ordered to do by the government, for the sea-coast. But, instead of embarking for Georgia, they made their way, by slow stages, to Pennsylvania. In this migration they were very generously aided by the

[1] *Ibid.;* p. 27.

Dutch Mennonites, and finally, to the number of about three hundred persons, they landed at Philadelphia in 1734, almost simultaneously with the Moravians, as previously narrated.

THE DUNKERS

The German Baptists, or Dunkers, are, as the name indicates, a detachment of the great Anabaptist army. They represent also the more strictly spiritual movement begun by Spener in 1690, and known as Pietism. Pietism originated within the Lutheran Church, to which Spener always remained attached, but it spread far beyond its original bounds. It was a reaction against the intolerant dogmatism and formalism of the state religion. The latter places its supreme and final emphasis on matters of intellectual belief, on correct doctrine; Pietism was chiefly concerned about the practical questions connected with daily Christian living. But the Dunkers were not alone in their identification with this Pietistic movement. Every nonresistant sect with which this account has to do represents in some way this same aspiration after a life of simple faith and genuine piety. But, just as the Schwenkfelders and Quakers represent the more mystical aspect of Pietism in this broad sense, so the Dunkers are typical of its more literalistic, non-mystical phase. In fact, the Dunkers have, throughout their history, looked upon every tendency toward mysticism as evil and have sedulously avoided it at every turn.

Professor Gillin, in his remarkable sociological interpretation of the Dunkers,[1] has applied to them the theory

[1] "The Dunkers; A Sociological Interpretation," by John Lewis Gillin; a doctor's dissertation, Columbia University, 1906.

of "consciousness of kind,"[1] and finds in it the clue to Dunker history. The principle seems to apply with peculiar force to those German Baptists, but doubtless much in the history of the kindred sects may be due to a similar, though less strongly developed, group feeling.

Their leader, Alexander Mack, and those who were to be his later companions, had noted the selfish greed, intolerant dogmatism, elaborate ceremonial, social pride, and general worldliness of those who were equally great and influential in both church and state. These simple Pietists felt the incongruity of such conduct with the meek simplicity of the Gospel teachings, and a keen sense of disapproval of the whole program of their oppressors came to fill their souls. They felt that the way of salvation was to obey the command to come out from among those who practised such wickedness, and be separate. Gradually they grew into a strong sense of their own unlikeness to these religious and social opponents; and this feeling was enhanced by a strong sense of their own similarity.

Gradually these primitive Baptist Brethren of Schwarzenau formulated their purpose, which was to found a distinct sect, based upon absolute obedience to the teachings of the Bible, as literally interpreted in every detail. It is in pursuance of this effort at literal obedience to all scriptural commands and precedents that, to this day, the Dunkers baptize in running streams, eat the Christian Passover as a real supper, wash one another's feet, and greet one another with the holy kiss of peace.

Having determined to form a true Christian church, they could not and would not receive baptism from the unregenerate churches by which they were persecuted. So

[1] See Giddings, "Principles of Sociology," for significance of these terms.

they cast lots, and, like the original Anabaptists at Zurich, baptized one another, "in the solitude of the early morning, in the Eder river, a small stream that flows past Schwarzenau, some time in the year 1708."[1]

Under the sense of joy and assurance that followed this action, they began to proclaim their doctrines and to gather adherents. Persecution immediately descended upon them, but the Dunkers "took joyfully the spoiling of their goods," and courageously continued their testimony, sowing the seeds of their teaching as they were driven from place to place. Four congregations were founded, two soon melted away under persecution, and finally the members of the remaining two congregations, after seeking vainly an asylum in Prussia, Holland, and Switzerland, left, first for Friesland and eventually for Pennsylvania. Thus, says Falkenstein, their historian,[2] "we have the unique example in history of the emigration of an entire religious denomination."

The movement in Europe seems to have died out completely with this emigration, which occurred in 1719. They left the usual good reputation of non-resistant citizens behind them. "The administrator of the Count of Schwarzenau in 1720 could say this only, 'that for a long time many pious people have lived around here, of whom no one heard anything bad, but perceived that they conducted themselves in a wholly pious and quiet manner, and by no one had a complaint been made of them. There were about forty families of them, about two hundred persons, that lately have betaken themselves entirely out of

1 Gillin, *op. cit.;* p. 61.

2 "The German Baptist Brethren, or Dunkers," by George N Falkenstein, in "Publications of the Pennsylvania-German Historical Society," 1900; Vol. X, Part viii, p. 23.

the land, of whom it is said of them that they were Anabaptists."[1]

The Dunkers have always been non-resistants and political non-participants. Both positions are in harmony with their Anabaptist antecedents. Moreover, they devoted themselves to the exemplification of a literal New Testament life. This yearning after the apostolic standard, as we have seen over and over, could hardly fail to lead them to the non-resistance position, and to this Professor Gillin has added a new motive, in the sense of solidarity with which the comradeship of persecution imbued them.

The Dunkers have made, not the communistic colony, but a close community of family and neighborhood, the basis of their existence. Their chief glory is the blending of piety, thrift, and domestic joys, which is characteristic of their history. Their strong consciousness of kind has expressed itself in this way. They have often preferred to worship in private homes rather than churches, because they were thus following the example of the early Christian disciples. The "home was a sanctuary. Here gathered parents and children, old and young, for the public preaching service. No other power on earth," continues Falkenstein, "can equal in far-reaching influence this combination of the home and the church."[2]

In connection with this home, which was usually a farmstead, they devoted the energies of their strong and populous families to agriculture, and are probably the best farmers in the world."[3]

In the light of these facts it is easy to see how it comes

[1] Gillin, *op. cit.;* p. 72.
[2] *Op. cit.;* p. 45.
[3] Gillin, *op. cit.;* p. 214, note. Falkenstein, *op. cit.*

about that the Dunkers have not been aggressive in politics or social reforms. Withdrawn into their quiet neighborhoods, they have been, like the Mennonites, political non-participants, and also non-litigants, as well as opposed to war. Their traits and utterances will appear more fully in the later discussions.

CHAPTER VI

THE QUAKERS AND THE PEACE IDEA IN POLITICS

ASIDE from the communistic non-resistants to be mentioned at the close of the present chapter, there remains only one more distinctive peace sect to be described: the Society of Friends or Quakers. Their history has long brought them into relations of very close mutual sympathy and helpfulness with the modern sects already described. Yet in several respects they stand somewhat apart. In the first place, the Anabaptists, Mennonites, Schwenkfelders, and Dunkers were all German or Holland-Dutch, while the Quakers are of English origin. In the second place, all the sects thus far described are strict non-resistants, while the Quakers are too aggressive to be correctly described by that term. That is, the German sects, with slight exceptions, repudiated the constabulary along with war. Hence they not only refused to fight, but also refrained from participation in civil government by voting or holding office, and they have usually held it wrong to sue in the courts. The Mennonites have given, perhaps, the clearest example of the non-litigant, non-political, non-resistance policy, but the Dunkers are hardly second to them. In all this, both sects have preserved unmodified the original doctrines of their Anabaptist progenitors. In a thorough and sweeping way they have obeyed literally the commandment, "Resist not evil."

The Quakers, on the other hand, are typical non-physical

resistants. That is to say, they do not resist evil by physical violence, but they are noted for their resisting of political and social wrongs by *political* and *social* means. They have wielded an influence in English and American history out of all proportion to their numbers, so that it is impossible to write the history of modern liberty and social reform without at the same time writing in part the history of the Society of Friends. The foregoing sects, especially the Schwenkfelders, sometimes display this active tendency also, but their characteristic attitude is that of *non*-resistance, as has been shown.

On the other hand, the Quakers and the other peace sects made common cause on more than one occasion, especially during the times of stress in Pennsylvania produced by the Colonial and Revolutionary wars. This sense of likeness was especially marked in the case of the Mennonites. In fact, it is impossible to be sure whether certain of the founders of Germantown, Pennsylvania, were Quakers or Mennonites. Smith [1] finds it convenient to use the term "Mennonite-Quaker," so closely identified were many pioneers with the two organizations. A high authority [2] in this field of history has shown the very close and affectionate relations that prevailed between the Quakers and Mennonites in Holland, and concludes that, "in fact, transition between the two sects both ways was easy." Pennypacker and others have pointed out that, according to Robert Barclay, the Quaker theologian, George Fox himself was "the unconscious exponent of the doctrine, practice, and discipline of the ancient and stricter party of Dutch Mennonites."

1 In his "The Mennonites of America"; Chap. IV.

2 The Hon. Samuel W. Pennypacker, in "The Settlement of Germantown, Pennsylvania, and the Beginning of German Immigration to North America," "Publications of the Pennsylvania-German Society," 1899; Vol. IX.

THE QUAKERS

It is out of question to attempt even a bare outline of the passive resistance aspects of the Society of Friends. But much of their history will appear, along with that of the other sects, as illustrative material in the later chapters. It has been said above that they are the typical non-violent resistants. In the popular mind the very name "Quaker" has become a synonyn for non-resistance and peace. Thus Roosevelt speaks of those Indians, who had been converted to Christian non-resistance by the Moravian missionaries, as "Quaker Indians"; and, a few pages farther on, he identifies the "Dunkards" as "Quaker-like Germans."[1] This is but one among many evidences that the sect now under consideration must, because of its peculiar prominence in history, furnish a large part of the materials for any theory of the social psychology of passive resistance. It is therefore important to seek first of all the origin of that spirit which has made the words "Friend" and "Quaker" synonyms for gentleness, peace, and non-resistance.

George Fox, the founder of the Society of Friends, was born in Leicestershire, England, about the year 1624. He was descended from honest and pious parents of the artisan class. His father was a weaver. "The neighbors called him Righteous Christer. My mother was an upright woman . . . and of the stock of the martyrs."[2] George Fox grew up from an innocent boyhood and a youth spent as a "Seeker," into a powerful man of God—a real prophet who shook the England of his day, and gathered around him not only such intellectual and moral giants as

[1] In his "The Winning of the West."

[2] "George Fox; An Autobiography," by Rufus M. Jones, (Edit.); pp. 65–66.

William Penn and Robert Barclay, but also a host of able preachers and public-minded leaders. Through their combined efforts almost the whole accessible world was visited, and a good part of it colonized within Fox's lifetime.

All the sects who had gone before them since the days of the apostles had testified nobly and clearly against war. There was nothing for Fox to add touching the formulation of that doctrine. In so far as he contributed anything new it lies in his terse characterization of the real root of the Christian peace principle, and in the organized movement which he set afoot. While Fox, as was not uncommon for reformers in those days, lay in the "house of correction" on some false accusation in connection with his religious activities, Cromwell's commissioners were seized with the idea that it would be good to make a captain out of this man, so uniquely endowed with powerful physique and commanding presence. The soldiers also cried out, saying that they would have none but Fox. His "Journal" records: "I told them I knew whence all wars arose, even from the lusts, according to James' doctrine; and that I lived in the virtue of that life and power that took away the occasion of all wars." Professor Jones remarks, with truth, "This is the true ground of opposition to war, namely, that a Christian is to live a life that does away with the occasion for war."[1]

This statement is brief, but it is fundamental. It makes of the peace doctrine a principle of present and living reality, as well as a sacred tradition. Fox substituted for the tradition its moral fountainhead, the *spiritual experience* that first gave it birth. In so doing, he really explained how it is unmistakably present in the New Testament, although no explicit statements are to be found there

[1] *Ibid.;* p. 128.

on the subject of war. This shows why the doctrine has appeared always wherever the New Testament was read, and disappears when it is neglected.

The history of passive resistance, as it has been traced in the preceding pages, has presented the three phases of the problem, viz., (1) the testimony concerning personal retaliation; (2) that concerning the magistracy and constabulary, or, in other words, the doctrine of the state; and, (3) the testimony against war. Each of these doctrines may be stated both as a negative and a positive principle, as follows: (1) The doctrine of retaliation teaches, negatively, that vengeance is forbidden; positively, it requires that one return good for evil. (2) The doctrine of the state, expressed negatively, is that the state is essentially violent and un-Christian and therefore that Christians can have no participation in civil government; the positive side is that Christian citizens must seize control of the state and make it the instrument of God's Kingdom. (3) The negative doctrine of war condemns it as organized murder and refuses to support the military establishment; the positive side is expressed in the modern peace and arbitration movement, with disarmament agreements as its most recent phase.

The doctrine of *personal* retaliation, as the preceding history has shown, was enunciated negatively, i. e., forbidding revenge, by Confucius, and positively, as overcoming through love, by Lao Tse, Gautama, the Stoics, and Jesus. The negative obligation of a life superior to personal spite and vengeance is enjoined by all ethical religions, and is not peculiar to Christianity, much less to the peace sects.

The doctrine of the *state* was expressed negatively by the apostolic writers, the Anabaptists and all the German peace sects, in the doctrine which deprecates participation in politics; its positive aspect of Christian politics is the peculiar contribution of the Quakers, partly in theory, but more especially in practice.

The testimony against *war*, even in its negative form, has not been made by Confucianism, Taoism, Buddhism, Stoicism, or the principal churches, either Roman Catholic or Protestant. It is the distinctive contribution of the apostolic church and the Christian peace sects, all of whom confined themselves to its negative aspect. Its positive side of peace and arbitration has been fostered chiefly by Quakerism, seconded, especially during the last century, by the general growth of humanitarian sentiment and international solidarity.

It thus appears that the significance of the Society of Friends in the history of passive resistance lies in their political activities and their public service along the line of peace and arbitration. To these two aspects this sketch will be confined. In this connection, an effort will be made to complete the history of the German peace sects whose European career has been previously outlined. They came to Pennsylvania under the urgent invitation of William Penn, and were not found in large numbers in any other colony. Their substantial contributions to the life of Penn's colony, as well as those of Germans who were not non-resistants, have been shown, of recent years, by the able historians of the Pennsylvania-German Society. Not the least of their services was the loyal support which, in so far as their anti-political principles allowed, these peace sects gave to the efforts of the Quakers to conduct the government along non-resistance lines.

To take only a few instances of Quaker social and political activity: When it was realized that the denial by colonial governments of the right of assembly could not be maintained except by actually exterminating the Quakers, there was nothing for the authorities to do but yield.

This carried the right of exemption from tithes to the established church, a concession which, as we are told, "was won only by a long hard fight, but when it *was* won, it was won for everybody. . . . But," continues their biographer, "they did not stop with passive resistance to the tithe system. They laboured for three quarters of a century by every method known to their intelligence, or 'revealed to the mind of Truth' to get the tyranny abolished by statute." And, again, "as fast as they won their freedom they took up the fight on behalf of other peoples who were oppressed and hampered, and they proved to be good leaders of what seemed at the time 'lost causes' and 'forlorn hopes.'" In Maryland, in 1681, "Lord Baltimore announced to both houses that *"moved by the frequent clamours of the Quakers,'*[1] he was resolved henceforth to publish to the people the Proceedings of all the Assemblies."[2]

But perhaps the best illustration of the Quaker battle for English rights is to be found in a quaint work published in London in 1670. The title runs, "The peoples ancient and just liberties asserted in the trial of William Penn and William Mead, at the session held at Old-Baily in London, etc." This little product of Quaker passive resistance describes in great detail the outrageous bullying of the court, which was composed of the mayor, recorder, and an alderman of London, and records the fearless and able defense of Penn and Mead, who acted as their own attorneys. The prisoners were indicted under the charge of having "unlawfully and tumultuously assembled with Force and Arms." The evidence, however, showed simply that Penn had been preaching to an assemblage in the street near the meeting-house, from which the Quakers

1 Italics mine.

2 Jones, "The Quakers in the American Colonies"; pp. 153, 167, and 333.

had been debarred by officers of the law. While they were thus peaceably engaged soldiers rushed upon and dispersed them, then trumped up the preposterous charge named in the indictment.

The defendants appealed to English charters and the common law, with an amazing knowledge of legal principles that probably not only mystified the learned court, but also irritated it.

The twelve "good men and true" were not so affected, however, and brought in a verdict to the effect that they found William Penn guilty of *preaching in the street*, and Mead not guilty of the same. The court promptly returned them to their cell without food, heat, or decent conveniences. For three days this continued, the court browbeating, and raging incredibly at both defendants and jurymen. Penn and Mead exhorted them to stand firm for the liberty and rights of Englishmen, and the sturdy commoners stood true. The court was simply forced to accept the unique verdict, and the prisoners went free, but not until the recorder had declared himself in favor of a Spanish Inquisition in England for such fellows![1]

The important thing for the present account is that the Friends were not content to come off free from the charge of riotous assemblage. They took up the battle for the threatened liberties of the English people and spread the account of the trial before the public. The

[1] It is interesting to note that a booklet on "The Trial of Penn and Meade" is announced (1921) by the Socialist "Appeal to Reason" in its "University in Print." The announcement pays the significant tribute: "Liberty, Equality and Fraternity have been preached through all time but it was left for William Penn, the Quaker, to come nearer establishing the ideal of this trinity than any other being called human before or since his day. Penn's defense in his trial . . . constitutes a mighty plea for the rights of men under Government."

document contains also "A Rehearsal of the Material Parts of the Great Charter of England," the "Confirmation of the Charter and Liberties" of Edward I, and the "Sentence of the Clergy against the Breakers of the Articles above-mentioned," along with considerable other material designed to arouse the English people to their endangered rights, affirming, in the introduction, that there cannot "be any business wherein the People of England are more concerned than in that which relates to their Civil and Religious Liberties." The essential point is that this is not *non*-resistance. It does more than seek to triumph by passively suffering. It is a form of resistance that comes back to the fight and takes the aggressive, but always abhors the use of brute force in moral conflicts.

A special student of this phase of Quakerism says: "The protest of the Quakers against their arbitrary taxation by the Duke of York, in 1680, includes most of the arguments used by the Americans in 1776 against 'taxation without representation' and is an early Quaker movement in favor of independence nearly a century in advance of the event." [1]

The accession of William Penn lent to Quakerism that public turn which has contributed so much to give the Friends their unique place in the history of passive resistance. But, since all the world knows the story of Penn, it need not be recounted here.

The founding of Germantown affords an excellent opportunity to observe the Quakers and Mennonites in close contrast, the latter as the typical non-political, the former as the typical political, passive resistant sect. Smith's account [2] is so suggestive that it is quoted in full. Speak-

[1] "The Quaker in the Forum," by Amelia Mott Gummere; p. 145.

[2] In his "Mennonites of America"; pp. 123 ff.

ing of the incorporation of Germantown (1680–91), he says: "It is one of the few times that the Mennonites of America had the opportunity to test the feasibility of non-resistant principles when applied to the establishing of a civil government. Here we have a group of men, all of whom inherit the Mennonite prejudice against the holding of civil office and the use of physical force in any form whatever when applied to government; they ask for separate incorporation which implies the establishing of a complete list of civil officers, the machinery for the making of laws, and the courts for executing them. Theory and practice were completely inconsistent with one another, and it was inevitable that an attempt to harmonize the two should end in failure." The Germantown government died a lingering death, until finally absorbed by the city of Philadelphia. The same authority continues:

> The loss of the charter was due largely to the fact that the Mennonites had very little taste for civil government. At first so long as the matter of local government was hardly more than the regulating of the family affairs of the brotherhood there seemed to be little objection to the holding of office. Out of eleven of the first officers named in the charter six and probably seven Mennonites and four of the remaining five were Mennonite-Quakers. But the village grew in numbers. Many came who were not in sympathy with Mennonite ideals. The making of laws and the administration of justice became more complicated. With the coming in of stocks and prison-houses the Mennonites lost their desire for politics. The offices were filled more and more by either Mennonite-Quakers, or by the Quakers, who seem never to have shared the prejudice of the Mennonites against the holding of civil office.[1]

The Quaker régime in Pennsylvania proved a success in times of peace, but, when the troubles with the French

[1] *Ibid.*

on the Indian frontier demanded military measures for the defense of the colonists, it went to pieces. The merits of the case will be discussed in a later chapter. The purpose here is simply to record the facts. The numerous Friends in the legislature came to feel their position untenable, especially as they were advised by London Friends, in England, to retire from the political field. Says Jones:[1] In 1756 "the Governor and Council declared war, bounties were offered for scalps of the male and female Indians, and the Quaker legislators resigned." But the Quakers found it exceedingly difficult to lay down their political power. They no longer held office, but "their opponents said that they still controlled the government through 'Quakerized' Episcopalians and Presbyterians.'"[2] The yearly meeting at Philadelphia, seconded by the local meetings, thenceforth urged upon the membership non-participation in politics, aside from voting and perhaps holding the local offices. A very similar movement occurred in Maryland and North Carolina. In the latter State it was proposed in the yearly meeting of 1809 that Friends holding offices which involved the judicial oath or punishment of crime should be disowned, and a similar situation occurred in Virginia.[3] In Maryland, "Friends in the eighteenth century contented themselves with sending petitions to the legislature instead of sending members to it."[4]

Simultaneously with their retirement from politics and their increase of membership, the now unified society began to take on that extraordinary zeal for moral causes which has marked Quakerism for a hundred years. "The

1 *Op. cit.;* p. 503.

2 *Ibid.;* p. 493.

3 "Southern Quakers and Slavery," by Stephen B. Weeks; pp. 117–118.

4 Jones, *op. cit.;* p. 334.

work of Friends by common consent was to be philanthropic only, so far as it touched the outside world, but mainly it was to be given to strengthen the body in its own principles and testimonies." The Friends had long felt that the principles of peace were at stake in Pennsylvania. They had felt, throughout the rank and file of the society, a deep sense of responsibility for the government founded, by their great leader, on the principles of passive resistance. They had long been the honored and powerful directors of the State. Now they were hooted at, despised, and their policy discredited. President Sharpless[1] eloquently observes: "They simply drew together as the world turned against them, more certain of their ground, more determined to maintain it at any cost of suffering and popularity. If all around had conspired, as it seemed, to annul Penn's Holy Experiment, they would renew it, not externally, that appeared hopeless, but in the hearts of a devoted band."

Much of this story of Pennsylvania is familiar knowledge, but it is not so well known that the Friends were governors of Rhode Island for the good part of a century, and that they gave the great Governor Archdale to North Carolina. Their work as rulers of Rhode Island will be referred to in later chapters, and so it will be sufficient at this time to remark that their policy there did not meet the sorrowful end that befell the Pennsylvania experiment. The Rhode Island Quakers were staunch peace men, but they distinguished between their public and their private duties. The result was some very interesting situations from the point of view of passive resistance, to be discussed in later pages.

The Quakers were very early settlers in New York

[1] In Jones, *op. cit.;* the chapters on Pennsylvania are written by Isaac Sharpless; cf. p. 579.

Colony, particularly upon Long Island. Here they came in conflict with the authorities, who referred to them rather plainly as "that abominable sect who treat with contempt both the political magistrates and the ministers of God's holy Word, and endeavor to undermine the police and religion."[1] This was a challenge to men and women of "the seed of the martyrs," and some of the best examples of victory through passive resistance occur in the history of Long Island Friends. These people who were so bent on building the state upon an enduring foundation of truth and right were everywhere received and branded as "turbulent," "attempting to destroy religion, laws, communities, and all bonds of civil society."[2] They were regarded then precisely as revolutionary anarchists were a decade ago, and much as all social liberals are regarded by the privileged and vested interests to-day.

Nowhere was this more true than in New England. The stern Puritan legalist, who prayed with one hand on the Bible, particularly the Levitical code, and the other on the sword, could not abide the thought of these "Antinomian" enemies of public order. Nor could their doctrine of peace appeal to the granite men of the old Massachusetts Bay Colony. Yet the Quakers felt that they had a special mission to these men of the Old Covenant, and they persisted in carrying their message into the very jaws of death. The result was their martyrdom, not less desired by the Quakers, to say the least, than by the Puritans themselves. When the Quakers came on undaunted, the Puritans had either to recede or push on to the bitter end; but we shall have occasion later to discuss the psychological aspects of that historic contest.

[1] Jones, *op. cit.;* p. 227.

[2] From the Virginia Act of 1859, quoted by Weeks, *op. cit.;* p. 17.

CHAPTER VII

THE GERMAN PEACE SECTS IN EARLY AMERICA

IN every case the sects previously sketched were left at the point where they turned their backs upon the cruel persecutions of the Old World, and set their faces toward America and the Wilderness, whither we must now note their fortunes. While the Moravians planted a colony in Georgia and another in Pennsylvania, all the others, Mennonites, Schwenkfelders, and Dunkers, were virtually confined to Pennsylvania, until they spread westward, following the usually traveled routes of the frontier movement. During their early years they were settled at Germantown and in the country lying to the west and northwest from that place. It is the purpose of this section to mention very briefly the part played by these exiles for peace in the history of passive resistance in the United States.

The *Mennonites,* who have been frequently mentioned already, have uttered their ancient testimony against participation in government on various occasions in American history. John Herr, a Mennonite reformer of about 1812, adduces, as a principal evidence of the corrupt and backslidden condition of the church, their sitting on the "seat of judgment"; and his successor, Daniel Musser, deplores their attendance upon elections and practice of electioneering. They also were accused by those prophets of using the courts of law to defend their rights! All these jeremiads, while probably exaggerated, indicate a tendency on the part of the rank and file to relax their original Anabaptist position. Along with the Friends and others, they suffered for their testimony during the Revolutionary and Civil wars. At a convention in 1776, "most of the Mennonites who were present took the position that since they were a defenseless people and could neither institute nor destroy any government, they could not interfere in tearing themselves away from the King." [1] During the Revolution they made contributions to the American cause in the form of money and supplies, which the Quakers held to be virtually a surrender of the peace principle. Smith thinks "the Mennonites were less consistent [than the Quakers]. While they would not carry weapons themselves, they appear generally not to have objected to supporting the cause by their means." [2] During the Civil War they assisted the Friends in the effort to obtain relief from the draft. It is interesting to note that their departure from their testimony against political participation enabled them to sustain their opposition to war, for by their solid Republican votes they had proved to be a valuable constituency to Congressman Thaddeus Stevens, and he helped to put the exemption bill through Congress largely for their sake.[3]

The *Dunkers* made a similar testimony and suffered for their faithfulness to non-resistance principles. Falkenstein [4] calculates that the little company who came to Pennsylvania in 1720 had traveled, in the aggregate, more than sixty thousand miles, in fleeing from persecution. They settled among the Quakers and Mennonites, but Falkner, one of their number, complains of "the melan-

[1] Smith, *op. cit.;* p. 259.
[2] *Ibid;* p. 380.
[2] *Ibid.;* p. 378.
[4] *Op. cit.;* p. 35.

choly, saturnine Quaker spirit" that prevailed in the province in those days.[1] They stood sturdily, however, along with the Quakers, for the ancient testimony against oaths and war, as when Christopher Sauer, the Germantown printer, "allowed himself to be despoiled of all his property, which was considerable for that day, and be dubbed a traitor . . . because he could not take the oath of allegiance to the new state of Pennsylvania at the close of the Revolutionary War. It was not because he was opposed to the state, or because he was a Tory at heart, but because he was conscientiously opposed to taking an oath."[2] The Dunkers have uniformly refrained from voting and from holding civil office, and their members are discouraged from using the courts of law, but in all these things there is a tendency, especially among the younger members, to do now as the world does; and the same is true of the Mennonites and all the other exclusive sects.

The *Schwenkfelders* emigrated in 1734, and therefore arrived some years later than the Quakers, Mennonites, and Dunkers. Consequently they found the land largely settled and were unable to secure a continuous tract large enough to permit them to form a distinct settlement. They were compelled to scatter more or less among the other German sectarians, and this fact, coupled with their former close relations with Zinzendorf and the Moravians, was partly the cause of their difficulty in forming a church organization. But it also saved them from the perils of the frontier during the Indian wars.

In the matter of participation in government the Schwenkfelders went with the Quakers rather than the Mennonites and Dunkers. "They did not strive for public office, since they preferred the freedom of private life;

1 *Ibid.;* p. 730.
2 Gillin, *op. cit.;* p. 207.

neither did they in general refuse to serve when called upon." The more public-spirited of them, such as David Schultz, did not deem it too much trouble to go forty miles to vote at a provincial election. They, like the Quakers and all true peace sects, were averse to the use of courts of law, but Kriebel says "they were ready even thus to maintain their rights if need be."

The Schwenkfelders shared in all the burdens of war except the actual bearing of arms. In a "Candid Declaration" of 1777, they "confess and declare that for conscience' sake it is impossible for us to take up arms and kill our fellow men." But they offer, "gladly and willingly," to pay the taxes, and their historian declares that "no Schwenkfelder ever refused to pay the fines imposed for non-performance of military service"; they stood solidly behind their representatives in the legislature when they voted "to defend the rights and liberties of America."

The *Moravians,* it will be remembered, were a missionary organization rather than a church, during their early days in America. They planted a large mission in Georgia, but later transferred their principal work to Pennsylvania. Here they devoted themselves to the conversion of the Indians. They established two missions called Gnadenhütten, which may easily be confused, inasmuch as events of importance occurred at both places during the French and Indian wars. The terrible massacre of non-resistant Indians by bloodthirsty whites occurred at Gnadenhütten on the Tuscarawas, as described in a later chapter. At Gnadenhütten on the Mahoning the Moravian mission settlement assumed very reluctantly a defensive attitude upon the outbreak of the French and Indian war. At first they merely built stockades and kept diligent watch, but after the massacre of eleven out of their fifteen members they accepted a supply of arms and ammunition sent from New York by the more belligerent friends of the mission.

In this juncture their leader, Bishop Spangenberg, felt called upon to set forth explicitly the Moravian position on the state, constabulary, and war. In so doing he said in part:

> We are of the opinion that governments ought to protect their subjects. Rulers are servants of God, and the sword is given to them by a Superior Power, who is King of Kings, and Lord of Lords. This sword given them they hold not in vain, but they are to protect the weaker ones and save the innocent. It is not only permitted unto them to oppose and punish all such as will hurt, kill, steal, etc., but it is their duty to do so, and if they neglect this office they will be answerable for it to their Master.

The minister of the Gospel must not, however, according to the bishop, be the one to wield these carnal weapons. He must conquer only "by the sword of the Gospel, by faith in Christ, by prayers and tears." But on the other hand "a common man such as they call a layman, if he have wife and children, is to provide for his family and to protect them against mischief. . . . It would be wrong in him if wicked wretches should fall upon his children and he be indolent and patient at the murdering of them."[1]

No fighting was found necessary on the part of the Brethren, and despite these defensive activities they have always been recognized as opposed to war. Therefore when, in 1749, the English Parliament legally recognized the Moravian Church, it granted to them certain concessions in Britain and the colonies, and among these were

[1] "Memorials of the Moravian Church," 1870; Vol. I, pp. 204 ff. Also "A History of the Unitas Fratrum, or Moravian Church," by J. Taylor Hamilton, Vol. VIII, in "The American Church History Series."

"relief from bearing arms and from taking judicial oath."[1]

THE COMMUNISTIC NON-RESISTANTS

Various ascetic, communistic sects have shown a natural affinity for the doctrine of non-resistance in its strictly negative form. They have repudiated civil government and have retired from the world, but they do not contribute much to the solution of this great problem, which, as has abundantly appeared, is inextricably bound up with the very nature and existence of the political state and the social order. Such semi-communistic sectarians hold the doctrine of non-resistance solely because of their "apostolic" simplicity of life and their general pacific disposition, while the perplexing questions of magistracy and war are very remote from their secluded lives and unsophisticated thoughts.

The *Shakers* are typical of this class. They hold that marriage is an institution inimical to true spirituality, and live apart in quiet ascetic "families" of the celebate "brothers" and "sisters." Their absolute non-participation in political affairs is well expressed in their petition to the President of the United States during the Civil War, in which they sought exemption from the draft. They aver that "this favor is asked of the Government for the following considerations: That non-resistance and non-participation in the affairs of earthly governments are primary and fundamental articles of the religious faith of the Shaker societies. . . . No Shaker has ever trained, voted or been voted for, or held any office of honor, trust or emolument (except Postmaster) under the Civil Govern-

[1] Taylor, *Ibid.;* p. 459.

ment, or participated in politics."[1] The Shakers originated in the eighteenth century in England, with the preaching of Mother Ann Lee, and, after considerable persecution among the hostile populace there, they came to America in 1774, and founded their first communities, a few years later, at Watervliet and New Lebanon in the State of New York. Since that time they have spread westward, and maintain "families" in various States. "They have suffered in person and property and even been imprisoned for their non-military testimony."[2]

The *Inspirationists* of Amana, in Iowa, are a direct outgrowth of the great German Anabaptist movement of the sixteenth and seventeenth centuries. "Its rise was one of the numerous protests against the dogmatism and formality that had grown up in the Lutheran Church."[3] Mrs. Shambaugh traces this particular sect back to John Philip Spener and "the early Mystics and Pietists—particularly of that little branch of the Pietists which arose during the last quarter of the Seventeenth Century and whose followers are said to have 'prophesied like the prophets of old' and were called the 'Inspirationists.'" The peculiar theological tenet of the Inspirationists is their absolute dependence for guidance in their affairs upon the revelations received by their "Instruments" (*Werkzeugen*), and which they accept as divinely authorized. It is therefore a modified mysticism; that is to say, the direct access to the Divine Mind is supposed to be limited to a few chosen instru-

[1] "Shakerism; Its Meaning and Message," by Anna White and Leila S. Taylor. The little story, "Susanna and Sue," by Kate Douglas Wiggin, gives a pleasing picture revealing the purity, peace, and gentleness of the Shaker communities, as well as their ascetic philosophy.

[2] *Ibid.;* p. 182.

[3] "Amana, the Community of True Inspiration," by Bertha M. H. Shambaugh; p. 21, Iowa State Historical Society, 1908.

ments, rather than taught as the privilege of every Christian, as in the teaching of the Quakers. The Inspirationists were like the Spiritual Reformers and the Quakers in their belief that God "will lead His people to-day by the words of His Inspiration if they but listen to His voice,"[1] but vastly different from them in their traditional spirit and the absolute subordination of the mass of the membership.

But the important thing for this sketch is the fact that "their cause soon encountered the opposition of the government, for the Inspirationists declined to perform military duty or to take the legal oath. 'We cannot,' they said, 'serve the state as soldiers, because a Christian cannot murder his enemy, much less his friend.' "[2] The Inspirationists were driven about by persecution, just as were all the kindred peace sects. Their history begins with the writings and teachings of Eberhard Ludwig Gruber and Johann Friedrich Rock in 1714. After the death of the early leaders there was a period of eclipse, but the movement lived and was revived a century later. Then their conflict with government broke out again. Although the age of bloody persecution had passed away, they suffered greatly for their peace principles and for their refusal to send their children to the state schools. Under these hardships they drifted naturally into a purely Christian communism, founded on mutual helpfulness rather than any theory of social equality, and they have maintained it to the present day, though on a vastly enlarged scale. Emigrating to America, they settled on the old Seneca Indian Reservation near Buffalo, New York, in 1843, but later removed to Iowa and founded, in 1855, the now celebrated Amana community, which still flourishes vigorously.

[1] *Ibid.;* p. 22.
[2] *Ibid.;* pp. 277–279.

The following passages will serve to indicate the root of their non-resistance principles, viz., the cultivation of a tranquil and benevolent state of mind, and personal salvation by an ascetic withdrawal from the "World." The following precepts were prepared in 1715 by Gruber, in his "Twenty-one Rules for the Examination of Our Daily Lives," and form the ideal standard of the Inspirationists to this day.[1]

V. Abandon self, with all its desires, knowledge and power.

VII. Do not disturb your serenity or peace of mind—hence neither desire nor grieve.

VIII. Live in love and pity toward your neighbor, and indulge neither anger nor impatience in your spirit.

XVI. Have no intercourse with worldly-minded men; never seek their society; speak little with them, and never without need; and then not without fear and trembling.

The Inspirationists and the Shakers, together with the Ephrata Communists (Pennsylvania), who were an offshoot from the Dunkers, and the Separatists of Zoar (Ohio), present the most successful examples of communism in history,[2] and they all rested on distinct non-resistance principles. Yet these two things are not cause and effect, as might at first appear. They are to be explained by a single cause in which both peace and stability were rooted. That was the attempt of the Inspirationists to reproduce the spirit and practice of the apostolic days.

THE DOUKHOBORS

The Doukhobors are the only *non-Teutonic* modern

[1] *Ibid.;* pp. 277–279.

[2] See Hinds, "American Communities."

peace sect to be described, with the exception of the Camisards of France.[1] The Doukhobors are Russian Slavs, and mystics, their name signifying "Spirit Wrestlers." They are partly communistic in their economic arrangements but have always maintained separate family life.[2] Doukhobor history runs back into the eighteenth century, but it is only in quite recent times that they have come into notice. Within the last decade or two the story of their heroic conflict with the Russian Government over military conscription became known largely through the efforts of Count Tolstoy and his followers. Aylmer Maude, a former disciple of Tolstoy in England, has given a thorough account[3] of their origins in the past and the political aspects of their philosophy. The Philadelphia Friends assisted the Tolstoyans in bringing these persecuted peasants to Canada in 1899, and one of these Quakers, Joseph Elkin-

[1] The Camisards came into prominence in France at the time of the Revolution. They were found chiefly in the Cevennes, at Congenies, but also in Languedoc. An English Quaker named Fox owned two luggers which, contrary to his protests, were converted into privateers during the war between France and England. The Quaker received fifteen hundred pounds as his share of the prizes. Investing this, "he advertised in the Gazette de France for the owners of the captured vessels. This account came to the body of Camisards, descendants of the original Huguenots, who held similar views upon war, and were greatly impressed by the action of Friend Fox. Through this incident, the whole French Community of Camisards at Congenies became Quakers." See the account in Gummere's "The Quaker in the Forum," pp. 259–270, from which the above quotation is taken. The account contains the petition of the French Quakers (including Americans who had settled at Dunkirk to revive the French fisheries) presented to the National Assembly, and also the remarkable adverse reply of Mirabeau, February 10, 1791.

[2] The Inspirationists of Amana have preserved the family life also.

[3] In his work, "A Peculiar People; the Doukhobors," 1904.

ton, has written, from first-hand knowledge,[1] about their doings in Canada.

Their significance for the history of passive resistance has special application to its modern aspects, namely, the militaristic state and its philosophy of government. As Maude pointedly observes, "Their doctrine that men gifted with reason and conscience should not use physical violence one to another, but should influence one another by the appeal of mind to mind and of soul to soul, is essentially anarchistic (in the best sense of that word), and it is naturally disliked by all authorities whose reliance is on sword or truncheon."[2]

When the Doukhobors first came into notice they were situated in the Caucasus region of southeastern Russia. But they had been transported thither as early as 1826, and had been fighting an intermittent war against the military draft for a great many years.

The English Quakers had known of the Doukhobors, and occasionally visited them during a large part of the nineteenth century.[3] There was much of the general spirit of George Fox in their attitude, but in two respects at least they found no sympathy from the Friends. The Quakers could not share their views on communism or on civil government. The Quaker has always been intensely individualistic, and has the English predilection for politics and constitutional government. But the Doukhobors, like the Anabaptists, and unmodernized branches of the Mennonites and Dunkers, have no place for civil government in their system of ethics.

[1] "The Doukhobors: Their History in Russia, Their Migration to Canada," by Joseph Elkinton, 1903.

[2] *Op. cit.;* p. 22.

[3] Stephen Grellet visited them, in company with William Allen, in 1819. Elkinton, *op. cit.;* p. 253.

Their leader, Peter Verigin, to whom, as an inspired prophet, they yield absolute and unquestioning obedience, was approaching the end of fifteen years in Siberia when some of Count Tolstoy's writings fell into his hands. The Doukhobors had not always kept up their testimony against war with unswerving faithfulness. Government enactments show that in 1834 they were allowed by law to provide Mohammedan substitutes, and they still had similar privileges in 1839;[1] yet in the main they had put up a marvelous resistance to the military encroachments of the government. Again and again in their history, cases of collective refusal of military service had occurred.[2]

However it might have been if things had taken their own course, Peter Verigin's reading of Count Tolstoy was shortly followed by a secret message from Siberia to his followers to resist the draft, and the command was obeyed with heroic firmness. It was because of the cruel oppressions that followed this bold stand that the Tolstoyans and Quakers came to the relief of the persecuted sect in 1898.

Since their settlement in Canada (January, 1899), they have given way to fanatical tendencies, the most striking of which was the pilgrimage made by a great company of people, without provisions, across the wintry Canadian plains to meet the Lord, on his Second Coming, which they believed to be immediately at hand. The Canadian authorities have used the utmost consideration toward these rather obstinate and troublesome subjects, who simply cannot comprehend how any governmental act can be prompted

[1] *Ibid.; pp.* 144–145. Maude says, p. 155, that during their later and more prosperous years in the Milky Waters, their former Crimean home, "they made no objection to conscription, and were in very good repute with the Russian authorities."

[2] *Ibid.;* p. 167.

by anything but sinister motives of exploitation or persecution—a most eloquent and richly merited tribute to the Russian autocracy! But on this occasion it was deemed necessary to coerce the wanderers in order to save them from self-destruction through their own fanaticism. In so doing an amusing example of non-resistance was given by the Doukhobors, as narrated by Maude: "At Minnedosa a special train pulled up, and after a stubborn struggle—in which many Doukhobors locked themselves arm-in-arm and showed all the passive resistance a sturdy body of men, resolved not to use aggressive violence, could offer—they were bundled into the cars by the police, or induced by less violent means to enter, and were sent back to Yorktown."

The non-resistance principles of the Doukhobors are drawn directly from their effort to reproduce the life and spirit of the early Christian communities. Although they have not always been entirely consistent in their policy, Maude concludes that, "when all their faults and errors are summed up, this remains: that in the irrepressible conflict, of which thoughtful men are becoming more and more conscious, between the imperialistic and military spirit of the age on the one side, and the spirit of peace on the other, the Doukhobors (by whatever motives actuated) have struck a conspicuous blow against the modern slavery of conscription." [1]

[1] *Ibid.;* pp. 230–231.

CHAPTER VIII

PEACE SECTARIANS AND CONSCIENTIOUS OBJECTORS DURING THE WORLD WAR: INDIVIDUAL ASPECTS

THE half-century of peace which preceded the World War had left its impress upon the peace sects whose history has been traced in preceding chapters, just as it had upon the whole world. The fathers had forged the doctrines of passive resistance in the very furnace of affliction, but their descendants held them, of necessity, as a matter of tradition, or at most as an abstract formula in which tradition and conviction were blended in varying proportions. Nevertheless, despite the fact that many adherents, as the sequel was to show, kept the faith more or less superficially, the central core of every one of these venerable organizations was rooted immovably in those underlying pacific principles, because they are the logical expression of an attitude of mind and heart which is as fundamental as anything in human life, possessing a perenniel power, wherever cherished by a group, to sway the lives of its members.

The opening scenes of the great conflict aroused the special advocates of peace, along with the whole of America's then pacifistic millions, to a horrified protest against the madness and wickedness of war, even though they then had little conception of the depths to which the world was about to descend. In those days, when Americans viewed the conflict from afar, and through all the conceptions, misconceptions, and valuations of prolonged peace, the peace sectarians were acceptable spokesmen. At that time they represented with practical accuracy the national attitude, even if not its fundamental philosophy. The hour was fast approaching, however, when traditional and academic theories would have to be translated into strenuous practice, as this vast, impersonal Purpose stalking through the world should roll onward to crush the bodies and wring the souls of men even beyond the farthest oceans.

As indicated in the title of this chapter, the exponents of peace, or perhaps more accurately the opponents of war, fell naturally into three groups. These we have designated by terms which will be more fully explained below, but we may observe in this place that the entrance of the United States into the war, and the consequent enactment of military conscription, struck them all with extraordinary consternation and dismay, although not for exactly the same reason. Those whom we here call political objectors were usually men of alien birth or connections, who did not necessarily hold any true peace principles, but were merely opposed to *this particular war* on America's part, and that solely because she chose to fight on the wrong side as they, very naturally, conceived it.

The "C. O.'s" on the other hand, were those persons who held abiding general principles which demanded the abandonment of warfare as a means of settling disputes between nations, not only in this case but in all cases. They did not, however, rest this objection upon religious tradition or idealism, but upon philosophical and humanitarian convictions. They were therefore correctly dubbed "C. O.'s" a convenient shorthand for "conscientious objectors."

Those whom we have called "peace sectarians" formed the third class, and they are sufficiently well known from the preceding chapters to require no further definition at this point, the next task being to notice how these various groups fared under the draft legislation.

The Selective Draft Law of May 18, 1917, explicitly provided that "nothing in this act shall be construed to require or compel any person to serve in any of the forces herein provided for who is found to be a member of any well recognized religious sect or organization at present organized and existing, and whose existing creed or principles forbid its members to participate in war in any form, and whose religious convictions are against war or participation therein, in accordance with the creed or principles of said religious organization."

By the terms of this law, which however was yet to be interpreted in practice, the peace sectarians were exempted, and by a later ruling the conscientious objectors were also provided for. Meanwhile the reaction of the three groups to the war situation was as diverse as their antecedents would have led one to expect.

As for the *political* objectors, no provision was made for them in the above-quoted act. The now well known, though misnamed, Epionage Law was really framed largely if not exclusively for "pro-German" residents of the United States, and for social radicals. This type of objector to the war program lacked, by definition, permanent significance, but it possessed an immediate importance as acute as it was purely temporary. The great and pressing danger justly felt by a nation at war from the presence in its midst of a very great number of aliens owing allegiance to the enemy governments, in the present as well as the past, and in their own persons or those of their forebears, called for a very prompt and vigorous, even drastic, suppression of words or deeds calculated to give aid and comfort to the enemy.

The non-religious conscientious objector, popularly known as the "C. O.," constitutes a new social type, possessing virtually no historic background, and consequently very little organization. The origins and social significance of this movement will be discussed in a later chapter, but it should be remarked at this point that the typical "C. O." is often associated more or less closely with organized religion or organized social idealism in some form or other. For example, many of them are international socialists, while others belong to the Fellowship of Reconciliation, which is frankly based upon Christian foundations.

Still, the conscientious objector was not entirely without a history. It is shown below [1] that the task of dealing with them had affected such legislation as the Defense of the Realm Acts in Australia, several years before the World War. Our own government was, moreover, not unaware of the existence of such a social species, and provision was made for them in the President's Executive Order of March 20, 1918. The purpose of that order was to define the "non-combatant service" provided for in the Selective Draft Act, and in defining this subject President Wilson announced that not only certified members of religious peace sects but also persons "who object to participating in war because of conscientious scruples, but have failed to receive certificates as members of a religious sect or organization from their local board, will be assigned to noncombatant military service, as defined . . . to the extent that such persons are able to accept service as aforesaid without violation of the religious or other conscientious scruples by them in good faith entertained."

These sentences specifically provide for those who objected to war as individuals, in complete detachment from

[1] See Chap. XI.

any social or religious group or organized movement. These are the "C. O.'s," whose fortunes will be touched upon in the following pages, along with those of their more numerous and better-known companions in passive resistance.

The third group of objectors, whom we have characterized as peace sectarians or religious objectors, were the representatives of a venerable and even honored tradition,[1] embodied for centuries in closely knit and sometimes even strongly clannish organizations. They thus had back of them the powerful moral support of their "beloved community," which even figured, in some cases, as an objective and collective conscience, affording them in their hour of trial the sustaining super-individual power which in the soldier's hard experiences was the outgrowth of patriotic devotion to the beloved country. The essential difference between the two was that one was cruelly torn by conflicting loyalties[2] while the other found his task a hard but relatively simple one.

The peace groups themselves were in many cases partly protected, in the popular mind, by what we elsewhere describe as the "badges of the sect"[3] such as the peculiar hat, coat-collar, or cut of hair and beard as worn by Mennonites and Dunkers; or by a distinctive form of speech and mode of worship, as used among certain of the Quakers. These outward peculiarities, possessing in themselves no importance for the world at large, nevertheless assisted in giving a distinctive character to otherwise obscure movements, and thereby helped them to benefit from social recognition. More specifically, these badges served as pegs on which to hang a more or less vague impression that these non-conformists were really good citizens, in fact "a

[1] See Chap. IV, V, VI and VII, above.
[2] See "The Philosophy of Loyalty," by Josiah Royce.
[3] See Chap. XII.

peculiar people, zealous of good works.'' Their long record of loyalty to government and devotion to human welfare was thereby gathered together, capitalized, and made to yield them a social return in the hour of need. Thus it was in recognition of their useful and consistent past that the various governments at war granted to these people an exemption, *as members of the sect,* which would have been denied them as citizens of the state.

This recognition itself was probably in part the more or less conscious acknowledgement of a moral claim which no honorable government could well afford to disregard. This claim in turn rested upon invitations to settle in America extended by rulers in the past, and upon the promise of exemption from militaristic burdens which accompanied those transactions.[1] Connected with this was a long history of public service on the part of some of the sects, and of very industrious, loyal, and godly citizenship on the part of all, not to mention a well-established expectation of freedom from that military conscription to escape which their fathers fled to America. All of these facts apparently disposed a liberal and peace-loving government to the utmost indulgence compatible with the tremendous crisis confronting the nation.

The presence of the conscientious objectors in relatively large numbers created, to be sure, a difficult problem for an administration already faced by superhuman tasks. Nevertheless the government at Washington adopted at the outset an enlightened and humane policy, which it tried steadily to pursue, despite the fact that the authorities, both civil and military, were hard driven by the urgent necessity of weeding out the pro-German and ''slacker'' tares from among the true non-resistant wheat. This liberal policy

[1] In Canada, this obligation was explicitly recognized in dealing with the Doukhobors.

was consistently followed throughout the war, not only by the higher officials of the civil administration but also by the superior military officers in the main. The deplorable barbarities perpetrated upon meek and unoffending young men whose inviolable convictions forbade them to engage in military activities were the joint product of an unfortunate interpretation of the law and the exasperated brutality of petty officers who were charged with the impossible task of carrying it out.

The passage of the Selective Draft Law, with its exemption clause for members of established peace sects, set a twofold task before the members of these organizations. The first, created by circumstances beyond their control, was to find a course of action that would enable their young men to comply with the demands of the law as administered, yet avail themselves of the exemption allowed. The second, entirely self-imposed and highly characteristic of certain of these societies, was to find some way of sacrifice and service permitted by conscience, and comparable, so far as possible, with the admittedly incomparable sacrifice demanded of the young manhood of the nation.

The experiences of the objectors of all types were greatly varied according to the local circumstances, particularly their own personal peculiarities and the temper of the military authorities with whom they had to deal. This treatment varied all the way from extraordinary tact and forbearance to the most brutal outrages. As already remarked, the general policy of the administration was just, and even liberal, to a high degree, and this applies to the military as well as the civil authorities. The situation, however, was an impossible one. Compelled to steer between the two pitfalls of persecution and indulgence of these troublesome recalcitrants, while extremists on the side hostile to the "C. O." watched every step with unwearied eye and tongue, the task of doing justice to all the antagonistic interests involved was really a superhuman one. The "C. O." was naturally unpopular and very little understood, even among the best informed of those who were required to deal with him. Even after more specific orders were issued these were not always at the ready command of his custodians, who, even if fully informed on the side of instructions, were often perplexed and exasperated beyond endurance. If to this be added the fact that occasional objectors felt impelled to make an issue of refusing to remove the hat (not as a military salute) when being examined in the presence of an officer, and to raise other archaic traditional issues having no living connection with the great moral questions at stake in this crisis, it need not appear strange that patience sometimes seemed to be no longer a virtue.

Furthermore, the popular contempt and hostility, always characteristic of the conforming majority toward any unyielding minority, was immensely magnified by the prevailing conviction, often fully shared in by the "C. O." himself, that the war then being waged was the most justifiable and most altogether righteous ever fought by men. Under such circumstances the man who could persistently refuse to strike a blow for the righting of monstrous and perfidious wrongs was naturally regarded as a coward or fanatic, or both, deserving of no consideration whatsoever. On the other hand, the conscientious objector, often realizing, as fully as his tormentors, the tremendous moral appeal of the hour, found his almost superhuman task so much the harder to perform, not only on account of the crushing disapproval of the multitude of his fellows, but even at times because of the misgivings or at least the chivalrous and indignant heartburnings within his own bosom; for in many a case the conscientious objector, as must appear on every page of this book, was not dead or even a stranger to the things that move other men.

So it was that, impelled by that imperious master which we call "conscience"[1] and armed only with the certificate of his sect and the statement of his local exemption board, or without even these in some cases, the conscientious objector was caught up with the vast human tides which, under the resistless mandates of world-wide war, were sweeping from every corner of the globe through the great mobilization camps and upon the mighty stage of conflict by land and sea.

Like multitudes of soldier-boys, these lads had many of them never ventured beyond their county line at home, and, also like their non-objecting associates, many a hard and cruel experience, inconceivable in the long and happy days of peace just ended, was to be their lot. This fate was governed, as already remarked, partly by the requirements of conscience in each particular case; and in this respect there was great diversity. Some refused to bear arms, but accepted any military task short of that, including the military drill. Others refused to drill, but donned the uniform. In other cases the objector accepted the soldier's suit but balked at wearing his cap. Some refused to perform any command whatsoever if issued by a military officer, while others obeyed when the task could be accepted as a punishment for earlier disobedience, and not as an act of war, direct or indirect.[2]

After the particular nature of non-combatant service was eventually defined, many objectors found themselves able to enlist for hospital work or other activities of the Medical Corps, while still others engaged in the duties of the

[1] Discussed, as to its nature and social significance, in a later Chapter.

[2] *Ibid.;* pp. 90–99.

Quartermaster's Service or similar tasks. As the war continued and the policy of the War Department was developed, many were found willing to accept the farm furlough, or reconstruction work in France; while in one case, at least, the Government assigned a number of drafted religious objectors to work at home.[1] This was in the case of the Inspirationists of Amana, Iowa, where the extensive woolen mills of this communistic peace sect were engaged in the manufacture of army blankets and other war materials.

Thus the response of the conscientious objector to the war situation varied all the way from the near-conformists who "were satisfied if they themselves are personally free from the responsibility of killing," [2] through the genuinely enlightened objector who was willing to ignore technicalities but determined to keep himself clear from the most indirect complicity in even "the hindermost parts of the military machine," [3] down to the clearly fanatical or merely obstinate and cantankerous individual, like some who, according to press despatches, having refused everything demanded of them in the way of service, objected even to leaving when finally discharged!

It would seem that the "C. O.'s" fared best in the United States and Great Britain, in which countries a long tradition of religious and civil liberty was not entirely eclipsed even during the darkest days of the war. Judge Kellogg [4] mentions a report to the effect that they had been put to death in Germany, and also in France, where they were classed as deserters. It is not supposed that the

1 Personal correspondence of the writer with Dr. Charles F. Noe, M. D., of the Community of True Inspiration, Amana, Iowa.

2 Jones, *op. cit.*, pp. 90–99.

3 *Ibid.*

4 "The Conscientious Objector," by Walter Guest Kellogg, New York, 1919.

phenomenon assumed very large proportions or was given much consideration in these lands, or in Belgium, Italy, or other Continental countries.

It is in accord with the genius of the British people that they should have given most thoughtful attention to the problem presented by the conscientious objector. In fact, the British experience largely paved the way for American procedure. As revealed in the discussions in the House of Lords, in May, 1917, the British plan was originally to treat conscientious objecting and related matters as civil offenses. Lord Kitchener is quoted as having explicitly declared: "The genuine conscientious objectors will find themselves under the civil power."[1]

The conscientious objectors in England numbered nearly five thousand, apparently, out of which hundreds proved to be unflinching absolutists who went through the rigors of repeated convictions and imprisonments at hard labor for the same offense.[2] Conditions in British jails and prisons, not unlike those in America, are marked at all times by many medieval barbarities of equipment and management; and the conscientious objectors, especially during a time of unprecedented national strain and peril, naturally saw the worst of them. In fact, Mrs. Hobhouse's remarkable book, referred to above, was written largely in protest against these cruelties, and the proceeds of its sale were pledged by the author to "the cause of prison reform." An English "C. O.," writing on "the horror of repeated imprisonment," says: "No man or woman who has not experienced this test of sincerity can be expected to form an estimate of the torment of its silence and loneliness. The only men who seem able to develop

[1] Remarks of Lord Parmoor, reported in "I Appeal Unto Cæsar, the Case of the Conscientious Objector," by Mrs. Henry Hobhouse; p. 11. London, Fourth Edition. No date.

[2] *Ibid.;* pp. 74, 41, passim.

a true understanding of its terror are the soldiers who have faced the dangers of the trenches and who shrink from the very thought of the alternative of prison.''[1]

It thus appears that between the trenches and the dungeons the choice was not so easy as has been supposed by the ''C. O.'s'' critics, even if these had actually been the alternatives before him. One of them, an English objector, speaking from ''The Cells,'' Salisbury Plain, says: ''It is not the fear of physical death in the trenches that has led to our remaining in prison, but rather a fear of spiritual death which we believe must follow our assent to any conscription scheme, military or civil.''[2] This is quite in accord with the facts, for under the operation of the English law, which, like the American, was ostensibly enacted to provide exemption for the sincere objector, the latter was first sent to the army, there court-martialed and consigned to prison, delivered at the end of his term by the prison to the army, thence to the court-martial and through it back to the cell, and so on *ad infinitum,* until madness, death, or the armistice interposed to halt the process.

Professor Gilbert Murray gives a very illuminating account, in the introduction to Mrs. Hobhouse's book, of the purpose and workings of the selective draft and exemption laws in Great Britain. Recognizing that a considerable number of persons, comprised among the Society of Friends, Christadelphians, Plymouth Brethren, Tolstoyans, and others who ''looked upon war as murder and on military service as a training in deliberate evil,'' would refuse to respond to the draft even at the forfeit of life itself, the British Government faced the difficulty ''with tact and prudence. They introduced compulsory service gradually, reluctantly, and not until the great majority of the nation

1 Quoted by Hobhouse, *Ibid.;* p. 74.
2 *Ibid.;* p. 73.

was ready to acquiesce in its necessity."[1] They provided exemption clauses for the conscientious objector, both religious and otherwise, and planned for the same to be administered on a generous scale by the local tribunals. The law provided for total and absolute exemption for those whose consciences required it, but offered also a qualified exemption conditioned upon engagement in non-military work of national importance, or non-combatant service in the army itself.

The local tribunals, from a natural desire to please the more turbulent newspapers, or the War Office, or to "display their own patriotism by sending other people to the trenches," granted very few absolute exemptions, and even few exemptions conditioned on the performance of work of national importance. They thus tended to excuse very few and even in those cases usually demanded non-combatant military service; but this alternative was little else than a mockery to most conscientious objectors, pleasing no one except the War Office and a few sectarians who objected only to the act of killing in itself, without scruples at becoming accessories to the act. But, on the other hand, as Professor Murray testifies, "The vast majority of the Conscientious Objectors were willing and anxious to accept alternative service. They were ready for any service that was not military, and on the whole showed a preference for ambulance work; or relief and reconstruction work, under the Society of Friends. I know," he adds, "two objectors who specially sought out employment in mine-sweepers, because it was at least as dangerous as ordinary fighting, and at the same time it aimed at saving life, not destroying it."[2]

But the extreme "C. O.," or "absolutist," was not really

[1] *Op. cit.;* p. vi.
[2] *Ibid.;* p. x.

provided for in all of this, for these "logicians of conscience," as they have been aptly styled, could "not accept their freedom at the price of recognizing and obeying the orders of a Tribunal which in its very essence their whole conscience condemns." In this they, like "all the Conscientious Objectors known to history, have been exasperating."[1] In some cases it may even seem childish and obstinate for a man to refuse to do, at the order of a tribunal, the very thing he would otherwise choose to do; but Professor Murray wisely thinks it "much more childish, and infinitely worse than childish, to send him, and to keep sending him again and again, to prison with hard labor until we achieve the sorry triumph of breaking his spirit or destroying his sanity."[2]

This is the punishment, condemned over their own signatures (in the volume referred to), not only by Professor Murray, but by the Earl of Selbourne, by Lord Parmoor, by Lord Hugh Cecil, and Lord Henry Bentinck, which befell those conscientious objectors who took what is known as the absolutist position, and demanded, justly or unjustly, the complete exemption provided for in the law. In July, 1917, they numbered in Great Britain between 800 and 1,000 men, in all stages of the "breaking" process,[3] which is described above.

[1] *Ibid.;* p. xi.

[2] *Ibid.;* p. xii. The usual sentence in England was 112 days in prison at hard labor. Mrs. Hobhouse refers to an increasing number of objectors who felt obliged to refuse to do work in prison "on conscientious grounds, practically identical with those which lead them to refuse the House Office Scheme [of national service.] The punishments for this offense are such that most of those who have adopted this policy for any considerable length of time have become mentally deranged." *Ibid.;* p. 46.

[3] *Ibid.;* pp. 3 and 14. Mrs. Hobhouse gives a detailed account of nineteen of these men, most of them persons of much more than average mentality, character, and social usefulness before the war, whose accustomed civil activities were the very kind that the mili-

In the United States this unhappy conflict between the majority and minority conscience followed largely the course of the British experience, but did not assume such drastic features on the whole. Major Kellogg says that "the conduct of the majority of objectors cannot seriously be criticised." As chairman of the government board of inquiry, Judge-Advocate Kellogg, in collaboration with Dean Harlan F. Stone of the Columbia University Law School and Judge Julian W. Mack of the United States Court of Appeals, traveled from one end of the country to the other examining hundreds of conscientious objectors in dozens of army camps, thereby acquiring the right to speak on this question from a comprehensive point of view attained by very few men in any walk of life. This might be less true if the board had shown a superficial or perfunctory attitude, which fortunately it did not do. Its personnel inspired confidence, and its history justifies the same, for nothing about Major Kellogg's book is more striking than the broad and liberal spirit with which he handles, often from a most exasperating angle, the whole problem of the conscientious objector. It is plain to be seen, between as well as in the lines of his story, that the board made a very sincere attempt to do its largely impossible task, which was to determine the sincerity of the individual conscientious objector. Consequently one is convinced that a large measure of success attended their efforts, and at any rate the distinguished ability and eminent fairness with which these agents of the Government conducted the inquiry is probably in part responsible for the tributes which the administration, both civil and military, received from leading members of objecting groups. Thus a prominent Dunker writes to the author, "At the War

tary authorities were now vainly and inanely trying to force them to do as an act of war.

Department and with the President himself, and generally with the higher officers in the camps every courtesy and consideration was extended to our pleas."[1] A leading Quaker testifies likewise that he and his official colleagues "had the most polite and sympathetic treatment on every hand. Everybody seemed to *understand.* They met us with fair and open minds. Officers accustomed to command, and raised to a pinnacle of dignity, talked with us on a basis of easy freedom and allowed us to debate every point at will."[2] This is in accord with the attitude deliberately adopted by the board of inquiry, namely, "to disregard military discipline during the conduct of the examination" of objectors. To this eminently wise and most truly dignified course they resolutely adhered, disregarding the concern and ridicule of certain army officers. The latter declared that the whole camp was laughing at the board for allowing "these dirty slackers" "to appear before it without standing at attention and saluting." This plea was fittingly rejected by Major Kellogg in his reply "that while functioning on the Board of Inquiry my first and only duty was to determine the sincerity of objectors and that it would be contrary to the spirit of the orders were I to insist upon military observances from a class of men who strenuously insisted that they were not to be regarded as soldiers at all."[3]

Dr. Jones adds some suggestive remarks on the underlying motives of this more liberal policy which happily prevailed. "Whatever the officials with whom we dealt may have thought of war in general," he says, "they appeared to be glad that there was a group of Christians left

[1] Letter of the Rev. W. J. Swigart, July 22, 1920.

[2] Professor Rufus M. Jones, in "A Service of Love in War time"; p. 124.

[3] Kellogg, *op. cit.;* p. 55.

in the world who still took Christ's way of life seriously and who in the face of grave difficulties were endeavoring to practice it." "Most of the officials with whom I had frequent dealing in Washington, and many unofficial people, were convinced that we who took this position were consistent in our course and were doing right when we kept unswervingly on the path of life which our fathers had walked before us. Again and again I was told: 'You are doing what you ought to do. We need to have in the world, especially now, some people who believe in the conquering power of love and who express in deeds the conviction that Christ's Kingdom of God is something more than a dream or an illusion to be surrendered at every hard pinch. Some day we shall all be glad that you stood out, held on and would not yield to the mighty appeal of the hour."[1]

It would be misleading, however, to make it appear that conditions touching the conscientious objector were idyllic in America during the war, or that military men and peace advocates constitute at present a mutual admiration society. The truth is that much bitterness existed and still exists, with immeasurable promise of evil in future in case we should be led into another war. Even Judge Kellogg is severe in his characterization of certain "C. O." types, and of course neither the militaristic temper nor the popular mood has aught for pacifists but ruthless suppression. But the infinite menace of this situation must be reserved for the discussion of a later chapter.[2]

[1] Jones, *op. cit.;* pp, 124 and xiii.
[2] See Chap. XV, below.

CHAPTER IX

PEACE SECTARIANS AND CONSCIENTIOUS OBJECTORS DURING THE WORLD WAR: GROUP ASPECTS

HAVING traced the experiences of the drafted members of the peace sects, attention must now be directed to a brief review of the official acts of these historic organizations themselves. Here the outstanding fact is that not one of the peace sects has modified its ancient testimony against war as being essentially un-Christian. On the contrary, Mennonites, Dunkers, Quakers, and others have steadily reiterated their long-standing conviction on the subject, in some cases even during the excitement of the war, without equivocation or modification. Their statements of the underlying ground for their common objection are not, however, identical.

The *Inspirationists* of Amana, Iowa, republished, in July, 1918, their belief that "arming is not permitted to any Christian, much less that it belongs unto a Christian and Godly Community. According to our faith we are not permitted to bear arms under any circumstances, nor make use of the same either in times of peace or war, not even in self-defense against our fellowmen, but rather to suffer wrong as a disposition of God, than to resort to violence."[1]

A leading member of this communistic peace group says,

[1] Official leaflet of the Amana Society, or Community of True Inspiration, July, 1918. Amana, Iowa.

however, that while "there has been no modification in the stand taken by our society in regard to war . . . this has never been carried to the extreme viewpoint of the Mennonites."[1] This statement is corroborated by the official literature of the society, as in the leaflet quoted above, where the stress throughout is laid upon "the bearing of arms" exclusively. The important thing, however, in the present connection is to note that on this somewhat restricted peace-ground the Inspirationists still stand unshaken by the distressing experience of the World War.

Similarly, we are told that whatever formal official action was taken by the *Dunkers* "was a restatement of the principles and testimony expressive of the attitude the church has maintained steadily and continuously since its organization."[2] Illustrative of this "restatement" is the following, from among similar annual utterances: "We take this occasion to renew . . . an expression of our abhorrence of war and our testimony in favor of peace and the furtherance of those sentiments that make for peace. . . . And we most respectfully but most earnestly and specifically protest against the enactment of laws that contemplate enforced training. . . ."[3]

The *Mennonites* likewise reaffirmed their ancient testimony in their general conference of 1917, and the various branches of the church united in addressing a signed "Appeal to the President" (undated) in which they say, "Because of our understanding of the teachings of Christ and the New Testament generally against war in any form, we can render no service, either combatant or noncombatant, under the military establishment, but will rather be amenable to any punishment the government sees

1 Letter of Dr. Charles F. Noe, July 23, 1920.

2 Letter of the Rev. W. J. Swigart, July, 1920.

3 Minutes of the annual conference of the Church of the Brethren, held at Winona Lake, Indiana, June 10–11, 1919.

fit to lay upon us as a penalty." These steadfast opponents of war also presented to Congress a petition against the passage of the Selective Service Act, which was signed by about twenty thousand persons of that sect, scattered throughout the various commonwealths of the United States.[1]

In all these utterances there is manifest a desire to make the ground of opposition as clear and as reasonable as possible, but no disposition to retreat before the astounding growth of military conscription which recent years have witnessed.[2]

The same may be said for the *Friends* and all the other historic passive resistant sects. The position of the former has been recently restated with great clarity and fullness.

1 This "Petition," which makes a good-sized volume, is without date also. See also the "Report of the Tenth Mennonite General Conference held at the Yellow Creek Church, near Goshen, Ind., Aug. 29 and 30, 1917"; pp. 3–6.

2 At the close of the World War the current magazines gave considerable discussion to the "problem" of Mennonite migrations. Certain Mennonite communities in South Dakota moved to Canada, under encouragement from real estate interests and the comissioner of immigration, in order to escape military conscription under the exemptions allowed there, and especially to be rid of public supervision of their own German-speaking schools. But the Great War Veterans' Association in Canada protested against their reception. They next chose to settle in Alabama and Mississippi, but the Democratic state committee of the latter State opposed their settlement, and at last accounts the wanderers were looking toward Mexico and Argentina.

The popular antipathy in this instance was aroused by the statement, attributed to a leader of the colony in question: "We are not a religious sect; we are a nationality; we are German." The discussion that ensued might leave the impression that the Mennonites as a whole were under attack, which would be an injustice, since comparatively few of them, apparently, have shared either the sentiments or the unpleasant experience of this particular colony. Most of the sect are abiding quietly in their accustomed rural neighborhoods, where their long-standing reputation as peaceable and industrious members of society will not be questioned seriously

Not only did the English Friends and certain groups of American Quakers issue addresses to their fellow-countrymen during the war years, but a general conference of all Friends throughout the world occurred in London during August, 1920. This was the most widely representative gathering of Quakers ever held, there being 350 delegates from America and Canada, with other leaders from various parts of the world sufficient to raise the list of delegates very close to a thousand.

This highly authoritative gathering issued a "New Statement of the Quaker Position" on war, which opens with these significant words: "The fundamental ground of our opposition to war is religious and ethical. It attaches to the nature of God as revealed in Christ and to the nature of man as related to Him. . . . The only absolute ground for an unalterable and inevitable opposition to war is one which attaches to the inherent nature of right and wrong, one which springs out of the consciousness of obligation to what the enlightened soul knows ought to be."

This position, as the statement goes on to explain, is such that one who takes it "may, quite sanely and even rationally, maintain that he can make his single life count for the most in the long run by preserving an uncompromising loyalty to the kind of world that ought to be"; yet he who does this "may be no less devoted to the ideals of his country, no less ready to surrender all that attaches to himself as an individual." This peace testimony, says the statement, "never was 'adopted.'" Moreover, "it is not a policy; it is a conviction of the soul. It cannot be followed at one time and surrendered at another time. . . . The Christian way of life revealed in the New Testament,

so long as the public mind is free from the excitement and dangers of war.

See "The Nation," November 9, 1918; The Literary Digest," September 4, 1920; and other current periodicals.

the voice of conscience revealed in the soul, the preciousness of personality revealed by the transforming force of love, and the irrationality revealed in modern warfare, either together or singly, present grounds which for those who feel them make participation in war under any conditions impossible."[1]

These propositions are integral parts of a closely reasoned argument covering seventeen printed pages, and are bound to lose force by being torn from their context. The sentences quoted express nevertheless the most notable aspect of the Quaker position, which is profoundly religious without being traditional, in the narrow sense in which that word is commonly used. The Friends stand, in consequence, on middle ground between the more strictly traditional and literal religious sectarians, on the one hand, and the non-religious, philosophical opponents of war, on the other hand. They do not adhere to their unyielding opposition merely because one finds, even in the sacred writings, any particular form of words, yet they do stand primarily upon the New Testament. In the words of the statement referred to, the Friends "do not rest their case on sporadic texts. They find themselves confronted with a Christianity, the Christianity of the Gospels, that calls for a radical transformation of man, for the creation of a new type of person and for the building of a new social order, and they take this with utmost seriousness as a thing to be ventured and tried."

Virtually all of these peace groups recognized the peculiar moral appeal under which this particular war was presented, and many of them were not a whit behind their fellow-citizens in their support of the high ideals pro-

[1] "Friends and War: a New Statement of the Quaker Position, adopted by the Conference of All Friends, 1920," London and Philadelphia; pp. 6, 7, 18, 23.

claimed in the noble utterances of President Wilson. In fact he simply gave expression from the vantage-point of a great political leader to ideas and sentiments for which they and their forebears had toiled and suffered for centuries. Nevertheless they denied, as it were, their own hearts, and refused to compromise, even in the service of the most righteous war in history, those principles divinely enjoined, according to their own view of the matter, which morally outlawed all war, even for the most holy ends conceivable, to the end of time.

In one respect, however, their historic attitude has been clearly altered by these modern experiences, and that is in their indulgence of individual members who have chosen to engage in the military activities demanded by the exigencies of the great crisis. Whereas in former times members were "disowned" for the bearing of arms and similar activities, the writer has observed no disposition to consider such action at the present time. On the contrary, the practice has been to leave the individual free to follow the dictates of his own conscience. Among the Friends, for example, young men subject to the draft were made the objects of solicitous care in such ways as explaining to them the traditional attitude of the society, its spiritual grounds, the possibilities, as was hoped from the start, in humanitarian service at the front and elsewhere as an alternative to the bearing of arms, and similar matters, yet the atmosphere was one of freedom, and those who chose to enter military service were in no way made the subjects of ecclesiastical discipline, either before, during, or after their warlike activities.

The same may be said for the other sects with few exceptions. One such is that of the English *Christadelphians,* whose official representative is credited with the statement that any Christadelphian joining the army in any capacity had his name expurged from the Christadelphian register.[1] On the other hand, the Amana Society states in an official leaflet, published in reply to charges of disloyalty, that, among many other loyal activities, "twenty-eight members of the Society served in the Army. Two of the four active physicians of the Society served in the Army as commissioned officers and the other two were members of the Volunteer Medical Service corps." Hundreds of members of all the peace sects in the aggregate served in every branch of the Army and navy, while other hundreds made their stand as conscientious objectors and suffered the consequences. Each was free to choose for himself in so far as any man is free to disregard the powerful, even if silent, pressure of his own most intimate group, and he was left to make his own decision for two reasons: first, because there was some confusion even in the minds of the leaders, in certain churches and communities; and, secondly, because the Government objected to any action which seemed to partake of the nature of "urging" upon men a certain course of conduct; the War Department by this action rendering a liberal policy toward militant members a practical necessity.

The attitude of all the peace sects on the whole was to regard the so-called non-combatant service as morally equivalent to actual fighting, although individual members might and did accept it in cases as justifiable. Perhaps the Inspirationists of Amana were least scrupulous on this point, as one might infer from the fact that their conscientious objection is rather specifically, perhaps exclusively, against "the bearing of arms." Moreover, one of their leading authorities writes: "The members of our society have not refused to serve in the branches of the army classed

[1] Cf. Mrs. Hobhouse, "I Appeal Unto Cæsar," fourth edition; p. 2.

as non-combatant, such as the quartermaster's corps, the medical corps, etc. In the recent draft the Society asked that its members be assigned to agricultural work, to government work in our mills, and to non-combatant branches, claiming this as its right under the constitution and the draft law. . . . The government finally recognized the claims of the society and assigned a number of the drafted men to work at home and others to the non-combatant branches.''[1]

In the main the conscientious objectors of every type rejected non-combatant service, but many of them accepted the farm furlough later provided for.[2]

No account, however cursory, of the conscientious objectors' part in the World War could claim a semblance of completeness without some mention of their relief and reconstruction work. It constitutes one of the significant accomplishments of a period of very big things, and it is peculiarly expressive of the passive resistant's point of view. If one were to indulge in a somewhat questionable but suggestive analogy now growing in vogue, he might fall back upon the Freudian psychology and say that the reconstruction service represents the sublimation of instincts and emotions aroused in the non-resistant by the tremendous appeals of the war, in which he could have no active part, but which must seek an outlet in some form of self-sacrificing and heroic endeavor. This was

[1] Dr. Chas. F. Noe, in personal letter to the author.

[2] Perhaps the following estimates for the conservative Dunkers may be taken as fairly representative of all the peace groups: "A few of our members enlisted. Some with agreement that their service should be limited to forestry or something of that sort that would not require the bearing of arms. I think one-eighth of those who were drafted accepted regular military service. Probably three-eighths accepted non-combatant service of various kinds. The remainder, one-half, refused all service, and went to the detention barracks." Letter of the Rev. W. J. Swigart.

found in a form of service at and near the front which afforded a very good moral equivalent for war, being strenuous and not devoid of hardship and peril, while it called forth his constructive instead of his destructive endeavors. Moreover, its magnitude, and more especially its unique spirit., challenged the attention even of a war-distracted world.

This work was begun by English Friends during the opening weeks of the war, with such expedition that "less than a fortnight after the Battle of the Marne, George Henry Mennell, accompanied by his wife, who is a Frenchwoman, started for Paris armed with the actual passport and brassard with the red and black star carried by his father Henry Tuke Mennell in 1870–71 when a member of the Friends' War Victims' Relief Expedition in the Franco-Prussian War."[1]

From this beginning the relief work of the British Quakers developed to large proportions at home, in Holland, France, and elsewhere. One of the most striking features was their volunteer ambulance units which operated within the battle area, and which were supported with both men and money by American Quakers long before the United States became involved in the struggle. So it came about that American Friends were in active coöperation with this work, though in a very minor capacity at first, almost from the start. They caught the inspiring spirit of the English Quakers and learned from their experienced and efficient workers the methods of this expanding service. For the task very early passed beyond ambulance work and civilian relief to include what became known as "reconstruction work" within the

[1] Jones, *op. cit.;* p. 29, quoting J. Thompson Elliott of London. This red and black star was adopted as the emblem of the Friends' Service, and is now familiar throughout Europe.

devastated areas. This service consisted in the construction of cottages, the restocking and cultivating of ruined farms, and the reconstruction, as far as possible, of the morale and social life of the disheartened people.

Upon America's entrance into the war the work of the American Friends was greatly expanded and organized upon a semi-independent basis, remaining always, however, in very close touch with that of the British Friends. Soon the movement spread beyond the Society of Friends, and enlisted the active and generous support of the Mennonites, Dunkers, and others. [1]

Extensive as this work is, especially when compared with the numerical strength of the organization responsible for its inception and support, its chief significance is moral rather than material. It presents a bright page in a dark history, and the extent to which it has been featured and commented upon in newspapers and magazines shows that it appeals to the masses of men in a peculiar way, including army officers, French mayors, and many

[1] See "A Service of Love in War time," by Rufus M. Jones; p. 75 and passim. A detailed and impressive account of this work in European countries is given in this authoritative book, upon which the following account is principally based. See also files of the "British Friend" (London); the "Friend" (Philadelphia); and the "American Friend" (Richmond, Indiana); also articles in other periodicals of the period. A similar work in Austria, Poland, Russia, and Germany was prosecuted, with special attention to children, until the autumn of 1922, when steps toward withdrawal were taken. A German food-ticket of August, 1920, bears the image of a broad-hatted Quaker dispensing food to the children, with the inscription, "Thanks for the help of the Quakers." It should be said, however, that the Quakers were appointed by Mr. Herbert Hoover as official dispensers of certain *public* funds in Germany; and the Russian Soviet Government later singled them out for a similar service. In both cases the reason assigned was their unquestioned freedom from partisan bias and ulterior designs.

others both old and young who have paid their tribute to the work.

The people of France among whom this work was done have made many expressions ("compliments") of their gratitude in their own stately yet graceful way. While these show sincere feeling, one is left to wonder whether the Gallic mind, especially in its present situation, is prepared to grasp the deeper significance of the Quaker faith and the passive resistance philosophy to-day any more than it did in the time of Mirabeau.[1] The same is probably true of the mass of German and Austrian people among whom they are laboring, but there are those in Germany who see the mission in its larger aspects, the more easily so if it be true that passive resistance is congenial to the psychology of national defeat, as some allege. For instance a writer in the "Frankfurter Zeitung," June 27, 1920, uses these significant words: "We all know that, however considerable this distribution of food and clothing may be, this work of itself is small in comparison with the actual need. But we also know that the spirit from which it springs contains something which could solve the problem of the nations with a single stroke. It is universal good will which has become as absolute as a divine commandment."

Another contributor to the same paper of July 11, 1920, says, with impressive directness: "What moves me most of all is the feeling that you are the only ones in these unhappy times who have stood your ground. . . . As I recognize in you the only group in European life that was strong enough to withstand the shock of fate, my thoughts linger about you with the old question— Are ye they that should come, or look we for another? . . . Before the stroke of fate came upon us, you were among

[1] See above, p. 114, n. 1.

us an almost unknown sect: now your presence among us is overshadowing all the churches. Neither the Papal bishops nor the Protestant superintendents have been able to keep themselves pure from the war's hatred, nor can they now point to any fundamental principle for life, as you can. Let me ask, wherein lies your power, and let me try to give an answer which has also a bearing upon the destiny of Occidental civilization."[2]

The work in Europe was prosecuted with a conscious endeavor to avoid propagandism and to preserve "the deep religious spirit" with which it was first undertaken by the English Friends. A leader in that service, addressing the newly arrived American workers, said: "By the very nature of the trust imposed upon us, we cannot speak as we might in times of peace of some aspects of our faith, but we can in our work demonstrate some aspects of humanity and brotherhood, lessen a little the terrible bitterness of war, and bring something of the spirit of comradeship and love into lives bruised and battered by the wrong that has been done."[2]

[1] "The Quakers, by Alfons Paquet, and a letter to the Quakers, by Wilhelm Schafer," translated and reprinted by Henry J. Cadbury and Carl Heath, at the Orphans' Printing Press, Ltd., 10 and 12 Broad Street, Leominster, England. No date.

[2] Jones, *op. cit.;* p. 67.

CHAPTER X

PSYCHO-SOCIAL TRAITS OF NON-VIOLENT RESISTANTS: HISTORICAL EVIDENCE

SYMPATHY, sociability, and the sense of justice are, as Professor Ross remarks,[1] moral sentiments of the person acting. His fourth factor of social conduct is the *resentment* of the person acted upon, in case of personal or group aggression. Here we strike the root of the problem of this essay. Passive resistance is, as we have seen from the very beginning, a matter of personal reaction. Elsewhere we have examined its program and the grounds on which the passive resistant justifies and directs his course. The question now arises: Is the non-resistant lacking in pugnacity, resentment, or other elements of belligerency? are the instincts that lead other men to retaliate not present in this type of humanity, or, if present, by what processes are they suppressed, or diverted into channels so different as to make him at once an object for the commiseration, ridicule, admiration, and envy of mankind? The answer must be sought in several ways: first, by an examination of the nature of resentment; secondly, by an appeal to the actual conduct of passive resistants as recorded in their history and literature; thirdly, by reference to the statistical evidence brought forth by the army examinations in the World War.

1 In "Social Control"; Part I.

As Ross, Westermarck,[1] and others[2] have shown, resentment is an instinctive protective reaction, a reflex that is built up in the species by natural selection. In the merely brute struggles which are constantly being waged on the lower reaches of existence, the creature that fails to react toward aggression by some defensive operation, either counter-attack, concealment, or flight, is promptly destroyed, leaves no descendants, and is eliminated from the race. Westermarck traces a long chain of evolution in which "there is no missing link. Protective reflex action, anger without intention to cause suffering, anger with such an intention, more deliberate resentment or revenge—all these phenomena are so inseparably connected with each other that no one can say where one passes into another."[3]

Professor Ross traces the wider social consequences of this biological process. "Resentment," he observes, "in its lower forms is an instinct; but in its higher forms it is simply the egoistic side of the sense of injustice. The more one recoils from *doing* an unjust action, the more he resents *suffering* such an action. On its altruistic side,

[1] "The Essence of Revenge," by E. Westermarck, in "Mind," Vol. VII, New Series, 1898; pp. 289–310. April, 1922.

[2] E.g., Cooley, "Human Nature and the Social Order," Chap. VII; McDougall: "Social Psychology," pp. 59, 277–279; Thorndike: "The Original Nature of Man"; Vol. I of his "Educational Psychology," Chap. VI and VII.

Professor Cooley finds three levels of "hostility" which are distinguished "according to the degree of mental organization they involve." These are as follows:

"1. Primary, immediate, or animal.

"2. Social, sympathetic, imaginative, or personal, of a comparatively direct sort, that is, without reference to any standard of justice.

"3. Rational or ethical; similar to the last but involving reference to a standard of justice and the sanction of conscience." *Ibid.;* p. 239.

[3] *Op. cit.;* p. 297.

the sense of justice lessens aggression by inspiring respect for the claims of others. On its egoistic side, it lessens aggression by prompting to the energetic assertion of one's own claims. Resentment is, therefore, a moral quality,—elementary, no doubt, but not without its value.''[1] But, as Professor Ross proceeds to show, the attempt to remedy violence by counter-violence leads not only to constant disorder, but to an entailed hatred which, in the form of private warfare, vendetta, and feud, tends ever to compound its interest, until the very stability of the social order is threatened. Then the state interposes, gradually extends its function from that of mediator to umpire, and finally to the rôle of sole guardian of peace and order.

Now it would be unnecessary to argue that non-resistants are equipped with the same instinctive capacity for resentment and revenge as are all other men, if certain hostile writers and the vast majority of their readers did not assume the contrary. The fact that the phenomenon in its best developed form has appeared among the most aggressive races would seem to carry with it the implication that these meek men of peace bear within their own beings the capacity for vigorous warfare. A further consideration is that the non-resistance of these Western nations, which are the only ones that have produced conscientious objectors, falls within the Christian era, which is a negligible period of time for the purposes of biological evolution. This should dispose of the notion that non-resistants are fundamentally different *by nature* from the mass of their fellows. The typical non-resistant himself would very promptly inform one that it is by no means a matter of *nature* but a work of *grace*. And, even in a strictly scientific sense, this is true; that is to say, it is a matter

[1] *Op. cit.;* p. 37.

of ideas, *ideals*, and of an inward, spiritual experience.

Yet, while he is thus equipped with all the physiological machinery of active resentment, modified and controlled, to be sure, by a special set of ideas, there is still room to inquire whether the passive resistant belongs to this or that temperamental class, or psychological type. Thus Patten, Giddings, and others have distinguished various "original differences in population,"[1] based on the predominance of different emotional and intellectual elements; and there can be little doubt that the typical non-resistant belongs to the psychological type called *stalwart* by Patten, and *austere* by Giddings. The Quakers represent in some respects the extreme wing of English puritanism, the leading stalwart species; and the Dunkers, who may be taken as representative of the *German* peace sects, are described by Professor Gillen as austere, deductive, and domineering: "Deeply religious," he remarks, "the Dunkers are not the rationally conscientious but rather the austere type of character."[2]

After all allowance is made for racial, social, and temperamental factors, the one controlling fact that stands out is that the passive resistant is an ordinary mortal with an extraordinary idea, and animated by an uncommon spirit. Passive resistance is that peculiar attitude held by otherwise unobtrusive men which springs from the conviction that personal violence is absolutely wrong; which conviction is supported by certain mental dispositions and moral qualities to which attention must now be directed. In so doing the first step will be to notice for a moment some of the more famous non-resistants of history.

[1] See the discussion under the above title in Ross, "Foundations of Sociology"; pp. 290–309. Also Giddings, "Inductive Sociology."

[2] "The Dunkers: a Sociological Interpretation"; p. 205.

RESENTMENT AND INDIGNATION

Warren says of Buddha, "Anger . . . had no place in his character"; and "his epithet for one of whom he disapproved was merely "vain man."[1] Bigg refers more than once to the "docile" temper of Marcus Aurelius. His persecutings the same author attributes to his "harsh creed," and believes he "would have been a better man if he had had no philosophy at all and simply followed . . . the guidance of his own *excellent disposition.*"[2] Kriebel, in speaking of the last days of Caspar Schwenkfeld, a life-long exile for conscience' sake, says that his soul was "calm, peaceful and at rest. No undercurrent or eddy of ill-will, hatred, or revenge to others disturbed the surface, and the grace of heaven was reflected from his entire being."[3] The Stoics, as well as the Buddhists, are constantly teaching the folly and sin of anger. All these considerations might seem to corroborate a popular impression that non-resistants are of a peculiarly mild and gentle disposition. If "disposition" is taken to mean mental habit and attitude of will maintained, the popular view is correct; but if it is taken to mean the absence of irascible qualities the idea is false.

The fact is that passive resistants, especially in cases where the *moral* aspects of the situation seem to admit of "*righteous* indignation," have shown themselves by no means lacking in healthy and vigorous resentment. The famous controversy between the Quakers and the Puritans of Massachusetts offers an excellent illustration. The Quakers who came to Massachusetts felt that they had a special message to the Puritans. The latter clapped the

1 "Buddhism in Translations"; p. 1.

2 Introduction to Jackson's "Marcus Aurelius"; p. 34. Italics mine.

3 "The Schwenkfelders in Pennsylvania"; pp. 5-6.

first party of Friends into prison, later banished them from the colony, and when they, along with others, persisted in returning time after time, the Puritans were forced, for the sake of consistency with their own earlier threats and promises, to execute the unwelcome visitants, both men and women. The Quakers suffered cruelly at the hands of their opponents, but, with all their meek and patient suffering, the men and women of peace showed themselves capable as a class of a very strong and enduring resentment.

In the duel that raged for several bitter years between the Quaker and the Puritan, one sees exhibited a contest between two peoples equally sincere and equally spirited, but who chanced to belong to "two different spiritual empires." It would be interesting to examine the theological grounds of that difference, but attention must be steadily centered here upon the psycho-social traits, rather than the theological beliefs, of those barehanded but fearless men and women who persisted in going up, as they put it, "to look the bloody laws [of the Puritan] in the face." In the mere sketch that is permitted here we may say with Jones, from whom the above passages are quoted, that the essential difference between these two remarkable opponents was that "the central truth on which the Quaker of that period staked his faith and to which he pledged his life, was the presence of a Divine Light in the soul";[1] whereas, as Fiske has clearly stated it, this "ideal of the Quakers was flatly antagonistic to that of the settlers of Massachusetts. The Christianity of the former was freed from Judaism as far as was possible; the Christianity of the latter was heavily encumbered with Judaism."[2] In

1 "The Quakers in the American Colonies"; p. 32.

2 "Dutch and Quaker Colonies"; Vol. II, p. 112. Quoted by Jones, *op. cit.;* p. 35.

this conflict between the Old Covenant and the New, the Quaker followers of the latter had come in the name of a spiritual empire from which the rule of bigotry, violence, and persecution had been cast out forever. The legalistic Puritan still clung to those departing ways of earlier and harsher times. In this respect, Puritan and Quaker were ages apart; in all other respects they were alike—of the same race, people, temperament, and moral purpose. When they confronted each other it was by no means the man of iron and strong conviction against a cringing, negative being, destitute of the moral fiber that makes for resentment, lofty indignation, and vigorous aggression. It was, on the contrary, like the clashing of steel on steel, though the one opponent faced the conflict with no weapon save the sword of Truth as he conceived it.

The first Quakers who braved the Puritan wrath were women, and later a woman suffered brave martyrdom on Boston Common for her persistence. It is impossible, and also unnecessary, to rehearse here the details of that long, grim contest, with its whippings, ear-croppings, brandings, foul imprisonments, and hangings. The point to be emphasized just here is that the Quakers could *resent* as well as endure their cruel persecutions.

The essential kinship of the passive resistant with our common humanity appears in the evident relish with which the Quakers applied the verbal lash when doubly reassured by the righteousness of their cause and the non-physical character of the means employed. Gummere says: "Certainly the Quakers were never guilty of any violence, although, as Dr. Ellis remarks, 'there was good cause for dreading their sharp tongues.' "[1] The governor of the Barbados said that "as to Friends' lives . . . they were inoffensive and unblamable, but their judging of others

[1] "The Quaker in the Forum"; p. 63.

he could not bear."[1] Jones powerfully sums up the matter when he says: '"They could be as tender as a woman toward any types of men who were low down, hard pressed and sore bestead, but they were relentless against what they called 'hireling ministry.' They used very vivid phrases to describe it, and they were as intolerant of it as the writer of Deuteronomy had been of the idolatry of his day. They hewed it as fiercely as Samuel had hewed Agag."[2]

AGGRESSIVENESS

The career of William Penn is so uniquely identified with the idea of gentleness and peace that it is of especial interest to notice in his character the aggressive qualities that probably would have insured his success even as a man of war, just as they did in the case of his own father, an efficient admiral of the British navy. It was not their difference in nature, but the dissimilarity of their spiritual experiences, that made the father a warrior and the son the world's greatest man of peace. President Sharpless, in speaking of Penn's traits, says: "There was, too, in his composition a good share of fighting spirit. He was to have difficulties, but he never quailed. The temper which declared that he would never yield a jot, even though he died in prison, served him in good stead in other contests. 'Can my wicked enemies yet bow? They shall, or break, or be broken in pieces before a year from this time comes about, and my true friends rejoice,' he declared in a crisis with Lord Baltimore. 'If *lenitives* will not do, coercives must be tried,' he announced in another emergency."[3]

[1] Jones, *op. cit.;* p. 42.
[2] *Ibid.;* p. 36.
[3] Jones, "The Quakers in the American Colonies"; pp. 431–432.

In 1657 the Massachusetts authorities appealed, through the commissioners for the United Colonies, to the authorities of Rhode Island, exhorting them to expel the Quakers, who had settled under the liberal Baptist régime in the latter colony. The Puritans pleaded to be freed from the danger of "contagion" from "such a pest." In their noble and dignified reply the rulers of Rhode Island drop this significant little observation on Quaker psychology: "We find that in those places where these people aforesaid in this Colony are most of all suffered to declare themselves freely, and are only opposed by arguments in discourse, there they least of all desire to come." Jones goes on to say that "this was, however, not because they liked opposition and enjoyed a fight, but because they believed that they had come to America under a commission from the Most High to sow their seed and truth in the soil of Massachusetts."[1] The whippings, finings, ear-croppings, brandings, etc., inflicted in Massachusetts only increased the number of these unwelcome visitors. "When John Rous and Humphrey Norton heard of William Brend's terrible sufferings, they started at once for Boston . . . because they could not eat or sleep for their desire to bear their part with the prisoners of hope, for a testimony of Jesus."[2] Gummere thinks that "righteous *indignation* at the increasing intolerance of those who first came out to Massachusetts with the meekness of martyrs, no doubt led the pioneer women, Mary Fisher and Anna Austen, to the Bay."[3]

At this stage the Quaker founder, George Fox, himself a prisoner in Launceston, England, sounded forth a clarion call that can hardly fail to thrill the heart of

[1] *Ibid.;* p. 56.
[2] *Ibid.;* p. 76.
[3] *Op. cit.;* p. 44. Italics mine.

every lover of a good fight for truth and righteousness. Fox trumpets to his followers: "Let all nations hear the sound by word or writing. Spare no place, spare no tongue nor pen, but be obedient to the Lord God; go through the work; be valiant for the truth upon earth; and tread and trample upon all that is contrary."[1]

The heroic soldiers of peace rallied to these trumpet tones and pressed the battle to the very gates of puritanism. They were really the *aggressors* from the start. The Puritans could have desired nothing more devoutly than to be left alone. They had built up their wall of orthodoxy and claimed the right to rule without molestation behind it. But their dream was not to be realized. "Two days after Anna Austen and Mary Fisher, without bedding and without Bibles, sailed out of Boston harbour, that is, August 7, 1656, a ship carrying eight Quakers—'pretty hearts, the blessing of the Lord with them and His dread going before them'—sailed in."[2]

The Puritans, harassed and cornered, did everything in their power to escape the final bitter conclusion of their own logic, and escape from staining their hands with blood. They banished the Friends, particularly the women, over and over. Mary Dyer in particular was banished, reprieved, and rebanished, and was finally offered clemency on the very gallows, but "she stubbornly refused to accept her life, if the law was still to remain against 'the suffering seed.' "[3]

COURAGE

A whole chapter could easily be given to the bare enumeration of examples of the extraordinary courage of the

[1] *Ibid.;* p. 78.
[2] *Ibid.;* p. 36.
[3] *Ibid.;* p. 86.

meek who refused to fight, yet could not be hired to run away; who stood undaunted far from the excitement and enthusiasm of numbers. A cool and yet fierce courage is manifested in the case of Josiah Southwick. He turned from banishment in 1661, and at once, with what Jones calls "almost excessive Quaker frankness," "appeared before the authorities and announced his return to this country. He was . . . whipped through Boston, Roxbury, and Dedham, and then carried fifteen miles and left in the wilderness. The next morning he fearlessly returned to his home in Salem, having told his torturers that he cared no more for what they could do to him than for a feather blown in the air." The same writer says that it was William Leddra's "brave manner," as well as his "saintly bearing," that so impressed the Puritan magistrates that Governor Endicott was long prevented, by a division in the court, from getting a capital sentence.[1]

A good example of cool courage coupled with refusal to fight occurs in connection with the career of a follower of John Wesley. The founder of Methodism himself was not a non-resistant in any degree, as regards either the constabulary or war, for he appealed to the courts, and took pride in the good military reputation of the Methodist soldiers.[2] But he shared the universal feeling that *personal* retaliation is incompatible with the Christian religion, and he enjoined, as a matter of wise policy, non-resistance towards the mobs with which the Methodist street preachers had to contend. His biographer exclaims: "Certainly, it is not superstition to find something supernatural in the religion which enabled these humble Methodists to bear with such patience the indignities to which

[1] *Ibid.;* pp. 103 and 96.

[2] See "The Life of John Wesley," by C. T. Winchester, 1906; p. 140.

they were subjected. For these men were not cowards. Most of them came from that tough English peasant class which, since the days of Robin Hood down, has always been able to give a good account of itself wherever any fighting is to be done."[1] The following incident in the life of one of these non-resistant itinerant preachers of Methodism shows the kind of courage that may go with non-resistance even when it is sustained, not by fanatical frenzy, or mob psychology, but simply by an enlightened zeal for a moral cause: "Thomas Olivers, on his big bay horse,—which he used proudly to say had carried him over a hundred thousand miles,—when surrounded by a mob in Yarmouth, pushed his way down one of the narrow 'rows' to a main street, and then, disdaining to put spurs to his horse and fly from the howling crowd, dodging the sticks and stones thrown at him, walked his horse deliberately down the street and made as he says, 'a very orderly retreat.'"[2] George Fox, on a similar occasion, while a howling mob endeavored vainly to drag his herculean frame from the saddle, continued calmly in the singing of psalms!

Wesley himself came in contact with the *Moravians* on his voyage to America and was much influenced by them. He records in the following passage from his "Journal" an interesting observation on this very question of non-resistance and courage:

> Every day had given them [the Moravians] an occasion of showing a meekness, which no injury could move. If they were pushed, struck, or thrown down, they rose again and went away; but no complaint was found in their mouth. There was now an opportunity of trying whether they were delivered from the spirit of fear, as well as from that of pride, anger and revenge.

[1] *Ibid.;* pp. 139–140.
[2] *Ibid.;* pp. 128–129.

In the midst of the psalm wherewith their service began, the sea broke over, split the mainsail in pieces, covered the ship, and poured in between the decks, as if the great deep had already swallowed us up. A terrible screaming began among the English. The Germans calmly sung on. I asked one of them afterwards, "Was you not afraid?" He answered, "I thank God, no." I asked, "But were not your women and children afraid?" He replied mildly, "No; our women and children are not afraid to die."[1]

The evidence suggests that the passive resistant is neither more timid nor more brave than others, but simply that he is indistinguishable from them in his native endowments, though quite diverse in social heritage. The experiences of the World War, particularly those aspects which pertained to the creation and maintenance of what was known as "morale," sustain this conclusion, for they have amply demonstrated that courageous conduct is very largely a matter of discipline and ideals, or, in other words, a social or cultural trait.

CONTENTIOUSNESS

Aggressiveness varies greatly from sect to sect among them, being especially marked in the Quaker type. Resentment, being a natural instinctive reaction common to all moral persons, is necessarily shared by all passive resistants in about equal proportions, but is usually transmuted into moral activities. Along with ordinary human nature there goes a capacity for contention by word and blow, which is the invariable concomitant of association among human beings. We, therefore, purpose now to inquire whether or not these quiet little communities where

[1] "The Heart of John Wesley's Journal," by Percy Livingstone Parker (Edit.); p. 7.

the men of peace dwell together are ever disturbed by the ripples of clashing opinion and purpose, or whether their still waters reflect always undimmed the depths of a heavenly tranquillity.

The beautiful story of Prince Dirghayu was told to allay a factious disturbance among the Buddhist monks; the New Testament speaks of "quarrels and fightings" among the Corinthian Christians; and ample provision is made for the settlement of quarrels between the members of the early church. The modern peace sects reveal a similar absence of idyllic conditions, as the following facts will show:

The *Dunkers* are said by Gillin to be of a "domineering" disposition. As a consequence of this, we are told, their leaders have been men "who ruled by coercion rather than by their superior mental and moral qualities. . . . The principles set forth in Matthew 18:17, 'And if he will not hear the church, let him be unto thee as a heathen man and a publican,' has been the controlling principle in the thought of the Dunker church." This phrase occurs so often in the minutes of the annual meeting as to become wearisome, in the opinion of Professor Gillin. He might have said with equal truth the same concerning references to "trouble in the local church";[1] and in at least one instance there comes up the rather ominous query whether a minister and some members of an irregular congregation should not *"fall into the hands of the brethren*[2] of adjacent districts, as offenders, and be dealt with as such."

The *Schwenkfelders* were long deterred by internal disagreements, and still more by the fear of them, from forming an organization of their own in Pennsylvania. Their

[1] "The Dunkers"; p. 205.

[2] Italics mine.

leader and minister, Balzer Hoffman, resigned his position twice because of "want of harmony" between himself and his brethren. A conference held in 1762, to consider the feasibility of a formal organization of the scattered Schwenkfelders, gave serious consideration to this remarkable query: "Will we be able to bear with one another, if a closer union is formed, so that what is undertaken may not be ended in strife and works of evil?" Kriebel says, however, that "the favorable answers given indicate plainly a decided departure from the position assumed by men of the type of Weiss and Hoffman," who had opposed organization. Christopher Schutz, another leader of these bellicose pacifists, also had misgivings, which he voiced as follows: "The most serious question, indeed, with me is, whether at this time such a plan can continue to exist among us. Let us not flatter ourselves. For this purpose it is necessary that we place plainly before our minds the nature and marks of love as described by the Apostle Paul."[1]

A vastly more flagrant and quite recent instance is at hand in the conduct of the "Christian Community of the Universal Brotherhood of Doukhobors in Canada" toward their former brethren who had seceded and formed the non-communistic branch known as the "Society of Independent Doukhobors." During the World War the question arose whether the latter, who had rejected the communistic program and had taken out naturalization papers in order to be able to hold their lands in severalty, had not by that action forfeited their right to exemption from military service as granted under the earlier order in council. While their fate was hanging in the balance the "Universal Brotherhood" petitioned the Government to regard the "Independents" as regular citizens and

[1] *Op. cit.;* pp. 64–78.

hold them strictly to all duties and obligations as subjects of the king, even to the extent of drafting them into active military service.

This statement is made upon the authority of one of the aggrieved parties, from whom the above clause is quoted, but there is no occasion to question the accuracy of his testimony.[1] He very appropriately writes:

> Here is a group of people who have deprived themselves of many worldly comforts, who have suffered untold persecutions and subjected themselves to incredible hardships and deprivations, and whose forefathers had borne the lash, the knout, the icy prison cell, and unflinchingly submitted themselves to strips of flesh being cut from their backs, in short to persecutions of every conceivable nature even unto death in the name of the Prince of Peace and in hope of furthering the cause of Peace among men at least one step if no more,—deliberately instigating a power to undo with one stroke the little that was won at the expense of so much blood and heart-rending sacrifice, and without any provocation and for no reason other than to satisfy the feeling of ill will towards their brothers.

Apparently in this case the power of resentment and contentiousness proved stronger than the love of peace. It must be admitted, however, that this striking example is too flagrant to be really typical of the spirit of true passive resistants, as their entire history has shown. Moreover, it will be recalled that the Doukhobors of this branch have exhibited for decades little if any power of intelligent self-direction, taking up not only their communistic program in Canada in slavish obedience to their leader, Peter Verigin, but having originally adopted their conscientious objecting in response to his commands trans-

[1] Mr. Peter G. Makaroff, in a letter to the writer. Mr. Makaroff is an able solicitor of Saskatoon, Saskatchewan, well educated and most fully conversant with affairs among the Doukhobors of both branches. During the war he served as interpreter for them.

mitted from Siberia while they were still living in Southern Russia.[1]

It is not pleasant to record these things, and it is needless to say that they are not pointed out in any spirit of captious criticism. Yet we do seek to know the exact truth concerning the traits of those who have maintained so conspicuously the difficult rôle of passive resistance; and we find them handicapped, but also, if we may so say, reinforced, with the same active propensities that burst into full and deadly fruitage in the lives of less devoted men. Passive resistants seem to know this to be true, and their one point of difference from men of violence is that they deliberately fortify themselves against those temperamental outbursts which carry less "guarded" men into actions destructive towards others and ruinous to their own peace. Hence, it is significant that in the "Constitution or Fundamental Principles of the Schwenkfelder Church, as Adopted in 1782,"[2] after an enumeration of the various duties and obligations incumbent on the members, these frank words should occur: "The practice and maintenance of such discipline and regulations will always have their temptations, *since we all carry these by nature in our own bosoms.*"[3]

It would, however, be erroneous to assume that the spirit and doings of the rank and file represent in every instance the true policy and spirit of passive resistance. "False brethren," grow up within, or creep privily into, every organization known to men. Every war has brought a sifting of the chaff from the wheat in all the groups of passive resistants; therefore it would not be strange to find the tares sprouting at all seasons. This is well

[1] See above, Ch. VII.
[2] Quoted in Kriebel, *op. cit.;* pp. 74–77.
[3] Italics mine.

shown in the published records of two meetings of Friends in Virginia at the close of the eighteenth century.[1] A struggle between the pugnacious propensities of the average member and the high Quaker ideal of personal non-resistance and peace is strikingly evident in the long list of "*disownments.*" The fact that a healthy fund of contentiousness and pugnacity is often housed beneath drab-clad bosoms may be graphically shown by a simple compilation of the reasons assigned in the following cases of disciplinary dealing or disownment. Out of a total of eighty-nine separate "minutes of disownment" and twenty-eight "letters of confession and condemnation" between 1794 and 1813, in these two meetings, the offense acknowledged is "fighting" "or beating a man" in sixteen cases, "profane" or "abusive" language in twelve instances, and "military" activities in nine.

The picture is drawn from dark and boisterous times, marked by rude manners and unrefined ideals in the mass of the populace, the Friends not excepted, but we see at the same glance the Quaker meeting as a center of sweetness and light, where the message of peace, forbearance, and good will was never allowed to languish. It is the same faithfulness to pacific ideals which leads the other sects quoted in the preceding pages to go on record in condemnation of practices which may pass unchallenged in other groups, the record thus being more to their credit, after all, than otherwise.

In the light of the historical and biographical facts adduced in this chapter the conclusion seems warranted that the natural endowment of the passive resistants is the same as that of other men of their generation; and the

[1] "Our Quaker Friends of Ye Olden Time, being in part a transcript of the minute books of Cedar Creek Meeting, Hanover County, and the South River Meeting, Campbell County, Va.," by J. P. Bell (Compiler), 1905.

psychological and statistical evidence of the following chapter will lead to the same conclusion by a different road. They are not moral ciphers or social negations, but people ruled by a compelling *idea* which, though often expressed in negative ways, is the great constructive, affirmative program and ideal along which any hopeful view of the future requires us to believe the ethical life of the world is slowly but irresistibly moving. So it is not without significance that the men we have been describing speak seldom of non-resistance, which is negative, but often of the "principles of peace," which are a positive thing. In the long war against war, first inaugurated by passive resistants of the Christian faith, the sects mentioned in this and preceding chapters fought for centuries single-handed under the hatred of the world, the contempt of the church *military*, and the secret admiration of both.

CHAPTER XI

PSYCHO-SOCIAL TRAITS OF NON-VIOLENT RESISTANTS: STATISTICAL EVIDENCE

It is improbable that any one, before the World War, should have raised the question of "intelligence" in connection with the personnel of any social class or movement. That great crisis, straining to the last extremity the resources of nations, gave tremendous impetus to a movement which had already been gaining headway for several years in psychological circles. That is the attempt to determine the relative mental levels of human beings by means of an objectively valid system of standardized measurements, giving what is known among psychologists as the "intelligence quotient" (I. Q.), and the "coefficient of intelligence," (C. I.).

It is no part of the province of this work to evaluate the accuracy of such methods. That is a task for psychologists, and, while they have arrived at a working agreement, some problems remain unsolved, among them being the question, perhaps not always sufficiently considered by specialists in psychometry, whether "intelligence" and *native mental capacity* are not radically different things, especially in their important social aspects. In a word, the "intelligence" ratings probably measure native capacity *plus* environmental contributions, and not native endowment alone, as seems to be all too commonly supposed. The word is therefore correctly chosen, [1] but inaccurately used in much popular and some scientific reasoning on the

[1] See Ward, "Applied Sociology"; pp. 39, 115, and 267.

subject. But, whether the psychologists are actually measuring inborn intellectual capacity or simply intelligence, the significant fact is that they have done and are doing a vast amount of it with very practical results, and the practice has assumed such proportions that we must now submit the passive resistant to this distinctly modern form of scrutiny, and inquire concerning the relative intelligence of this social type as measured by the rigid and unbiased methods now so much in vogue. Is the passive resistant on the average higher or lower in mentality than that vastly greater multitude of his contemporaries from whose opinions and purposes he presumes to dissent so conspicuously, and, oftentimes, so disastrously for his own fortunes?

During the five months beginning with May, 1918, approximately 1,300,000 men were tested in the various army cantonments of the United States. The system in use was devised by a committee of the American Psychological Association and the National Research Council, and comprised the so-called Alpha test for those who could read and write English; the Beta test for illiterates; and various individual tests.[1] Upon the basis of these examinations each man was given a letter rating (A, B, C, +, etc.) of definitely recognized significance ranging from "very superior" to "very inferior" intelligence.

With these ratings as a guide the personnel officers sorted the men into groups requiring different degrees of mental ability, and the army experience showed that their selection of men corresponded very closely to the results obtained by experienced officers using their own less scientific but practical first-hand estimates.

[1] Cf. the government report on "Intelligence Ratings," October, 1918, being Chap. X of the "Personnel Manual." Also "Army Mental Tests," by Clarence S. Yoakum and Robert M. Yerkes, New York, 1920.

In connection with these and other activities of the military camps, the so-called "C. O.'s," i. e., conscientious objectors, early began to attract especial notice, inasmuch as they were recognized as presenting a difficult problem. In some, if not all, of the army camps they were examined with particular care and their records kept distinct for the purposes of comparative study. All told there were at least two thousand of them in the camps, [1] thus providing a number adequate for sound generalization.

At the close of the war a special study was made of the more than three thousand military prisoners at that time confined in the United States Disciplinary Barracks, at Forth Leavenworth, Kansas. Among them were included upward of four hundred conscientious objectors, who were thus made the subjects, along with the other prisoners, of this more intensive examination, which was conducted by Major Herman M. Adler, Lieutenant Edward A. Lincoln, Lieutenant John K. Norton, and others. Doctors Adler and Lincoln later published the results of this work in two significant papers. Dr. Adler's paper, entitled "Disciplinary Problems of the Army," was read before the National Conference of Social Work, and appears in the "Proceedings" for 1919. It thus constitutes the first important contribution to the subject before us, but will be treated later in this discussion more conveniently because it represents a distinctly different classification.

Lieutenant Lincoln's article, which was entitled "The Intelligence of Military Offenders," appeared in the "Journal of Delinquency" for March, 1920. In this no-

[1] Cf. "The Psychological Examination of Conscientious Objectors," by Professor Mark A. May, in "American Journal of Psychology," April 1920; p. 153.

table study Lieutenant Lincoln detected at the outset the significant trend of the facts which the army examinations had amassed concerning the conscientious objectors, although they constitute only a small section, numerically speaking, of his data.

A few months later Lieutenant Mark A. May attacked directly the particular problem itself under the title, "The Psychological Examination of Conscientious Objectors,"[1] in a very thorough study based upon about thirty reports sent to the surgeon-general's office by the psychological examiners stationed in the various army camps. In this study Lieutenant May pushed still further the analysis begun by Lieutenant Lincoln and his associates.

About the same time the present writer, as yet unaware of the studies referred to, had begun by correspondence an effort to ascertain the facts concerning "C. O." mentality from the above-named officers and others connected with psychological examining during the war. It therefore seems best, before proceeding to an examination of the published literature of the subject, to introduce this correspondence for several reasons: first, because it will enable us to hear the testimony of other army examiners who have had first-hand experience with conscientious objectors, but who have not published their conclusions; secondly, in view of the fact that it touches points, such as physical and emotional traits, not measured by the army mental tests; and, thirdly, because it will thereby appear how exactly the present writer's classification, based entirely upon the historical studies recorded in preceding chapters and supplemented with some considerable first-hand acquaintance with passive resistants, was found to agree with that of the army ex-

[1] In "American Journal of Psychology," April, 1920.

aminers based only upon direct contact and examination in the camps, in virtually complete detachment from any historical background.

The nature of the inquiry will perhaps best be shown by the following passages from a letter of inquiry which was sent, early in June, 1920, to a number of trained psychologists who had been, or then still were, connected with the psychological work of the United States army, [1] and to one medical officer, Colonel Munson, in close touch with the general problem.

In the letter of inquiry the object was stated as twofold in character, namely, to solicit the personal judgment of the correspondent, and to secure references to persons and records. Before specifying the points of inquiry it was stated that it had seemed best to divide the objectors into three groups, as follows:

1. Those who were opposed to this particular war and in favor of peace not because of permanently held peace

[1] Those addressed, upon information furnished by Dr. Bird T. Baldwin, Director of the Iowa Child Welfare Research Station, and formerly major in the Reconstruction Division of the United States Sanitary Corps, were as follows: Colonel E. L. Munson, Medical Corps, General Staff, chief of the Morale Branch; Major Harold C. Bingham, Sanitary Corps, Section of Psychology, office of the surgeon-general; Professor Mark A. May, Syracuse University, formerly first lieutenant, U. S. Army; Dr. Edward A. Lincoln, Harvard University, formerly first lieutenant, U. S. army; Dr. John K. Norton, Bureau of Research and Guidance, Oakland Public Schools, California, formerly captain, U. S. army; Dr. Carl C. Brigham, Washington, D. C.; formerly lieutenant, U. S. army; Professor William S. Foster, University of Minnesota, formerly major, U. S. army; Dr. Reuel H. Sylvester, director Des Moines Health Center, Des Moines, Iowa, fomerly captain, U. S. army; Miss Margaret V. Cobb, National Research Council, Washington, D. C.; Dr. C. S. Yoakum, Director Bureau of Personnel Research, Carnegie Institute of Technology, Washington, D. C., formerly, major, Psychological Division, U. S. army; Dr. Herman M. Adler, criminologist, Department of Public Welfare, Springfield, Illinois, formerly major, Medical Corps, U. S. army.

principles, but because of certain racial, sentimental, or economic reasons bearing upon the particular war in question. Among these the *Pro-German* element formed the nucleus.

2. Members of religious peace sects, ancient and modern, who hold an unalterable religious conviction that *all* wars are forbidden of God. The *Mennonites* may be taken as the type under this head.

3. The modern "C. O.," whose objection to war is both permanent and sweeping as well as conscientious, but is based upon philosophical and humanitarian grounds instead of upon religious tradition. The *international socialist* is the type under this category.

Let it be said here in passing that this division of the subject, which the history of passive resistance before the World War demanded in the interest of accuracy and logical consistency, was found to tally in detail with the classification which practical experience in the army camps suggested to the experts of the War Department. Major Bingham finds the present classification "particularly interesting because it is so similar to the one which we found convenient to use in this office."[1] Dr. Lincoln used a similar subdivision in his article referred to above, and observes that the two classifications are "practically the same." He adds, however, "I cannot truthfully say that I ever found an objector whom I considered really pro-German."[2]

On the other hand, Colonel Munson, while pronouncing the classification "good," goes on to say that "it overlooks a considerable class which was purely political"; but inasmuch as he specifies "Russians or Russian Jews, who were in touch with people and ideas of their home

1 Personal correspondence of the present writer.

2 *Ibid.* Cf. also Dr. Adler's remarks on this point, below.

country," such cases would be included under our first category, if taken as broadly as it was intended.[1] Another correspondent who suggests a modification or expansion of the classification is Lieutenant Brigham, in the following very interesting comments based upon his study of a group of 150 conscientious objectors at Camp Meade in the early part of 1918: "The group as a whole," he writes, "contained an abnormal number of psychotics. There were a few distinct cases of insanity, where the C. O. reaction was part of the symptom picture. . . . It seems to me that this group falls outside of your three groups. I am almost certain that there is a definite group of cases showing inferior mental make-up before the war, who on failure to meet the army situation, reacted by assuming the conscientious objector attitude. The reasoning of these individuals was not clear and the whole reaction was bizarre. I remember very distinctly one case of hebephrenic dementia præcox—a terminal case—whose reactions were very striking.

"I also believe that there were other cases, members before the war of groups 1, 2, or 3, who on meeting the tremendously difficult army situation, developed psychotic trends. This hypothesis is the only one which to me will explain the particularly strong reaction of some cases. It is almost a "triple plus" reaction.

"After these two groups have been eliminated the genuine cases are found, probably falling in the three groups which you enumerate."[2]

This testimony from a specialist of highest authority requires us to add a fourth subdivision, giving the following classes: (1) religious objectors; (2) social objectors; (3) political objectors; (4) psychotic objectors—the first

[1] Correspondence of the present writer.
[2] *Ibid.*

three representing normal attitudes, the last named a pathological condition. These latter cases fall outside the province of this study, being proper subjects for the psychiatrist and alienist. The three normal groups, on the other hand, being cultural phenomena, can be understood only in their historical and social setting, and can be adequately investigated only by the methods of the social sciences, which is the procedure which we have attempted to apply throughout this book.

But, after all, classification is merely a means to an end, and it was so used in the present inquiry, the principal object being to obtain the most expert testimony available on the question of distinctive passive resistant traits, if such exist. The traits sought after were designated as "physical, mental, and moral," and information was sought concerning all three of the normal "C. O." classes in the following question, addressed to the army examiners and their associates: "Were they, particularly those numbered 2 and 3, of noticeably smaller chest-capacity, lower muscular development, or otherwise poorer physique than the average run of the men who entered military service without objection? In other words, did they, as a class, show physical deficiency in any respect, or physical superiority, or were they part and parcel, anthropologically and psychologically speaking, of the stock which produced the fighting forces?"

Major Bingham, writing from the office of the surgeon-general, replied that the inquiry "opens up aspects of this problem which we were unable to touch in this Division, and on inquiry, I find that other divisions do not have the data you desire. It seems that the physical measurements have never been considered by the division in charge of that work with any particular reference to conscientious objectors. A joint study of the divisions of Neuropsychiatry and Psychology is probably the most comprehensive that was attempted. . . . That study was directed at the emotional stability and mental capacity of the men.''[1]

It is thus evident, upon the highest authority, that no official data exist on this question, and our reliance must be placed upon the testimony of direct and personal observations. Fortunately we have the statements of a few very competent witnesses, who have enjoyed exceptional opportunities for observation in this field. For example, Lieutenant May says;[2] ''I know of no anthropometric measurements taken on C. O.'s that would merit being called scientific. . . . The routine physical examination of the C. O. was taken and recorded in the usual way and no special labels were put on them as far as I know.

''From my personal observation of 60 or more of these men I noted nothing that would suggest that they are of an inferior stock. In fact, I should say that they possess *no physical stigmata whatsoever* that would brand them as non-resistants, or 'sissies,' etc.''

Lieutenant Lincoln's reply is completely corroborative. After pointing out the fact that no studies have been made showing the physical characteristics of the objectors, and remarking that ''many of these men did not submit to the physical examination,'' he adds; ''From my personal contact I should not say that these men differed from the general run of the Army. I realize at the same time that statistics might show a very different case.'' From the point of view of scientific caution it is perhaps wise to recognize this possibility, but as a matter of fact it is utterly improbable that statistical evidence of the most thorough character would reveal anything that has escaped

[1] Letter of June 8, 1920.
[2] In his reply dated July 12, 1920.

personal observation, since we are dealing in this matter with a social, rather than a physical or even psycho-physical problem in the narrow sense of the terms.

Dr. Norton's opinion[1] coincides with that of others when he says: "None of the three groups you mention showed any noticeable physical inferiority or superiority. . . . A group of religious objectors quartered just across the street from the psychology building in Camp Taylor seemed to play base ball as well as the average native American group of similar age."

Upon the suggestion of Dr. Bingham the writer communicated with Dr. C. B. Davenport, whose notable anthropometric report on the first million drafted men, prepared in collaboration with Colonel Love, is known to students of this subject; and through Dr. Davenport the inquiry was extended to include Dr. A. J. Rosanoff, of King's Park State Hospital, New York. The question put was whether the conscientious objectors observed by them "were marked by any stigmata of physical or mental degeneracy or abnormality." In addressing these specialists, who conducted the neuro-psychiatric work at Camp Upton, it was felt that the inquiry on this phase of the subject would thereby be pushed to the farthest point feasible in the present state of knowledge. Their personal opinions are therefore of the utmost interest.

Dr. Davenport says: "The general conclusion I reached in regard to conscientious objectors was that they were

[1] He refers to his answers as "mere opinion unsupported by any data in my possession." The same undogmatic attitude is maintained more or less explicitly by all the correspondents, and it should be clearly understood that there is no purpose here to attach to them any significance which their character does not warrant; and least of all should any such intention be imputed to these scientific men who have had the generosity to express their own personal impressions in the absence of statistical evidence.

not so much characterized by physical or mental defect as by certain moral defects, including an exaggerated fear reaction and a comparative absence of self-control. A certain proportion of the conscientious objectors, however, were mentally constitutionally opposed to going with the crowd. There was a sort of anti-herd instinct. Sometimes combined with an *amour propre* or, at least, a fondness for independent action and a carelessness of the opinion of others, sometimes combined with a paranoiacal trend. However, these are mere opinions.''[1] Dr. Rosanoff's reply, which he characterizes as ''only a general impression from memory,'' is that ''conscientious objectors seen at Camp Upton were not, as a group, characterized by a higher prevalence of physical defects or abnormalities than would a group of recruits selected at random.''

The testimony of these trained minds in more immediate contact with the conscientious objectors during the war experience exactly coincides with common observation, whether it be that of the man on the street or those who have personal and intimate knowledge of them in their daily walk and conversation. The evidence is as negative as it is harmonious and uniform—so consistently negative as to attain the greatest positive value. It amounts simply to this, that if there is any physical difference between the conscientious objector, or ''passive resistant,'' to use the older and better term, it is one that no one has been able to detect, even under closest scrutiny. Moreover, while men of this social and religious persuasion were subjected in large numbers to a rigid physical examination along with some millions of other men, *no one seems to have noticed the slightest difference between them and their fellows.* Under such circumstances it

[1] Letter of March 31, 1921. Italics mine.
[2] Letter of April 8, 1921.

would be a refinement of scientific circumspection to proceed upon any other hypothesis than that no physical difference exists.

This position is vastly strengthened by the fact that in the statistical data gathered by the *mental* examinations on the other hand a marked difference was apparent from the first. This same divergence of mentality was noted also by eye-witnesses, so that in both cases statistical analysis and personal observation exactly agreed. But in the one case it was positive, in the other negative in character. In other words the army "C. O." was physically like but mentally unlike the average run of his draft associates. This would not militate against the opinion of one correspondent,[1] whose observations led him to "suppose" that "the C. O.'s are not an unselected group anthropologically or psychologically." So far as the draft is concerned, it took a random sample, within the requirements of age, physical condition, and social circumstances, from the "C. O's," just as it did from other citizens. The objector and conformist were thus far on a common basis, suitable for valid comparison, although it is no doubt true that passive resistants as a whole represent a group *selected* historically and socially in very much the same sense that is conveyed by the saying in reference to the Pilgrims that "God sifted three nations for this planting." The truth of this assertion will be clear to all who have read the preceding chapters of the present work, wherein the history of the passive resistant sects is traced, and their philosophy of conduct is analyzed.

Passing from the question of physical stigmata to that of mental and moral characteristics, the following question was asked:

1 Professor William S. Foster.

In their mental and moral traits did they show, on the average, a higher or lower intelligence as shown by the army mental tests or otherwise? Did they seem to be either lacking in, or unusually endowed with respect to pugnacity, self-assertion, energy, contentiousness, obstinacy, courage, endurance, or any other neural traits, instincts, or sentiments? In a word, was there any evidence to warrant the popular idea of them as "sissies," "mollycoddles," or something of that kind?

The question is somewhat inclusive, even indefinite, but was naturally so in a letter designed merely to invite observations and suggestions on a subject concerning which, as the writer correctly anticipated, no considerable mass of data exists, except on one or two points, particularly that of intelligence. The army examinations covered this ground very extensively, and quite accurately, provided the individual is considered in the lump as a complex working unit, with no attempt to distinguish hereditary and environmental factors in the production of the working efficiency actually measured. Into this result there will probably creep the influence of vital and emotional elements, including something of the driving force that comes from sentiments, ideals, and "character" in general; and even where the Alpha and Beta tests are regarded as a measure of strictly intellectual capacity it is admitted that "they do not measure loyalty, bravery, power to command, or the emotional traits that make a man 'carry on.' However, in the long run these qualities are far more likely to be found in men of superior intelligence than in men who are intellectually inferior. . . . *A man's value to the service should not be judged by his intelligence alone.*"[1] Again: "While it has been well enough established that such factors as these are not present in a sufficient degree to invalidate seriously the

[1] "Personnel Manual"; Chap. X, loc. cit.

test results, their presence cannot be denied. It can hardly be claimed that the mental or physical condition of the subject and the circumstances under which the test is given have no effect upon the score. Similarly, it would be unreasonable to suppose that the result is wholly uninfluenced by educational advantages.''[1]

It is thus clearly stated by the most competent authority, and recognized by all properly qualified examiners, that the mental tests do not, and as thus far perfected cannot, measure affective and volitional qualities, such as were inquired about in the letter above quoted. For our knowledge of these less strictly intellectual and most important personal traits we are thrown back again upon direct observation and inference. In this situation the opinions of specially qualified and very favorably situated observers possess the highest value, even though they are submitted as nothing more than opinions. The remarks of our correspondents in this matter fulfil these favorable conditions of origin, and to them we now turn for the most significant available evidence.

Colonel Munson expresses the opinion that ''the real *religious* objectors were honest pacifists. I think that the *political* objectors were mostly cowards or were egocentrists who saw in objection an opportunity to escape danger or for sensational notoriety which flattered their vanity. The religious class made little trouble, as they honestly believed in non-resistance. . . . Inasmuch as there were several varieties of C. O.'s, whose diverse motives and qualities were cloaked in the common appearances of objection, I don't think you can fairly draw any general conclusion [with respect to] their relative endurance, self-assertion, contentiousness, or other traits you mention.''

Lieutenant Lincoln points out that ''the moral side is a

1 "Army Mental Tests," by Yoakum and Yerkes; p. 49.

matter of conjuncture. Certainly, no one who has knowledge of the severe punishments to which these men are subjected, could doubt their sincerity, courage and endurance. I did not find evidence to warrant the popular idea of the objectors as mollycoddles."

The opinion of Dr. Norton is in the same vein. He says: "The obstinacy or courage, whichever you choose to call it, that the religious objectors showed in supporting their belief was remarkable. They resisted efforts of all types, persuasion and compulsion to the point of torture, that were used in efforts to force them to accept military service. . . . I saw nothing to justify the application of the term 'mollycoddle' or 'sissy' to the religious objectors.

"Regarding the pro-Germans, I came in contact with comparatively few of these as a class. So far as I noticed, their moral natures were no different than might have been expected considering their past environment and racial ties."

Major Foster is fully corroborative, saying: "My own impression, whatever that is worth, is decidedly contrary to the popular idea you quote, namely, that they were 'sissies,' or 'mollycoddles.' I lay much greater stress upon education and other environmental factors in the causation of conscientious objection than upon any native endowment of traits such as you mention. I do not doubt that in some cases such traits played a part and possibly a large one, but I do doubt very much if such is the case in general."

In these sentences Professor Foster touches what, in the opinion of the present writer, is the key to the interpretation of this problem, as the entire discussion of the present work amply demonstrates.

The testimony of all the psychological observers whom

we have quoted is remarkably uniform on this, as on every other point of the inquiry. The only exception appears in the experience of Captain Sylvester, who says, speaking specifically of the *religious* objectors, that "nearly all were lacking in 'self-assertion,' 'contentiousness,' 'obstinacy,' 'courage,' and 'endurance.' They were not 'sissies' or 'mollycoddles' but were meek and passive, and at Camp Dodge at least they were largely dependent as to their conduct on two or three leaders . . . men of ability and initiative."

It will be noticed that the divergence of view in the case of this single correspondent is only partial, while he is in complete agreement on the main point, which is that the conscientious objectors "were not 'sissies' or 'mollycoddles"; and he adds the important remark, "I do not believe that these[1] conscientious objectors were using their religious beliefs as a means of saving themselves personally from the danger of war."

Thus the weight of evidence goes to show that the popular conception of these much misunderstood objectors as "sissies," "mollycoddles," or cowards is without foundation in fact.

There remains to discuss only one other trait inquired after in this study, namely, that of *intelligence.* In considering it we leave the realm of casual observation and direct description, and turn to more impersonal and objective methods. This is possible because of the fact that the army mental tests did measure *intelligence* principally if not solely, thus leading to the accumulation of accurate statistical data covering a vast number of cases.

Very early in the examinations the mental superiority of the conscientious objectors became noticeable. It is a fact quite generally recognized among the army psychol-

[1] The passage is discussing only the religious type.

ogists, if the passing references to it in the above-described correspondence are to be taken as a criterion. About the time of that correspondence and during the succeeding months several very valuable reports and discussions found their way into print. Foremost among these is the article on "The Intelligence of Military Offenders," by Lieutenant Edward A. Lincoln, which appeared in the "Journal of Delinquency" for March, 1920, Dr. Lincoln being at that time still connected with the Psychological Division of the surgeon-general's office at Washington.

The study was based upon data secured in a mental examination of the military prisoners confined at the United States Disciplinary Barracks, at Fort Leavenworth, Kansas, early in 1919. The psychological examinations were conducted in exactly the same way as were all the army examinations, thus providing a valid basis for comparison.

While Lieutenant Lincoln's primary object was to study military offenders in general, he was by no means unmindful of the conscientious objectors from the start. In fact, the tendency for the prisoners' grades to run slightly higher than the army average having caught the attention of the investigators, Lieutenant Lincoln says that "further study of individual records suggested that the distribution of grades might be influenced by the inclusion of the records of the conscientious objectors, who, as a group, tested very high."[1] The records were therefore separated into two groups, whereupon it became clear that the distribution of grades for the non-objectors was virtually identical with that for the white draft as a whole, while the objectors made "a considerably larger proportion of higher grades than the other prisoners."

In the study referred to the conscientious objectors were

[1] *Loc. cit.;* p. 32.

divided into the three groups which have emergd in our own consideration of the subject, namely, (1) the religious, (2) the political, (3) the alien objector; and the records are tabulated upon the basis of this division. A glance at the figures reveals the fact that the religious objectors at Fort Leavenworth were equal to the average for the army, the political objectors distinctly higher, and the alien objectors distinctly lower than the average.[1]

The average for the conscientious objectors as a whole yielded 32.6 in "A,"[2] Upon the basis of these figures Lieutenant Lincoln very justly remarks: "Conscientious objectors of the religious and political types are high grade men very distinctly above the other groups. This superiority is especially noticeable in the case of the political objectors.

"The men classed as conscientious objectors because of being alien enemies, having alien relatives, etc., are decidedly low in intelligence. This seems to be one group in the institution whose troubles may be ascribed to low mentality. The men in this group were largely foreign born, many could speak or understand very little English, and a large proportion of them were illiterate.

"A supplementary study was made of the conscientious objectors who have continually and consistently refused to do any work either before they came to the institution or afterwards. . . . The superiority of these men as a group

[1] For example, the largest, or modal, group for both the white draft and the Leavenworth prisoners made the grade of "C" (interpreted in all examinations as "average intelligence"); the religious objectors at Leavenworth also cluster about the "C" point, (with almost the same percentage under "C"+); the political objectors from a distinct modal group under "A," the highest grade ("very superior intelligence"); while the alien objectors massed themselves under "D" (indicating, according to the psychological interpretation, "inferior intelligence). See Table VII, *ibid.*

[2] *Ibid.*, Table VIII.

to any other group in the institution is very apparent.'' Furthermore, Lieutenant Lincoln notices in his comparison of previous criminal records that ''very few of the objectors got into trouble before they came into the army,'' and surmises that ''possibly these previous difficulties were also the result of political or religious activities.''[1]

Shortly after the appearance of Lieutenant Lincoln's article, another study, based upon the same records, then on file in the archives of the War Department, was made by Mr. Winthrop D. Lane, and published in the ''New Republic'' for April 14, 1920. This briefer and more popular article is chiefly to be mentioned for its graphic presentation of the essential facts concerning the conscientious objectors. The following table is quoted from Mr. Lane's article, which is entitled ''Who Are the Conscientious Objectors?''

Groups Compared	Percentages showing ''average'' and better than ''average'' intelligence
Theoretical normal company	65
Approximately 20,000 white men drafted and sent to Camp Lee in one month	45.1
Enlisted privates, all illiterate—86,936	68
Sergeants—3,393	95
Candidates for officers' training-corps—9,240	94
Commissioned officers—8,819	97
Political objectors—84	82.2
Religious objectors—218	81.4
Objectors who were ''alien enemies,'' etc.—135	27.3

In commenting upon this table its author points out that it shows that ''both political and religious objectors

[1] *Ibid.;* pp. 37–38.

excelled their fellow-inmates at Fort Leavenworth, the white draft at Camp Lee, the theoretical normal company and the enlisted men; in other words, they excelled their own associates both in prison and camp. When the comparison is made upon the basis of the first four grades, the conscientious objectors are excelled by the sergeants, the candidates for officers' training corps and the commissioned officers." It is true that these figures apply only to persons in the disciplinary barracks, but, as Mr. Lane justly remarks, "conscientious objectors in prison differed in no essential respect from other objectors."

One other fact of special importance emphasized in the article quoted is the exceedingly small number who had made a previous criminal record. It appears that more than 10 per cent. of the military prisoners had served terms in prisons or reformatories for more serious offenses, "whereas only *six-tenths of one per cent* of conscientious objectors—two or three individuals at most—had served such terms." This is all the more significant when it is remembered that the reference is to objectors of all types, and not alone to the religious objector, who might reasonably be expected to show a criminal record lower than the average.

Shortly after the appearance of the articles quoted above, the problem of the conscientious objector was more extensively treated in a paper by Professor Mark A. May in the "American Journal of Psychology" for April, 1920. This study, which bears the title, "The Psychological Examination of Conscientious Objectors," was based upon about thirty reports sent by the various psychological examiners to the surgeon-general's office, and covering about one thousand objectors distributed among about twenty camps.

One of the interesting features of this valuable study is the following table, which shows at a glance the superior average intelligence of the conscientious objectors:

		White Draft (94,000 Per Cent	Conscientious Objectors (1,000 cases) Per Cent
A	Very superior	4.1	8.7
B	Superior	8.0	15.2
C+	High average	15.2	22.6
C	Average	25.0	24.8
C–	Low average	23.8	16.8
D	Inferior	17.0	8.7
D–	Very inferior	7.1	3.1

On another page Lieutenant May apportions the grounds of objection, showing that "out of 958 cases, 90 per cent object on religious grounds; 5 per cent on social grounds, 3 per cent on political grounds, and 2 per cent on ethical grounds."[1]

The article thoroughly analyzes the data, which admit of only one conclusion, as we have already seen, and that is the distinct mental superiority of the average conscientious objector. But it is in his insight and sympathetic understanding of the point of view of the conscientious objector that Professor May especially contributes to this subject, as every one who has read their history as set forth in earlier chapters of this work will appreciate. He distinguishes, and characterizes with penetrating insight, these types: the religious-literalist, the religious idealist, and the socialist.[2]

[1] *Loc. cit.;* p. 156.
[2] *Ibid.;* pp. 160–161.

One finds a distinctly different classification in the article by Dr. Adler, already referred to above.[1] This is the one used in the personality study conducted by Major Adler and his associates at the United States Disciplinary Barracks at Fort Leavenworth, Kansas, in 1918. The survey was not directed at the conscientious objectors, but it included a large number of them within its scope, there being about five hundred "C. O.'s" in the barracks at that time, or shortly thereafter.

Dr. Adler says:[2] "We started with the assumption that all were sincere in their conviction. We divided them into two groups, namely, those who were conscientious objectors on religious grounds and those who were conscientious objectors on political grounds." In so doing the "pro-German" or "alien" class used by both the present writer and some of the army authorities is eliminated. This category, numbered (1) in the correspondence already described, Dr. Adler holds to be ambiguous, and he frankly expresses the opinion: "There is reason to believe that a number of men whom you would class under (2) or (3) really should belong under (1). How can you determine," he asks, "whether a man is sincere in his belief, especially if he has only recently joined a sect, such as the Quakers or Mennonites? Just because it happened recently is no justification for the assumption that he was not sincere; nor just because it happened under war conditions."

Dr. Adler points out with pertinence that the Government found it necessary to appoint a special board to determine in each case whether the objector was sincere or not, and he very justly remarks that it was a question-

[1] Disciplinary Problems of the Army," by Herman M. Adler M.D., criminologist, Illinois Department of Public Welfare; Pamphlet 227, National Conference of Social Work.

[2] In a personal letter to the present writer, January, 1921.

able expedient, since it is "unwise for a government to set up qualifications the possession of which cannot be objectively determined."

The history of conscription in Australia before the World War had pretty well illustrated the futility of such an occult policy, as is pointed out in a later chapter of this essay,[1] and on the whole there is much force in Dr. Adler's elimination of the "pro-German" or "alien" group from the classification. But in any case it does not effect seriously the present discussion, since our own treatment of this type is admittedly of a purely cursory character, it being, as remarked at the outset, a merely temporary, and even fortuitous, grouping. The present writer's thought has been from the start that objectors of this kind are to be found in connection with every war, their particular grounds for objection varying with the circumstances, whereas the two other types are of permanent significance, being exponents of self-consistent, enduring, and very fundamental forces in modern social life.

However, the most significant aspect of Dr. Adler's analysis is to be found in another passage as follows: "An analysis of the personality reactions of the prisoners was made, dividing the prisoners according to their findings into three general groups: 1. Those who had been in difficulty as a result of the lack of intelligence or judgment, or of some other marked mental defect. 2. Those who showed no decisive defect, but whose difficulties either in the army or previously could be traced back to emotional instability either in the direction of violent temper or loss of control, or of discouragement and depression. 3. Those whose difficulties could be traced to a marked egocentric characteristic or trait."[2]

1 See Chap. XIII below.

2 "Disciplinary Problems of the Army," National Conference Pamphlet 227; p. 5.

This analysis was based upon the psychological principle that "each individual human being has his threshold value; his breaking-point at which the balance between himself and his social environment may be upset. When it is upset, however, the inherent personality will manifest itself and the reaction will be more or less consistent with his makeup." [1]

In the study based upon this principle the approach was consciously made from "the point of view of the psychopathologist," according to which "it is sufficient to give an explanation and not to attempt an evaluation."

In his letter referred to above Dr. Adler emphasizes his belief in the importance of the definitions and personality classification set forth in the article quoted, and regards it as very encouraging that the more intelligent conscientious objectors "were interested in this classification and felt that there was a good deal to be said for it."

One cannot help but feel, however, that the conscientious objectors were in this case more gracious than accurate. It does not appear whether the particular conscientious objectors so testifying were of the religious type or not, but if they were it would seem that they should not have been included without qualification in the personality study used at Fort Leavenworth. For that method, splendid as it is, rests upon the assumption that "the conscientious objectors . . . represent a heterogeneous group of men. They had only one thing in common, namely, their resistance to the selective service act and their unwillingness to bear arms. The reasons, the underlying motives, the previous experiences and training, the advantages or difficulties of each individual's career that lay back of the stand they took, are almost as many as there are individuals

[1] *Ibid.*

in the group."[1] If this is really true of the objectors studied at Fort Leavenworth it creates the presumption that they did not represent a fair sample, certainly as far as the religious objectors are concerned, and possibly with reference to the social objector type also, although the evidence is not so clear in the case of the latter.

As for the religious objectors, it would be hard to find anywhere a type of reaction which is to such a small degree a matter of individual motive, experience, or training, and so clearly a case of group tradition and group idealism expressing itself in a stereotyped response to a given social situation on the part of its various members. When the mild-mannered and simple-hearted Mennonite, Dunker, or Quaker lad placed himself in the attitude of passive resistance to the war-impassioned myriads of his disapproving fellow-countrymen, very much as a reed opposing a tornado, it was by no means his own private, individual personality that set itself in contradiction to the general purpose, but himself as the representative of a social tradition which had its sources in some quiet sectarian circle or community, where was kept green and fresh the memory of some almost medieval movement long forgotten by the world at large; and even beyond that the vision of another community where apostolic men, and even the Son of Man himself, had lived and taught a Way of Love which could admit of no compromise with the ways of violence and war to the end of time.

In other words the religious objection to war and military service is essentially a group phenomenon, as all the evidence reviewed in the present essay goes to show. It would be hard to find a more distinctly cultural, as opposed to a psychological, attitude, or reaction-type. Perhaps the same is largely true of the social objector

[1] Adler, *op. cit.;* pp. 2–3.

also, but the group aspect of his philosophy is harder to detect, its social origins more difficult to trace.[1] Moreover, it is quite possible that the war situation, in conjunction with the contagious example set by the traditional religious objector, may have brought to the camps many social and political objectors whose reaction was more of an individual than a group affair, more psychological than cultural. These individuals could consequently be regarded as actually constituting a random sample suitable for statistical analysis, and there was doubtless much validity in classifying them as either egocentric, mentally inadequate, or emotionally unstable.[2]

But the *religious* objectors as a whole, probably the socio-political objectors in so far as they acted as convinced adherents of a group tradition and ideal coming to them with moral authority and power out of the past, were not a random but a highly selected sample; so much so that the attempt to analyze them by purely psychiatric and statistical methods may be justly questioned as inadequate, since it assumes a heterogeneity in the specimens which does not exist in fact. The view here maintained, on the contrary, is that the religious objectors, at least, were, in the first place, a selected and homogeneous group in so far as their attitude toward military service is concerned, which is the sole point at issue in their case; secondly, they were not military offenders in any true sense of the word, and their inclusion within a psychiatric survey of military prisoners was a purely fortuitous circumstance due to a legal fiction; thirdly, the army physical examinations had failed to discover in them the slightest physical or

[1] See Chap. XIV, below.

[2] "When classified in this way it was found that 66 per cent. of the cases fell into the ego-centric group; 24 per cent. into the inadequate group; and 6 per cent. into the emotionally unstable group." Adler, *Ibid.;* p. 5.

emotional defect not equally common to the draft as a whole; fourthly, the army mental tests had shown, or were then showing, them to be *superior* to the average for the entire draft and hence furthest removed from mental inadequacy. This leaves only one psychopathic class to which they could possibly be assigned, but to place them in that category would make it appear that to be a conscientious objector is equivalent to being an egocentrist. If this is in accord with the actual situation there is no occasion to quarrel with the facts. This, however, raises the question of definition, since it is obvious that it would be possible to define egocentrism in such terms as should necessarily include conscientious objecting and non-conformity in general.

We do not intend, however, to press this point unduly, and would recall here, upon the other side, that in Dr. Davenport's statement, quoted above, the conscientious objectors at Camp Upton were credited with "an *amour propre* or, at least, a fondness for independent action and a carelessness of the opinion of others." This opinion is partly corroborated by the following from one of the most prominent of the conscientious objectors themselves: "All were probably egotists of a sort, though I use this term without in the least implying the condemnation that usually goes with it. I mean they were egoists in the sense that they were filled with a sense of their own individual responsibility for their own conduct along certain lines at least; also of their own importance. We all took ourselves quite seriously and were n't ready to admit that ideals must wait for their realization upon the indifference and ignorance of the masses."[1]

The question is whether the *amour propre* of Dr. Davenport and the "egotism" of our C. O. correspondent both

[1] Personal correspondence of the present writer.

refer to the same kind of self-regard. There is of course an egocentrism which is clearly pathological, while on the other hand there is that normal aspect of it, in the form of the "self-regarding sentiment," which constitutes, according to Professor McDougall, the very foundation of the moral life,[1] including not only conscientious objecting but conscience itself.[2]

At any rate, it is highly probable, if not entirely certain, that among any considerable group of objectors there would be found some egocentric, mentally inadequate, or emotionally unstable individuals, but the more important fact would seem to be that these individuals reacted as they did to the war situation, not because they were mentally inadequate (or mentally superior), or emotionally unstable, or egocentric, but largely because they were convinced exponents of a group ideal and tradition which had been transmitted to them out of the past. Many of them were members of their respective non-resistant sects by virtue of birth within the religious community, so that their membership therein was more or less automatic; and where they had become members by deliberate choice it is probable that their choice was as much or more influenced by superior intelligence as it was by inadequate mentality. But the most plausible hypothesis is that membership in the Mennonite community, the Quaker meeting, or the Socialist International is not a function of any of the personality factors used at Fort Leavenworth, namely, mental inadequacy, emotional instability, or marked egocentrism. That is to say, these conditions were not primarily causal in their relation to the "C. O." reaction. They were concomitants more than causes, if our present

[1] Cf. "Social Psychology," by William McDougall, London and New York, 1914; Chap. VII and VIII.

[2] See the discussion of conscience in Chap. XV, below.

understanding of this problem is correct. The real cause of sectarian conscientious objecting is neither biological nor psychological, but essentially cultural.[1] The writer is pleased to think, however, that Dr. Adler himself, despite the emphasis laid upon psychiatric considerations and methods in his article, seems to make room for the position taken here when he concludes that "the solution of the behavior problems of the individual depends upon as accurate possible a knowledge both of the individual and of his environment; . . . [which] knowledge can be obtained by the mental studies of the neuro-psychiatric officer and the social investigations of the social worker."[2] While he is here speaking particularly of the professional welfare worker in relation to delinquents in general, this remark applies with equal force to the army studies of the conscientious objector in his alleged rôle of military offender. In studying this type of "criminal" the investigators were in danger of being misled by their too exclusive dependence upon the methods of clinical psychology, without an adequate picture of the conscientious objector's historical, social, and spiritual background. This picture furnishes the key to the whole situation, and it is the most deplorable feature of the objector's experience that the Government found itself compelled to deal with him in complete detachment from that environmental setting, in the light of

[1] The reader interested in the theoretical aspects of this question, particularly the implications of the term "culture," is referred to the following, among other discussions of this principle of social interpretation: Lowie, "Culture and Ethnology," New York 1917; Wissler, "Psychological and Historical Interpretations for Culture," in "Science," N. S. XLIII, No. 1102; also "The Psychological Aspects of the Culture-Environment Relation," in "American Anthropologist," N. S. XIV; Elwood, "Theories of Cultural Evolution," in the "American Journal of Sociology," Vol. XXIII, No. 6; Kroeber, "The Superorganic," in "American Anthropologist," April-June, 1917.

[2] *Ibid.*; p. 6.

which alone it is impossible to understand him at all.

In conclusion it should be said that while all the available evidence points to the soundness of the cultural, or historical, interpretation here adopted, it is to be regretted that the army examinations did not provide the data for an exhaustive analysis of the anthropological and racial characteristics of the conscientious objectors as a whole. It would be still more conclusive if this were supplemented by evidence concerning their occupational and class affiliations, as well as by a personality study such as that employed by Dr. Adler and his colleagues; especially if it were possible in such a study to grasp the elusive factors of *emotion* and *sentiment*. While the present writer is convinced that the results would not alter the conclusions here arrived at with respect to the entire normality of the average conscientious objector in his native physical and mental equipment, it might throw some light on another difficult question, namely, that of the fundamental ground or origin of that non-religious objection to war and military service which is growing naturally and steadily in modern life. This problem must be faced in a later chapter.[1]

[1] Certain discussions at the meeting of the American Sociological Society, in December, 1921, directed attention to the investigations now being conducted by physiologists into the effects of the ductless glands, or endocrines, upon human dispositions and behavior. The new knowledge being unearthed here will probably yield, under the hands of psychological and sociological enthusiasts, a crop of novel and even bizarre theories concerning the causes for different mental and social types, and the conscientious objector will have to be analyzed along with the rest. In the end some new and fruitful principles for the interpretation of such problems as the one before us may possibly be evolved, but pending such a remote possibility the case for the psycho-physical normality of the conscientious objectors as a *class* may be regarded as clearly established. Cf. the address of Professor Arthur Keith before the British Association for the Advancement of Science, Anthropological Section, 1919, Vol. LXXXIX, pp. 275–281; also "Publications of the American Sociological Society," Vol. XV, pp. 102–124.

CHAPTER XII

PASSIVE RESISTANCE IN THEORY AND PRACTICE

THE meek and lowly-minded men and women whose story makes up the history of passive resistance have been working at one of the bravest tasks ever undertaken by vessels of clay, and we, in essaying to narrate and estimate their conduct, are attempting to solve the *most difficult problem of conduct to be met in human experience.* This startling conclusion forces itself upon the mind as one follows the struggles, sufferings, defeats, and triumphs of the advocates of moral resistance in a world of conflict and violence. It is so supremely difficult because it involves what we may call an *antinomy* of practical judgment. The reader of Kant's "Critique of Pure Reason" will recall that the German seer finds in the transcendental dialectic, wherein pure reason discourses of things above human experience, four propositions, each of which is perfectly sound in its logic, yet has each its direct contradiction in a counter-proposition, which also is logically unanswerable. In other words, the thesis and the antithesis are both convincing to the pure reason.[1] Now, in the problem before us we are facing a similar antinomy,

[1] "Immanuel Kant's Critique of Pure Reason," translated by F. Max Müller. Centenary Edition, 1907; pp. 328 ff. The Kantian antinomies, it will be recalled, deal with conceptions of the universe with respect to such questions as (1) its limitations in time and space; (2) its resolvability into simple parts; (3) casuality and freedom; and (4) the existence of an absolutely necessary Being.

that is to say, an irreducible contradiction; but, instead of dealing with those transcendental ideas which overstep the limits of all human experience, this antinomy has to do with one of the most immediately pressing problems that practical experience can present, namely, how should a morally developed human being or a civilized social group react toward the aggressions of other individuals and groups? And it is this baffling problem that we have termed an antinomy of *practical judgment.*

The *thesis* of this contradiction affirms that evil should be met by resistance. This satisfies the instincts and feelings, but disturbs the reason, which sees that by such conduct evil multiplies itself. The *antithesis* teaches non-resistance toward him that is evil. This satisfies the reflective reason, but outrages the deepest feelings, which chafe at evil unrebuked.

Professor Giddings has searchingly discussed this problem in his "Democracy and Empire."[1] He finds it "a curious phenomenon,—this growth of conviction among intelligent people that the world would be better off if it accepted literally the gospel of non-resistance, while yet each civilized nation is strengthening its military resources and its armaments, and is intently watching every move of its rivals." This anomalous situation leads him to ask "whether there is not an inherent contradiction in the moral nature of man." He finds in Nietzsche and Tolstoy "the opposite poles of nineteenth century thought," and seeks to reduce the tremendous contradictions, which they incarnate, by a searching analysis of Nietzsche's idea of physiological power. He thinks that Nietzsche is right in making it the fundamental consideration for progress, but shows that it is too narrowly conceived. The "might" that makes "right" is not, in the thought of Professor

[1] Chap. XX, "The Gospel of Non-Resistance."

Giddings, the undifferentiated might of sheer, crude, physical power. The triumph of such might is *wrong.* Physiological power becomes the might that makes for right when it becomes differentiated into various forms without diminishing the total amount. Among these differentiated forms are "sympathy and all its products. . . . All the higher virtues—philanthropy, compassion, and forgiveness." In these passages the thought is carried from worship of sheer brutality to moral levels. In the clearer light of this analysis the non-resistant figures as something more than a weakling, or the deluded victim of a suicidal obsession. In a sense he may be really the true superman, for, when viewed on the physiological side, even *altruism,* according to Professor Giddings, "is a mode of expenditure of any surplus energy that has been left over from successful individual struggle."

But it would be misleading to imply that the essay referred to is a plea for non-resistance at any cost. Professor Giddings expects these two principles to continue to operate; and "only in the spiritual brotherhood of a great secular republic created by blood and iron not less than by thought and love, will the kingdom of heaven be established on earth." This inadequate statement of Professor Giddings' argument will serve its purpose if it helps to impress upon the reader the tremendous difficulty of the problem before us.

Not only is it a duel between Neitzsche and Tolstoy, as Professor Giddings remarks, but the antinomy involves a whole array of antagonistic forces and systems deeply rooted in two contrary aspects of human nature. It seems almost, at times, to be the conflict of instinct with reason, of race against the individual life. The group purpose often ruthlessly demands the sacrifice of the private conscience, and competition, survival, ethnocentrism, and evolution array themselves against coöperation, self-sacrifice, humanitarianism, and revelation.

This dual aspect of human experience brings to pass many strange alliances and unexpected situations. Thus it is narrated [1] that during the plundering, raiding, violent border struggles of our Civil War the Shakers of Pleasant Hill, in Kentucky, dwelt in peace and security under the powerful protection of a most "unlooked for protector, no less a personage than the notorious guerrilla leader, John Morgan." It developed that Morgan had grown up in the vicinity of the Shaker community, and cherished a profound respect for those quiet, kindly people. Hence, when the Confederate foragers were hatching a design against the well-stored Shaker larders and barns, he peremptorily forbade the foray. He then informed his troops that he had known the Shakers from long acquaintance, as "a harmless, inoffensive people; that they took no part with either side, injured no man and had no desire so to do, and none under his command should injure them in any way." The friendship thus formed was permanent, and Morgan "has ever been held, by all Shakers, in grateful remembrance." [2]

This incident has been narrated, not for its seemingly unique picturesqueness, but because it typifies a universal human experience. The wild life of a border raider expressed one side of Morgan's nature; the quiet village of non-resistant Shakers embodied the other. This concrete historic incident reveals the two motives in conflict upon the outward visible stage of human social action. They are

1 "Shakerism, Its Meaning and Message," by White and Taylor; p. 202.

2 *Ibid.*

forever in silent conflict in every human heart, and the pathos of Morgan's conduct is typical of all thoughtful human experience.

The plan of the present Chapter is not to evaluate, or even explain, the contradictory experience of passive resistants as revealed by history. That must be attempted in later pages. For the present the method to be pursued is that of an inductive study of the actual sayings and doings of various advocates of passive resistance, in which its exponents will state the theory in their own words. Then some contradictions between the theory and its practice will be observed. But before so doing, the remarkable tendency of non-resistance toward logical degeneration and expansion in theory will be traced.

THE PATH OF LOGICAL DEGENERATION

Professor Ross shows, in his "Social Psychology,"[1] the path of degeneration by which a discussion tends to descend "from the realm of social psychology into that of pugilistics." The process in the case before us is different, but the line of descent is fully as marked. In the passage referred to we are shown the *social* dialectic of two disputants, who first reason, then wrangle, next vituperate, and finally fall to fighting. In this instance we shall observe the individual dialectic of a single mind, or of many minds acting more or less separately, and the logical process by which this inherent contradiction in human nature forces the thinker down a path of degeneration in which the doctrine becomes self-destructive because all-destroying.

The initial proposition of non-resistance is, "Thou shalt

[1] See pp. 313-314.

not kill." Starting with this injunction, the first and natural interpretation is that one should commit no murder. All civilized and socialized men hold this command as inviolable. Many of the more highly enlightened extend it to forbid all *retaliation,* in the sense of personal revenge. Violence against human life is thus completely forbidden. But the next step is to inquire whether it should not include the life of animals also—at least the higher, more sentient forms. The Buddhist answer is found in the "Story of the Goose-Killing Priest,"[1] as it is quaintly entitled. The Albigensian Perfecti also were forbidden to slay any beast, and the modern Doukhobors have at times taken the same position. They do not limit it to a priestly class, as in the other instances mentioned, but enjoin it upon all. In the case of *Van der Ver,* the hero of Tolstoy's essay, "The Beginning of the End," it is of significance here to observe that the young Hollander flatly refused to train simply because he did not wish to murder his fellowmen, and remarked that he could not bear to see an animal killed, much less kill one himself. So in order to avoid the necessity he had become a vegetarian.

Here we have a process by which abhorrence of murder descends, or, if the reader prefers, ascends, step by step, into vegetarianism. It may not be contemptuously dismissed as a case of fanaticism or abnormal mentality. There are a great many sane and healthy vegetarians in the world who constitute a sort of standing refutation of such dogmatism. In styling it a "dialectic," however, it is not assumed that this is a purely intellectual process. On the contrary it would deem to be due to a growing refinement of *feeling,* which may still further increase as civilizations become older.

1 Cf. Warren, "Buddhism in Translations," Harvard Oriental Series, Vol. III, Second Issue, 1900. p. 433.

A faction[1] among the Doukhobors in Canada took the next step along the path of logical degeneration, and concluded that since it was wrong to utilize the animals for food it must be equally wrong to exploit their labor. Therefore they promptly turned their beasts of burden loose to roam the plains in glad freedom while their masters harnessed themselves to the plow.[2]

The next scruple would logically attach itself to the destruction of plant life, and, sure enough, we observe that among certain Buddhist zealots "carpentry, basket-making, working in leather, and other respectable occupations were held in disrepute, because they could not be carried on without a certain cost of plant and animal life."[3] The Doukhobors went a step further, and objected to tillage because they did not want "to spoil the earth."![4]

Thus far attention has been centered upon the effort to avoid aggression, but at this point, if logical sequence is to be followed, our thought should turn to the question of *resistance toward the aggressions of others.* As fully illustrated in their writings, the Roman Stoics, and the Buddhists also, start out to resist no evil. This passes into an extreme asceticism, in the case of the Buddhist, and a ruthless casting off of useless baggage (impedimenta that might hinder the stern will) in the case of the Stoics. In both cases the individual shifts from resisting no evil to a position where he desires no good. Then, with Mar-

1 The illustrations taken in this connection do not represent the Doukhobors as a whole, but a considerable number were involved in these extremes.

2 Elkinton's "Doukhobors" contains a photograph of this strange scene.

3 Aiken, "The Dharma of Gotama the Buddha and the Gospel of Jesus the Christ"; p. 38.

4 The Buddhist extremists also "went so far as to question the blamelessness of tilling the ground," but this was "on account of the unavoidable injury to worms and insects in ploughing." *Ibid.*

cus Aurelius, he comes to count even *surprise* at the course of events as unworthy. Reaction having diminished to a point, it now ceases altogether. Complete passivism finally triumphs. The Hindu announces that one should "abandon [not only] all wish, passion, delight, desire, seeking, attachment, [but also all] mental affirmation, proclivity, and prejudice in respect of sensation, perception . . . the predispositions . . . consciousness. Thus will all consciousness be abandoned, uprooted . . . and become non-existent."[1]

This looks like mental self-destruction, and as a matter of fact this last step in their logic brings both the Buddhist and the Stoic to suicide as a door of escape. For the Buddhist, Nirvana, the paradise of Nothingness, awaits the soul that has thus trod the pathway of absolute non-resistance to its logical conclusion.

THE TENDENCY TO EXPANSION IN THE CHRISTIAN TRADITION

It will be noticed that the above description has dealt largely with the Hindu religion and the Stoic philosophy. We must now turn to the Christian tradition and observe a somewhat similar logical elaboration; but in this case it is one of *expansion*, though based on the same prohibition, "Thou shalt not kill." In the first instance again this refers to murder, and applies to a personal foe. But the primitive Christians extended it to forbid the killing of a public enemy, a group antagonist in battle. Thus war is prohibited, and, as we have seen, was very early branded as murder, by Lactantius.[2] The same writer and

[1] Warren, "Buddhism in Translation"; p. 298.

[2] It is of interest to recall here that Buddha, when confronted with a direct question by Simha, the general, explicitly refused to include war or official executions in his prohibition of physical coercion.

a number of later non-resistants, notably one wing of the Anabaptists, extended the prohibition to include the official act of a magistrate in executing the judgment of the law against a criminal. The next logical addition was to forbid the preferment of a capital charge, and it duly appeared in regular sequence.

All these are valid inferences from the prohibition against taking human life, where the same is received as absolute and sweeping. But still more difficult situations, real and imaginary, have confronted the advocates of non-resistance. The most distressing problem is that one which has been put to peace advocates time and again in the long history of that movement.[1] This is the question whether it is right to resent with violence a murderous assailant of one's own person or life. Even thorough peacemen writhe under this situation, but the absolute non-resistant stands firm and interprets literally the saying, "Resist not him that is evil: but whosoever smiteth thee on thy right cheek, turn to him the other also." Yet when the final and truly crucial test is applied, and the hypothetical assailant is pictured as a murderous ravisher of the helpless, human nature usually proves unequal to the terrific strain, fundamental instincts and emotions refuse longer to be confined, and it is a rare advocate who can endure his own logic. For the steady advance of an *idea* has its limits, and, when confronted, in fact or fancy, with outraged innocence, is now rolled backward under the irresistible uprush of chivalrous *feeling;* for in actual life the result in such situations is usually vigorous reaction. In the purely imaginary situations that figure in discussion there is, to be sure, usually some logical fencing, or a more or less precipitate dialectical retreat, to avoid facing the hideous dilemma even in thought.

[1] See the published addresses of the American Peace Society.

THE SOCIAL PSYCHOLOGY OF NON-RESISTANCE, AS STATED BY ITS ADVOCATES

The considerations that demand attention at this point are not those of the private convictions and spiritual experiences of the non-resistant himself. We seek now to find the clue to his own *social* psychology, that is, the laws and principles by which he expects his peculiar rule of conduct to affect the other personalities with whom he finds himself in contact. To be sure, one need not hope to see a thoroughly rationalized system. It is always to be borne in mind that the true non-resistant has usually been governed by a compelling conviction of the eternal rightness of his course, inasmuch as he believed it to be the divinely ordained and only way of salvation for mankind, and he would be among the last to attempt to justify the ways of God to men. Nevertheless one does find, in the sayings of the great teachers of the non-resistance ethics, the rudiments of a social psychology, that is, some laws, actual or alleged, of mental interaction among men.

The first formulation is negative, and affirms, in substance: *Evil aggression thrives only on the resistance which it meets.* Lao Tse said of the sage that "it is because he is free from striving that no one can strive with him." Seneca carries the same thought further when he observes that "the displeasure suddenly quaileth whenas the one part forbeareth to contend. No man fighteth unless he is resisted." This last is very explicit. Epictetus decided that this world offers very few things that are significant enough to warrant resistance if assailed; therefore, he asks, "why do you not make public proclamation that you are at peace with all mankind, however they may act; and that you chiefly laugh at those who suppose they can hurt you?" Gautama put the thing with amusing pithiness when he said to his reviler, "I decline to accept your abuse." In this remark, along with all the noble sayings above quoted, one sees simply the more elegant and systematic formulation of a truth familiar to the common sense of Western races, and expressed in the old saw, "it takes two to make a quarrel."

The second principle is positive, and declares that *Evil is overcome by good.* Every one knows that Solomon said: "A soft answer turneth away wrath"; although the Wise Man of Israel is not to be reckoned among the non-resistants. The Sutra of the Chinese Buddhists enunciates the same thought in the striking words: "He will reply to thee in the same tone." In the story of *Prince Dirghayu* we have seen an exemplification of Gautama's principle that "Hatred is appeased by not-hatred. This," adds Budda, "is an eternal law." No one who enjoys the least comprehension of the New Testament needs to be told that the very spirit of those writings, and of the apostolic church which was their living embodiment, is contained in the saying of Paul, "Be not overcome of evil, but overcome evil with good." It was his faith in the efficacy of this principle that led the great medieval humanist Erasmus to the proposition that "the most effectual way of conquering the Turks would be if they were to see the spirit and teaching of Christ expressed in our lives; if they perceived that we were not aiming at empire over them."[1]

The third principle formulated by the advocates of non-resistance is designed to prevent retaliation. It observes that *Rational reflection allays resentment and prevents strife.* Epictetus understands that your neighbor has been throwing stones, and seeks to determine what kind of conduct is proper in return. "If you are considering yourself as a wolf, then bite again. . . . But if you ask the

[1] Drummond. "Erasmus: His Life and Character"; Vol. I, p. 408.

question as a man, then examine your treasure; see what faculties you have brought into the world with you. Are they fitted for ferocity; for revenge?" In this reflection attention is fixed on the matter of fighting *equipment,* of fang and claw. In another passage Epictetus proposes that the aggrieved person should reflect upon his fundamental *nature* before going vehemently to the attack: "Remember to say first that you are constituted gentle, and that by doing nothing violent, you will live without the need of repentance, and irreproachable." In this passage Epictetus sounds the very depths of the problem on its moral side. The essential nature of man, the very law of his being, demands that his conduct be shaped, not in response to the moment's passion, but comformably to the standards of that ideal self in whose clear light conscience will eventually be heard, even though one take the wings of the morning and fly to the uttermost parts of the sea.[1]

In their individual lives men come to guide themselves by the recollection that conscience never fails to have the last word. Therefore it is probably true that numberless incipient deeds of violence have failed of completion because their prospective perpetrators "remembered," and there are those to-day who propose to extend this principle of preliminary examination of the merits of the case to such group struggles as labor conflicts and international war.[2] The idea was naïvely expressed ages ago in this legend of Gautama and the kings who were preparing to war for possession of certain fortifications:

" 'The Blood of men, however,' said Buddha, 'has it less intrinsic value than a mound of earth?' 'No,' the kings

1 Psalms; CXXXIX, v. 7–10.

2 For example, the peace pacts of Secretary Bryan. Cf. the twenty-fifth "Mohonk Report"; p. 18. Also the Canadian Industrial Disputes Act.

said, 'the lives of men, and above all the lives of kings, are priceless.' Then the Tathagata concluded: 'Are you going to stake that which is priceless against that which has no intrinsic value whatever?' The wrath of the two monarchs abated, and they came to a peaceable agreement.'' The reader may smile at the sweet reasonableness herein imputed to humanity, yet the underlying principle is not so guileless as the form that it assumes in this instance.

Summarizing, we have three propositions. The first *checks* antagonism and aggression already begun; the second actively *overcomes* it with good; the third *prevents* a retaliatory evil-doing in return.

PASSIVE RESISTANCE AND THE STATE

The Pauline doctrine of the state, as contained in the New Testament writings, was simply one of accommodation to the actual conditions of an evil world. Moreover, it was a purely temporary arrangement. The world was passing away and its rulers were coming to naught. Since the end of all things was so close at hand, the best thing was for all to abide as they found themselves in the social order. Rulers were recognized as the agents of God against evil-doers, so that the state gained by assumption a certain validity; but the whole thing was believed to be of such an ephemeral nature that no positive theory of political science can be deduced from New Testament sayings. Christian men had no conception of themselves as a legitimate part of a social order which was not only to last for centuries but was also to work out its earthly salvation by the political participation of all its members.

Nevertheless, many thinkers of the middle ages tried to ground their political practice on certain Bible sayings. Among these the most prominent were the principle of non-resistance and that of passive obedience to rulers. The two together erected a tremendous barrier against all insurrections, yet the inner spirit of Christianity and the general tenor of the New Testament gave, at the same time and to the very same men, a powerful impetus to social and religious revolution. In the last analysis the problem became one of how to bring about the inevitable revolutionary changes when the only two avenues, constructive reform and insurrection,[1] were both closed; the former by the stupid tyranny of the ruling classes, the latter by the doctrine of passive obedience to rulers and the principle of non-resistance.

As has been shown in the words of Balthasar Hübmaier, a large wing of the Anabaptists taught that there are two swords, one, the spiritual, given to the true church, the other, the temporal, placed by divine commission in the hand of the magistrate. As he quaintly observes, "if there are two swords, of which one belongs to the soul, the other to the body, you must let them both remain in their worthiness, dear brother."[2] Hübmaier held that these two swords were not opposed to each other, but not all Anabaptists were so liberal. The general theory of the movement and of the sects into which it differentiated was distinctly negative. The Anabaptists were especially intent upon denying the power of the civil magistrate to coerce men in matters of faith and conscience, since they had good reason to be hostile to government because of their persecutions. But, in their zeal thus to disarm the intolerant state church, they swung to the opposite extreme, and ended in a doctrine of complete political non-participation on the part of the Christian.

1 See Perry, "The Moral Economy," Chap. IV, for a discussion of these terms. Cf. also C. Delisle Burns, "The Principles of Revolution," London, 1920.

2 Vedder, "Balthasar Hübmaier"; p. 194.

THE QUAKER THEORY OF THE STATE

The theory, and especially the practice, of the Friend was precisely the opposite of the Anabaptist, for the Quaker's political doctrine was all positive. He spent no time arguing about the state, pro or con. He simply accepted it as a tremendous agency for good if administered in the fear of God. Mention has already been made of a few of the contributions of the Quakers to English and American liberty, since it is in the field of actual civil experiment that the Quaker view of political science must be studied. Assuming some things and taking others for granted, they plunged into the active work of government, where, however, their trying experiences forced them to some political reflections, and finally into a policy of political non-participation, from which however they have rallied in more recent years.

We refer here particularly to the Friends in Pennsylvania, but on the other hand the Rhode Island Quakers, who gave a line of governors to their colony, when in office subordinated their non-resistance scruples to the imperative demands of the office, yet at the same time pursued an ever-vigilant policy of peace and passive resistance. Jones states the situation finely when he says: "There have always been in the Society of Friends two groups of persons. One group held it to be imperative to work out their principles of life in the complex affairs of the community and state, where to gain an end one must yield something; and where to achieve ultimate triumph one must risk his ideals to the tender mercies of a world not yet ripe for them. . . . Another group was pledged unswervingly to the ideal. 'If there comes a collision between allegiance to the ideal and the holding of public office, then the office must be deserted.' "[1] The Rhode Island Quakers exemplify the former attitude, but it would be a mistake to infer that they thus tamely consented to lower their standard of peace. While loyal devotion to public duty in public position might dictate certain un-Quakerly tasks, in the Quaker meetings there was no wavering. No man could remain a Friend if he participated in the spirit of war. "Even so blue-blooded a Friend," says Jones, "as Nathanael Green of Rhode Island,—a patriot of the patriots—had his name expunged from the list of members for the offense of 'taking arms.' "[2]

In Pennsylvania the same irreducible contradiction between theory and practice appeared. Mrs. Gummere[3] points out the incongruity which placed the Quaker governors of Pennsylvania, as well as those of Rhode Island, with their well-known testimony against fighting, in the office of captain-general of those provinces. They could hardly hope to come free of coercive violence in some form, since even William Penn himself had to issue a commission to establish a fort on the Delaware. He could not have received the charter for his colony without accepting command under the king. That was the price he had to pay in the very outset for the bare opportunity of trying to establish peace in a world where violence ruled. As Mrs. Gummere points out, he performed his "martial acts through deputies who were not Quakers and who had no scruples."[4]

In their official capacity Friends had to meet also the question of capital punishment, but here they squarely upheld the power of the sword. Thus in 1778 the Quaker

[1] *Ibid.;* pp. 175, 176.

[2] *Ibid.;* p. 151. This was the celebrated Revolutionary general of later years.

[3] "The Quaker in the Forum"; p. 134.

[4] *Ibid.*

assembly passed an act, drawn up by a Quaker lawyer, which added a dozen or more offenses to the list of capital crimes; and the meetings did not protest against it. The assembly itself, though controlled by Quakers, was unable to resist the powerful tide of group sentiment, and, "recognizing their duty 'to give tribute to Cæsar,' voted £4,000 [in 1745] for 'bread, beef, pork, flour, wheat and other grains' in lieu of military supplies. The Governor is said to have construed 'other grain' to mean gunpowder.' "[1]

Observing more closely the diverse expressions of this "inherent contradiction in the moral nature of man," we see advocates of non-resistance manifesting an affinity for the affairs of government, with all its coercion, and, on the other hand, the exponents of the ruthless ethics of evolution and unlimited sovereignty often secretly admiring the men of peace, and covertly assuming their ideal to be the true goal of humanity. The Roman emperor and Stoic philosopher, Marcus Aurelius Antoninus, exemplifies in his self-contradictory career the union of these two antagonistic principles of conduct. Bigg says, "From his cradle he was a beautiful soul, delicate in mind as in body, tender, truthful, docile, sweetly melancholy, a virginal flower, shrinking from the world of which he was the master."[2] Yet the greatness of the Cæsars was thrust upon him, and this gentle dreamer, who penned the irenic passages of the "Meditations," wrote them in those precious moments of peaceful solitude which he was able to snatch from the crowding cares of the day. And what were the activities which consumed the days of this reluctant wearer of the purple? Directing the terrible Roman legions at the front, administering the machinery of coercion at home, and pursuing Christians with the

[1] *Ibid.*

[2] In John Jackson's "Translation"; Introduction, p. 13.

worst persecutions in the history of the church! Yet this was not the fruit of hypocrisy. "Marcus is a noble figure. Even the Christians of the ages of persecution could not speak evil of him, though he had smitten them very hard. Noble, beautiful and pathetic." He was simply that most incongruous thing, an absolute non-resistant on the throne of the Cæsars! Bigg picturesquely declares, "The gods had appointed him a task that was far beyond his strength; he wrestled with it, but he wrestled in vain. We may call him the most tragic figure in history."[1]

The conflict thus supremely set forth in Marcus Aurelius passive resistants in all ages since have endured in greater or lesser degree according to the extent of their implication in government. As a result every passive resistant movement has at some point been forced either to deny itself or repudiate the state.

During this transition period, this chrysalis stage of humanity, the passive resistant has suffered much, not only from the contradictions of men, but from the conflicts of his own heart. Therefore, the anomalous situations of actual life have naturally been matched by casuistical solutions in the realm of theory. Gautama justified the warrior who "moderates himself and, extinguishing all hatred from his heart, lifts his down-trodden adversary up and says to him, 'Come now and make peace and let us be brothers.'"[2] Emmanuel Swedenborg also presents a plan for handling the antinomy, as follows: "Where a person resists the assaults of an enemy, and in his own defense either beats him, or commits him to prison for his future security, at the same time retaining such a disposition of mind as to be willing to become his friend; in this case

[1] *Op. cit.;* p. 49. The career of Martin Luther also presents some interesting self-contradictions, as shown by McKinnon, in his "History of Modern Liberty." London and New York, 1906.

[2] Carus, "The Gospel of Buddha"; p. 128.

he acts from a principle of charity." So also it is with wars of defense for country or church, he argues, propounding his own peculiar solution as follows: "Since then charity, with respect to its origin, consists in good-will, and good-will resides in the internal man, it is plain that when a man possessed of charity resists an enemy, punishes the guilty, and chastises the wicked, he effects this by means of the external man, and consequently, when he has effected it, he returns into the charity which is the internal man, and then as far as he is able, or as far as it is expedient, wishes well to him whom he has punished or chastised, and from a principle of good-will does him good."[1]

A French writer wrestles with this same intensely tragic mental situation as it presented itself at the opening of the present war, and, like thousands of others under the stress of such harrowing situations, despairs of a solution. After narrating the story of a French Mayor in Alsace who had shown, according to the despatches, the utmost magnanimity toward German soldiers from whose alleged barbarity his own family had, according to the story, suffered terribly, the writer exclaims: "That is the divine vengeance of Christ on the barbarians. Nevertheless, let us not forget that we are at war, and that in order to survive the frightful shock,—for it will be that,—of the German masses, it will be necessary to apply the law of retaliation: eye for eye, tooth for tooth. That a municipal Magistrate, *representing the civil element of the country,* should conduct himself with an abnegation almost superhuman, that will be to the eternal glory of France. But if the Prussians continue to exterminate prisoners of war, the wounded, aged persons, women and children, the Darwinian law of the survival of the strongest demands that our army apply to the enemy the penalty of the law of

[1] "The True Christian Religion"; Chap. VII, pp. 443–444.

retaliation."[1] Here the effort to reduce the antinomy is abandoned for a permanent division of the social mind, in which the civil element expresses forgiveness while the military becomes the agent of condign vengeance.

[1] "Le Cri," (a little French war sheet published in London); August 21, 1914.

CHAPTER XIII

SUCCESSES AND FAILURES OF PASSIVE RESISTANCE

THE supreme interest for this study lies in the *uniform* ways of *mental interaction* which take place when passive resistance is practised. These, if ascertained, would constitute the social *laws* of passive resistance. A further interest is to be found in the effort to formulate the *principles* which *explain* these actual workings or laws.[1] The two together, i.e., uniformities and principles, would make up the social psychology of passive resistance.

Underlying the doctrine of passive resistance is a fundamental proposition which really amounts to an article of faith. It is that the constitution and purpose of the world are such that *rational* methods are the only right means, and also offer the most effective means, for attaining moral and social ends. This single principle of conduct, of reaction to social environment, operating under various human groupings and relations, gives rise to several derived principles, which we have already called the social laws, or social psychology, of passive resistance. In the attempt to work out the rudiments of these laws no superhuman agency is either assumed or denied, but attention is necessarily centered upon the purely mundane aspects, leaving the religious and metaphysical implications to those

[1] The terms "law" and "principle" are used with the sense given them by Ward in "Pure Sociology"; p. 169.

sciences whose special task it is to deal with them.

It is the purpose of this chapter to analyze the available material in a threefold way, as follows: first, to state some typical cases of passive resistance; secondly, to illustrate the same from history and literature; thirdly, to formulate under each case the principle that seems to govern the success or failure of the policy, as viewed in its outward and social aspects.

Before proceeding to this analysis a word may be in order respecting the literature of this phase of our subject. So far as the present writer is aware, less than half a dozen writers have directly attacked this problem. Mention has been made of the chapter on "The Gospel of Non-Resistance" by Professor Giddings. Aside from his essay, the direct discussion of the efficacy of this policy has been left to the earlier essayists of the peace movement. This is supplemented by incidental references in the works of historians and public speakers. We have, to be sure, the works of the historians of the various peace sects, but their interest has not lain in this direction. Being active members of the sect themselves, their attention has been centered on the more strictly religious life of the organization rather than upon its social influence and success. This reminds us again that the problem which we are investigating is, in the eyes of those who have practised it, merely the by-product of the principle. They would not have suffered as they did for considerations of mere social expediency; but, on the other hand, a demonstration of its failure from a worldly point of view would not have deterred them.

This subordination of temporal success to the testimony of a good conscience is reflected in the literature upon which we shall have to draw, and accounts in part for its comparative meagerness. Almost a hundred years ago, nevertheless, the questions we are seeking to answer were entertained by a mind competent to discuss them, with the result that Dr. Thomas Hancock published, in 1826, the second edition[1] of a work in which he clearly anticipated the present and similar inquiries. In his preface he says, "The time will undoubtedly come—and no one can say how soon it may arrive—when the Christian principles of peace will be more generally received and acted upon in the world than they are at present; every contribution, however small, pointing out the way in which the followers of peace have endeavored to obey their Lord and Master's literal injunctions on this fundamental point, and commemorating the blessed effects of their obedience, may have some little weight in the balance, to determine the minds of hesitating Christians on the side of peace." And, further on, he reminds the reader that "the fact of their outward preservation would be no sufficient argument to themselves that they had acted as they ought in such a crisis" as that described, yet it nevertheless "affords a striking lesson to those who will take no principle, that has not been verified by experience, for a rule of human conduct, even if it should have the sanction of Divine authority."[2]

Dr. Hancock's work represents, however, simply the detailed study of a particular historical situation, whereas the most thorough and systematic development of the *theory*

[1] The date of the first edition is not given. An edition of the same work was published by the American Peace Society, Boston, 1843. The cover-title of this edition is "Hancock on Peace."

[2] The title of this truly remarkable book presents, in the quaint fashion of those times, a sufficiently full description of its character: "The Principles of Peace Exemplified in the conduct of the Society of Friends in Ireland, during the rebellion of the year 1798, with some preliminary and concluding observations. By Thomas Hancock, M. D. Second edition. Revised and enlarged. London, 1826."

of non-resistance in its general aspects known to the writer was published by Adin Ballou, in 1846, under the title, "Christian Non-Resistance in All Its Important Bearings, Illustrated and Defended."[1] In this able exposition the author, after pursuing with clear and relentless logic every conceivable objection to the scriptural authority and moral consistency of the doctrine, turns to the question of its social expediency, and marshals the most imposing array of illustrations and anecdotes to be found in the entire literature of this subject.[2]

The one other work which is devoted to an extended investigation of the social workings of this principle was published, apparently by William Ladd, the "father of the American Peace Society," under the pen-name "Philanthropos," in 1831. The self-explanatory title runs: "A Brief Illustration of the Principles of War and Peace, showing the ruinous policy of the former, and the superior efficacy of the latter, for national protection and defense; clearly manifested by their practical operations and opposite effects upon nations, kingdoms and peoples." From these and various other works less directly devoted to this problem it is now proposed to analyze the actual workings of the policy of passive resistance, and to deduce some laws that govern the same.

[1] A second edition was published in 1910 by the Universal Peace Union, Philadelphia.

[2] Virtually all the incidents cited in the present study, along with many more, are gathered together in Ballou's volume, but, inasmuch as this chapter in its original form was written before the author became acquainted with the work of Ballou, the following citations to the scattered peace pamphlets are allowed to stand. Moreover the writer has been unable to determine which is the original source, Ballou's book or the peace literature referred to, especially since they all appeared at about the same time. Ballou was himself a minister of the Universalist faith.

I

The first case is that in which a non-resisting individual confronts a hostile aggressor. Under this head would fall the various anecdotes of deliverance from highwaymen and other assailants, narrated of the men of peace. For instance, it is related of the Archbishop Sharpe that, when riding alone in a secluded spot, a "well-looking" young man suddenly confronted him, placed a pistol to his breast, and demanded his money. The archbishop, gazing upon him with the utmost composure and steadfastness, asked him to remove the dangerous weapon and tell him frankly and honestly his condition.

"Sir! Sir!" with great agitation, cried the youth, "no words, 't is not a time—your money instantly."

"Hear me, young man," said the archbishop; "you see I am an old man, and my life is of little consequence; yours seems far otherwise. I am named Sharpe, and am Archbishop of York; my carriage and servants are behind. Tell me what money you want, and who you are; and I will not injure you, but prove a friend. Here, take this," giving him his purse, "and now ingenuously tell me how much you want to make you independent of so destructive a business as you are now engaged in."

"O sir, replied the man, "I detest the business as much as you. I am—but—but at home there are creditors who will not stay; fifty pounds, my lord, indeed, would do what no tongue besides my own can tell."

The money was given him and he departed, agreeing to call upon the archbishop as requested. This he actually did two years afterward, when he returned with the money, and with great emotion related to his benefactor how he had been driven by misfortune from a respectable career to that former desperate enterprise in order to retrieve his fortunes, which had since turned for the better. ''By your astonishing goodness,'' he exclaimed, ''I am at once the most penitent, most grateful, and happiest of my species.''

This account [1] suggests the thought that the safety of the non-resistant depends in some cases upon the question whether the assailant is playing his normal rôle or is in a condition of mental and moral instability. Yet the large number of recorded cases of this kind would seem to indicate that the basis of pacific appeal is often present Robert Barclay, the celebrated Quaker apologist, when attacked by a highwayman offered no resistance, but calmly expostulated. ''The felon dropped his presented pistol, and offered no farther violence.'' Again, Leonard Fell, a Quaker minister, was assaulted by a highwayman, ''who plundered him of his money and his horse and afterward threatened to blow out his brains. Fell solemnly spoke to the robber on the wickedness of his life. The man was astonished; he declared he would take neither his money nor his horse and returned both.'' [2] George Fox relates a similar experience in his journal. These, and numerous other examples of the kind, are not cases of sheer *non*-resistance, which is much rarer than is commonly supposed. They represent a form of resistance which Professor Cooley calls, with keen discrimination, an ''attack upon the higher self'' of the assailant, and which is be-

1 Published by the American Peace Society in "Views of Peace and War," No. XL, under "Safety of Pacific Principles." Also Ballou, *op. cit.;* p. 144.

2 "The Book of Peace; a Collection of Essays on War and Peace," Boston, 1845; cf. p. 542. The essay referred to is entitled, "Efficacy of Pacific Principles."

lieved to be the enemy's weakest point.[1] It might be called a moral flanking movement, and is perhaps possible only to a real spiritual general.

In each of these instances we have a man of superior moral character and spiritual power confronting an assailant who is in the very act of offering him violence. Ballou gives twenty-one instances of this character, all being designed to show that Christian non-resistance is "preëminently safe." This is because, as he has previously sought to show by a dozen or more examples, it is not incompatible with human nature, but itself follows "a law of universal nature," namely "that like must beget its like—physical, mental, moral, spiritual."[2] In other words, we have here again the modern expression of an experience which ancient wisdom embodied in these sayings (all spoken in Asia, by the way):

"He will reply to thee in the same tone";[3] "The displeasure suddenly quaileth when the one part forbeareth to contend"; and "A soft answer turneth away wrath."

Among the examples which illustrate the persuasive power of non-resistance, apart from the question of personal danger, are to be found the numerous stories of sudden softening on the part of recalcitrant children, ferocious inmates of penal institutions, and others, under the melting effect of unexpected kindness.

We have presented only a handful from a long list of

[1] "Human Nature and the Social Order," by Charles Horton Cooley; pp. 246–247. The entire chapter on "Hostility" is vigorous and discriminating.

[2] *Ibid.;* p. 115.

[3] A former teacher of the writer's tested this principle some years ago while driving through several counties of Indiana. To some he spoke or nodded curtly and invariably received a curt reply. To others he spoke cordially and received a cordial response.

anecdotes which could be narrated, all showing the efficacy of non-resistance, or, better, of moral resistance, to abolish animosity, allay strife, and disarm aggression. On the whole, it is abundantly shown to be the truly human method, for in many instances nothing less is compatible with the dignity of a true spiritual stature, as is seen in the magnificent speech in which Buddha *declined to "accept"* his reviler's abuse.

Yet, numerous as are the instances of its successful workings in the ordinary manifestations of social friction, or even in the many cases of deliverance from violent aggression, candor compels the observation that the unwritten records of human life would probably show unnumbered instances where the non-resistant did not live to testify to the success of his principle. In circumstances where one is threatened with violence and bodily injury, non-resistance can hardly be said to be in accord with "human nature," because it requires the suppression of the most deep-rooted of all motives, that of self-defense, which is popularly recognized as "the first law of nature." The power of this impulse is so irresistible that few, even among ardent non-resistants, are able to practise the principle uncompromisingly when personally assailed with physical injury.

The fundamental faith of those who advocate non-resistance is that there resides in every human breast a chord that is capable of responding to generous treatment. Hence the practice of the principle by the Quakers was entirely in harmony with their teaching of "a seed of God," a "light of Christ," which they believed was the possession of every human being, however degraded. It was this divine spark that they expected to see kindled by the divinely gracious conduct made possible to the followers of Christ. But in so far as they depended upon a special intervention of God to assist them by direct operation upon the assailant's conscience they introduced an element which falls outside the realm of social psychology, which limits itself to strictly human interactions.

On the whole the conclusion is that, in the case of the non-resisting *individual* confronting a hostile aggressor, non-resistance is a powerful socializing force, and the conduct most truly dignified and worthy, provided that it does not degenerate into abject submission, but takes on the noble aggressiveness of an exalted moral and religious character. But, admirable as it is, the policy has not been successfully shown to be the safest from a physical point of view, although a very strong case is made out by those who have sought to uphold it by such considerations. But physical preservation is not the sole criterion of success for any form of resistance. Viewed in its personal aspects, that type of resistance would seem to be best which preserves most fully the self-respect, highest interests, and true worth of the assailed personality. In this light Christian non-resistance, i. e., moral resistance, enters a very powerful claim, but must reckon always with the fundamental and socially valuable impulses of self-preservation and resentment of injury.

Generalizing from the rather numerous cases of this type, it appears that *the success of passive (moral) resistance in these dyadic, or man-to-man relations, is due to a rush of generous emotion such as gratitude or shame, aroused by an unexpected act of kindness, magnanimity, or fearless interest in the moral welfare of the offender.*

II

The second case is that wherein the passive resistant individual comes in contact with the requirements of the state. In this group would fall the persecutions of the early Christians, as previously described, and those of the later peace sects before the time when the sect and its peculiar tenets became clearly impressed upon the social mind. When this occurred, a different principle came into play, as will be shown in the following section. But, before the sect as such became known to the public, those who were later to compose its membership succeeded or failed as individuals, that is to say, as *separate* recalcitrant members of the community at large. It is known to all that the passive resistants who represent this type have usually suffered severe hardships, and in some cases a terrible death. Thus, for example, the animosity of the populace urged on the civil authorities against the early Christians with results fearful to contemplate.[1] Many individuals thereby suffered martyrdom, although the new faith triumphed in the end. In the more recent case of the incipient peace sects their clash with government usually arose from the refusal of individuals to train for military service, take the oath of allegiance, or perform other acts pertaining to the duties of citizenship.[2] In all these struggles we find the same sufferings on the part of the individual, particularly during times of public danger from invasion or insurrection, and the same final triumph, after years of hardship, as the *sect* became favorably known as a group, and was thereby enabled to secure exemptions for *its own members as such.* However,

1 Cf. "The Early Christian Persecutions"; by D. C. Munro (Edit.)

2 See "The United States versus Pringle: The Record of a Quaker Conscience," in the "Atlantic Monthly"; Vol. III, pp. 145-162 (February, 1913). Also "An Account of the Sufferings of Friends of North Carolina Yearly Meeting, in Support of Their Testimony Against War, from 1861 to 1865," published by North Carolina yearly meeting.

since the historical citations of earlier chapters have so often referred to the experiences of the well-known peace sects, the space must here be devoted to a few more modern examples.

Mention belongs first to the socialists, the most modern of all peace groups, and one of the most active. Their hatred of war, which rests upon humanitarian grounds, as stated in Tolstoy's case of Van der Ver, expresses itself along the lines of political activity and public agitation.

Mr. Robert Hunter's careful study, "Violence and the Labor Movement," is a profound and truly philosophic analysis of the problem of the present essay, but proceeding from a different angle. He shows the long and heroic struggle which the socialist movement has waged against the use of violence in its own ranks, and in the face of the organized violence long directed against the working class, first by venal governments, and more recently by the private mercenary armies of capitalist employers. At the outset those laboring men who sought to better in a permanent way their social condition had to wash their hands of such terrorists as Henry and Vaillant, whose violence destroyed all reason and sympathy in the public mind, and placed reactionary governments in the saddle elsewhere. The earlier terrorist practice of removing officials by violence, Mr. Hunter declares, "has hardly caused a ripple in the swiftly moving current of evolution."[1] In fact, so futile are such methods that the police of European countries have long made it a practice to send secret emissaries and spies among the discontented laborers with treacherous counsels of violence and terrorism, knowing full well that such methods, when adopted

[1] "Violence and the Labor Movement," by Robert Hunter, 1914; p. 103.

by the laboring man, produce a profound reaction in the public mind which favors the enactment of drastic laws in the interest of conservatism and privilege. A socialist speaker, referring to the trade-union activities of 1815–16, declared, as quoted by Hunter, "It was not until we became infested by spies, incendiaries, and their dupes—distracting, misleading, and betraying—that physical force was mentioned among us. After that our moral power waned."[1]

The meaning of the working-class movement for the last one hundred years is found, for the purposes of this essay, in the successive efforts of two conflicting tendencies or principles to gain control of the forces of social discontent. These two contending ideas are, on the one hand, the principle of *violence,* as expressed in the early "propaganda of the deed" by Bakounin and Netchayeff, in the organized anarchism of later years, and in its logical descendant, the syndicalism of to-day; and, on the other hand, the principle of passive, or *moral resistance,* as consistently pursued by the Socialist party, and shown in its dependence solely on the education of the masses and the appeal to the ballot-box. It is the long and dramatic contest between these two principles of social action that Mr. Hunter's book portrays. The superior power of moral resistance may be shown by the following striking instance:

In pursuance of the determination on the part of the German autocracy to crush the growing party of Social Democracy, Bismarck, having rendered unlawful all socialist organizations, meetings, or publications, then tried to provoke retaliation on the part of the socialists through the use of the well-known Russianized methods. "Again and again," says Hunter, "Bismarck's press declared: 'What

[1] *Ibid.;* p. 313.

is most necessary is to provoke the Social-Democrats to commit acts of despair, to draw them into the open street, and there to shoot them down.' " But, as Hunter declares, "If this was actually what Bismarck wanted, he failed utterly."[1] An underground movement grew, hampered by occasional terrorist acts on the part of misguided working-class fanatics, or their enemies, but the Social Democrats steadfastly refused to appeal to brute force. During twelve years of suffering, the movement increased, gaining a million adherents and a tenfold representation in the Reichstag.[2] The Government could no longer withstand this increasing volume of moral and political power, and so, on September 30, 1890, the anti-socialist law was repealed. A wave of popular rejoicing and celebration swept over Germany, and Liebknecht was able to say to the socialist conference in 1891: "He [Bismarck] has had at his entire disposal for more than a quarter of a century, the police, the army, the capital, and the power of the state—in brief, all the means of mechanical force. *We had only our just right, our bared breasts to oppose him with, and it is we who have conquered! Our arms are the best. In the course of time brute power must yield to the moral factors, to the logic of things.* Bismarck lies crushed to the earth—and social democracy is the strongest party in Germany! . . . *The essence of revolution lies not in the means, but in the end. Violence has been, for thousands of years, a reactionary factor.*"[3] To this impressive testimony to the might of passive resistance let us add some of the last words of Engels to his socialist followers: "We, the 'revolutionaries,' are profiting more by lawful

[1] *Ibid.;* p. 219.

[2] Cf. Ogg, "Economic Development of Modern Europe"; pp. 521–523.

[3] *Ibid.;* p. 226.

than by unlawful and revolutionary means. The parties of order as they call themselves, are being destroyed by their own weapons."[1]

The celebrated Defense Acts of New Zealand and Australia illustrate, in some of their workings, the method and social significance of passive resistance. The laws were so framed that the Government ignored the parental authority with impunity, and dealt directly with boys of adolescent years. In consequence we have in this extraordinary instance a case of passive resistance against a sovereign state on the part of the children! "Many of the boys who had been imprisoned formed," we are told by contemporary observers, "a Passive Resister's Union." This, in 1913, numbered 450 youths in the town of Christchurch alone. Every one of them was pledged to resist compulsory military training. Under the influence of this new approbational organization punishment by the military authorities became a badge of honor instead of a disgrace. "Those who have worn the broad arrow, picked oakum, and had their fingerprints taken, are looked upon by their fellows as leaders and heroes," says a contemporaneous pamphlet. "They organize meetings, address large crowds in the streets, and circularize members of Parliament."

The military authorities met this opposition with prosecution in the civil courts, later followed up, in persistent cases, with rather drastic punishment in detention-camps, culminating, in some instances, in solitary confinement of the stubborn lads, and even, according to the weight of the evidence, in physical punishment upon occasion.

But, despite these harsh measures directed against the legal infants and wards of the state, probably indeed, as a consequence of them, the opposition grew more open and

[1] *Ibid.;* pp. 347–348.

wide-spread. The courts were swamped with cases to such a degree that the "New Zealand Times" proposed that an extra magistrate be added to the bench for the exclusive handling of such cases. Criticism of the Government's policy was voiced in the public press and in the legislature, while popular protest vented itself in pamphleteering and such demonstrations as that at Footscray, in 1912, where "over 100 Cadets were sentenced, and a crowd of from 300 to 400 cheered each Cadet as he left the building."

The cause of the "passive resisters" seemed, nevertheless, to be losing ground even before the World War became an acute danger, and it was lost from sight very early in the war through the vast extension of military activities which was rendered popularly acceptable by the agitated state of the public mind.[1]

The war cloud engulfed another passive resistance movement, which, however, was already losing ground in 1914. This was the organized opposition to the English Education Act of 1902, which extended the private school system of the Anglican and Roman Catholic churches at the expense of the general taxpayer. The interest of the matter for the purposes of the present discussion lies in the fact that it was *explicitly* an example of passive resistance, inasmuch as the agitators called themselves "passive resisters" and published, for a decade or more, a periodical called "Passive Resistance," from whose pages this account is drawn.

Their method was to refuse to pay the school tax, which

[1] The above account is drawn from the columns of the "American Friend," the "London Friend," and two pamphlets, both published in Australasia, entitled respectively, "A Blot on the Empire," and "A Stream of Facts"; also from clippings from the Australian public press and some personal correspondence with the military officer charged with the administration of the law.

they held to be grossly unjust to dissenters, but to submit obediently to the penalty prescribed by the law for delinquency. This punishment came with great regularity in the form of fines, which the passive resisters steadfastly and consistently refused to pay; whereupon their goods were distrained, or, in default of goods, the recalcitrant was cast into prison. The magnitude of the movement is shown by the fact that within two and one half years of its inauguration the league had on file reports of seventy thousand summonses and 254 commitments to prison.

The character and social standing of the members of the movement are facts of significant interest. According to the secretary of the organization,[1] "The men and women whose goods have been sold belong to all classes and ranks. They are clergymen and ministers, journalists and teachers, manufacturers and magistrates, members of Parliament and candidates for Parliament, farmers and gardeners, aged women and young men."[2]

The movement was losing momentum in 1914, in response, as was supposed, to a feeling on the part of some that the Liberal victory of 1906, for which the Passive Resisters seem to have been more or less responsible, insured the repeal of the obnoxious law. But the decline was doubtless due also to the proverbially early exhaustion which overtakes all sudden expressions of popular indignation. The secretary admitted in 1913 that the Passive Resisters were "fewer in number compared with the hosts which at first resisted the fraudulent legislation of 1902."[3]

In cases where the passive resistant individual conflicts, in his individual capacity, with the policy of the

[1] "Passive Resistance," June, 1913; p. 7.
[2] *Ibid.*
[3] *Ibid.;* p. 4.

state, his success is usually doubtful, and depends solely upon the tone of ethical thought and the liberal public opinion existing at the time, and upon the degree in which, by means of communication, this favorable public opinion affects in the interest of leniency such institutions of social control as government, the press, and organized religion.

By way of a corollary to the above it follows that the imminence of war, whether as a present fact, or merely in imagination or memory, is the decisive factor in every instance.

III

The third typical case is that wherein a passive resistant sect seeks to maintain a policy of peace and perfect neutrality toward the contending parties of war or social revolution.

Into this group fall the experiences of all the modern peace sects during the American Revolution, the Civil War, and the recent world conflict.

In cases of the kind now under consideration, the sect, in order to serve as a palladium for its members, must not only be popularly recognized as producing the qualities of character and citizenship universally admired, but it must also be able to command absolute confidence in its perfect neutrality and freedom from partisan bias. Just in proportion as this confidence is lacking, to that extent is the popular wrath in such times of excitement visited upon it. Thus, in places where the Quakers and other peace people were suspected of Tory sympathies they suffered mistreatment at the hands of the rabble; but such cases are comparatively rare.

The most melancholy example of this kind on record is that black blot on American frontier history, the Moravian Massacre. The affair has been described from two entirely different points of view by Roosevelt in his "Winning of the West" and by Professor Taylor in his "History of the Moravian Church in the United States." These two divergent writers agree, however, in attributing the foul deed to a loss of confidence on the part of the enraged frontiersmen toward the Moravian Brethren and their Indian converts on the Tuscarawas. Roosevelt declares that "their fate was not due to the fact that they were Indians; it resulted from their occupying an absolutely false position. This is clearly shown," he argues, "by what happened twenty years previously to a small community of non-resistant Christian whites. They were Dunkards—Quaker-like Germans—who had built a settlement on the Monongahela. As they helped neither side, both distrusted and hated them. The whites harassed them in every way, and the Indians finally fell upon and massacred them. The fates of these two communities, of white Dunkards and red Moravians, were exactly parallel. Each became hateful to both sets of combatants, was persecuted by both, and finally fell a victim to the ferocity of the race to which it did not belong."[1]

Taylor really assigns the same cause when he says of those same Moravians: "Despite their serious losses and openhanded hospitality, the Brethren themselves were denounced, by those inimical to their missions, as being secretly in league with the French and the savages. . . . Again the Brethren were falsely charged with supplying the savages with powder and ball. . . . The influence of Zeisberger [the Moravian leader] had been steadily employed to restrain [the Indians] from sweeping down upon the colonies . . . but their very neutrality exposed the missionaries and their converts to the hostility of both parties. . . . Although [the Moravian Indians] had re-

[1] *Op. cit.;* Vol. II. p. 146.

peatedly shown their consistent adherence to non-combatant principles, they were mistakenly identified with the perpetrators of the raids and massacres that had horrified the border settlements during the winter.''[1]

Under the exasperation, suspicion, and thirst for vengeance engendered by all these conditions, a party of frontier militia visited the peace Indians at Gnadenhütten, on the Tuscarawas, and accepted the hospitality of their unsuspecting hosts; and the next morning ''ninety Christians and six heathen visitors, offering no resistance whatever, were butchered in cold blood in two buildings wantonly named 'slaughter-houses.' '' Such is Taylor's account. Roosevelt narrates how the Christian Indians, ''usually very timid, merely requested a short delay in which to prepare themselves for death. They asked one another's pardon for whatever wrongs they might have done, knelt down and prayed, kissed one another farewell, 'and began to sing hymns of hope and praise to the Most High.' Then the white butchers entered the houses and put to death the ninety-six men, women and children within their walls.''[2]

The preceding examples would seem to indicate that passive resistance is always a failure in cases of this type, but such a conclusion is precluded by the following account of the experience of the Moravians and Friends in Ireland, as well as by that of the latter in Pennsylvania:

In the year 1788 Ireland was devastated by a widespread war between the party of the United Irishmen, largely but not wholly Roman Catholic, and the Orangemen, or Constitutional party, composed of Protestants. The conditions were therefore most distressing, since nothing can be worse than a war in which neighbor

[1] *Op. cit.;* pp. 479–481.
[2] *Op. cit.;* p. 156.

is set against neighbor, especially where the intense passions of religious bigotry, and social animosity caused by class oppressions, are turned loose to run riot without even the discipline of well-ordered armies. Buildings everywhere were burned, property plundered, and scores of people of all ages were cruelly murdered. In the midst of all this carnival of ignorance and brutal passion, the Moravian mission at Gracehill, in the North of Ireland, was preserved in impartial neutrality, and yet unquestioned loyalty, and suffered no loss except the appropriation of the stock of green ribbons from the shop, with meat and drink for the foraging party. After the battle of Toome Bridge, Gracehill became the general asylum, and, as the fugitives came flying through the streets, "some . . . threw their purses and money into the houses, and made sure of their being restored by the unknown inhabitants. Such was the confidence of all, in these honest Christian people."[1]

During this same rebellion, the Quakers were widely scattered, sometimes in remote neighborhoods, in both the North and South of Ireland. The account of their experiences, based directly on the reports of participants, has been given by Dr. Hancock in his work, "The Principles of Peace Exemplified," which has already been quoted. This little volume is probably the most remarkable book ever written on the subject of peace, and its authenticity cannot be questioned. Its tone is notably temperate and cautious, with that extreme carefulness of statement which has always characterized the typical Friend. The plan of treatment here pursued will be to sum up, under separate headings, the incidents that seem to the present writer to throw light upon the actual workings

[1] From the letter of the Moravian secretary (1828) quoted by Hancock in "Principles of Peace Exemplified"; p. 76.

of passive resistance under this severely trying test. The principles of success in this case, considered solely from the point of view of social psychology, seem to have been: (1) inflexible neutrality; (2) unfailing benevolence; (3) complete sincerity and confidence in God; (4) the reputation and badges of the sect. As consequences of these principles we shall notice: (1) the hardships and reproaches endured; and (2) the remarkable preservation and influence of the Friends.

(1) INFLEXIBLE NEUTRALITY

The approaching storm being discernible from afar, the Friends began as early as 1795, three years before, and upon recommendation of their meetings, to destroy all fowling-pieces and other weapons, "to prevent their being made use of to the destruction of our fellow-creatures,—and more fully and clearly to support our peaceable and Christian testimony in these perilous times." The members as a whole complied willingly, and one Quaker, a member of the committee appointed to oversee this disarmament program, "took a fowling-piece which he had, and broke it in pieces in the street opposite his house; an example of fidelity to his principles, and a spectacle of wonder to his neighbors." This action of the society became widely known, and later, in the search for arms by both parties, their houses were not disturbed.

(2) UNFAILING BENEVOLENCE

So undiscriminating was the hospitality of the Friends that on various occasions their houses were crowded to the limit with a motley throng, including officers' wives, wounded soldiers, fugitive neighbors, and whatever human flotsam and jetsam the waves of civil war brought to their doors. Being threatened with reprisals for sheltering some Protestant women, one Friend replied that as long as he had a house he "would keep it open to succor the distressed; and, if they burned it for that reason, he must only *turn out* along with them, and share in their affliction." The constant endeavor of the Quakers was, as Hancock words it in describing a Friend at Ballitore, "to steer a course of humanity and benevolence, which qualified him to interpose his good offices, with effect, on several occasions, for the preservation of those, of both parties, who were in imminent danger from their enemies."

(3) SINCERITY, AND CONFIDENCE IN GOD

The Friends, even in the most embarrassing and perilous circumstances refused, virtually without exception, to compromise their principles. Thus one refused to sell ropes and linen to the militia for purposes of torturing and killing the rebels, while Friends in general refused to accept gifts tendered by the rebels when they were known to be the spoils of war and plundering. In a town where the officer in charge had ordered the inhabitants to place lights in their windows to illuminate the streets, in case of a night attack on the town, with the threat of "severe and instantaneous punishment" for failure, another Friend, more scrupulous than his fellow-members, went to the officer and said that, "as I could not fight myself, I was not easy to hold a candle for another to do it for me." As a result all the Friends were exempted from the order. Another Friend, captured by the rebel army, stood uncovered while the army knelt in the service of mass. Others refused to take the less conspicuous and hence safer back way to meeting. All over Ireland they scarcely, if ever, failed to hold a meeting even when threatened with destruction, although they sometimes had to remove the dead bodies of non-Quakers from the road in order to pass. Under such circumstances Quaker women went unattended, yet unmolested, for miles, through a country in flames.

(4) THE REPUTATION AND BADGES OF THE SECT

Numerous instances occurred which make it perfectly clear that the absolute confidence of the people, on both sides, in the integrity and peaceable neutrality of the Quakers, was a principal source of their protection. But, as this will more amply appear in the next section, it may be omitted here. We simply note in this place the testimony of one Friend, who remarked afterward that "the more he attended to what he conceived to be right in his own conduct, the more he seemed to be respected by the contestants."

The term "badges of the sect" refers to the garb peculiar to the Friends, as well as their mode of speech, or any other distinctive traits. Its recognized importance is illustrated in the case of a fleeing Roman Catholic priest, who begged for a Friend's coat as a means of protection, but was soon convinced that it could not conceal the lack of genuine Quakerly qualities. The plain Quaker garb proved also a strong armour during the Pennsylvania Indian troubles, and it is of significance to note that the Shawnee Indians, in later times, addressed a letter to North Carolina yearly meeting, in which they deplored the departure of Friends from their ancient garb and manners, says the report upon the incident, adding that "in former days, they knew us from the people of the world, by the simplicity of our appearance, which, in times of war, had been a preservation to us."[1]

The Irish Quakers, however, did not enjoy complete social approval, and in consequence of the above-described *neutral* policy the Friends suffered some sharp criticism from their fellow-citizens and neighbors. In one case the rebels proposed to let some of them stop bullets in the front rank if they would not fight, complaining that it was unfair for the Quakers to allow their neighbors to risk their goods and lives, unaided, for the common liberties. In another instance the commander of the government troops allowed a Friend's house to be plundered, along with those of other people, remarking, "He is a Quaker, and will not fight, therefore the men must be allowed to take his goods."

But instances of this kind were rare; and throughout Ireland the Quakers suffered very little from plundering, and only one young man, who insisted on arming himself, was killed. Yet at the same time their own Protestant neighbors were ravaged and slain by the score. In the horrible massacre of the "Scullabogue Barn" a whole company of Protestants was shut up within the building and all were burned alive.

On the other hand, the Quakers in numerous instances acted as protectors of both sides in turn, and also as mediators. In some cases a certificate from a Friend was sufficient to save the lives of prisoners. In other instances the officers set guards over the property of Friends; a soldier pronounced a eulogium on the Quakers; and on two occasions favorable official action was determined by the belief that "Quakers will not lie." As a result of this confidence the Friends were dismissed, after trial, while others tried with them were sent to execution.

1 Weeks, "Southern Quakers and Slavery"; p. 131.

While the insurgents were in control, the homes of Quakers were invaded, and their lives narrowly imperiled, but they themselves invariably were spared. Guns were leveled and even snapped at some; a rope was placed about the neck of another; threats and plots were made, only to die from lack of momentum. On several occasions a word, such as "Desist from murder!" or "Thou canst not touch a hair of my husband's head, unless Divine Providence permit thee," was sufficient to cause the uplifted sword to fall to the ground and the would-be assassin to withdraw in discomfiture.

The indicated conclusion is that probably the most striking success has been won by moral resistance in the cases of this third type, where the *sect* as such, instead of more or less undifferentiated individuals, is maintaining a testimony against the use of violence. That sphere of freedom for the legal exercise of its peculiar views, previously obtained by the patient might of endurance under persecution, as in the case of the early Christians,[1] comes to be reinforced by a powerful public opinion, which the good repute of the sect has engendered, as in the case of the Friends in Ireland. This reputation for industry, sincerity, neighborly kindness, and unswerving good will toward all men is distinctly the product of a process which possesses significance for social psychology. The economic connections of both the sect and its members come to bind the latter to their neighbors in mutual understanding and cordiality. The sectarian thus finds an opportunity to impress the public with a sense of his solid worth as a

[1] For example, the edict of the Roman Emperor Galerius, issued in 311 A. D., frankly confesses that, since many of the Christians "have continued to persist in their opinions" despite persecution and death, it is deemed advisable for the state to let them enjoy legally that which they seem determined to have. See Robinson, "Readings in European History"; p. 12.

citizen. We have seen in earlier chapters how the modern peace sects were everywhere acknowledged, by those who had daily dealings with them, as most estimable neighbors and subjects. The names Dunker, Shaker, Friend, etc., have come to stand for distinct virtues, both individual and social. Moreover, their peculiarities attract attention, and their willingness to suffer becomes itself a token of power. All this stimulates the popular imagination, which finds convenient crystallization points in the quaint dress, distinctive speech, and customs of the sect. About these oddities there comes to cluster a set of associations, some true, some erroneous, partly unfavorable, but mostly friendly. These are the badges of the sect. They have a more or less definite spiritual and social content, and the individual member of the sect is promptly fitted wherever he goes into this psychological pigeon hole. Whatever fund of good will has been accumulated by the sect as a whole in the public mind is placed to his credit, and he draws upon it, to his advantage as well as his detriment.[1]

The tendency of all the peace sects at the present time is to do away with their badges and peculiarities and to emphasize their essential resemblance to other Christians. At the same time their peace doctrine is being taken up by other churches. As a result they may lose, along with their distinctiveness, some of the psychological basis of their success, but this may be offset by a corresponding increase in the voting power and social influence which the united force of all the Christian churches is able to muster.

[1] This social significance of the good repute and badges of the sect has assumed such proportions in the case of the Friends that a determined but futile effort has been made by them in the United States to prevent by law the extended and constantly increasing use of the Quaker name and costume as a trade-mark upon commercial products.

Generalizing from the instances presented under this third class, we conclude that

Success in such cases depends upon the reputation of the sect for benevolence, square dealing, and peaceable intentions, combined with neutrality in the existing struggle.

IV

The fourth typical case of passive resistance is that where a passive resistant political group is threatened by foreign aggression.

The following extract[1] indicates in part the principle which was once erroneously supposed to be in operation in cases of this class. The argument of those peace advocates who adhered to this fallacy was usually illustrated by the experience of *individuals,* as in the following passages, and applied to *political groups* by an easy but specious analogy. Thus we read: "Professed and consistent peace advocates and non-combatants have always been respected and left unmolested, except by a few desperadoes, who became outlawed thereby. . . . So in the case of duelling in its worst prevailing days; the man who possessed the high rational principle and true moral courage to refuse and denounce it, was not molested; that man would sink into infamy who dared to challenge him. The most violent fire-eaters dared not challenge J. Q. Adams, though in argument he lashed them severely."

The traveler Raymond declares, in his "Travels in the Pyrenees,"[2] that he had many a time put this principle of disarmament to a successful test. Speaking of the assassins and smugglers who infested the mountains, to

[1] From Daniel S. Curtis, in an address before the Arbitration Anti-War League, published in "The National Review" (newspaper); Saturday, August 9, 1881.

[2] Quoted by Hancock in "Principles of Peace Exemplified"; p. 94. Also by Ballou, *op. cit.;* p. 140.

the terror of travelers, he says: "Their first movement is a never-failing shot, and certainly would be an object of dread to most travelers. . . . As for myself, *alone* and *unarmed,* I have met them without anxiety, and accompanied them without fear. . . . Armed, I should have been the enemy of both; unarmed, they have alike respected me. In such expectation, I have long since laid aside all menacing apparatus whatever."

These incidents illustrate in individual instances the proposition that armament may tend to provoke, as well as serve to allay, attack. But the essential question is whether the dealings of political or national groups will follow the same laws. This we shall have occasion to question later, in part, but let us notice first some further evidence in *favor* of disarmament, in cases more directly illustrative of *group* hostilities. Says the author of "The Safety of Pacific Principles": "Even savages feel the charm of this principle. About the year 1812, Indiana was the scene of Indian hostilities, but the Shakers, though without forts or arms, lived in perfect safety while the work of blood and fire was going on all around them. 'Why,' said the whites afterward to one of the Indian chiefs, 'why did you not attack the Shakers as well as others?' 'What!' exclaimed the savage, 'we warriors attack a peaceable people! We fight those who won't fight us! Never; it would be a disgrace to hurt *such* a people.'" Furthermore, regarding the Indian troubles in the later history of Pennsylvania, it is related by the Quaker minister and traveler, Thomas Chalkley,[1] that among the hundreds slain he heard of only three Friends who were killed. Of these, two were men who, contrary to the Quaker custom, went to their work with weapons, and the third was a woman who had sought refuge in a fort. An exactly

1 Quoted by Hancock, *op. cit.;* p. 86.

similar fate met the only Friend who took to arms during the Irish rebellion.

A persistent but unauthenticated anecdote has been often quoted to show the efficacy of disarmament. It is that of a Tyrolese village of Christian non-resistants who were informed by courier that troops were coming to take the town. "They quietly answered, 'If they *will* take it, they must.' Soldiers soon came, riding in with colors flying, and fifes piping their shrill defiance. They looked around for an enemy, and saw the farmer at his plow, the blacksmith at his anvil, and the women at their churns and spinning-wheels. Babies crowed to hear the music and boys ran out to see the pretty trainers, with feathers and bright buttons, 'the harlequins of the nineteenth century.' Of course none of these were in a proper position to be shot at. 'Where are your soldiers?' they asked. 'We have none,' was the brief reply. 'But we have come to take the town.' 'Well, friends, it lies before you.' 'But is there nobody here to fight?' 'No, we are all Christians.' Here was an emergency altogether unprovided for by the military schools. This was a sort of resistance which no bullet could hit; a fortress perfectly bomb-proof. The commander was perplexed. 'If there is nobody to fight with, of course we can't fight,' said he. 'It is impossible to take such a town as this.' So he ordered the horse's heads to be turned about, and they carried the human animals out of the village, as guiltless as they entered, and perchance somewhat wiser."[1]

This rather fantastic account may have no foundation in

[1] "Safety of Pacific Principles," *loc. cit.;* p. 352. Quoted also by Ballou, *op. cit.*, p. 156, where it is credited to Lydia Maria Child, in her letters to the "Boston Courier" in the first half of the nineteenth century. It is quoted here as an example of a style of argument often used by peace and disarmament advocates, especially a generation ago.

fact, but it nevertheless expresses a conviction which was uttered ages ago by Lao Tse in the saying, "It is because he is free from striving that no one can strive with him," and which refuses to die because it expresses a certain measure of truth. Nevertheless illustrations of this kind fail to carry entire conviction when used to support national disarmament, because they do not seem to tally completely with the known facts and laws of *group* life. Therefore, for the elucidation of this, our fourth typical case, we must assign little weight to such arguments and seek an example where political units, rather than individuals, actually confronted one another in hostile attitude, and observe there the workings of passive resistance, if such an instance can be found.

Only one solitary experiment in government without arms is presented by history, but this is as impressive as it is unique. William Penn stands out as a mountain-peak character even among those towering men who have made the history of political pioneering, whether along the line of theory or of experimentation. The more one studies his ideals and efforts, the more majestic appears the elevation of his simple yet richly endowed and forceful nature. His remarkable "Plan for the Peace of Europe" explicitly outlined the present League of Nations.[1] At this point it is to his Holy Experiment in Free Government that we must turn for the only example of a determined and consistent effort to conduct a state without military forces to support either its internal authority or its external independence. In calm disregard of the expostulations of the English king, who marveled at the Quaker proprietor's resolve to plunge into the American wilderness without soldiers or muskets as a protection against the fierce native inhabitants, Penn departed with the ex-

[1] Published as No. 75 of the "Old South Leaflets." Boston.

press intention of founding the colony on simple truth, fair dealing, and good will.

In a former chapter we have already traced some of the difficulties of this Quaker attempt at government. In the main, Penn and his followers were thorough and consistent in carrying out their purpose. The generous response of the Indians to Penn's gracious overtures, the celebrated treaty under the elm at Shackamaxon, the sacredly guarded tradition of eternal friendship on both sides, the long years of amicable dealing between the two races—all these things make one of the brightest pages in American history, and form really a part of the spiritual treasures of humanity. They constitute an epic written by the white man and the red in deeds which shine with the inward light of human nature transformed by divine truth.

More closely analyzed as a political experiment it resolves itself into an internal and an external aspect, and the two phases are equally instructive. On the side of its own internal affairs and the semi-domestic relations with the Indians the experiment was an instance of that positive moral resistance which is inseparable from the Quaker movement. In this aspect it was an entire success during all the early stages, and a less complete one for a long period of seventy years, with increasing complications as it drew toward its close.

The story need not be rehearsed here. The whole world knows it well, as the one bright page in the dark history of American aggression against the aboriginal inhabitants of this continent. When war with the French and Indians at last became imminent, the Friends, as has been fully noticed in an earlier chapter, relinquished their control of the assembly. All that need be added here is a few words on the real merits of the success and failure of Quaker government in Pennsylvania. Sharpless says "the glowing words of Andrew Hamilton, when giving up his place as speaker of the Assembly in 1739, were undoubtedly true: 'It is not to the fertility of our soil or the commodiousness of our rivers that we ought chiefly to attribute the great progress this province has made within so small a compass of years . . . it is all due to the excellency of our Constitution . . . and this Constitution was framed by the wisdom of Mr. Penn.' "[1]

The Quaker peace régime was good while it lasted, and it produced no bad after-effects. The illogical attempt to connect it with the present-day corruption of Pennsylvania politics has been fully refuted.[2] President Sharpless attributes "the breakdown of Quaker policy, in 1756 . . . to the injection into the political situation of the non-Quaker management of the Proprietors. As long as exact justice prevailed peace existed, and this is the lesson of Pennsylvania."[3]

To this may be added the consideration that the policy of peace and fair dealing was hampered greatly by the ruthless aggressions of the non-Quaker and non-German inhabitants of the frontier. Having insisted on appealing to the sword, they came inevitably to perish by the sword, and then it was that the Friendly régime was loudly proclaimed a failure. It was a success in all its constructive work; it proved, to be sure, a failure when it came to rescuing by violence the men of violence from the evil fruits of their own aggressions. The massacre of the Moravian Indians indicates the temper of these frontiersmen.

[1] "A History of Quaker Government in Pennsylvania," by Isaac Sharpless; Vol. I, pp. 55–56.

[2] See "Ills of Pennsylvania," by "A Pennsylvanian" in the "Atlantic Monthly," Vol. LXXXVIII (October, 1901), and the reply of "A Pennsylvania Quaker," "The Causes of Pennsylvania's Ills," *ibid.*, Vol. LXXXIX (January, 1902).

[3] "History of Quaker Government in Pennsylvania"; Vol. I, p. 247.

The celebrated raid of the "Paxton Boys" presents another gruesome case, where the last surviving remnants of the Conestoga tribe were wiped out in cold blood. These are extreme examples, to be sure, but they imply a large and steady current of hostility and thirst for violent aggression which undoubtedly hampered the Quaker program all the way along. William Penn's policy, so far from being a failure in its domestic aspect, might, if pursued throughout our national history, have solved the Indian problem from the start.

In attempting now a final conclusion under this fourth typical case, that of hostile relation between political groups, we have the following:

In cases where a non-resisting political group is threatened by foreign foes, its success or failure will hinge upon the mitigating influence of a non-provocative attitude in the one attacked and the strength of its non-resisting appeal to the sense of fair play in the aggressor. But inasmuch as the doings of social groups are unusually low in moral tone, actuated only by instinctive impulses, and ruthless in carrying out the group purpose, the probability of success is very slight, and actual examples almost entirely lacking.

It is therefore evident that this last case of non-resistance, considered as the policy of political groups, involves problems of *group psychology* and various economic and political principles which would require a separate chapter for even a cursory discussion. At this point, then, the ancient question of non-resistance, which, before the dawn of modern nationalistic predation and its systematic militarization of vast populations on the grand scale, was largely a matter of scattered individuals and sects, merges itself with that gigantic problem of international war upon whose early solution the fate of civilization depends.

V

As one reviews the evidence adduced in this chapter he is impressed with the fact that few contemporaneous or even very recent examples are instanced. Moreover, there is something unsatisfying about some of the most favorable instances, as in the notable case of the Friends in Ireland. It is hard to escape the feeling that even the most benignant *neutrality* does not constitute, in some situations, the completest social *morality*. That is to say, there seems to be a loss to moral idealism when men are prevented by their just abhorrence of the methods of violence from taking sides in any way in a struggle over great issues of truth, liberty, or justice. The thought impresses itself that there ought to be some means by which the idealism of passive resistance might become a more positive and immediately effectual force for righteousness.

As for the *modern* instances, they are not entirely lacking, and they seem to display more of that character of active championship which we have missed in earlier examples; but they will also seem, in the eyes of some beholders, to be marred by a corresponding excess of partisanship. We have in mind here such very recent measures as the proposed international refusal of metal-working trades to produce munitions of war; the Chinese boycott of Japanese goods; and the non-coöperation movement led by Gandhi in India. These matters will be more fully discussed in following chapters, so it will be sufficient here to point out merely that they are new and modern expressions of the principle of passive resistance—so very modern that their success or failure cannot yet be estimated.

There remains then one other situation that should come under this analysis. It is that which adheres to non-violence but is no longer a form of non-resistance in any sense. On the contrary it may partake of resistance to the point of *coercion,* but strictly refrains from the use of physical force.

The fifth typical case is therefore that of non-violent coercion, wherein a nation, or classes and other minor groupings within nations, attempts to bring desired social conditions to pass by exerting social pressure upon other nations, or sub-groups and individuals within their own or other nations.

The examples illustrating this type of situation are fully set forth in subsequent chapters on the strike, the boycott, and non-coöperation. As those accounts will show, such movements have considerably affected the course of industrial and political history. The essence of this method, i. e., of non-violent coercion, consists in the withholding of certain economic or social relations deemed valuable by those at whom the movement is directed, and in leaving them to choose between the action demanded and the hardship thus presented as an alternative, which is intended to figure as the worse horn of the dilemma.

Success in such cases depends first of all upon the ability of those attempting this form of coercion to control the essential social contacts by their own action or that of themselves plus their relatives and friends. For example, a boycott by laboring men involving the refusal to purchase tobacco might be effective, where a boycott against high-powered touring-cars would fail; for the reason that they and their associates form an important market for the one, and virtually none at all for the other. Success depends, in the second place, *upon their ability to stand firmly and steadfastly behind their particular program of non-dealing, and endure the unavoidable provocation and hardship involved, without resorting to violence or intimidation.*

CHAPTER XIV

GROUNDS OF CONTEMPORARY CONSCIENTIOUS OBJECTION

THE purpose of this chapter is to indicate the sources of the more recent conscientious objection, particularly that which disclaims any religious motive; while the following one will seek to show the bearing of these newer tendencies upon certain current problems.

This phase of our inquiry was suggested by the fact that alongside the religious sectarian objectors in the army camps there appeared in considerable numbers men whose antecedents were by no means so easy to recognize, but whose opposition to participation in war-like acts was no less clear and unyielding. In fact they seemed to bear the hardest brunt of the situation, although provided for in the law, because they lacked the prestige of a well-known historic sect behind them, and their refusal to serve seemed in consequence to be more clearly a case of personal egotism and stubbornness setting itself up presumptuously against the general judgment and will of the nation. In reflecting upon the underlying cause or grounds for their abhorrence of war it seemed probable that there are at least three sources from which, in the absence of a religious tradition transmitted to them through the agency of the sect, they might have derived their inspiration. First among these we may mention the influence of Count Tolstoy and other great personalities of pacifistic and anarchistic bent. In the second place there is the philosophy of international socialism and proletarian solidarity; and thirdly we have certain pacifying conditions and influences characteristic of modern industrial life apart from any philosophy of reform connected with it. That is to say, men working by modern industrial processes with the materials and forces of inanimate nature, in a large-scale, impersonal way, tend to experience a decline or softening of the predacious, fighting, killing propensities. Moreover, the fact that they no longer live by hunting, much less by forays and plunder, and do not in most cases slaughter their own meat animals or even kill their own table fowls—all this may operate to increase that profound abhorrence of the brutalities of war which is undoubtedly growing in the modern world.

With this threefold explanation in mind as a working hypothesis, the writer addressed an inquiry to a dozen or more of the conscientious objectors who had attained greatest prominence during and since the recent war. The list included a few religious leaders, but was principally composed of men whose objection had been made upon avowedly non-religious grounds. If the list seems short it must be remembered that the number of such objectors as a whole was small. A leading religious objector, one of the best authorities in this country on the subject, remarks, "The type of objector whom you wish to reach was not as common as you might think";[1] while another, himself the most outstanding of the non-religious objectors, is even more emphatic, as follows: "I want to emphasize the fact that there were only a handful of objectors in the U. S. who counted in making the issue,—about 500 out of the three and a half million men drafted. The others (3,500) all accepted some form of service under the Administration's elimination policy, and therefore raised no issue. Only a few of those 500 came to public attention

[1] Dr. Norman Thomas, in personal letter to the author.

as individuals, and the group as a whole did so chiefly as victims of brutality in the prisons and camps. These 500 counted out of all proportion to their number because of the savage attacks on them in the press and by so-called patriotic organizations. These attacks aroused widespread comment, and enlisted a body of support for the issue, which included practically all the labor and liberal movements of the country.''[1]

These authoritative statements support the opinion that the relatively limited number of witnesses whom we are able to bring forward on this phase of the subject is nevertheless a highly representative one, and adequate for the purpose in view. That purpose was to detect the underlying grounds and present drift of this most modern of all phases of passive resistance. The method pursued was to submit to the persons selected a request for their assistance in a quest for ''the historical and personal origins of modern, non-sectarian, conscientious objection,'' and the correspondent was asked, with reference to the professedly non-religious objection, ''to what source should it be traced? to Tolstoy and other great personalities? to the philosophy of internationalism? simply to the conditions attending on modern industrial life? or to some other source?'' Other questions, dealing with the present tendencies of conscientious objectors along the line of social radicalism, were also included, but their treatment will be reserved for the next chapter.

Taking up first the question of origins, the outstanding fact is the heterogeneous character of the non-religious objectors. They seem to be as varied as the sectarian objectors are homogeneous and stereotyped. One correspondent says ''the motives back of passive resistance are many

[1] Roger N. Baldwin, in a memorandum prepared for the writer, April, 1921.

and complex when it comes to analyzing them in individuals. . . . The 'non-religious' objectors to war can be traced in part at least to all of the sources you mention.'' And this statement in corroborated in one way or another by all the testimony. It seems, moreover, quite clear that the non-religious objectors formed no cult of personal followers traveling in the wake of some towering pacifistic thinker like Tolstoy. It is true, as the correspondent above quoted says, that every idealistic ''absolutist'' was ''influenced in some way or another by Tolstoy.'' But he adds that Kropotkin also had his followers, among the objectors of more anarchistic type.

Professor Gilbert Murray probably states the actual situation for the United States as well as for England when he says: ''Tolstoy's doctrines were so extreme that actual Tolstoyans were rare; but almost every young man and woman in Europe who possessed any free religious life at all had been to some extent influenced by Tolstoy.''[1]

But it is also true, as another correspondent points out, that, while many of the ''C. O.'s'' respected Tolstoy, he was ''seldom the determining cause for their stand.''[2] The larger truth, upon which all these divergent statements rest, is that partly formulated by still another of the correspondents, namely, that when the objectors of certain type were once convinced of the unfairness of the modern industrial system, and its working partnership with militaristic aggression, they ''turned to Tolstoy, Kropotkin and others for the way out,'' or in other words for an interpretation and a remedy for the situation. Among those quoted by objectors of this type, in addition to Tolstoy and Kropotkin, were Thoreau, Jefferson, Lincoln, and Romain Rolland. But they, confessedly, turned to these

[1] In his Introduction to Mrs. Hobhouse's "I Appeal Unto Cæsar."
[2] Letters of Mr. Evan W. Thomas and Mr. Carl Haessler.

thinkers somewhat as to a referee, and "very few of the objectors rested their philosophy on personal allegiance to some great moral character."[1] The only personality primarily and directly responsible for conscientious objection is Jesus of Nazareth himself, and, since that was in the case of the religious, sectarian objectors, it falls outside the scope of this chapter.

The query concerning the influence of the philosophy of internationalism brought forth divergent answers, but they may be harmonized in the statement that while this was a factor in the situation it was effectively formulated only by the socialist objectors. In other words, while it is probably true, as one correspondent avers, that "the philosophy of internationalism in one form or another influenced every objector," as shown by the fact that they were often observed to be "internationalists, in feeling as well as intellectually, to a far greater extent than is the average man," it is equally true, as another maintains, that the philosophy of internationalism "played almost no part in determining objection, except as reflected in the international solidarity of the socialist movement, a purely class concept."[2] These assertions simply emphasize two different aspects of the case, making between them a complete picture. That is that most conscientious objectors are imbued with a humanitarian spirit that gives them an international outlook, which, however, they do not explicitly avow as a definite program unless they have been trained in socialistic ways of thinking and speaking. Hence it is seldom professed except by members of the last-named movement. This definite, articulate socialistic internationalism is strictly class-conscious and anti-capitalistic, while the vaguer internationalism is much more conscious of

1 Roger N. Baldwin, *ibid.*
2 Roger N. Baldwin, *ibid.*

human brotherhood than it is of proletarian solidarity.

While the divergence of view among conscientious objectors of non-sectarian antecedents is very great, there seem to stand out three quite distinct types which we shall designate as the Socialist, the Individualist, and the Humanitarian objector, respectively. The truth or falsity of this classification will appear as we proceed next to sketch the characteristics of each.

THE SOCIALIST OBJECTOR

The most marked trait of the socialist is his extreme class-consciousness, coloring as it does his every utterance on the subject of war and peace. This is very clearly shown in the valuable "Documentary History of the Attitude of the Socialist Party toward War and Militarism Since the Outbreak of the Great War," issued by the Department of Labor Research of the Rand School of Social Science.[1] In the introduction to this work, Mr. Morris Hillquit, as international secretary of the Socialist party of America, makes this significant statement: "The Socialist opposition to war is based not merely on humanitarian grounds, potent and compelling as these are, but principally on the deep-rooted conviction that modern wars are at the bottom sanguinary struggles for the commercial advantages of the possessing classes, and that they are disastrous to the cause of the workers, their struggles, and aspirations, their rights and liberties." This is exceedingly clear, but if there remained a vestige of ambiguity it is dispelled a little further on by the explicit declaration that "It is this fundamental conception which largely deter-

[1] Edited by Alexander Trachtenberg, New York, 1917. The phrases quoted constitute the subtitle, the principal title being, "The American Socialists and the War."

mines the Socialist opposition to the war and the Socialist program of peace.''[1]

While the sentence last quoted might seem to refer specifically to the war then in progress, the socialist opposition appertains ''to this and all other wars, waged upon any pretext whatsoever.''[2]

The official declaration just quoted characterizes war as ''a crude, savage and unsatisfactory method, destructive of the ideals of brotherhood and humanity to which the international Socialist movement is dedicated,'' but this represents a more broadly humanitarian statement than is usually met in socialist documents. As a rule the anti-capitalistic note predominates, as in the manifesto ''Starve the War and Feed America,'' of August, 1914, which opens with the declaration '' . . . Unscrupulous *capitalists,* using the European War as a pretext, are increasing the cost of food so that millions are threatened with starvation.''[3] Not only did the socialists perceive that capitalism was fattening off the situation created by the war, but they definitely and repeatedly charge it with responsibility for the tragedy itself. In its first proclamation of the war the Socialist party of the United States expressed its ''condemnation'' of ''the ruling classes of Europe.'' In September the national executive committee, in its call for an International Socialist Congress, pointed out that ''Whatsoever rewards and advantages will come from the War will go to the ruling classes; all the sacrifices, sufferings and sorrows it will entail will fall to the lot of the workers''; and it is explained that the catastrophe occurred because ''Capitalist militarism proved stronger than the young spirit of Socialist brotherhood.''

[1] *Ibid.;* pp. 3 and 5.

[2] "Proclamation of the National Committee on Immediate Action," published August 12, 1914; *ibid.;* p. 8.

[3] *Ibid.;* p. 9. Italics mine.

In the "majority report" presented at the St. Louis convention of the Socialist party, in April, 1917, it was explicitly declared that the European conflict was "the logical outcome of the competitive capitalist system," and that the immeasurable sacrifices entailed by the gigantic conflict "have not been sacrifices exacted in a struggle for principles or ideals, but wanton offerings upon the altar of private profit."[1]

It would be easy to multiply examples in support of the assertion that in socialism we behold a movement against war and militarism which constantly analyzes and views the whole problem from the point of view of class-consciousness and the class struggle, stating its denunciations always in terms of capitalism and its idealism always in the name of the laboring class. Thus in the platform of the Socialist party in the Presidential campaign of 1916 the problem of peace is set forth as the task of disarming the capitalistic class, as it were; that is, of depriving them of the means and power to continue to embroil the world in such calamitous struggles. More explicitly, the party "urges upon the workers in the mines and forests, on the railways and ships, in factories and fields the use of their economic and industrial power, by refusing to mine the coal, to transport soldiers, to furnish food or other supplies for military purposes, and thus keep out of the hands of the ruling class the control of armed forces and economic power, necessary for aggression abroad and industrial despotism at home." Not only is it clear to the socialist that war is the work of the *capitalist* class; it is equally clear that it is *labor* that must build the foundations of world peace. This conviction is clearly expressed in the manifesto of May, 1915, wherein

[1] *Ibid.;* pp. 9, 12, 41.

it is proclaimed that "the supreme duty of the hour is for us, the Socialists of all the world . . . to summon all labor forces of the world for an aggressive, an uncompromising opposition to the whole capitalist system, and to every form of its most deadly fruits—militarism and war—to strengthen the bonds of working-class solidarity, to deepen the currents of conscious internationalism, and to proclaim to the world a constructive program leading towards permanent peace."[1]

The more universal note which appears in the last sentence is not without parallel elsewhere in socialist official literature, predominantly class-conscious though it is. Thus in the "Call for the Revival of the International," already quoted, a profoundly human note is struck in these words: "Upon the blackened ruins of this greatest of human tragedies must be laid the foundations of the greatest of human ideals, the federation of the world." Again, in the majority report of the St. Louis convention, while the appeal is addressed not to all *men*, but to "all the workers," to end wars by establishing socialized industry and industrial democracy the world over, the goal is nobly described as "a new society in which peace, fraternity, and human brotherhood will be the dominant ideals."[2]

After his extreme class-consciousness, the most striking thing about the socialistic objector is the fact that at bottom he is not conscientiously opposed to violence or to war in and of itself, but specifically to international wars as waged by and for the capitalist class. The socialists are not really pacifists, if that word means abhorrence of physical force by military methods without regard to the

[1] *Ibid.;* pp. 28, 17.
[2] *Ibid.;* p. 43.

object in view. A typical socialist "C. O." writes: "I never was a pacifist and frequently told my investigators that I would gladly fight in a class-war revolution or for the present government of Russia, but not for the present [that is the then, Wilson] government of the United States."[1] In this position he is entirely supported by the official declarations of his party, as in its proclamation on the Mexican crisis of March, 1916, wherein the workers were urged to "serve notice on them that if you must fight you will fight your real enemy and not the workers of this or any other land"; or in the majority report at St. Louis, in which it is said that "the only struggle which would justify the workers in taking up arms is the great struggle of the working class of the world to free itself from economic exploitation and political oppression. . . ."

The two attitudes thus far set forth constitute the most essential facts about the socialist objectors, but along with these traits we must notice a third, namely, their bold stand against the governmental war policy, in which they clearly exceeded all other bodies of objectors. That anxious solicitude to leave no room for a suspicion of disloyalty, which we have noted in the various peace sects during the war period, is entirely absent from the policy pursued by the socialists. Less concerned in this respect, they constituted the most active and numerous protesting group in the world, despite the fact that they were temporarily disrupted and alined more or less vigorously with the various governments at war. Moreover, the socialist objectors, and the party as a whole, constituted, in sharp contrast to many of the traditionally minded and clannish sectarians, a positive force for constructive social idealism, no matter how narrowly class-conscious or economically unorthodox it might be shown to be.

[1] Personal correspondence of the present writer.

THE INDIVIDUALIST OBJECTOR

A type of objector less numerous than the preceding, but hardly less clearly defined, is the one who directs his protest against *conscription* in and of itself, without regard to the right or wrong of war in general or of the particular war in question. In this case we seem to have an outstanding social rebel of peculiarly exasperating quality in the eyes of many who fail to perceive that, so far as America is concerned, such a one has simply maintained unshaken the attitude of abhorrence formerly held by themselves, and by well-nigh the entire nation. In thus standing steadfastly (stubbornly, if preferred) upon the abandoned ground of the ancient national tradition, the individualist objector kept alive one of the greatest issues of the war—in fact one of the most far-reaching and momentous problems of the modern world, inasmuch as it is this newly asserted power of governments to force every last resource of nations into the business of destruction that has made of modern war incomparably the greatest menace to human freedom and progress in the history of mankind.

It is not infrequently asserted that objectors of every type were unanimously opposed to conscription. If this is true it is so only in an incidental way, because of the fact that it was the actual operation of the selective draft that provided the occasion for their conflict with the government, and not because they held, in most cases, such a fundamental philosophical opposition as we find in the individualistic type now under consideration. It is indeed possible that, as a leading authority observes,[1] "conscientious objection by radicals was based rather on an objection

[1] Dr. Norman Thomas, in a letter of February 8, 1921.

to conscription than to killing," but some *religious* objectors would probably have no objection to conscription for non-warlike purposes such as the operation of railroads dur ing a strike; and, so far as *socialist* radicals are concerned, we have seen that their opposition is directed primarily against the aggressions of the capitalist class, both actual and alleged, and they would probably acquiesce in conscription by a proletarian state. A socialist objector's remark is illuminating on this point: "Not the method but the present purposes of the sovereign state were principally repudiated."[1]

Mr. Reginald Clifford Allen, a prominent English objector, expresses the quite divergent point of view of the *individualist* objector most clearly in his defense before his third court martial. After stating his belief, as a socialist, that warfare is socially and morally wrong, and that peace could be had at once by negotiation if desired, he goes on to say:

> Such being my attitude to all war, and to this war, I can, of course, in no way acquiesce in conscription, which is designed to equip the nation for war. I have an additional reason for this. I shall continue in prison to refuse every offer of release which demands from me *any sort of acceptance of conditions which originate in conscription, even though they may be of a civil character.* I resist war because I love liberty. Conscription is a denial of liberty. . . . This country is faced with the most insidious danger that can confront a free people in the claim of the State to dispose of a man's life against his will, and what is worse, against his moral convictions, and of his service without his consent. A war which you can win only by the compulsion of unwilling men and the persecution of those who are genuine will ultimately achieve the ruin of the very ideals for which you are fighting.[1]

1 Mr. Carl Haessler, in letter to the present writer.
2 Hobhouse, *op. cit.;* pp. 29-30. Italics mine.

The most typical example of the individualist objection produced by the war, either in England or America, was that of Mr. Roger N. Baldwin. This case was rightly deemed so important that it was presented to the public by twenty-seven liberal American publicists, of both sexes, with the statement of their conviction that to do so "would be a genuine public service." This was apart from any indorsement on the whole of Mr. Baldwin's philosophy, but because his clear statement of his reasons for deliberately refusing, with no attempt to escape the consequences, to obey the Selective Service Law, taken in conjunction with Judge Mayer's "logical and uncompromising statement of the opposite position in imposing sentence," constituted a most notable conflict of ideas "above the plane of personal anger or bitterness."[1]

Mr. Baldwin, highly educated, and a social worker of wide experience and recognition, resigned his position as secretary of the Civic League in St. Louis and came to New York when America entered the war, in order to give all his time, without other compensation than his expenses, to work for the preservation of civil liberties as director of the National Civil Liberties Bureau. This is important for our present purpose, which is to show that the essence of this type of conscientious objection lies in its resistance to the encroachments of the state upon the sphere of civil rights and personal ideals. Mr. Baldwin's statement is unmistakable touching this issue: "The compelling motive," he declares, "for refusing to comply with the draft act is my uncompromising opposition to the principle of conscription of life by the State for any purpose whatever, in time of war or peace. I not only refuse to obey the present conscription law, but I would in future refuse to obey any

[1] "The Individual and the State: the Problem as Presented by the Sentencing of Roger N. Baldwin," New York, November, 1918.

similar statute which attempts to direct my choice of service and ideals. I regard the principle of conscription of life as a flat contradiction of all our cherished ideals of individual freedom, democratic liberty and Christian teaching."

In this case, as in all others, we do not find any single argument standing absolutely alone, but the various objections inevitably reinforce one another, the basis of classification used in this chapter being that of the principal emphasis stressed. Thus in the present instance the speaker adds that he is "the more opposed to the present act, because it is for the purpose of conducting war," and does "not believe in the use of physical force as a method of achieving any end, however good"; although he "would, under extreme emergencies, as a matter of protecting the life of any person, use physical force." It was thus made plain that in this instance we are not dealing with an absolute non-resistant. Nor, on the other hand, is it a case of class-conscious socialist objection, the defendant not being a member of any radical organization, although professing to "share the extreme radical philosophy of the future society." On this phase also the central note struck is the individualistic idealism which we have taken as the distinguishing mark of this class of objectors, as shown in the following words: "I look forward to a social order without any external restraints upon the individual, save through public opinion and the opinion of friends and neighbors."[1]

THE HUMANITARIAN OBJECTOR

There remains to notice one other group of the non-religious conscientious objectors, which we have chosen to

[1] *Ibid.*

call the *humanitarian* type. Perhaps at bottom this point of view is inseparable from religion rightly defined, but its advocates make no religious profession; and they are not in any way identified with the sectarian objectors.

Mrs. Hobhouse, in her very illuminating biographical account of English objectors, describes several cases which seem to fall under this category. For example, Mr. Walter H. Ayles, a Labor leader and parliamentary candidate, informed the court martial: "I cannot consent . . . to be involved in the administration of the military system in any way. For many years my life and work have been governed by certain definite principles, based on the sanctity of human life. They have governed my political work as a Guardian of the Poor in Birmingham, as a City Councillor of Bristol, and as a member of the Socialist Movement. They have governed my attitude with regard to war, both social and international."[1] In similar vein it is recorded of Mr. G. H. Stuart Beavis, sentenced to "death by shooting," but commuted to ten years' penal servitude,[2] that "his convictions [were] the results of his early training and his intimate association with men of various nationalities. It was his intense belief in the brotherhood of men of all nations which led him to study languages and the literature of other lands, and, presumably, to engage as a volunteer teacher of languages in the Working Mens' College in the city of his residence.[3]

Mr. Beavis had lived in Germany and France before the war, which may help to account for his cosmopolitan attitude, and the case of Mr. A. Fenner Brockway is still more suggestive along this line. As shown in Mrs. Hob-

1 Hobhouse, *op. cit.;* p. 37.

2 No conscientious objectors were actually executed in England. A number were given the death sentence, but it was commuted in every case. The same is true of the United States.

3 *Ibid;* p. 24.

house's account, he was born in Calcutta, in a family of marked humanitarian temper, his father, grandfather, an uncle, and an aunt all being missionaries, and his mother an active temperance and educational worker in India. Mr. Brockway himself was formerly a settlement worker, then subeditor of the "Christian Commonwealth," and when arrested was editor of the "Labour Leader."[1] Widely traveled and well educated, he ably represents the type now under consideration, and his statement to the courtmartial indicates, as its fundamental ground, the humanitarian attitude which we find to be characteristic of this subgroup. He says: "I believe that mankind is in reality one; that the universal spirit dwells in all men and unites all men. I believe that human personality is sacred, because it is an expression of the universal spirit. War violates the spiritual amenities of the human race, degrades human personality, and destroys human life Therefore, holding the faith I do, I cannot participate in the war under any circumstances."[2]

That inadequacy of terminology which besets this subject is especially in evidence at this point, because the humanitarian and idealistic spirit characteristic of this type of objector is indistinguishable from that of the higher ethical religions. In fact, many of these men are confessedly religious, although not identified with any historic creed or institution; and it would therefore be more accurate to speak of the three subgroups of this chapter as constituting the non-*sectarian* rather than the non-*religious* objectors. But, since the latter term is the one used during the war and in the government reports,[3] its retention will probably

[1] *Ibid.;* p. 19.

[2] "Brockway's Defense," a leaflet without date or place of publication, sent to the present writer by a "C. O." correspondent.

[3] E. g., "Statement of the Secretary of War on Treatment of Conscientious Objectors," June, 1919.

lead to least confusion. It may be logically justifiable, however, to make reference here to a non-sectarian, broadly religious attitude represented by certain objectors who seem to classify most naturally under this humanitarian category. Thus, in his defense before the court martial, Mr. Erling H. Lunde, an American objector, confessed himself "out of the rut of orthodox thought" and as belonging to no established creed, yet affirms that his "actions, in refusing to become a soldier, have been prompted by deep religious and moral convictions against war, which includes militarism and conscription." That this religious attitude, "solidly grounded upon the teachings and example of Christ" though it was, rested at bottom also upon the humanitarian temperament, is suggested by the further testimony that the defendant "as a boy . . . never took any pleasure in shooting either with a rifle or a slingshot and was always taught to respect animal as well as human life." He also refrained from fighting for leadership as a boy, and was active in abolishing "hazing" in his college fraternity.[1]

On the whole the position taken by these "non-religious" objectors raises some very difficult problems. As for the formulas of the class-conscious *socialist,* they are too narrowly framed but they express a very fundamental truth which may help to lay bare the factitious character of war in the modern world, and point the way to a social renovation that will render international warfare not only unnecessary but morally impossible.

The protest of the *individualist* objector hurls a challenge, not to be ignored, against the current militaristic regimentation of national life in countries long boastful

[1] "Defense of Erling H. Lunde, Conscientious Objector to War, made before a Court Martial at Camp Funston, Kansas, October 15, 1918"; a pamphlet,—Chicago.

of their civil and political freedom; but it rests, like philosophical anarchism, upon an exaggerated conception of the nature of personality and individual rights. It fails to recognize that, so far as we can observe, not only the physical existence, but also the mental and moral life of the individual, is the direct product of the *group*, of *society;*[1] so much so that isolation usually means either imbecility or insanity, sooner or later. Consequently no such inviolable and self-subsisting individuality as the anarchistic philosophy posits can be found to exist in fact. Personality is as fully social as it is individual. Indeed, as Professor Cooley shows, the individual and the group cannot be separated except in thought, and for purposes of analysis.

On the other hand no group can afford to ride roughshod over personal convictions and ideals, especially when shared by intelligent and benevolent people, since there is always the chance that these social mutations[2] may point the way to the social progress of the future. This applies with especial force to the *humanitarian* objector. Not only may it be true, as Tolstoy suggested in the case of Van der Ver, that the spontaneous multiplication of this temperament may mark "the beginning of the end" for war,[3] but it raises the whole question of the nature and rights of conscience, which must next be very briefly noticed.

[1] For a notable statement of this truth see the chapter on "Association," by Professor E. A. Ross in "Principles of Sociology," New York, 1920. Also Cooley, "Social Organization," New York, 1915; Chap. I, II, and III.

[2] For this use of the term, see "Has Human Evolution Come to an End?" by Professor Edwin H. Conklin, "Princeton Lectures," Vol. I, No. 1, Princeton University, 1920. Also his "The Direction of Human Evolution," New York, 1921.

[3] l. See Tolstoy's essay by the title quoted.

CHAPTER XV

SIGNIFICANCE OF CONTEMPORARY CONSCIENTIOUS OBJECTION

PROFESSOR PERRY, in his vigorous little volume, "The Free Man and the Soldier," wields a trenchent pen against the objector type of conscience. After pointing out that a man who might hold conscientious convictions against paying his taxes, educating his children, or submitting to vaccination would find that the state would "penalize his action without respecting his conscience," and possibly deliver him to martyrdom if he were to incite to riot on behalf of his peculiar ideas, Professor Perry goes on to say: "No way has been found of avoiding this tragedy: it is simply the price which is paid for the benefits of social order." The citizen, he holds, "must bear his share of the burden which the national exigency imposes . . . he cannot expect to reserve liberty of action in the presence of the enemy. If his conscience is offended, so much the worse for his conscience. What he needs is a new conscience which will teach him to keep the faith with his fellow until such time as their common understanding and their controlling policy shall have been modified."[1]

Professor Perry, stressing as he does the inherently higher moral claims of the *larger*, more *inclusive*, organization of life,[2] goes so far as to assert that "a man with

[1] "The Free Man and the Soldier," by Ralph Barton Perry, New York, 1916; pp. 36, 37.

[2] See his book, "The Moral Economy," New York, 1909.

a conscience, or a sense of mastery, or a self or some other inner authority by which he justifies himself, is a menace to any neighborhood." This sweeping statement would seem to dispose not only of the conscientious objectors of to-day but many of the greatest spirits in all the history of the past, applying with peculiar fitness to Socrates, for example. It is quite true that his own little Athenian community voted him a menace, and prescribed for him the fatal cup, who has been voted by all succeeding generations a blessing to the larger life of the world. So true it is, as Professor Perry affirms, that "society finds it necessary to suppress any man who is too exclusively concerned with being himself, and has to be especially firm with those who take themselves seriously." This he holds to be true especially in its application to the recent crisis, because of his feeling that "the belief that when a man has struck an attitude, and has braved it out in the midst of a rough and vulgar world, he has somehow solved the problem and done his duty, underlies much of the pacific sentiment that is now abroad. It is a dangerous error," he is convinced, "because it makes the difficulties of life seem so much simpler than they really are, and may teach a man to be perfectly satisfied with himself when he has really only evaded the issue."

The substantial truth of this passage will be evident to all, but especially to those who, reading in no matter how receptive a frame of mind the various statements and declarations of individual objectors and of the peace sects themselves, have been impressed with a painful sense of futility which is inseparable from even the noblest of these usually fine utterances. This is most evident when such statements take the form of what Professor Perry aptly styles a "philosophy of inner rectitude," which he declares to be "self-centered and individualistic," so that "life becomes an affair between each man and his own soul, a sort of spiritual toilet before the mirror of self-consciousness."[1]

On the whole, despite the seeming overstatement already pointed out, Professor Perry's arraignment seems to leave the conscientious objector very little ground to stand upon. But the problem is not so simple as that, and any clean-cut solution for this irreducible contradiction in the moral nature of man is justly subject to question by reason of its very neatness. We must therefore notice some considerations that fall upon the other side.

Without accepting the older view that conscience is some transcendental and unerring voice of the absolute implanted in the soul, we may justifiably reject also the opposite extreme, which would accord to it no greater moral dignity than a mere intellectual opinion. The truth seems to be, as Professor Hayes well puts it:[2] "No man is born with a conscience any more than one is born with a language. But just as we are born with the predisposition to communicate and so to learn a language if one is spoken by our associates, otherwise to begin to make one, so also we are born with the predisposition to acquire from society a conscience or to begin the making of one. . . . Conscience is not a single faculty but the combined resultant of individual and social reactions that ultimately shape the mental state which the individual has toward his own conduct." Conscience, so understood, may therefore be regarded as both innate, in the sense of being antecedent to social experience, and acquired, i. e., as the product of the community experience. Upon one side it is profound enough to satisfy the most religious conceptions, and upon

[1] "The Free Man and the Soldier"; pp. 97, 98.

[2] "Introduction to the Study of Sociology," by Edward Cary Hayes, New York, 1916; p. 226.

the other it is such a transparently simple social phenomenon as to afford ground for that purely naturalistic account by which some erroneously imagine the earlier view to be entirely superseded. In short it may be regarded as natural or supernatural, according to the aspect held in view.

Professor Cooley treats the problems of *right* and *conscience* as matters of "organization," and in his chapter on "The Social Aspect of Conscience"[1] he shows that the right is the *rational,* in a very profound sense, dealing with "the whole content of life, with instincts freighted with the inarticulate conclusions of a remote past, and with the unformulated inductions of individual experience." In this view, "conscience must be regarded as of a profounder rationality" than a superficial ratiocination, in case the two should chance to conflict, which is not usually the case. "The question of right and wrong," he continues, "as it presents itself to any particular mind, is, then, a question of the completest practicable organization of the impulses with which that mind finds itself compelled to deal. . . . It is useless to look for any other or higher criterion of right than conscience. What is felt to be right *is* right; that is what the word means." Consequently, "for the individual considering his own conduct, his conscience is the only possible moral guide, and though it differ from that of everyone else, it is the only right there is for him; *to violate it is to commit moral suicide.*"[2]

[1] In "Human Nature and the Social Order," by Charles Horton Cooley, New York, 1902.

[2] *Ibid.;* p. 329-30, 333-334. Italics mine. It may be of interest to note that this exact expression was used in one objector's defense, in these words: "For me to participate in such a conflict would be nothing short of moral as well as intellectual suicide." (Jacob Wortsman to the military court, quoted in "Who Are the

So it seems clear that when the social group conscripts a man for any purpose which requires a violation of his conscience it really demands that he destroy his own moral life. Nothing could be worse, and among those who hold to the religious conception of conscience there will always be found some who prefer, if need be, physical destruction to moral suicide. Their attitude is clearly expressed in the following from the recent Conference of All Friends: "We feel that the State in giving true service may well demand a loyal response, which the individual will gladly render. There may come, however, a point beyond which the claims of the State do not carry, where the enlightened conscience cannot bow to its commands, and where the individual gives the best service to the State by refusing to obey that which violates the august authority of conscience. This does not imply disregard of the State or free us from the obligation of service to it. This obligation we gladly and freely recognize, and it is of the greatest importance that we should make our policy positive, practical and helpful, not merely obstructive and negative."[1]

Such is the nature of religious conviction that it can not be laid aside as an obsolete garment, nor even be remodeled easily to fit the prevailing fashion of the social mind. Space forbids any elaboration of this thought, but to those who have reflected on the essential nature of the religious attitude none is required, since it will be perfectly understood that religion holds none of its tenets lightly—*if it did so it would not be religion.*[2]

Conscientious Objectors?" a pamphlet published by "A Committee of 100 Friends of Conscientious Objectors," Brooklyn, 1919.)

[1] "Official Report"; Minute 14.

[2] Religion, as the word is used by the present writer, may be briefly defined as one's completest response to his largest view of life and the universe.

One might possibly find an alternative in some process of *socialization* by means of which these side eddies and backwaters of conviction and social outlook would be drawn into the larger current of the national life, but the means and methods of such an educational undertaking do not readily suggest themselves. For one thing it would be necessary to eliminate the New Testament from their lives, since most passive resistants are as prone to lean upon its precepts as are militarists to flee from them to the more comfortable shelter of the Mosaic code and the imprecatory psalms. It will be recalled in this connection that earlier pages have noted the tendency of the passive resistance view of life to appear spontaneously wherever the New Testament writings are subjected to interpretation by earnest and exegetically uncorrupted minds bent upon reproducing the spirit of the apostolic life.

But even if the education of the *religious* objector's conscience presents peculiar difficulties, that of the *non*-religious ought by theory to prove more amenable, since it is, as above defined, no more than the most rational judgment which its possessor has been able to attain on a given subject or situation. Having no reference to any supernatural and absolute sanctions, one with this type of conscience might well be taught to reflect that his judgments can hardly lay claim to infallibility, that there is always, presumably, a possibility of his being mistaken, and of his perceiving a higher rationality in the prevailing judgment of his group. Unlike the religious objector, he does not even rely upon the super-individual and collective wisdom embodied in some great tradition or organization which springs from the life of generations of men; and the more purely individualistic the objector's philosophy the more need he will find to reflect on Professor Perry's assertion that "the man who refuses to obey the law or play the game because he has been outvoted is more likely to be afflicted with peevishness or egotism than exalted by heroism."[1]

No matter how the problem of conscientious objection is handled, it involves at bottom the very foundations of *democracy*. To the trained political philosopher it seems to be no such simple matter of summary suppression as it is to the man on the street corner, with his new dogma of the infallibility of majorities. Thus so eminent an authority as Professor Laski asserts that the power of the state to crush an opponent by brute force is no evidence of right or title to success. "The only ground for state-success," he justly affirms, "is where the purpose of the state is morally superior to that of its opponent. The only ground upon which the individual can give or be asked his support for the state is from the conviction that what it is aiming at is, in each particular action, good. . . . It deserves his allegiance, it should receive it, only where it commands his conscience." Among numerous passages of utmost significance for the present problem, this brilliant master of political theory expounds that conception of the internal limitation upon the action of the state which "insists upon the greatest truth to which history bears witness that the only real security for social well-being is the free exercise of men's minds. Otherwise, assuredly, we have contracted ourselves to slavery. The only permanent safeguard of democratic government is that the unchanging and ultimate sanction of intellectual decision should be the conscience. We have here, that is to say, a realm within which the state can have no rights and where it is well that it should have none."[2]

In most discussions of the individual and the state one

[1] *Ibid.;* p. 37.

[2] "Authority in the Modern State," by Harold J. Laski, New Haven, 1919; pp. 46, 55.

meets with a succession of *absolutes.* The absolute theory of state sovereignty locks horns with the absolutist conscience, while a more or less absolute notion of democracy, i. e., as the infallible majority, attempts to mediate between the opponents and finds itself unable to work with either in the end. Apparently in despair of breaking this deadlock, Professor Laski concludes that "a democratic society must reject the sovereign state as by definition inconsistent with democracy," and points out that a pluralistic state in which the rights of the minority and the judgments of conscience will be respected is not only the ideal for the future but to a growing extent the actual situation in the present.[1]

In view of the very evident fact that the whole question of passive resistance is inseparable from the problem of sovereignty, it would be interesting to know what part is being taken by conscientious objectors in that wide-spread revolt against the iron-clad dogmas of the sovereign state which is under way at the present time, in the political pluralism of Professor Laski and his school, the growth of gild socialism, at least in theory, and the other more or less unrecognized ways by which a profound reorganization of thought like this takes place.[2]

The communication addressed by the writer to certain conscientious objectors included an inquiry concerning the post-war attitude of the "C. O.'s" toward social radical-

[1] *Ibid.;* pp. 65, 45 and *passim.*

[2] Cf. Laski *op. cit.;* Bertrand Russell, "Why Men Fight" and "Proposed Roads to Freedom"; also "The New State," by Mary Parker Follett; "The Guild State," by W. R. Sterling-Holt; "The Economics of Syndicalism," by W. K. Kirkcaldy; "Social Theory," by G. D. H. Coles; "Reflections on Violence," by Georges Sorel; "Direct Action," by William Mellor; "Authority, Liberty, and Function," by Ramiro De Maeztu.

ism in its various forms, particularly whether their experience during and since the war had given them any impetus in the direction of socialism on the one hand, or a tendency on the other hand to repudiate the agency of the state and to embrace political pluralism, philosophical anarchism, or any other form of social protest and political non-participation. The answers are interesting, and seem to indicate a slight drift in the non-political direction. Says one: "Undoubtedly some objectors were driven more towards anarchism and opposition to the state and all institutions of coercion because of their experiences under the military. On the other hand, I believe the movement which has caused many anarchists to adopt Marxism because of the historical example of the dictatorship of the proletariat in Russia has also caused many objectors who were individualists to embrace the Marxian doctrine."[1] Another says that "the almost universal experience of objectors was that they left prison much more radical than they entered. A number have embraced Communist doctrines, many are Socialists who were not before. . . . The state came to be looked upon as an instrument of class oppression, quite in the character of the Leninist teaching. . . . Philosophical anarchism, professed by some at the beginning, usually gave way to eager Communism at the end."[2] A third corroborates the preceding testimony, as follows: "The contact of objectors in camps and prison had a most decided effect in converting men to modern socialist concepts. Many men who went in as religious objectors came out radicals as well. The socialist objectors and many of the I. W. W. objectors, too, tended to more extreme views, and many have since joined the Communist

[1] Letter of Mr. J. B. C. Woods.

[2] Letter of Mr. Carl Haessler.

parties. A considerable number of the 'intellectuals' [college men] have gone into the labor movement or radical activities. . . . I do not think that the experience of most objectors resulted in theorizing about the State or about 'coercion' by the State. . . . I believe the result is more pragmatists and fewer theorists. Some of the most articulate of the group have announced their utter loss of faith in political methods and in the State as an institution, and have severed relations with it by not voting and by resolving not to accept jury service. Their *positive* testimony, however, is in their allegiance to the labor movement and to international radicalism of one of the several schools."[1] Still another correspondent writes, in similar vein: "Among the real 'non-resistants' there is naturally a strong tendency to repudiate the agency of the sovereign State. This is a natural outcome of their philosophy of passive resistance, and where the individual concerned is clear headed enough to think through the implications of his position and adopt a political philosophy it generally leads to philosophical anarchism in some form or another. . . . Such individuals refuse to vote and if not entirely repudiating all coercive measures . . . they are very skeptical with regard to them." This correspondent adds the following very interesting confession: "In general I think the objectors so far as I know them are a puzzled group to-day. The problem of realizing one's ideas and ideals in society and as a member of society is so vastly much more difficult than going to prison or defying the sovereign State and taking the consequences no matter what they may be. The latter is simple, clear cut, and satisfying to an ego believing in that sort of thing. The former is complex, entailing endless problems of adjustment in the relation of the individual to society, and ir-

[1] Letter and statement of Mr. Roger N. Baldwin.

ritating in the extreme in its constant failures and compromises and falling short of the ideal."[1]

There is practical unanimity among the answers on this point, namely, that the non-sectarian "C. O.'s" were impelled toward radicalism, and loss of faith in the sovereign state as an agency of justice and progress, by their war experience. But how about the sectarian objectors? The following quotation from a communication by Mr. Norman Thomas doubtless states the essential truth on this question. After expressing the prevailing opinion, namely, that "there is a decided drift on the part of C. O.'s to socialistic ideas or, to be more accurate, toward radical ideas, including philosophical anarchy," he adds: "How far that drift characterizes the conscientious objectors who never went to prison I do not know. It is this latter class I refer to, and of course among them many of the Mennonites and others have gone through camp and prison experiences practically unchanged in their way of thought." This is no doubt equally true of the Amana communists and all the other traditionally insulated groups, but, as the reader of the foregoing history might easily infer, it holds least true in the case of the Quakers. As a leading Friend writes, "It seems quite clear that pacifism [in the Quaker sense] and social radicalism are closely associated among the younger people here and in England. The radical tendencies are at present away from state socialism. In England the tendency toward Guild socialism seemed very marked last summer. In America the tendency is more toward 'democratic control' of industry, running all the way from joint committees of workers and managers to Syndicalism—at least in its non-political program."[2] This opinion will be found corroborated in slight but sig-

1 Letter of Mr. Evan W. Thomas.

2 Letter of Professor Elbert Russell, April, 1921.

nificant ways by one who will review the sayings and doings of the Young Friends Movement during the last five years.[1] A spirit of constructive *liberalism* is evident, but whether it should be called *radicalism* depends entirely upon one's own particular interpretation of that extremely ambiguous term.

But there may be those who will question whether the subtle disputations of those whom they are pleased to call "the logicians of conscience" are of sufficient importance to justify this discussion. In other words, the question may be raised whether the more recent conscientious objection is of great significance from any point of view. Certainly it cannot be so regarded from the point of view of *numbers,* since we are told in the published statement of the secretary of war that "the ratio of men professing conscientious objections in the camps to the total inductions is as 3,989 to 2,810,296, or 0.0014 per cent." It is further reported upon the same authority that only about four thousand men inducted into the military service made claim in camp to conscientious objections to any kind of service. This figure represents only about 20 per cent. of those making such claims before the local boards and receiving certificates of such claim to exemption. In other words, "more than 80 per cent. of religious objectors whose claims were recognized by the local boards . . . changed their minds before or after reaching camp and failed to claim the advantage of exemption from combatant service."[2]

[1] See "Jordans, 1920. Being the Report of the International Conference of Young Friends held at Jordans (England), August 24–30, 1920." London, 1920; also the files of "The American Friend," "The Quaker," and other periodicals.

[2] "Statement Concerning the Treatment of Conscientious Objectors in the Army, Prepared and Published by Direction of the Secretary of War, June 18, 1919"; pp. 9, 16.

It thus appears that the relative number of conscientious objectors of all types taken together was exceedingly small, and the number of non-religious objectors, of the types principally discussed in this chapter, constitutes an exceedingly small fraction of this small fraction. Thus for example we read that out of 113 prisoners released in January, 1919, from the Disciplinary Barracks at Leavenworth, 103 were classified as religious, six unclassified, and only four non-religious. Professor May found that out of 958 cases 90 per cent. objected on religious grounds, 5 per cent. on social grounds, 3 per cent. on political grounds, and 2 per cent. on ethical grounds. He concludes that "it is quite obvious that the problem of the conscientious objector is a problem of dealing with religions."[1]

There is no doubt a large measure of truth in this assertion, but the peace sects are not growing even at best, and one should not overlook the significance of the *socialist* objector. While it may be true that his objections are often not "conscientious" in the same sense as are those of other types, his numbers are great and increasing, his policy more bold than that of the others, and his mental attitude more flexible. That is to say that it may be quite possible for the socialistic, radical objection to war to grow in all nations, without involving any religious or even non-resistance principles in any sense as the basis. Such persons will not be hindered by their private conscientious convictions from bearing arms personally, when conscripted and forced to do so. But at the same time their hatred of international warfare and their eagerness for the war of the classes may be rendered still more bitter even while their hands are being trained in the use of arms. Their opposition to war being primarily class-conscious and rationalistic, objection with them is more of an impersonal,

[1] American Psychological Review"; April 1920.

mass, or at least class, attitude, and only to a slight degree if at all a matter of private conscience and personal conduct. This class-conscious war against war may be further strengthened by the growing *humanitarian* horror of the slaughter of men to which we have several times referred. As a consequence of all these influences, not excluding, of course, that of religion, it may come to pass that war, like slavery, will eventually fall to be wiped out of existence by a general revolt or strike against it on the part of the multitudes who will be driven to do so by the simple fact that, like human slavery at an earlier crisis, it has become an intolerable outrage on the modern conscience, that is to say, on the modern rationalized view of life.

The foregoing discussion, fragmentary though it is, will serve to make clear why it is impossible to frame a terse and confident statement concerning the significance of conscientious objecting for the future. Judge Kellogg well says, "The question: What shall be done with the conscientious objector? has never yet received a satisfactory answer." He is confident that a solution will some day be found, but "not . . . until the subject is given the thoughtful and sober consideration which it deserves." He rightly fears, however, that the problem will easily be forgotten in times of peace, "only to present itself, in the event of a later war, as full of knots and perplexities as ever."[1] That this is true may be indicated in some degree by the fact that three or more years after the close of the war one heard almost simultaneously of meetings of the "World War Objectors" in New York, of the "C. O. 's" in the South of England, and also in Germany.[2]

[1] *Op. cit.;* p. 5.

[2] "The American Friend," May 5, 1921, p. 363; and correspondence of the present writer.

There is danger of overestimating the significance of these movements in themselves, but on the other hand it is probably true that they are symptoms of a permanent conflict in modern life.

Another consideration which renders confident prediction in this field impossible is the fact that passive resistance has shown a tendency to pass beyond the meek endurance of injustice, extending first to its abolishment by the use of educational and political methods, as in the history of the Quakers, and more recently to the employment of economic power, especially the strike and boycott, as a method of social constraint, and even control of governmental policy. Now, there will doubtless be those ready to say that in so doing it has ceased to be passive resistance, but that is precisely the point in question. Earlier chapters have abundantly demonstrated, by appeal to history, that passive resistance never was mere passive submission. That would be *non*-resistance, about which we are not now speaking. Whatever else it may be, it is a form of "resistance," as the name indicates. We have to deal here with a phase or aspect of *conflict*. Although it moves on the impersonal and non-violent level it is conflict just the same, and, being conflict, it naturally merges into constraint and coercion. The crucial test for its ethical evaluation must therefore be sought neither in its generic nature as *conflict*, nor in its bearing upon constraint and coercion, which are ever-present and inescapable aspects of social pressure inherent in group life itself, but in the *methods* which it brings into use and the ethical spirit in which it is employed. In short, it is the word "passive" rather than "resistance" that must engage attention, and it would be virtually meaningless if it did not tend to translate itself into such phrases as "moral," "non-violent," or at least "non-injurious" resistance. In the end we shall probably be forced either to widen in this way the meaning of the word, or to interpret it as exactly synonymous with *non*-resistance. In the former case the strike and boycott will be included, while if the other alternative is chosen it excludes such active peace groups as the Quakers, who are *not non*-resistants, as earlier chapters have shown, whatever else they may be.

The temptation is strong to attempt a further analysis of the term at this point, but that would be contrary to the method we are trying to follow, which is to pursue the principle into all its apparent ramifications, to test our original concept, and thereby to arrive, if possible, at a renovated conception which will bear the flavor of reality. It must be remarked at this point, nevertheless, that even the more extended phrase "non-injurious resistance" may have to be further widened to read "personally non-injurious resistance," in order to make room for the boycott, and for non-coöperation in the broad sense currently used in connection with the Indian revolution. These qualifications are prompted by the reflection that the destruction of economic goods and of human life cannot, by any logic more robust than legalistic and political fiction-mongering, be placed under one and the same ethical category. But this thought may well remain purely tentative while we explore somewhat further the hitherto unmapped frontiers of passive resistance.

CHAPTER XVI

NON-VIOLENCE AS THE DEMONSTRATION AND THE STRIKE

AT this point it is necessary to call attention to a two-fold implication in the term "passive resistance." In the primary sense it is almost purely negative, and it is this aspect of the matter that has determined the use of the word in the dictionary and the terminology of the sciences. In this usage, "to resist" means simply *to stand against, to stop, to obstruct, to endeavor to counteract, defeat or frustrate, oppose, antagonize,* or *prevent.* All these expressions agree in denoting activity which is not primarily self-initiated, self-motived, or self-directed, but which is aroused and determined mainly by the actions of others. In a sense it is merely the rebound or echo to another's action, and little or nothing more.

This meaning, conveyed by common-sense usage, is reflected in the technical language of the schools. Thus, in physics "resistance" is a force tending to prevent motion, as the *resistance* of the air to a body passing through it. In electrical science it is the opposition offered by any substance to the passage of an electrical current through the same, while in nautical science it denotes the *retardation* of a vessel passing through the water.

In the history of that social phenomenon known as passive resistance it is this negative, non-active idea that has prevailed, and the discussions of our preceding chapters have been devoted principally to this aspect. The earlier term "non-resistance" has been used occasionally in these pages, but it is almost useless because of its inherent self-contradictions. If "resistance" means merely some kind of opposing, obstructing activity at the most, and it is then further negatived by the prefix "non," which indicates the absence of the thing qualified, it is plain that "non-resistance" means simply nothing at all, and one using it is about as explicit as the Irish judge who demanded "nothing but silence in court, and but little of that." The stubborn child who converts himself into a limp meal-bag in the hands of an elder who would drag him home against his will is a perfect example of passive resistance in this narrow sense. Similar instances are of course rare among adults, but we have recorded on an earlier page the action of the Canadian Doukhobors, who locked their arms together and thus resisted the soldiers, who were seeking to entrain them, by nothing more than the limp dead-weight of their collective avoirdupois. The moral and social attitude typified by this physical incident is exactly what one finds in passive resistance of the traditional, negative, and orthodox type.

In glancing back over the earlier chapters of this study one will observe that attention has been centered largely upon these negative aspects, such as non-retaliation of the assailed individual, or the refusal of the conscript to bear arms for the state. The attitude is well summed up in the phrase, "conscientious objector," which stresses the more negatively protesting aspect of this particular social rôle. But there is another side to the matter, and it is this more positive implication of the term that will engage attention for most of the chapters that follow. While completely overshadowed by the other idea, this meaning has not been entirely absent from even the current usage as reflected in dictionary statements, as when resistance is defined as "opposition, passive or active." But this is all that one can find in formal definitions, and it is only in the actual facts of history that we may hope to discover the more positive meaning of passive resistance. Thus in the course of the present inquiry it very early appeared, contrary to the accepted notion with which the study was begun, that the Quakers could not be classified along with Mennonites, Dunkers, or Doukhobors with reference to one most important characteristic. While they are all of them alike religious peace sects and conscientious objectors to military service, they differed greatly, as we had to recognize, in their attitude of resistance to it, the one group being more or less *non*-resistant, going so far as to eschew public agitation and even political participation, while the Quakers have been unusually active in both. While the distinction is not absolute, there being some exceptions on both sides, it seems to be on the whole the view most truly in accord with the facts of earlier history.

In more recent events this positive aspect of passive resistance stands out with much greater distinctness, in such mass reactions as the strike, the boycott, and non-coöperation in general. These phenomena may not turn out to be, in every instance, true expressions of passive resistance, but they must be examined impartially from that point of view, which is the task immediately before us. Toward such an undertaking the very recent history of Korea offers a most fitting approach, in view of the fact that it presents a concerted mass movement falling exactly between the passive submission of the traditional non-resistance and the active aggression, or at least the coerciveness, of the boycott and the strike.

THE KOREAN "DEMONSTRATION"

The story of Korea indeed stands in a class by itself. This movement did not, as in the case of the strike, aim to coerce the opponent by cutting off his supply of labor; nor by diverting his business customers as in the use of the boycott; nor by withdrawal of social support from his enterprises and institutions in the largest sense, as in what is known as "non-coöperation" in India. Korea's policy is most accurately described as a national non-violent demonstration, by which the despairing and desperate people of that unfortunate country sought to attract the attention of the powers, assembled at Versailles, to the fact that they had *not,* as many then assumed, passively submitted to Japanese domination, and that they desired the assistance of the liberty-loving nations in extricating themselves from a foreign yoke. Without going into the details of Korean history, it should be said that that country had suffered for some decades a constantly increasing aggression on the part of Japan. As a result their independent existence, of which Koreans love to boast as enduring for four thousand years, had been brought to an end, and the ancient kingdom was ostensibly incorporated with the empire of Japan.

Korea, like her next of kin, China, has always been, and is to-day, a land whose people and traditions are "eminently pacific," described as "mild" and "good-natured," although "full of contradictory characteristics" . . . among which is the capacity for "great bursts of passion."[1] All these traits are clearly manifested in the events we are about to relate.

[1] "Korea's Fight For Freedom," by F. A. McKenzie, New York, 1920; p. 17.

Japan, seeking steadily to supplant China in her protectorship over Korea, seized the issue that arose over the sending of Chinese troops, in alleged disregard of an earlier agreement, into Korea to quell disorders there. The war between the two ancient empires followed, in 1895, and Japan emerged triumphant. From that time the process of subordinating and assimilating Korea has gone steadily forward, inch by inch, until it provoked the remarkable but apparently futile expression of passive resistance narrated below.

After the Russian war, a decade later, or even during its successful progress, the hand of Japan bore down ever more and more heavily upon Korea. Japanese advisers were substituted for other official foreigners; the control of administrative functions was next assumed; then the Japanese acquired the Korean postal and telegraph systems in their entirety; and in this way a progressive subjugation steadily proceeded. But these are external facts of political history, while we are interested in the inward, moral aspects of the drama, or more exactly the tragedy, of Korea. At every step the aggressor was met with protests, but they were devoid of either persuasive or coercive power, and the situation grew steadily worse, for the Japanese in Korea proved to be as belligerent as the Koreans were pacific.

In 1907, while the emperor still sat upon his tottering throne, he saw a hope in the Hague conference, then in session, and secretly sent three emissaries of high rank, who reached that court only to be refused a hearing. But the hope of gaining the ear of the world did not completely perish, and when President Wilson thrilled the subjected peoples of the whole world with the declaration that one great object of the league of nations would be to provide for the freedom of small nations, by preventing the domination of weak governments by strong ones, the Korean patriots clutched at it as their last opportunity. They sent, or tried to send, leaders, one of whom succeeded in reaching France, although the peace conference did not receive him.

Meanwhile the Korean people, under the guidance of their leaders, decided to make a concerted, nation-wide *demonstration,* with the object of supporting their delegate, and impressing the powers, then assembled for the ostensible purpose of guaranteeing to weaker nations the self-determination which, after so many scores of centuries, seemed just then slipping from their own possession. The method to be employed was strictly one of passive resistance, or non-violent coercion, and that for several reasons. In the first place they were entirely without munitions of war, even if the national temperament had been inclined to that line of conduct, which it manifestly was not. All the historical experiences, traditions, and present arrangements of the nation were against it. In the second place, no national or international machinery for the exercise of the will of those twenty millions by *constitutional, political* methods was then in existence. The only remaining alternative, aside from complete submission, was some form of passive resistance, and this must be the typical procedure of seeking, by means of their own sufferings, to attract the intervention of the bystanders, as it were, who in this case were the nations of the Western world. Kendall's account is very explicit on this point. "The general plan," he says, "was to make Seoul the center of activities, inasmuch as the foreign legations were there and the whole purpose of the movement was designed to gain recognition and publicity." And we read, further on, that when the demonstration actually began the paraders "divided into the groups of three thousand each, as prearranged, and went to the foreign consulate buildings."[1]

The old deposed emperor had just died, and his approaching funeral was seen to offer the very occasion required, since the people would then be in national mourning, with all hearts turned toward the capital at Seoul, while scores of thousands of feet would also be turning thitherward, unsuspected, to attend the funeral exercises. With remarkable speed and secrecy organizations were formed from end to end of Korea, and plans were laid for a concerted "demonstration" throughout the length and breadth of the land. Says McKenzie: "A Declaration of Independence was drawn up in advance and delivered to the different centres. Here it was mimeographed, and girls and boys organized to ensure its distribution. Meetings, processions and demonstrations in all the big cities were planned." At these meetings the procedure was simply to read the declaration of independence, and to shout "Mansei!" (the Korean for "Hurrah") amid the waving of the old Korean flags brought forth from their hiding-places for this occasion. "It was the old national battle cry, 'May Korea live ten thousand years,' " says the writer quoted above; and he rightly adds, "A new kind of revolt had begun."[2] This occurred on the first day of March, 1919.

It is important to note that this was no mere blind frenzy of protest, but a carefully planned pacific demonstration directed expressly at the ear of the peace conference—a nation's appeal for intervention. The methods used, while essentially pacifistic, were astonishingly bold, especially when one considers the helpless condition of

1 "The Truth About Korea," by Carlton W. Kendall; pp. 26, 29. Pub. by the Korean National Association, San Francisco, 1919.

2 *Ibid.;* pp. 245, 246. Cf. Kendall, *op. cit.;* p. 27.

the whole nation. Thirty-three men, dedicated to martyrdom, if that should be required, became the original signers of a remarkable document entitled, "The Proclamation of Korean Independence." This was first promulgated by being produced and coolly read before some leading Japanese residents, who had been invited in to dine with these Koreans, if McKenzie's account be correct, but at any rate in a restaurant where the "signers" took a last meal together. After the reading it was despatched to the governor-general. Then the "signers" called up the central police station, reported what they had done, and stated that they would await the arrival of the police if it was desired to arrest them, which was promptly done.

The declaration generously announces: "We have no wish to find special fault with Japan's lack of fairness or her contempt of our civilization and the principles on which her state rests. . . . Let us not be filled with bitterness or resentment over past agonies or past occasions for anger. Our part is to influence the Japanese government, dominated as it is by the old idea of brute force which thinks to run counter to reason and universal law, so that it will change, act honestly and in accord with the principles of right and truth." The document closes with three "items of agreement," the first of which contains the following unusually clear enunciation of both the spirit and method of passive resistance: "This work of ours is in behalf of truth, religion and life, undertaken at the request of our people, in order to make known their desire for liberty. Let no violence be done to any one."

Notwithstanding the attempted suppression, which was carried out with greater or less severity in the various parts of the country, the people everywhere continued their demonstrations.

One experiences a misgiving, however, that in their courageous devotion to liberty, for which they were so willing to die contending with naked hands, these "signers" and their followers might have been actuated by a misunderstanding with respect to the real nature of the greatly admired American independence movement, which no doubt served, in part at least, as a source of suggestion to them. Perhaps they did not sufficiently realize that the American Declaration was announced at a time when those in whose name it was uttered were *actually resisting* their opponent with a fair measure of success, and with the intention and prospect of continuing that resistance to a successful conclusion. Consequently the essential meaning of the American Declaration was that it shifted the moral and political basis of their resistance, changing it from an insurrection for the "rights of Englishmen" under the empire to a war for independent political existence. In the case of America the fundamental fact was that she was in position to use some coercive pressure by various means, while the Koreans either could not or did not organize coercive pressure, either violent or non-violent, but simply made a futile gesture of protest and despair.

Aside from the morally significant fact that men who had been ennobled by the Japanese resigned their titles, there were, it is true, some slight tendencies in the direction of an employment of coercive economic and social pressure, but they did not take on effective proportions. The merchants closed their shops in some places, Korean employees on the state-owned railroads and the street railway employees came out on a strike, and farmers, meeting in their respective districts, threatened to refrain from planting their crops unless independence was granted.[1] None of these, however, was carried out with the unani-

[1] "The Case of Korea," by Henry Chung; pp. 209, 210. New York. 1921.

mity and persistence necessary to render it a decisive factor in the struggle, which began and ended purely as an appeal, or at most a protest, not only non-violent but also non-coercive in character.

This remarkable movement thus seems to have been in fact a clear and explicit attempt at passive resistance on a national scale. It possessed the attributes of the older, more negative conception of that policy, namely the rejection of violence, the direct appeal to the conscience of the aggressor, and the indirect appeal to the sense of justice of the beholder (in this case the peace conference) as a moral tribunal. On the other hand, it lacked the coercive power of the economic forces as one sees them used nowadays in the strike, in the boycott, and in non-coöperation on the grand scale. It is true that in the "resolution" appended to the "constitution" such positive measures were clearly suggested, as follows:

> That the Koreans in the employ of the Japanese Government shall withdraw.
>
> That the people shall refuse to pay taxes to the Japanese Government.
>
> That the people shall not bring petitions or litigations before the Japanese Government.

These three resolutions do virtually formulate a program of non-violent coercion similar to that which arose in India about the same time. They may even have been a reflection of the Gandhi movement, discussed in a later chapter; but they were announced too late to be effective in Korea, even if the organization of national thought, purpose, and industry had been such as to render them feasible. As it was, the movement in Korea was destined to remain a purely pacifistic, virtually non-resistant protest and appeal, which very accurately described itself by the term "demonstration." In so far as it was *resistance* at all, either passive or active, it consisted solely in a call for help, and was not calculated to exercise coercion by either economic, military, or social pressure. According to its historian, "It was expected in Korea that there would be an immediate agitation in America to secure redress for the Koreans."[1] This hope was sadly misplaced, for their self-sacrificing demonstration was studiously ignored in the Japanese press, proved unable to gain a moment's attention from war distracted Europe, and became barely known in America. It resulted in adding one more to the list of failures wrought by pure non-resistance as a principle of conduct for national and social groups.[2] That is to say, while it took the form of passive resistance, it scarcely displayed the substance, that is to say, the constraining if not coercive pressure, necessary to bring it under that category. It furnishes an excellent transition, however, to the discussion of those more drastic, yet essentially non-violent, methods of coercion which we have yet to examine, first among which is the *strike,* especially in its political aspects.

THE STRIKE

This topic really challenges the student of non-violent coercion, because of the objection raised by some leading non-resistants to the principle of the *strike* in industrial disputes, their contention being that it is incompatible with passive resistance. This is a vital issue because, as has been shown, the conscientious objectors produced by the recent war represent a group of passive resistants who have received a specially powerful impetus toward active

[1] Kendall, *op. cit.,* p. 308.
[2] See Chap. XIII. above.

participation in the great liberal and radical social idealism so characteristic of these times. Nothing, therefore, could seem more fitting than for those who so utterly abhor war to ally themselves with the modern crusade against the unjust and corrupt economic order which is as closely related to warfare and strife at home and abroad as the root is to the branches.

Furthermore, since their fundamental philosophy and their hard experiences worked together to teach passive resistants of the more negative type to distrust and repudiate the state centuries before the political pluralists and gild syndicalists began their brilliant and effective assault on the dogmas of sovereignty, one should naturally expect to find them particularly friendly to the method of the industrial strike, inasmuch as it aims to secure social justice without resorting to state action on the one hand or to plain violence on the other. But passive resistants even of most progressive and idealistic temper are far from agreement on this matter. Upon this subject the discussions recently conducted by leading passive resistants are extraordinarily interesting and informative:[1]

In the course of their able argument, the conscientious opposers of the strike take the stand that it is wrong in the last analysis simply because it is a method of *coercion*. Not because one is forbidden to kill, as the earliest non-resistants in both Orient and Occident envisaged it, nor because one is not permitted to use *injurious* physical force, according to Ballou and his peace-society colleagues of the middle nineteenth century, but because of their "conviction that compulsion is not God's way nor the method he wished men to use—not coercion but conviction"—this is declared to be what made pacifists in the first place of

[1] See "The Strike: A Discussion," in "The World To-morrow," May, 1920; also "The Strike: A Symposium," *Ibid.*, June, 1920.

those who now take the anti-strike position. Indeed, the pacifistic objection to *physical force* is branded by this most recent school of pacifism as "doctrinaire,"[1] while the evil of *coercive methods* is elaborated and stressed, and the rejection of all coercion declared to be the essence of the non-resistance philosophy. The strike is condemned because it is held by them to be "not passive resistance to, but aggressive attack upon, injustice. It is revolt in terms not of suffering but of battle and conquest. The strikers are now an army, organized for warfare against those who hold them in subjection. Which means that at the bottom of the strike to-day is the principle of coercion—coercion of the worker to join the union and the strike, coercion of the employer to yield to an ultimatum of terms; coercion of the whole body of citizenship to the support of labor at the cost of indescribable misery and social peril! Coercion, of course, is force, and therefore do we see the strike, originally a method of peaceful protest and agitation used in the spirit of martyrdom, developing into a weapon of violence used in the spirit and to the ends of war."[2] This is held to be not only evil but unnecessary in "a spiritual universe inhabited by men sensitive to the influence of spiritual forces," where "the real triumph is always a triumph of ideas."

This astonishing turn on the part of the "logicians of conscience" has been well and promptly met by their fellow-pacifists, one of whom confesses that he is "growing more and more afraid of 'absolutes' in human conduct"; another is reported as now realizing "that an absolute pacifist philosophy such as he held or thought he held during the war implies a repudiation of all coercion and au-

[1] Professor Henry J. Cadbury, *loc. cit.;* May 1920.

[2] Dr. John Haynes Holmes in "Is Violence the Way Out?" quoted *loc. cit.;* June, 1920.

thority which subsequent experience makes it impossible to hold''; while still another says, ''many of us who took the absolute stand against the last war are finding difficulty in finding ourselves satisfactorily in the work-a-day world with its hates and stupidities of to-day.''[1] This testimony could doubtless be multiplied many times with ease, and it possesses the greatest meaning for this debate. It simply shows that modern passive resistants are repeating the experience of their predecessors throughout the past in finding that the theory of absolute non-resistance will not work out in actual life. Supremely, even superhumanly, logical in the various parts, it proves so utterly illogical on the whole that it cannot find itself, nor bring the two halves of its world together. There is no need to elaborate this point, since preceding chapters have abundantly illustrated it before ever this newest issue arose.[2]

Aside from these admissions concerning personal bewilderment, the more objective arguments are urged that the deprecators of the strike are purely negative, offering no substitute whatsoever; that one becomes inevitably a partner of the one side or the other; that the objectors to the strike are delivering those who were pacifists during the war into the hands of the ''economic imperialists who made the war''; that the concerted refusal of conscientious objectors to serve in the recent war itself resembled in every way an organized strike; that the strike is no more a form of coercion than is all organization and all government known to man; that he who denies the ethical validity of the strike must, if consistent, deny himself the right to use the courts or to hold private property under the existing capitalistic system; and that the absolute non-resistant should consistently refrain from political partici-

[1] *Ibid.* May, 1920; and correspondence of the present writer.
[2] See Chap. XII and XIII, above.

pation, the rights of private property, and the enjoyment of the fruits of capitalistically organized machine industry, and, like Tolstoy, turn his back on machinery and science and feed himself by hand labor.[1] This last is in fact what the non-resistants of the Amana communistic colonies, the old-style Mennonites, conservative Dunkers, and others have done with varying degrees of thoroughness, and it has already been remarked that they are really the most logically consistent of the peace sects, so long as they hold to the principle of *non*-resistance instead of passive or moral resistance as distinguished in this book. The method of the strike is rightly, as the writer believes, held by the more positive party to this debate to be a clear case of *passive*, or non-violent resistance, and if so it can no more fit into the logic of absolutist *non*-resistance than can a thousand other things of daily life, most of which are nevertheless illogically participated in more or less directly every day and hour by the most thoroughgoing objectors.

Now the question of the strike in connection with conscientious objection to war is not an academic one, since the socialists actually proposed such a mass movement in connection with their efforts to keep America out of the World War, exhorting the workers to every exertion, "even to the final and extreme step of a general strike and the consequent paralyzation of all industry."[2] But a general strike means unavoidably the quick approach of starvation for the laborers, with consequent bread-rioting and looting, and the inevitable battle with the militia in the streets. From these horrors of a general class war it is not strange that the true men of peace should recoil. But if sufficiently wide-spread and unanimous, so as to in-

1 "The World To-morrow," loc cit.; *passim.*

2 "The American Socialists and the War: A Documentary History, etc."; p. 25.

clude the police forces also, it might succeed without bloodshed; or likewise if, on the other hand, it were to avoid the always dangerous attempt to rely on unanimity, and were made sufficiently intermittent to avoid a drawn battle, yet persistent enough to prove finally effective. A step in this direction is noticeable in the report that a world agreement of metal-workers to prevent war by refusing to manufacture munitions has been proposed in the international circles of that craft.[1]

In such an event it would be of utmost importance for national freedom that action be simultaneous in the several countries, since it is obvious that a general strike by laborers in a single warring nation might amount to a betrayal of their country into the hands of a foreign and more militaristic power. That *concerted* action is now seriously under consideration is shown by the following resolution:

> "The International Congress of the Federation of Trades Unions (24,000,000 members) declares it to be the task of the organized workers to counteract all wars which may threaten to break out in the future by means at the disposal of the labor movement and, if need be, to prevent the actual outbreak of such wars by proclaiming and carrying out a *general international strike*."[2]

The problem of passive resistance is not, however, simply that of conscientious objection to war, as the above discussion of the industrial strike has shown. We have seen that those passive resistants who deprecate the strike have pointed out that when it takes this form the policy is extended beyond resistance to aggression by passive suffering, which had become the typical passive resistance

[1] Press despatches of April 14, 1921.

[2] Adopted at Rome, April 20-26, 1922.

and "C. O." attitude. They further argue that passive resistants who indorse the strike method are undertaking to carry out social purposes by means of coercion rather than by persuasion. In the process, we are told, passive resistance is "developing into a weapon of violence used in the spirit and to the ends of war."

Such reasoners perform a service in so far as they help us to see that we may have here a principle of social action which contains implications much wider than has commonly been supposed. Since the present study may lay claim to scientific detachment only in so far as it seeks to pursue the subject wherever it leads, the clue here presented must not lie neglected.

If now one were to define passive resistance more widely, as the exercise of social constraint by non-violent means, all the essential elements in the principle would seem to be taken into account; yet the policy so conceived reveals a surprisingly wide application. At one stroke it becomes thereby more positive and more impersonal. Originally the term "passive resistant" meant simply one who endured personal abuse without retaliation, in which case it was really non-resistance, that is, no resistance at all, Later the term was widened and the typical case became that of the *conscript* who refused to bear arms at the command of the State. In both cases the method of resistance was simply that of nonconformity and of passive endurance of the suffering inflicted—for failure to defend oneself in the one case and refusal to obey in the other. In none of these instances do we see the passive resistant playing the rôle of one who seeks to further a positive social policy, either by persuasion or coercion. On the contrary he asks only to be let alone, whether "he" be a private person, or a retired and more or less socially isolated sect.

In the case of the strike, on the contrary, one beholds a positive and active effort to modify the policy of others, such as a capitalistic employing group or even the state itself. An example of the last named occurred in the recent conflicts between the British Government and the Triple Alliance of Great Britain, which comprises the Miners' Federation, the Natonal Union of Railwaymen, and the Transport Workers' Federation. In these struggles the workers were not limiting their efforts to the resistance of actual or alleged injustices against themselves, but were engaged also in the advocacy of certain policies which they desired the Government to pursue. The particular measures urged by the British Triple Alliance included:

1. The withdrawal of the Conscription Bill then (April, 1919) before Parliament;
2. The withdrawal of all British troops from Russia;
3. The release of 'C. O.'s'' then in prison;
4. The raising of the blockade against Russia.[1]

In this, and similar cases, we see illustrated the attempt to obtain political victories by means of so-called *direct action,* which is defined by its advocates as ''the use of some form of economic power for the securing of ends desired by those who possess that power.''[2] The particular form of economic power consists in this case of control over the supply of labor force. This control depends in turn upon the *organization* of laborers, and it constitutes a new social factor of great significance. This is clearly understood by the labor leaders themselves, as when, for example, the joint conference representing the Trades-union Congress, the Labor party, and the Parliamentary Labor party ''Warns the Government that the whole industrial power

[1] Cf. "Direct Action," by William Mellor, London, 1920; p. 144.
[2] *Ibid.;* p. 15.

of the organized workers will be used to defeat this war.''[1]

The rather numerous cases of this kind are more recent than new or original, for, if Mr. Wells is right in so denominating it, there occurred a "general strike of plebeians" at Rome in 494 B. C. On this occasion the plebeians, thoroughly aroused by the systematic exploitation of the patrician profiteers, twice "marched right out of Rome, threatening to make a new city higher up the Tiber, and twice this threat proved conclusive." Let it be noted also that this was the work of the original *proletariat,* and that it was done without disorder.[2] One reads also that some years ago the Belgians obtained the reform of their constitution by the threat of a general strike. Moreover, as far back as 1890 the Guesdist party of French radical socialists passed, in its national congress at Lille, "a resolution by which it declared that the general strike by the miners was actually possible" and in itself capable of accomplishing all the objects to be hoped for from a general strike of all the trades. The same thing was not only proposed, but actually attempted later, in connection with the railway service in France.[3] The significance of the "political general strike," to adopt a phrase of Sorel's, lies, therefore, less in its novelty than in a recent tendency to extend its applications, to use it more freely, and, especially significant for the present inquiry, in its relation to the principle of passive resistance. In other words, we are now raising the question whether passive resistance and direct action do not possess some sort of logical and even ethical affinity. The anwer can emerge only as our examination

1 *Ibid.;* p. 152.

2 "The Outline of History," by H. G. Wells, New York, 1921; p. 391.

3 Cf. the chapter on "The Political General Strike," in "Reflections on Violence," by Georges Sorel, New York, 1921; first published in 1906.

and analysis of facts proceeds. For the present let us observe that the Council of Action, in presenting the demands of the British Labor Movement upon the Government, as described above, made use of a very suggestive phrase when it announced that the council was "authorized to call for any and every form of withdrawal of Labor which circumstances may require" to give effect to its policy. This expression "withdrawal of Labor" sounds strikingly similar in effect to the term "non-coöperation" as used in India, and described in a following chapter; while both these policies are akin to the much more venerable *boycott.*

CHAPTER XVII

NON-VIOLENT COERCION AND THE INDUSTRIAL BOYCOTT

IT is common knowledge that the word *boycott* originated in Ireland as late as the year 1880, but it may not be so widely recognized that the policy itself was in use on a much greater scale more than a hundred years earlier in the British colonies of North America. Moreover, the word itself lacks etymological content, although it has come to stay, and has even been incorporated into the French (*boycottier*) and German (*boykottiren*) languages. It perpetuates the name of the particular land agent, one Captain Boycott, against whom the struggling peasant tenantry of Mayo County directed their economic and social protest in 1880, but the word conveys no meaning in itself. Consequently, even if sound method did not so dictate one would be compelled to seek the correct definition of the term in the facts of history itself. In other words, it is purposed to take this specific term as used to denominate the act of concerted refusal of economic and social intercourse in a particular instance, and try to see how much or how little, according to the actual practice of history, should be included in the term. For such an inquiry the experience of colonial America is especially instructive.

In his notable study of the part played by colonial merchants in the American Revolution,[1] Professor Schlesinger

[1] "The Colonial Merchants and the American Revolution, 1763–1776," by Arthur Meier Schlesinger; Vol. LXXVIII, Whole Number

has presented a most illuminating body of evidence concerning the actual operation of this form of social coercion. His method is strictly historical, however, and the present writer is responsible for the attempt to interpret those events under the categories of passive resistance.

The boycott of colonial days did not, of course, go by that name, but was expressed in the words "non-importation" and "non-consumption," as applied to those goods taxed by the mother-country, and in some cases all, or many, of the goods originating in English trade. In virtually all cases exceptions were made in favor of imperative necessities or goods required for the support of colonial industries, notably the fisheries of New England.

The original opposition to the obnoxious laws, viz., the Stamp Act and the Townshend Acts, was strictly economic and limited to the merchant class, who weighed the measures solely from the point of view of their effects on trade. As time went on the non-commercial elements of the population became more actively interested, and the idea that constitutional rights were being infringed began to engage the minds of the people. But this class-conscious movement on the part of the mercantile element constituted, according to Professor Schlesinger, "the one tremendous fact of the revolutionary movement prior to the assembling of the First Continental Congress."[1]

From the very beginning the allegiance of the populace to the "utilitarian revolt" of the merchants, as the same authority aptly styles it, lay in their participation in and complete sympathy for smuggling and smugglers, this form of law evasion having become a settled social habit throughout the colonies.

182, of "Studies in History, Economics, and Public Law," edited by the faculty of political science of Columbia University. New York, 1918.

[1] *Op. cit.;* p. 105.

The entire story of this matter bristles with suggestions to the student of social constraint in its various forms and phases. The merchants, true to the intuition of their class, were by no means revolutionary or even reckless as regards the foundations of law and order, although in this case they permitted their zeal for prosperity to encourage social forces which, in turn, eventually raised a tempest that they could not quell. Their intention, both real and apparent, was the organization of a boycott against British trade, particularly in commodities subjected to taxation or other restrictions under the recently enacted revenue laws. This boycott was planned with clear comprehension of the inter-play of interests that obtains in human affairs, and particularly the dependence of political policies upon personal and business influences. Consequently the colonial merchants did not aim a general broadside at the whole British Empire, but planned to reach particular interests with a well-directed blow. More specifically, they hoped, by means of their boycott measures, to give the British mercantile and manufacturing people a motive, in the person of their own imperiled interests, for seeking the ear of Parliament with a demand for the repeal of the objectionable legislation.

The straight, or primary, boycott was the method used to impress the minds of the British trading class, which *was*, of course, the British *government* for practical purposes. The *secondary* boycott, as now known, was in turn brought to bear upon Americans who failed to observe the original agreement and resorted to dealing within the limits prescribed, either as to persons or goods. For instance, in the earlier struggle, waged against the stamp tax, communities that paid the same were made to feel the disapproval of their neighbors, as in Charleston, South Carolina, where a radical fire company agreed that "no provision should be shipped 'to that infamous Colony Georgia in particular nor any other that make use of Stamp Paper.' "[1]

During the later boycott, directed against the Townshend taxes, Rhode Island yielded to that temptation which constitutes the greatest peril for any concerted movement of this kind, namely the impulse to reap a rich harvest by seizing the opportunities deliberately left to go begging through the self-denial of one's competitors. This incident also discloses another weakness inherent in such organized "voluntary" efforts, which is that they are really seldom, if ever, completely voluntary. Enthusiasts for every cause, however worthy, almost invariably make use of coercion by means of the hundred and one devices known to social pressure, and thereby incorporate the seeds of their own disintegration. Thus a contemporary Rhode Islander wrote that they "were dragged in the first place like an ox to the slaughter, into the non-importation agreement," and that adherence to the same "would have been acting out of character and in contradiction to the opinion of the country."[2]

The resistance of the colonists was destined, however, to run the entire gamut of forms known to social opposition and constraint. *Evasion of law* had long been an established business in the form of smuggling; the peaceable *boycott,* both primary and secondary, was now well under way; but *political* action, *litigation,* social *ostracism,* mob *violence,* and *armed revolution* were either already coming into play or waiting to enter the stage as the historic drama proceeded. And this list makes no mention of those subtle methods of *persuasion* and *"influence"* which operate between friends and relatives, business and scientific asso-

[1] *Ibid.;* p. 82.
[2] *Ibid.;* p. 215.

ciates, boon companions, and numberless other channels of daily intercourse, not to mention the more overt persuasion of pulpit, press, and platform. And one of the most significant aspects of it all is the tendency of any one of these situations to transform itself into one or more of the other members of the series, so that one method can hardly be used without sooner or later invoking the others. This truth is clearly exemplified in the events now before us.

For example, in the secondary boycott directed by Charleston against Georgia, as quoted above, the resolution threatened death for future offenders, with destruction of their vessels.

In Boston, especially during the earlier contest over the Stamp Tax, the disturbances were most serious. The rioters were led by one Mackintosh, a shoemaker, endowed by nature for "government by tumult." Under his leadership, the mob, which was currently reported to include "fifty gentlemen actors" partly disguised in workman's attire, not only razed the stamp office but also attacked the house of the registrar of the admiralty, and even the residence of Governor Hutchinson himself. In all these scenes the Sons of Liberty, composed largely of workingmen, did the strong-arm work. Meanwhile the merchants, ostensibly committed exclusively to the boycott and orderly methods, lent in private an anxious but effective moral support. One of them testifies in a private letter of the time that they were endeavoring "to keep up the Spirit" of resistance but were "not a little pleas'd to hear that McIntosh has the Credit of the Whole Affair."[1]

The anxiety felt by the merchants grew into genuine alarm lest they might not prove able to control the destructive social forces their own reckless policy had unleashed. Governor Hutchinson's sarcastic analysis of the

[1] *Ibid.;* p. 72.

mob government against which he, as royal governor, had to contend links the merchants, with apparent truth, with these riotous demonstrations. He refers, in bitter humor, first to "the lowest branch . . . [which] consists of the rabble of the town of Boston, headed by one Mackintosh." These, according to the governor, did the actual work of pulling down houses, burning effigies, etc., but were, in this systematic mob government, controlled by a superior set of skilled mechanics. Both these groups, he avers, were "under the direction of a committee of merchants," while back of the whole stood the general meeting of all the inhabitants of Boston, "where Otis, with his mob-high eloquence, prevails in every motion."[1] In similar vein is the testimony of a member of the customs board before the British privy council in 1770, when he declared himself unable to call the disorders riots, because "the Rioters appear to be under Discipline."[2]

Despite these circumstances, or rather on account of them, the merchants experienced a change of heart, and sought to wash their hands of violence when they took up their second contest. Leading speakers and writers in all the colonies made it a point to condemn riotous methods and to counsel a strict adherence to the forms of law. Violence having alienated some of their most influential associates, constitutional methods should henceforth be their sole reliance; but first among these they still named the boycott, and thereby gave a pawn to fortune, inasmuch as subsequent events proved that the two methods could not be kept apart.

The element of time figured largely in this affair, as it must in all such cases. The longer the struggle the greater the economic inconvenience and social strain, and

[1] Quoted *ibid.;* p. 72.
[2] *Ibid.;* p. 103.

the more intense the pressure of accumulated irritation, until finally this emotional pressure breaks out in explosive violence at the weakest point. This weak point, so far as the pacific resistance of the colonial merchants is concerned, lay in "the increasing restlessness and self-confidence of the radical elements," which, as Professor Schlesinger points out, "made the introduction of mob methods inevitable." Gaining its entrance through the activities of smugglers, "there occurred the usual vicious sequence: evasion of the law leading to defiance of the law, and defiance of the law breeding violence."[1]

Economic pressure through the boycott and physical force in the form of violence were constantly supported by the more subtle forms of social coercion. Thus the Boston agreement of 1767 was to be enforced by a *discountenancing* "in the most effectual but decent and lawful manner" of all who should fail to aid the movement. At Philadelphia, any person failing to support the boycott was to be branded "An Enemy of the Liberties of America," and it was the plan to publish such names in the newspapers. The commercial resisters of Savannah likewise agreed that "every violator should be deemed 'no Friend to his Country' "; while in South Carolina nonsupporters were "to be treated with the utmost contempt." In 1769 the Boston boycotters circulated thousands of handbills throughout their own and neighboring provinces calling on the inhabitants to have no trade relations with persons whom they named as lacking in regard for the public good. While this is apparently merely a case of the secondary boycott already described, the publicity methods connected with it are of interest just here. Public disapproval, aside from withdrawal of patronage, was a factor held in view. It was an effort to revive the ancient

[1] *Ibid.*; pp. 96, 97.

pillory upon its mental though not its physical side that prompted some of these acts—perhaps that of the Harvard College seniors who resolved never again to deal with Editor John Mein, who championed the non-boycotters.[1] The town meeting went a step further, and ordered the names of seven persistent offenders inscribed on the town records in order "that posterity may know who those persons were that preferred their little private advantages to the common interest of all the colonies."[2]

Boston, the scene of so many stirring activities, staged a prototype of our present-day "peaceful picketing" on a mass scale, when, during the struggle to prevent disintegration of the boycott forces, in 1770, a procession of more than a thousand persons proceeded, in what Professor Schlesinger describes as "impressive and orderly array," to the homes and shops of the recalcitrant merchants, among them two sons of the governor, whom they sought under the roof of the executive mansion itself. Having made their demonstration and protest, in every place the multitude quietly dispersed.[3]

All these legal, extra-legal, and illegal modes of social pressure exerted in combination an effect so powerful and overwhelming that in both North and South men cowered and wept before committees possessing no authority whatever except that of public opinion. This, however, was powerful enough to drive from the colonies the able and fearless South Carolina publicist, William Henry Drayton, for his unyielding opposition, on constitutional grounds, to non-importation; and unverified tradition has it that the doughty Boston editor, John Mein, also sought peace in flight, for a time at least.

[1] *Ibid.;* pp. 112, 130, 148, 149, 158, 172.
[2] *Ibid.;* p. 173.
[3] *Ibid.;* p. 176.

When all the taxes except that on tea were repealed in 1770, the merchants abandoned their "utilitarian revolt" with even greater alacrity from the fact that the more turbulent Sons of Liberty and other political radicals were coming to look upon them as the champions of imperiled constitutional rights. In their case it would seem to be exemplified, as a Quaker merchant of Philadelphia had predicted, that "Interest, all powerful Interest, will bear down Patriotism."[1] Yet under the leadership of men of different interests and temper the movement of protest which the merchants had started was to continue, and to pass through the increasingly violent scenes of the Boston Tea-Party, the Boston Massacre, and the sacrifice at Lexington, culminating in seven long years of rebellion and war.

The foregoing account of the boycott in one of its earliest manifestations clearly reveals that it is inextricably entwined with other methods of coercion, so that one who pulls this string can never be quite sure how much of a social tangle he will find on his hands in the end. This is due to two conditions: first, the logical connection between the various forms of social pressure; and, secondly, the fact that every social movement, no matter how honestly devoted its leaders may be toward the aims and methods avowed, is liable to draw into its constituency elements that hold different scruples and opinions concerning the means proper to be employed. Thus it came about that the conservative, utilitarian colonial merchants, honestly deeming themselves especial sponsors of "law and order," came to figure in the end as harbingers of a violently radical political movement which eventuated in full-blown revolution and war.

Aside from some sporadic instances to be mentioned in a later paragraph, the boycott figures, during the interim be-

[1] *Ibid.;* p. 212.

tween the events just recited and its very recent expansion in the Orient, as an instrument of coercion in labor disputes; and it is to that phase of the story that we now address this discussion.

The boycott as a weapon of labor in industrial disputes, like that of the colonial merchants, is indigenous to America. This was perceived by the earliest students of the subject. Thus a writer in the first number of the English "Economic Journal," as far back as 1891, pointed out that the boycott had been little used by English laborers, while the United States had witnessed a great and rapid expansion of the policy.[1] A German writer somewhat later referred to the United States as "the classic home of the boycott."[2]

These expressions are borne out by facts, for the Knights of Labor, so prominent in the earlier industrial history of the United States, made such extensive use of this weapon in their struggles with employers that a careful student of the subject concludes that they were "primarily a boycotting organization." Indeed their absorption in this method of coercing employers became so great that in 1887 it was deemed advisable to establish a "boycotting department" in the national order.

At this time, however, the Knights were beginning to decline, and within the next decade they were virtually displaced by the American Federation of Labor. The latter was more conservative from the very beginning in its use of the boycott, but only for prudential, and not ethical, reasons.[3] This organization grew up under the intense

[1] "The Boycott as an Element in Trade Disputes," by John Burnett, in the "Economic Journal"; Vol. I, No. 1 (1891).

[2] Quoted in "The Boycott in American Trade Unions," by Leo Wolman, "Johns Hopkins University Studies in Historical and Political Science, Series XXXIV., No. 1 (1916); p. 41.

[3] Wolman, *op. cit.;* pp. 25, 27, 34.

hostility of the Knights, so that there was presented in those days the spectacle of the older organization imposing boycotts upon the products of those younger rival unions which afterwards came together in the new American Federation of Labor.[1]

The first labor boycott in the United States, according to a leading authority in this field, was conducted by the hatters of Baltimore in 1833.[2] During that decade the growth in its use was very rapid, and it early showed a tendency to elaborate itself into the various forms distinguished by those who practise or study this remarkable movement in detail.

The history of boycotting in the United States is a long and devious story, marked by such exciting events as the great Pullman strike, the Danbury Hatters' Case, the bitter struggle with the Bucks Stove and Range Co., and similar incidents. It is no part of the present task to set forth this account, but merely to indicate the enormous importance of the boycott in the history of American Labor, as a basis for some further analysis of the policy as a method of non-violent coercion, and, in that sense, a form of passive resistance.

Students of the boycott itself, entirely apart from any connection with passive resistance or kindred conceptions, have perceived its coercive aspects, although they are not always in agreement concerning these. The earliest of them all asserted that throughout history in some form or other it "has been used as a sort of impalpable weapon for the purpose of spiritual, social, or moral intimidation. . . ."[3] Dr. Wolman, in the monograph already quoted, attempts to narrow the definition for the purposes

1 *Ibid.;* p. 29.

2 "Boycotts and the Labor Struggle," by Harry W. Laidler, New York, 1914; p. 69.

3 Burnett, *loc. cit.;* p. 163.

of the student of industrial disputes. He therefore challenges the assertion of certain other students that coercion of disinterested third parties is an essential element in the term "boycott" as applied to trade disputes. His own conclusion is that it may be defined as "a combination formed for the purpose of restricting the markets of an individual or group of individuals."[1] The same writer distinguishes the boycott from the strike by the fact that in the strike the employer "may obtain a fair hearing and take measures to protect his business," whereas "in a boycott the union acts as judge, declares the employer guilty, invokes to its aid a vast power foreign to the dispute—the membership of affiliated unions—and, if the boycotted commodity is sold for the most part to workingmen, it succeeds in destroying the employer's business."[2] Yet we find Dr. Laidler, on the other hand, saying: "When picketing is brought into play . . . and third parties are induced to abstain from offering their labor power to the employer, the methods of the strike and the boycott show a marked similarity. When strikers bring to their aid the sympathetic strike, all distinctions between the boycott and the strike on the ground of immediate and ultimate effects are found to be without merit."[3] The two, especially in the case of the secondary boycott, where those who fail to support the original movement are themselves boycotted, thus merge together. For by the secondary boycott the boycotters accomplish the same thing that is achieved by picketing in the case of the strike, and that is the coercion of the employer by bringing such economic and social pressure upon third parties as will cause them to aid, abet, and make the original coercive effort effective.

[1] *Op. cit.;* pp. 11, 12.
[2] *Op. cit.;* p. 212.
[3] *Op. cit.;* p. 212.

The boycott becomes in this way an exceedingly powerful means of social pressure and has shown itself capable of some very wide applications. Those which represent the efforts of whole populations or national groups will be discussed in the following chapter, while for the present we confine ourselves to industrial disputes, where a more or less limited section of the laborers seeks to carry out a policy of economic or social coercion.

Dr. Wolcott thinks that the boycott was practised so extensively by the Knights of Labor partly because they needed to rely on "spectacular and effective, but cheap, methods of aggression." Moreover, being poorly supplied with funds, but controlling a strong economic force in the purchasing power of its members, it logically seized upon the boycott as its most likely means of coercion.[1] This factor is especiallly effective when the boycott is laid, not upon materials used in a trade, but upon the finished commodities actually used by all the working people. In such a situation it has recently been estimated that the American Federation of Labor, with its two million members and their eight million relatives, friends, and sympathizers, controls a really vast purchasing power in certain situations, and it is known that it has been effectively wielded in some instances. In fact, the strength of the boycott depends upon the coercive potentialities that lie, not only in enlistment of possible purchasers with those engaged in the boycott, but also in "those groups of consumers who feel that labor can in turn bring to bear upon them effective pressure of a political or economic nature."[2] The boycott has therefore been aptly likened, by the writer quoted, to "a mailed hand over the head of a recalcitrant employer," in those very frequent cases where it is held

[1] *Ibid.;* p. 27.
[2] Wolman, *op. cit.;* p. 86.

in *reserve* as an impending but not too frequently utilized chastisement.

The kind of coercion used in the non-violent boycott is well characterized by Dr. Laidler, when he says that it "simply gives a merchant a choice as to whether he desires to continue his dealings with the boycotted firms, thus losing the custom of unionists and their friends, or whether he prefers to cease his profitable relations with the firm and retain a certain patronage." And he very pertinently adds: "Every day merchants are forced to just such choices by their competitors. . . . The man has to choose between two evils, but his choice is left free."[1]

These are true words, for such situations are the very stuff that social life is made of. The experience of such an organization as the Consumers' League, in a city like New York, is entirely corroborative, particularly in connection with its attempt to bring about better working conditions by means of the publication of "white lists" containing the names of the fairly managed department-stores. The secretary, Mrs. Florence Kelley, declared: "The experience of twenty years is conclusive that wages cannot be dealt with by the method of persuasion. There must be coercion, either through efficient organization of the wage earners . . . or by legislation for minimum wage boards."[2]

Next to violence itself, its accomplice, secrecy, is the essentially evil aspect of any form of coercion. This feature in itself tends to render the black-list more harmful than the boycott. Thus Mr. John Mitchell observed that "The black-list . . . is generally covert and secret," using devices and signs so slight as to baffle detection. He also clearly perceived the affinity that always holds between

[1] *Ibid.;* 232–3.
[2] Quoted by Laidler, *ibid.;* p. 33.

the secret and the malicious in human conduct when he said: "The only safeguards against the occasional abuses of the boycott are openness and publicity, and if the law forces the boycott to become irregular and secret, it will undoubtedly be used to serve the purpose of malice and spite. . . ."[1]

Our conclusion on the side of method is that the boycott is a form of passive resistance in all cases where it does not descend to violence or intimidation. The fact that it is coercive does not place it beyond the moral pale, for coercion, as we have remarked before, is a fact inseparable from life in society. On the side of the object in view, it need hardly be said that, as Justice Holmes has argued, "the true grounds of decisions are considerations of policy and of social advantage, and it is vain to suppose that solutions can be attained by logic and the general propositions of law which nobody disputes."[2] It is upon the ground of similar reasoning that Dr. Wolman concludes: "The question of the morality or immorality of the boycott as an industrial weapon cannot, however, be settled by referring merely to the abstract rights of those affected by its exercise. Another important element must . . . be considered, namely, the function of the boycott in modern industrial life."[3]

Any attempt to set forth the character of this function in further detail would carry the discussion entirely beyond the scope of the present study. Attention is called to this aspect of the problem merely to register the fact that here we again have to face the inability of absolutist theories of conduct to solve the concrete problems of daily life in the actual, striving, rough-and-tumble world.

1 Quoted by Laidler, *ibid.;* p. 331.
2 *Ibid.;* p. 193.
3 *Op. cit.;* p. 138.

CHAPTER XVIII

NON-VIOLENT COERCION AND THE NATIONALISTIC BOYCOTT

THOSE who have studied most intensively the boycott as a definite, highly specialized instrument characteristic of the conflicts of organized labor and capital have been nevertheless well aware of the more varied applications to which this form of social pressure has lent itself. One striking summary of its wider manifestations runs as follows: "The general public resorts to the boycott to force a reduction of monopoly prices; the class conscious capitalist uses it to silence the organs of public opinion; the employer ruthlessly employs it to crush the union spirit among his workmen; the merchant wields it to cut the market from beneath unmanageable competitors; the citizen uses it to place his friends in office; the peoples of one country practice it to gain concessions from other countries or to prevent aggressions; labor, business, social, ethical, religious, political, educational associations fashion it to their ends—some for the weal of society, some to its detriment."[1] In this passage the term is given a wider meaning than that specifically treated by Dr. Laidler, but it is this wider significance that concerns the student of passive resistance. We do not, however, adopt completely this broader use of the word "boycott," because it leads to confusion of thought. For instance, the term is sometimes made to cover such things as the Jewish practice of shunning Samaritans and the refusal of the Pharisees to

[1] Laidler, *ibid.;* p. 55.

hold social intercourse with the publicans.[1] This would seem to be an unwarranted extension of the term, because the boycott, even in its widest application, means something more specific than mere lack of social intercourse. The same writers come nearer to the truth when they mention excommunication and interdict, as practiced by the Roman Catholic Church during the middle ages. The word "boycott" should be used neither so narrowly as to denote only the very definite measures of labor or capital in the industrial conflict, nor so widely as to gather under its scope all the more or less settled attitudes of avoidance between social groups such as Jew and Samaritan, Brahman and Pariah. It is not merely an attitude, but is an instrument—a method of social pressure designed for a definite purpose. That purpose is not, by any means, to sever relations, but to modify the type or character of the relations already existing. In his early essay, already referred to, Mr. John Burnett takes his stand very clearly upon this firm middle ground when he characterizes the boycott in its wider sense as "a sort of impalpable weapon for the purposes of spiritual, social or moral intimidation by one section of society against another, or by individuals against each other."[2] And he rightly adds that the interdict or excommunication of the medieval church was "the modern 'boycott' on a gigantic scale, applied to feelings and sentiments in human nature peculiarly sensitive to alarm." This is true because it was not a settled attitude of contempt and avoidance, as in many cases that merely resemble the boycott, but was a deliberately chosen measure of non-violent coercion used to produce a definitely specified form of conduct. We do not, however, interpret

[1] Thus Laidler, *ibid.*, p. 27; and quoted by Wolman, *op. cit.*, p. 16. But both these writers narrow the term for the purpose of their own discussion.

[2] *Loc. cit.;* p. 163.

these words so rigidly as to exclude a "spontaneous revulsion of feeling in large masses of people against a certain individual, with the result that they determine to cease all intercourse with him, social or economic," as Dr. Wolman accurately describes the boycott in its more generic form.[1] But in such instances, and the very affair in Ireland that gave birth to the name is a case in point, this wave of popular feeling is aroused by concrete acts, uses specific and concerted methods, and aims at definite results.

This limitation of the term by no means confines it to labor struggles. On the contrary, its very great development along the narrower line in the United States should not be allowed to obscure the fact that it began in the New England colonies, and later in Ireland, as a somewhat broad *social* policy; and it has been greatly extended by struggling national groups in very recent years. But before treating of those aspects an inherent weakness in the boycott method itself must be pointed out.

This is its tendency to fail from apathy on the one hand or to be betrayed into the use of violence on the other. For example, Mr. A. J. Portenar, after years of actual experience in the use of the boycott in labor disputes, found the method failing despite its abundant funds, and proposed to substitute for it "a great coöperative society controlled and directed by international unions." His argument for this change of tactics is as follows: "Far more than money, it must have the enthusiastic devotion of its members to the continuous, laborious and unpleasant work needful to make the expenditure of money effective. This, with a few exceptions, I found it impossible to get." The apathy of the members of the boycotting union, and of course still more that of the affiliated unions and the public, was such as to lose his great fight against the Butter-

[1] *Ibid.;* p. 18.

ick Co. "Therefore," he concludes, "my opinion is that no boycott can completely and permanently accomplish the result sought, and very few will do nearly as much in that direction as the one here spoken of, which finally became a failure."[1]

When apathy fails to quench the movement, it is very liable, on the other hand, to flare forth in deeds of violence, which we understand to be the unlawful or unregulated use of destructive physical force against persons or things. This has been noticed already in all the forms of passive resistance thus far described, and it will appear very clearly in those yet to be discussed. It has also dogged the pathway of the labor struggle, so that students of the subject have deemed it necessary to devise the term "compound boycott" to denote those that involve intimidation by means of threats or violence.[2] But, instead of thus widening the connotation of the word, it would seem better to recognize that whenever the line of violence is crossed the so-called boycott ceases to be such in reality, and should be treated under another category.

The boycott is essentially a form of coercion, but its non-violent character is also essential to its definition. In its origin it may be either "a spontaneous revulsion of feeling in large masses of people" or the deliberately planned policy of a small, centralized, or even autocratic group. In every case its procedure is to deprive the offending party of some kind of social contact or relation which he regards as desirable. Its method is thus privative and non-violent. When, on the contrary, physical force and intimidation are used, this introduces a new type of contacts instead of taking away the old, and it drags the conflict to a level

[1] "Problems of Organized Labor," by A. J. Portenar; quoted by Laidler, *ibid.*, p. 271.

[2] Cf. Laidler, *ibid.*; p. 64.

where an entirely different set of mental values and ethical standards prevails. The situation becomes one in which the boycotted party no longer finds himslf compelled to choose between this or that form of economic or social contact, but is faced with the perilous prospect of ceasing to have any contact whatsoever. In other words, he fears for his life, either its destruction or serious impairment through severe bodily injury. The alternative is no longer: "Choose one or the other of these types of contact, and experience such and such consequences in either case." It is now the peremptory challenge to live according to the challenger's formula or cease to live at all. The transaction might be called a social "hold-up" committed by a group, a class, or other section of society—a sort of collective crime. Whenever the thing we are talking about moves in this direction it ceases to that extent to be a boycott and becomes a persecution.

The boycott, as here understood, derives its coercive power from the fact that the boycotters possess sufficient directive influence over the necessary social contacts to place before the object of their social pressure a real pair of alternatives. Let us take the case of the *interdict* and *excommmunication* of the medieval church. This has been included under the wider view of the boycott, as we have seen; but it would be more accurately described as an ecclesiastical *blacklisting.* The analogy between it and the black-list policy of a great modern business corporation is striking. In both cases we see a centralized, autocratic organization wielding monopolistic control over a kind of social contact or relation which is held to be indispensable in the individual's scale of values. In the one instance he must have the opportunity to worship and in the other to work. In both situations one finds it possible to sustain those relations only on the terms laid down by the monopoly. Go where he might, during the middle ages in Europe, the excommunicant could obtain the bread of life for his soul by no means or power so long as the ban of the church lay on him; and, just in so far as the black-list of to-day is complete and monopolistic, just so will one bearing it seek in vain for the chance to earn bread for his body.

Some *differences* appear which are equally instructive. The medieval church, being unquestioned in its spiritual authority, was able to use its black-list against private individuals, rulers, communities, and nations (the *interdict*) with all openness and publicity. The monopolistic employer, on the contrary, has to manipulate his black-list with the utmost secrecy, for fear of public opinion, and of the law in some cases. But this is not the whole story, for the motives in the two cases are quite different. Despite a shameful lot of corruption and self-seeking at times, the purpose of the church was to discipline men unselfishly for the good of their souls. The purpose of the blacklisting employer and the boycotting employee is to discipline others for personal, if not selfish, gain. And the more indispensable the publicity the less liable is any of these measures to degenerate into the malice and spite that flourish in secret.

One other distinction may contribute to this analysis. The power of the ecclesiastical excommunication endured just so long as men really believed that by thus cutting them off from its prescribed ritual of worship the church could really shut men away from the divine source of spiritual life. When they ceased to think so, this form of boycott or black-list fell worthless to the ground, simply because the alternatives placed before the individual lost their sense of reality; they constituted no real dilemma. The same is true of the boycott in every form. Its power consists in its ability to control social relations which possess an impelling value for the individuals or groups directly or indirectly involved. The Korean "demonstration" owed its futility to the operation of this principle. The boycotters in that case were not organized in such a way as to control social contacts deemed important by the Japanese, who cared nothing for their protestations. On the other hand, these might have been of the utmost significance to Japan if the attention of the international public had not been engrossed with more immediately urgent affairs. Failing in this, the only other method would have been for the Koreans to render the Japanese game of "assimilation" not worth the candle, but they did not succeed in shaping their course to that end, with the result that all their heroism and suffering were without avail.

Aside from this demonstration in Korea, we have discussed one other national expression of passive resistance, namely, that of the American colonies of the eighteenth century. The latter, however, proved to be really a merchant-class, utilitarian movement in the beginning; and it lost much of the support of its profit-seeking promoters when it passed into a nationalistic political movement aiming at independence. From this quasi-class use of the boycott, as well as its strictly class-conscious exploitation by both sides in the labor-capital conflict, we turn now to consider it as a method of passive resistance and non-violent coercion on the part of whole populations, without regard to class divisions.

Beyond comparison the most extraordinary example of this social phenomenon is that of India, which is reserved for a separate chapter. It is mentioned here because we are indebted to that movement for a valuable survey of this aspect of the subject. More specifically, an anonymous writer in the official organ of the Indian National Congress printed, in the autumn of 1920, a series of papers on "Non-Coöperation in Other Lands," in which the passive resistance movements in Hungary, Egypt, and Korea are described.[1]

The Hungarian story, in its passive resistance aspects, centers around Francis Deak, a Catholic landowner, and belongs to the middle nineteenth century. The Emperor Franz Josef was then striving to subordinate the ancient Hungarian kingdom to the power of Austria. The account runs in this wise:

"What can we do?" said the moderates. "We cannot fight Austria with the sword—what, then, is there left but to submit and make the best of the situation?"

"Your laws are violated, yet your mouths remain closed!" Deak exclaimed in response, "Woe—woe to the nation which raises no protest when its rights are outraged! It contributes to its own slavery by its silence. The nation which submits to injustice and oppression without protest is doomed."

Deak proceeded to organize a scheme for national education and industry, and a boycott against Austrian goods was set in motion. As relations between the two governments became more tense, "Deak admonished the people not to be betrayed into acts of violence, nor to abandon the ground of legality. 'This is the safe ground,' he said, 'on which, unarmed ourselves, we can hold our own against armed force. If suffering be necessary, suffer with dignity.' He had given the order to the country—Passive

[1] See "India" for October 15, 1920, and succeeding issues. The articles are signed "A. F. B.," and are based upon "The Resurrection of Hungary," by Arthur Griffiths, "Korea's Fight For Freedom," by R. A. McKenzie, and similar literature. As a result, largely, of Griffiths' interest in the Hungarian experience, the Sinn Fein movement in Ireland was conceived on lines of non-violent resistance at the outset.

Resistance"; "and the order was obeyed. When the Austrian Tax Collector came to gather the taxes the people did not beat him nor even hoot him—they just declined to pay. The Tax Collector thereupon called in the Austrian police, and the police seized the man's goods. Then the Hungarian auctioneer declined to auction them, and an Austrian auctioneer had to be introduced. When he arrived he discovered that he would have to bring bidders from Austria also if the goods were to be sold. The government found before long that it was costing more to distrain the goods than the tax itself was worth."

When the Austrians attempted to billet their soldiers upon the Hungarian householders, the latter did not resist except in a passive way, but the Austrian soldiers themselves protested against the decree, after trying to live in houses where every one despised them. And, just as common soldiers could not endure an existence cut off from that minimum of social intercourse which is indispensable even to an oppressor, neither could the Imperial Parliament continue to exist when no representatives appeared from Hungary.

Finally, on February 18, 1867, the Emperor Franz Josef capitulated and recognized the constitution and independence of Hungary. It may well be questioned whether the passive resistance above described was responsible solely for Hungary's success, but it was doubtless a large factor, since we are told that the emperor tried in every possible way to give signal recognition to Deak, but the latter would accept neither presents nor honors, saying simply, in reply to a question concerning his real desires, "Sire, when I am dead you may say that Francis Deak was an honest man."[1]

In his discussion of the boycott Dr. Laidler refers to

[1] *Ibid.*

the case of Persia, where the shah aroused the anger of the people by giving a monopoly in tobacco to an English company for $75,000 a year. Armed rebellion in some parts was put down by the military forces, but when the nobility, and even the women in the harem, ceased smoking; when meetings were called off, stores were closed, and trade dwindled almost to nothing, the government found itself compelled to yield, and the concession was canceled.[1]

The Egyptian boycott against the mission of Lord Milner in 1919 offers an equally striking and successful example. The British Government sent Lord Milner and his associates out to make inquiry concerning the attitude and aims of the Egyptians. Establishing their headquarters at a leading hotel, they issued appeals to the people to come before them and testify "freely." Instead of doing so, a thoroughgoing boycott, led by the Nationalists, was launched against the inquiry, and drew after it, one after another, every section of the national life. Workers high and low went on strike; the students left their schools and picketed the hotel where the commission was sitting; the members of the Egyptian bar ceased their practice for a week, in protest against the coming of the commission; and the climax was reached in a three weeks' strike of the public officials in all departments of the government, which culminated with the act of the ministry, who joined the strikers and resigned their positions. In so doing, their resolution was doubtless fortified by the women, who picketed the offices of the ministry and paraded without regard to social distinctions, veiled upper-class ladies and courtesans from the lowest quarters marching through the streets together.

In this affair we see again the enormous social pres-

[1] *Op. cit.;* p. 53.

sure that can be exerted by even the lowliest and weakest when by some form of concerted non-violent action they shut off the supply of social contacts without which the mightiest tyranny must languish and die. So we read that "Lord Milner and his colleagues spent three months in Egypt, employing every device to secure the coöperation of the Egyptian people, and they returned to England without a representative Egyptian having consulted with them." The mission exhausted every effort "without succeeding in breaking the circle of silence around it. . . . Never in history," asserts the narrator, "has a nation revealed more united determination."[1]

In this episode the method of passive resistance was effective because it aimed at a definite object, which did not require too long a time for its accomplishment, and it operated by withholding social contacts that were within the control of the boycotters. For it is perfectly obvious that an inquiry into the state of mind of any community must be absolutely dependent on the willingness of its members to testify. Being so extremely simple, this may be taken as a type of non-violent coercion, illustrating most clearly the general truth that its power consists in withholding coöperation in situations where the specified kind of coöperation is indispensable to the boycotted party, and is at the command of the boycotter.

The Chinese, more than any other people, have shown a natural predilection for the use of the boycott for national purposes. In 1906 they were employing this method against the United States with such vigor that an American correspondent[2] credited China with "the distinction of having organized the most extensive boycott in the an-

[1] *Ibid.*
[2] Dr. W. A. P. Martin writing in January, 1906.

nals of history,'' and declared that it had ''fallen like a paralytic stroke on the commerce of two nations—amounting to war waged with the weapons of peace.'' At any rate it was important enough to occasion a hearing before the United States Immigration Commission on ''Boycott of American Manufactured Goods by the People of China.''

This boycott was caused by the indignation of the Chinese against the disabilities and hardships which their nationals of all classes, including students, were compelled to undergo in the United States. There was no effort in this instance to secure the admission of coolie labor, but to obtain more proper treatment of the classes privileged to enter.

While the boycott of 1906 was the work of the upper classes and represented the interests of the aroused student element, in 1908 there occurred a wide-spread movement among the masses. This time it was directed against Japan, because of her overbearing conduct in what is known as the *Tatsu Maru* affair.

The boycott, which was largely centered in the great coast towns, and affected chiefly marine products, particularly those imported from Japan and in many cases by Chinese merchants resident in Japan, was promoted in a most systematic way, and it declared its intention of inflicting a loss of $300,000,000 upon the offending Japanese before it should be abandoned.[1]

In numberless ways of communication, especially through personal emissaries of the so-called National Disgrace Societies, who were careful to keep within their recognized rights, the boycott was spread more or less widely throughout the empire, and even reached the Chinese then resi-

[1] Joseph Rice, in Canton correspondence of the "New York Herald," April 10, 1908.

dent in Australia. But, despite all these vigorous measures, and notwithstanding the fact that even the women held meetings in which they pledged themselves to non-consumption agreements just as their Occidental sisters did in American colonial days, the boycott soon passed its crest and declined. This was perhaps the more inevitable inasmuch as it was largely an expression of indignation and retaliation for indignities already suffered in the past.

In 1911 a boycott against British goods was planned, as a protest against British activities in Tibet. In 1915, another boycott against Japanese goods was organized by the Chinese merchants in the leading commercial ports, who were greatly incensed by the notorious Twenty-one Demands pressed upon China by Japan for acceptance.[1]

The boycott of 1919 began with a student strike, passed into a boycott, and was gradually merged again into the great movement for national regeneration of which it was really an overt expression in the first place. The movement had its birth on May 3, 1919, which had been set apart as a day of national humiliation, in commemoration of the acceptance of Japan's hateful Twenty-one Demands by the Chinese Government. Only three days before, the

[1] Statement of Mr. Ge Zey Wood, editor-in-chief of the "Chinese Students' Monthly," in letter to the present writer. In addition to this and other specific citations in the text, the author acknowledges the assistance in personal conference or by correspondence of Messrs. C. P. Cheng, C. K. Chen, William Hung. Y. Y. Tsu, Chiang Liu, T. M. Lau, Dr Joseph Shiang-Min Lee, all connected with the Chinese student movement in the United States; also Mr. Ralph A. Ward, acting executive secretary of the China Society of America; Mr. Perry O. Hanson of the North China conference, Methodist Episcopal Church; the Rev. Paul L. Corbin, Congregationalist missionary long resident in North China; Mr. Maurice T. Price, educational adviser to Edward Evans & Sons, Ltd., Shanghai, and Mr. G. Stanley High of the China Society, the last two of whom were in China during the height of the boycott also Mr. R. S. Kim (with materials for Korea).

peace conference had disappointed the eager hopes of China by awarding the port of Tsingtao, with the former German concessions, to Japan. The most dearly cherished desire of the Chinese people had been to purge their sacred province of Shan-tung, the birthplace and shrine of Confucius, Mencius, and other great heroes of their race, from the presence of foreign aggressors. The mental and moral aspects of the hour are thus vividly portrayed by a Chinese student writer:[1]

> Even the cradle of the nation was stolen. The masses of the people looked toward Peking. There they found only corruption and treason. They looked toward Paris. . . . There is no hope there. They looked toward their own enlightened young men who had studied abroad. They found that they were inadequately prepared to offer a practical plan to save the country. The merchants lacked initiative; they were looking for a leader. And the leadership came from school boys and school girls who were ready to sacrifice their future careers, liberty and life that China might continue to exist. The students of China refused to study, refused to participate in the usual affairs of life until China was free. They clogged the machinery of the nation. They brought the issue to a head. . . . These students were Chinese trained. They had never, most of them, left the country. . . . Their cry was, "Sell us, sell everything we have or may at any time have, but let the nation live."

Another Chinese student[2] has characterized the students' movement in China, in contrast with the prohibition and similar movements in America, as "a sweeping patriotic movement covering and stirring everything," and this is corroborated by Professor John Dewey's later as-

[1] Mr. F. C. Sze, University of Wisconsin, "Publications of the Publicity Bureau of the Chinese Students in the University of Illinois"; No. 2 (August 7, 1919), p. 9.

[2] Mr. H. S. Chow, of the University of Pennsylvania, *loc. cit.*, No. 7 (April, 1921).

sertion that, after the episodes we are narrating, it "was drawn into a multitude of side streams and is now irrigating the intellectual and industrial soil of China."[1] But at the time whereof we speak they had a very definite purpose, which was to recover Shan-tung Province from the Japanese and to drive from office three Chinese officials who were believed to be in traitorous negotiations with Japan. The student youth of China, ranging in years from twelve to twenty, held the clearest conceptions concerning national policy and were possessed of a sense of their obligation as the only element in the population having common ideals and the power to articulate them. Moreover, they had no political or personal axes to grind —a very unusual thing in the political life of China.

The first move was made by the students at the National University in Peking, who marched, to the number of three thousand, with a petition of protest concerning the Shan-tung award, addressed to the representatives of foreign powers. This happened on the fourth of May, and telegrams were sent at once to other student centers throughout China. On the seventh, or tenth according to some narrators, the students of Shanghai gathered "spontaneously" in the public recreation ground and formulated their demands upon the Government. There was formed the Shanghai Students' Union, consisting of eighty-three schools in Shanghai, and representing twenty thousand students among which were included five thousand girls. Similar action was taken in Tientsin, Nanking, Hankow, Canton, Hongchow, Soochow, Ningpo, and other cities of China.[2]

[1] In the "New Republic"; February 25, 1920.

[2] Sze, *op. cit.;* p. 10. A young Chinese woman student, in describing to the present writer her own part in the affair, put it thus quaintly: "We students went out into the streets and taught the people how to love their country."

When the arrest of students was reported at Shanghai, "the Chinese merchants, big and little, closed up their shops. It all happened in about thirty minutes on Wednesday morning, June 4th. . . . After the shops had been closed for two days word was received from Peking to the effect that the merchants' protest had been effective and that the students had been released. But with their power established the merchants naturally decided to make a clean slate of it and demanded the resignations of the pro-Japanese traitors at the Capital."[1]

By the combined efforts of students and merchants the offending officials were ousted, and the Government promised to refrain from direct negotiations with Japan.

Frequent clashes took place between students and agents of the government, and we are told that "bloodshed occurred on many occasions."[2] But, encouraged by their success, both merchants and students proceeded to extend their organizations by admirably systematic and effective methods.

The student-organization swept millions into its membership by a simple plan which lent itself to rapid and indefinite extension without dependence on a centralized authority or stimulus. This was the "Ten Men Group" arrangement of the National Students' League. According to this plan any ten students could form a unit by merely coming together and choosing out of their number a chairman, an inspector of goods, an editor of placards and newspaper broadsides, a treasurer, and five orators to speak in the streets and other public places. The duties of these officers were such as pertain to the functions indicated. The energy and zeal of the individuals composing these groups was the secret of their success. It is

[1] Ms. statement of Mr. Stanley H. High.
[2] Chow, *ibid.*

well emphasized by one of their critics when he says, "Every Chinese student took it upon himself to turn out a few thousand posters, and the city was literally plastered with signs and banners. Chinese employees in the correspondence departments of many foreign firms also got into the game and did a little posting and circularizing at the firm's expense for postage and stationery."[1] Besides these communications, personal emissaries of the National Disgrace societies and other affiliated organizations composed of lawyers, educators, and agriculturists, went out on every boat up the rivers into the interior, fervently preaching the boycott program to the passengers and the people. In all these activities the effort was not merely to exhort but to instruct the people, showing them just how to conduct the boycott with least disadvantage to themselves. Thus Mr. High relates, "When we were in Chengtu, the remote capital of Szechuan Province, we were told that the students in the University there had secured a full page in a native daily paper and on one side were printing the Japanese commodities which the Chinese had been accustomed to buy and on the opposite a list of those Chinese-made products which were a satisfactory substitute."[2] These activities represent only a few among many pursued by the students, such as teaching native industries to native artisans in night schools, and giving plays to foster the boycott—all having the threefold object of boycotting Japan, promoting native industry, and purifying the government of its pusillanimity and corruption.

The parallel methods of the merchants are well exemplified in the admirable measures adopted by the Peking

[1] "That Boycott Fizzle," in The Far Eastern Review, Jan., 1921, p. 22

[2] *Ibid.*

Chamber of Commerce, as reported in the *China Bureau of Public Information*, Shanghai, Jan. 16, 1920. The plan was surprisingly thorough and systematic, but its numerous subdivisions are grouped under four main heads, as follows:

A.—Measures for stopping the coming of Japanese goods into this country.

B.—Measures for dealing with the Old Japanese Goods.

C.—Measures to be carried out by the Chamber of Commerce.

D.—Measures to be carried out by the individual citizens.

From among the various directions included under these four heads, the following are quoted to show the popular bearings of their plan: The Chamber shall advise all the shops to have at their doors calendars on which are printed such notices as "Only Home-Made Goods for Sale," "Don't Buy Japanese Goods," "Don't use Japanese Banknotes," etc.

The business shops shall voluntarily hand calendars on which are printed the aforesaid statements to their Customers.

Boards or cards with such requests as "Don't Buy Japanese Goods," "Don't use Japanese Banknotes," etc., shall be posted at the entrance of every street.

It is more easy to trace the popular course of the boycott as reflected in current accounts than to estimate its ultimate financial effects. For example, a well-equipped department store in Canton was accused of selling Japanese goods, whereupon its throngs of clerks were found idle on every floor, waiting for the trade that had suddenly ceased to flow. A few days after the students struck, the inmates of the Municipal Reformatory disdainfully shoved aside their plates because the fish course was Japanese!

The populace in the streets jeered foreigners caught abroad in Japanese straw hats. Chinese store-keepers in Shantung province scandalized the Japanese consul by rejecting the Japanese military notes offered by soldiers in payment of bills. Coolie longshoremen refused, even hundreds of miles up the rivers of the interior, to unload vessels discharging Japanese goods. Many of the smaller Japanese stores and shops were compelled to suspend business. In other cases the tabooed wares were dumped into the street and burned, either by the inspectors or the owners, who in every case were Chinese, and did not care, or dare, to protest in face of the popular indignation. In other cases the offensive goods were simply sequestered till the storm should pass by. Mr. High relates the following experience which well illustrates this aspect of the matter: "Later in the same year while in Shanghai, we set out to purchase a foot ruler, and at the Commercial Press we were shown a whole drawer-full of the exact article for which we were searching, but our clerk courteously informed us that these had been purchased in Japan, and therefore were not for sale. Bribes proved ineffectual, and although we walked from shop to shop for the remainder of that afternoon we were obliged to leave Shanghai without the ruler."[1]

Like earlier boycotts, that of 1919 stirred Chinese circles throughout the world, ripples coming to the surface occasionally in such distant places as Chicago, where a Chinese merchant was fined heavily by a secret society of his fellows for selling Japanese goods; or San Francisco, where the Chinese are reported to have made a bonfire of such obnoxious goods as the boycott found in their possession.

As for the total loss to Japanese trade, various authori-

[1] *Ibid.*

ties have settled upon $50,000,000, which we may accept as a close approximation. At any rate the pressure was great enough to impel the Japanese merchants of Peking and Tientsin, with apparent ruin staring them in the face, to appeal to their home government for protection. They insisted that the boycott should be made a diplomatic question of the first order and that demands for its removal should be backed by threats of military intervention. To all this the government at Tokio "could only reply that it knew of no way by which the Chinese merchants, much less the Chinese people, could be made to buy Japanese goods against their will."[1]

But the correspondents quoted, and most friends of China, recognize that figures express the least important aspect of the boycott, especially when it is seen in its larger setting; and it is impossible, as has appeared at every turn of this narrative, to separate the student strike and the boycott movement. Both are doubtless in part symptoms of a growing national consciousness. "For the first time in the history of China," says a Chinese student writer, "the spirit of the Chinese people has been really aroused."[1] Another declares that "These are not merely aftermath following the track of the students' movement. They are the seeds sown in the blood that was shed during the last strike and they will mean the strength and glory of a reborn China when time is ripe."[2]

Our account of China, which has come to figure as the classic land of the *nationalistic* boycott, as America is for the *industrial*, may not be finished without some reference

[1] *The Christian Science Monitor*, April 7, 1920.

[2] Mr. C. C. Yu, in *Publications of the Publicity Bureau of the Chinese Students in the University of Illinois*. No. 3, (Nov. 3, 1919)

[3] Mr. H. S. Chow, *Ibid.*, No. 7, (April, 1921)

to the question of its fundamental sources. The problem is whether her pacifism is the result of the circumstances of the hour or is the natural expression of race temperament and national culture. The answer is so very difficult that this discussion must of course be largely tentative.

Many of the friends of China, including some Chinese students in the United States, seem to look upon her use of passive resistance as a last resort, in the absence of other and more conventional means.

Thus Mr. Hanson writes, "The Chinese had no efficient army and navy so that it was impossible to resort to arms to seek revenge and redress." He thinks, moreover, that "the results have been far and away more beneficial than would have been the case had the Chinese attempted to fight." Mr. High expresses the same opinion when he says. "The Boycott of Japan represented the only weapon at hand which the Chinese could utilize against Japan. Nevertheless he holds that "passive methods of resistance such as the boycott are characteristic of the Chinese people," and expresses the opinion that "such movements will have greater effectiveness in the future," in proportion to the increase of national consciousness in China. Again, Mr. Cze, in the article already quoted, explains that the Chinese students "adopted the principle of passive resistance" because "the only thing that could be done was to strike, peacefully, quietly, but effectively."

But while these competent witnesses are supported by others in their account of the matter, the question remains whether this sole and only expedient was not, after all, just the one most compatible with the Chinese national character. Going further, we may point out that the very situation wherein the Chinese people found themselves shut up to the use of passive methods was itself the result of their passive resistance in the past. We are raising no new issue just here, for Chinese group behavior, as contrasted with that of more militant nations, has been the theme of earlier writers on Chinese life. So far as the episodes of the student strike and the boycott are concerned, the evidence from China reinforces our earlier conclusion that heroism is essentially a *social* phenomenon, depending upon the attitude of a *group,* and the sentiments which serve in it as standards for approval and disapproval applied to the character and conduct of others.[1] The experiences of the World War demonstrated that martial courage is a practically universal trait, depending upon inculcation for its development; so much so that it would seem to be very much more a matter of nurture than of nature; more truly cultural than instinctive.[2] This is certainly true of that set of artificially stimulated virtues known as military heroism, whatever may be said of innate courage and fortitude. Fortitude represents courage in its more passive aspect, and is the basis of ability to endure hardship and suffering. In these qualities the Chinese display even more than average endowment. A few incidents from the recent boycott serve to illustrate this statement, as in the occurrences at Tsinan-fu, the capital of the province of Shantung. Here the striking students came into contact with Japanese soldiers, who had been ordered, by proclamation, to arrest all students found on the streets at noon of June 12, 1919. As the forces, consisting of mounted infantry led by an officer with drawn sword, advanced, "the lads knelt on the street, and with tears streaming down many a face they cried, 'This is a matter of conscience.' As they

[1] The social process involved is most clearly elucidated by Prof. E., C. Hayes, in "Introduction to the Study of Sociology"; Ch. 20. New York, 1916.

[2] The present writer has discussed this problem more fully in "The Am. Jour. of Sociology," vol. XXVII, (Jan. 1922)

saw this scene," adds the American narrator, "the soldiers refused to obey their superiors, and the students were safe."[1] In this successful episode the students practised passive resistance and displayed the passive courage and fortitude which it requires. In other instances they gave expression to more positively belligerent impulses, as when they bound, labelled and photographed the office force of the pro-Japanese military clique at the headquarters of their pro-Japanese newspaper, the *Chang Yen Pao;* or gleefully made bon-fires of Japanese goods; or threw Chang Tsung-hsiang, the obnoxious Chinese minister to Japan, into the street and left him half dead. These demonstrations of physical force were coupled with the use of such slogans as "Kill the Traitors!" "Revenge the Disgrace!" and others of similar threatening import.

The Chinese people do not, it is true, base their passive resistance practices upon any doctrinaire or absolute principles of non-resistance; but on the other hand it seems clear that there is a distinctly pacifistic strain in Chinese character, both individual and social. It may be primarily *practical* rather than theoretical, but that merely shows its essentially Chinese character. One of the earliest among scientific observers of modern Chinese life has the following suggestive words to say on "The Race Mind of the Chinese": "The more cheaply gotten-up races of men have a short mental circuit and respond promptly to stimulus. . . . But the races of the higher destiny are not so easily set in motion. They are able to hold back and digest their impulses. The key to their conduct is to be found, not in their impressions, but in their thoughts and convictions. . . .

[1] "The Students' Revolt in China, by Paul Jones, An American in Shantung," the *Independent*, Sept. 20, 1919. Accompanying the article is a photograph of this remarkable scene.

Their intellect is a massive fly-wheel by means of which continuous will power is derived from confused and intermittent stimuli. . . . Now, of this massive unswerving type are the Chinese. Fiery or headlong action is the last thing to be expected of yellow men. They command their feelings and know how to bide their time. . . . Instead of assassinating the high-placed betrayer of his country, the Chinese patriot sends his Emperor a plain-spoken memorial about the traitor and then kills himself to show he is in earnest."[1] Recent history in Korea witnessed episodes so exactly similar to this description that they are highly corroborative of Professor Ross's analysis, in as much as the Koreans and Chinese are very closely related in race and culture.

In another passage Professor Ross is more explicit, and highly suggestive for our present inquiry:

> The soldier has come from the dregs and contempt for him has gone so far as to quench the natural admiration for the martial virtues. No civilian carries weapons, the duel is unknown, and there is little shame in showing the white feather. . . . Under nocturnal attack many a villager takes to his heels leaving his family to the robbers. The latter give the foreign traveler a wide berth having learned the fellow will actually fight. The mere presence of the white passenger is said to brace the nerves of the boatmen in the perilous rapids of the Yangtze. It is not considered shameful to weep, and one often hears of men dissolved in tears. Yet the Chinese meet pain and death like Stoics, and Gordon and Wolseley declared they make brave soldiers when well led. "When well led," aye, there's the rub! For Chinese pusillanimity testifies not to want of natural grit but to the fact that the bold manly qualities have not been stimulated among them, as they have been among us, *by social appreciation.*[1]

[1] Edward A. Ross, "The Changing Chinese," New York, 1911; pp. 51, 52.

[2] *Ibid.;* pp. 307-308.

This particular estimate of the soldier's social worth is not simply a thing of the past, as is shown by the saying still current among the populace in many parts, specifically in Shansi Province of North China: "One does n't make nails out of good iron nor soldiers out of good men."[1] Furthering also the national disparagement of the military career there stands the traditional list of professions, which, arranged in the order of social worth and honor, runs, scholar, agriculturist, artisan, merchant—with the soldier not even mentioned. This list reflects the standards of social evaluation, and enables one to understand the very great influence of the *student* movement in recent Chinese affairs, both at home and at the Washington disarmament conference.

Professor Dewey finds the explanation for the pacifism remarked by him in the peculiar social environment characteristic of Chinese life. "It is beyond question," he asserts, "that many traits of the Chinese mind are the products of an extraordinary and long-continued density of populations."[2] To be sure, he is speaking here of Chinese traits in general, and not specifically of their pacific attitudes, but the latter are clearly included. As one result of this "constant living in close contact with large numbers, of continual living in a crowd," with "no relief from the unremitting surveillance of their fellows," and with no possible escape through "even the possibility of solitude that comes from being in a crowd of strangers"—the Chinese people have developed a conservatism and a passivism that are almost beyond the understanding of Americans or other comers from the sparsely settled ranges of the Western world. In China, we are told, as in an overcrowded vessel, innovations are unwelcome because probably danger-

1 Personal statement of the Rev. Paul L. Corbin.
2 "Asia"; May, 1920.

ous, and the accepted wisdom consists in sitting still and in refraining under all circumstances, as Professor Dewey picturesquely puts it, from rocking the boat. "The reformer does not even meet sharp, clear-cut resistance. If he did, he might be stimulated to further effort. He is simply smothered. Stalling has become a fine art." This is the essence of passive resistance in its more negative aspect, where it figures more as obstruction than as coercion.

Social control apart from government in the ordinary, political sense of the term has reached its highest perfection in China. The problem of social checks and balances, social contacts and social pressures, would seem to have been elaborated to the highest degree of perfection—not as a theory of social psychology, but as the actual functioning of the national mind. "The actual government of China," says Professor Dewey, "was a system of nicely calculated personal and group pressures and pulls, exactions and 'squeezes,' neatly balanced against one another, of assertions and yieldings, of experiments to see how far a certain demand could be forced, and of yielding when the exorbitance of the demand called out an equal counter-pressure. . . . Their social calculus, integral and differential, exceeded anything elsewhere in existence." One can well understand how he refers to the Manchu rule as "a game of exactions and resistance," and it is equally evident that in the main it has been passive resistance and non-violent coercion that have figured, not only in the very recent boycotts against Japan and other nations, but in the daily affairs of Chinese life for ages.

Furthermore, it is reported that leading spirits in China have contemplated the organization of a "wholesale exodus from foreign concessions"[1] as a still more drastic protest

[1] *Ibid.*

against the aggressions of foreigners. If this plan were carried out it would bring Chinese passive resistance very close to the pattern set by India in that extraordinary movement known as *non-coöperation.*

CHAPTER XIX

NON-VIOLENCE AS SOUL-FORCE

PERHAPS it was about the autumn of 1920 that the Western world began to grow aware that a great revolution was going on in British India, headed by a leader and conducted by methods which astounded and bewildered Occidental reporters. For example, leading American newspapers and magazines were talking in the spring of 1921 about "a *monk* who imperils British rule in India."[1] This "monk" was named as Mahatma Gandhi, and, it being known that "Mahatma" is the Indian word for *saint,* one need not marvel that Westerners should take him to be a monk instead of an international publicist and man of affairs, which he had been for two decades before "making the head-lines" of the American press. The misapprehension is all the more natural because of his personal appearance and mode of life. This now famous world figure is described as small and slight, variously estimated in weight at from one hundred to one hundred and twenty-five pounds. His eyes are said to be mild, and his photograph shows them to be large, dark, and soulful. With sunken cheeks, marked with constant fasting, his voice weak and mild of tone, his feet bare and body clad in coarse homespun, Gandhi is far from presenting that personal appearance usually associated with

[1] "Literary Digest," Apr. 2, 1921, p. 40, reviewing articles in "New York Herald" and "Manchester (England) Guardian." Italics mine.

the leadership of men, especially among the nations of the Occident.

But things are different in the Orient, and the very traits discounted here may figure as a positive asset on the other side of the globe. One unusually well qualified to speak concerning this aspect says, "He is a man who, by the very example of his ascetic life, would attract the masses of India whatever his policy might happen to be, and it is just because of the great influence which he exercises over the people that he is regarded as so dangerous an opponent of British rule in India."[1] A fellow-countryman of the politician-saint thus describes his mode of daily life: "He lives the life of an ascetic. He eats only vegetables, rice and nuts. By voluntary fasting he has reduced himself to a mere skeleton. . . . He sits on a mat spread on the floor and sleeps on hard planks. He dresses like a poor workingman, and he walks barefoot. He invariably travels by the third class. He has reduced his personal needs to the minimum."[2]

Such is the more physical aspect of one of whom the same writer says, in words that are corroborated in various ways by a host of witnesses, "The soul of the East has found a worthy symbol in Gandhi; for he is most eloquently proving that man is essentially a spiritual being, that he flourishes best in the realm of the moral and spiritual, and most positively perishes both body and soul in the atmosphere of hatred and gunpowder smoke." We have called him both politician and saint because he him-

1 W. W. Pearson, in the New York "Call"; magazine section, September 18, 1921. Mr. Pearson is a graduate of Oxford and Cambridge, has resided in India, and acted as secretary to the Indian poet Tagore on his American tour.

2 Besanta Koomar Ray, in "New York American"; May 8, 1921. More recent reports describe Mr. Gandhi as using a Ford car in his campaigns.

self has said: "Most religious men I have met are politicians in disguise. I, however, who wear the guise of a politician, am at heart a religious man."[1] The pages that follow will present some evidence for determining his claim to either or both of these titles.

Mohandas Karamchand Gandhi, commonly called Mahatma Gandhi, was born in 1869, and was just rounding his fiftieth year when he emerged in his full rôle as one of the few world figures created by a world war. His ancestors before him were politicians, his forefathers having served as prime ministers of Porbandar and other native states of India. The Gandhi clan belong to the third or commercial caste, known as the Vaishya, with the warrior and priestly (Brahman) castes above it, and Sudra, or domestic caste below. The family, his mother in particular, was devoutly and strictly religious according to the ceremonial and teachings of its own caste. Religion is taken to heart in India, and it meant no small thing to break with the religious traditions into which one was born. So when the young Mohandas proposed, with the consent of his parents and an influential uncle, to proceed to England, for the study of law, his caste associates, finding abuse and threatenings of no avail, called a meeting of their caste-men in Bombay and excommunicated him.[2]

After three years' study at the law schools of the Inner Temple in London, he was admitted to the English bar. Returning to India Mr. Gandhi began the practice of law, and continued his studies in the high court of Bombay. After eighteen months spent in this way, he was retained

1 Pearson, *ibid.*

2 M. K. Gandhi, An Indian Patriot in South America," by Joseph J. Doke, Baptist Minister, Johannesburg. With an Introduction by Lord Ampthill, G. C. S. I., G. C. T. E., etc., etc. First Indian Edition, Madras. 1909. Mr. Doke bases his autobiographical statements upon personal acquaintance with Gandhi.

by an Indian firm with a branch in Pretoria, South Africa, to proceed to that country and undertake the prosecution of an important lawsuit in which a number of Indians were involved. So it came about that Mr. Gandhi began, in 1893, the remarkable experiences which made his own name and that of passive resistance familiar words within the British Empire, almost two decades before those now world-famous events in India for which this South African experience directly prepared him.

His first day in Natal rudely awakened the Indian barrister to a world of color prejudice and racial hostility of which he had scarcely dreamed before. Says his biographer: "He himself was a high-caste Hindu, the child of an ancient and noble race. His father, grandfather, and uncle had been Prime Ministers of their respective Courts. His childhood and youth had been spent in India, familiar with all the splendour of an Eastern palace. In manhood he had known nothing of colour-prejudice, but had been granted free access to polite English society. Prince Ranjitsinhji was his friend. By profession he was a Barrister, trained in the fine old English Law Schools of the Inner Temple, called to the Bar in London—a cultured gentleman in every sense of the term."[1] Yet on the day following his arrival, as he sat in court wearing his barrister's turban after Eastern fashion as a sign of respect, he was rudely ordered to remove his hat. Shortly afterward, while traveling to Pretoria, he relied upon his sleeping-rugs in place of procuring a "bed-ticket," and was forcibly ejected from the train when he refused, having bought a first-class ticket, to ride in the second-class coach. Upon reaching the Transvaal, and continuing his journey by stage-coach, he again had to suffer for being an Indian.

[1] Doke, *op. cit.;* pp. 35, 36.

He was seated on the box when "the guard, a big Dutchman, wishing to smoke, laid claim to this place, telling the Indian passenger to sit down at his feet. 'No,' said Mr. Gandhi, quietly, 'I shall not do so.' The result was a brutal blow in the face. The victim held on to the rail, when another blow nearly knocked him down."[1] At this point the passengers interfered. But the new-comer had some bitter lessons yet to learn. In Johannesburg he drove to the leading hotel, but found there was "no room" for him. In Pretoria the sentry kicked him off the "footpath" in front of President Kruger's house, while the Natal Law Society crowned the whole series of rebuffs by attempting to exclude him from practice in the supreme court of the colonies, contending that "It was never contemplated that coloured barristers should be placed on the roll." But the court laughed at this silly objection, and he was admitted.

Three years later, in the course of a lecture delivered in Madras on "The Grievances of Indian Settlers in South Africa," Mr. Gandhi characterized these experiences in the following vivid words: ". . . the Indian is the most hated being in South Africa. Every Indian without distinction is contemptuously called a 'coolie.' . . . The railway and tram-officials . . . treat us as beasts. We cannot safely walk on the foot-paths. A Madrassi gentleman, spotlessly dressed, always avoids the foot-paths of prominent streets in Durban for fear he should be insulted or pushed off. We are 'Asian dirt' to be 'heartily cursed,' we are 'chokeful of vice' and we 'live upon rice,' we are 'stinking coolies,' living on 'the smell of an oiled rag,' we are 'the black vermin,' we are described in the Statute Books as 'semi-barbarous Asiatics, or persons belonging to the un-

[1] *Ibid.;* p. 37.

civilized races of Asia.' We 'breed like rabbits' and a gentleman at a meeting lately held in Durban said he 'was sorry we could not be shot like them.'"[1]

It was in such an atmosphere as this that Mr. Gandhi began his historic struggle for the rights of Indians in South Africa. At the close of the year 1893, as he was preparing to leave Natal for India upon the completion of his professional errand, he noticed in a newspaper that the Government was about to introduce a bill to disfranchise his fellow-countrymen in Natal. Perceiving that this would be simply the entering wedge for further disabilities, Mr. Gandhi urged his compatriots to make some concerted effort in defense of their rights. They confessed that they had known nothing about it, and it was evident that in their depressed and inert condition they could do nothing without strong leadership. But they were not only willing but glad to follow one whom they honored and trusted in the highest measure; so when Mr. Gandhi offered to draw up a petition they agreed to obtain the requisite signatures. This was done and the petition was duly presented, although it failed to defeat the measure in the legislature of Natal. But, encouraged by some admissions wrung from its advocates and the interest aroused in the public press, another petition, bearing ten thousand signatures, followed the bill to the imperial colonial secretary and prevented it from receiving the royal sanction. But the victory was only temporary, a substitute measure soon being formed to accomplish the same object by a different road.

Nevertheless, the moral effects of Gandhi's leadership

[1] "Speeches and Writings of M. K. Gandhi," Revised edition, Madras, 1919. The work contains, besides the writings of Gandhi, biographical and historical sketches by his secretary in South Africa, Mr. H. S. L. Polak, and "appreciations" and tributes by eighteen personages of international reputation in England and India.

proved to be of the greatest significance. The submerged manhood of the oppressed Indians was aroused, hope stirred for the first time within them, while the astonishment and concern of the ruling element in the colonies showed that they were aware that a new chapter had opened in South African history.

It was Gandhi's purpose to awaken the latent self-respect and "soul-force" of his fellow-countryman, and he proposed to do it by resisting with all his moral might everything both within and without the Indian community that was contributing to their degradation. This he recognized as more than the task of a day, and he went to work to effect a permanent organization among them. The result was the formation of the Natal Indian Congress, the Natal Indian Educational Association, and similar constructive work.

When the colonies became involved in war, in 1899, Gandhi, who had just returned from India with his wife and children, saw in it an opportunity to refute the charge that the Indian residents were lacking in loyalty and courage, and that they would run away when danger threatened the colony. With much difficulty he obtained permission to organize a volunteer company for any kind of service the Government might think the Indians competent to perform. When the way seemed closed to them it was opened by the dire need of the forces for assistance, and the Indian Ambulance Corps was authorized.

The Indians, on their part, fully justified their leader's faith, and a thousand, both free and indentured, quickly enlisted. We are told that they "entrained amidst scenes of unusual enthusiasm,"[1] and were soon performing their duty with unflinching courage, even under fire, at the front. An European correspondent, writing from the

[1] *Ibid.;* p. 57.

scene at the time, reported, "Their unassuming dauntlessness cost them many lives, and eventually an order was published forbidding them to go into the firing-line."[1]

In this we see still further evidence of the already well-established truth that no necessary connection exists between lack of physical courage and non-violent propensities. And once again it appears that martial courage is social rather than physical, an attitude *inculcated* much more than it is inborn. After the war these non-combatant heroes shared with the soldiers the temporary gratitude of the populace. The prime minister of Natal spoke of "our able and distinguished fellow-citizen, Mr. Gandhi."[2] General Buller had already referred to him as "Assistant Superintendent" in the Medical Department, saying that he meant it as "a title of courtesy." A massive stone monument was erected near Johannesburg, paid for by public subscriptions, to those Indians who died in the great war. Mr. Gandhi received a medal of honor at this time, and, when in 1906 a native rebellion in Natal called forth from him a similar service, every member of his Indian corps was rewarded with a special medal struck for the occasion.[3]

After the war of 1899, Gandhi went to India for another sojourn, and when he returned to Pretoria in 1903 he found a new Administration in power and himself systematically snubbed. This policy went so far as to strike his name from a committee, nominated by his own people upon request of the Municipal Council, for a conference over Indian interests in the community.

As Mr. Gandhi was settling down to the practice of his

1 "Speeches and Writings"; Mr. Polak's sketch, p. vii.

2 *Ibid.;* p. viii.

3 "Speeches and Writings"; Mr. Polak's account.

profession the Transvaal Government suddenly precipitated the struggle anew by promulgating various disabling measures, among which was an order for Indians to register, against immigrants from Asia. It was then that Gandhi began that career of leadership in South Africa, later to be continued in India, which has made his name pre-eminent in the history of non-violent resistance. The "passive resistance" movement, as it was known in British territories, began September 11th, 1906, when he took an oath not to submit to the law, and "by speech, pen, and example, inspired the whole community," says his biographer and former Secretary, "to maintain an adamantine front to the attack that was being made upon the very foundations of its religion, its national honour, its racial self-respect, its manhood."[1]

Mr. Gandhi and many of his followers were jailed for refusing to register under the terms of the obnoxious law, but General Smuts effected a compromise, according to which they agreed to register voluntarily, while he on his part undertook to have the law compelling it repealed. The details of the long struggle, covering the eight years extending from 1906 to 1914, cannot be rehearsed here, but attention must be given to only a few outstanding incidents. Aside from his numerous arrests, and his sojourns in the filthy Colonial jails, Mr. Gandhi made a journey to England and India in the interest of the demand for repeal. At various times "provisional settlements" were made, but the contest was always reopened sooner or later. One of the principal bones of contention was the head-tax of three pounds imposed on every Indian, and which constituted a grievous financial drain upon the slender resources of these humble workers. It

[1] *Ibid.;* p. XIII.

was in connection with this tax that there occurred the now historic "strike" conducted by the Indian laborers under the leadership of Mr. Gandhi.

For some reason General Smuts had not succeeded in redeeming his "promise," as Gandhi regarded it, to repeal the hateful law, despite the fact that the Indians, in their voluntary registering according to agreement, had even submitted to the indignity of having their finger-prints recorded as is done with dangerous criminals.[1]

Among the many picturesque incidents of Gandhi's career that would bear expansion are the launching of his own magazine, *Indian Opinion,* in 1903, as an organ not only of the passive resistance movement as such but as a voice for the Indian awakening in South Africa in the largest sense. Another is the founding of the Indian cooperative, communistic colony at Phœnix farms, in 1904. At every turn in the great contest Gandhi was accorded the most reverent and devoted support of his countrymen in South Africa, except the solitary disaffection of a handful of fanatical enthusiasts, one of whom murderously assaulted him, unresisting and later unretaliating even by law, under the mistaken impression that he was betraying the Indian cause by his concessions in the interest of harmony. Under his leadership in 1906, when the resolution of passive resistance, which would commit all its adherents to jail so long as the law remained unrepealed, was read in a meeting of Indians, "the whole vast audience of three thousand persons rose as one man, and shouted a solemn 'Amen,' when the oath of Passive Resistance was administered."[2] Ninety-five per cent of those at this meeting, and of the Indian community at

[1] Concerning this "promise" see "Speeches and Writings," pp. XIII–XIV, and Doke, op. cit., p. 65.

[2] Polak's account, *ibid.;* p. XXXIV.

large, held firm under the test, some hundreds being consigned to jail, but all presenting such an unyielding front that the Government found it best to offer concessions. They failed to resolve the dispute, however, which continued with such determination that Mr. Gandhi and Mr. Haji Habib were able to declare in a statement issued to the British public at London, in 1909, that "legal equality in respect of the right of entry, even though never a man does enter, is what British Indians have been fighting for, and according to the reports we have received from the Transvaal, is what some of them, at least, will die for."[1]

Perhaps the so-called "Wonderful March" of 1913, is among the most colorful events of Gandhi's picturesque career. It was instigated by the Indian women, whose marriages under Hindu and Mohammedan religious auspices at home had been ruthlessly declared illegal in South Africa. Smarting under a deep sense of undeserved disgrace and righteous indignation, the women picketed the coal mines in nothern Natal, persuading the men to strike until this and other objectionable features of the law should be repealed. The response was immediate and general, and the final result was an army numbering more than three thousand men, women, and children who marched into the Transvaal, determined to proceed until they should be arrested and sent to jail. Mr. Gandhi took command of this blind demonstration, and saved it from disaster by his moral prestige and practical efficiency. It was a passionate protest of moral indignation, though without offer or act of violence, and when the march ended at Charlestown the strikers were satisfied to find themselves under arrest and returned (either to jail or to incarceration in abandoned mines), with

[1] "Speeches and Writings," p. 57.

gladness, under the conviction that their demonstration would result in the appeal of the law sooner or later.

Late in December of the same year, 1913, Mr. Gandhi, in the course of an impassioned speech delivered shortly after his release from prison, advocated a repetition of this method in the following words: "My friends, . . . are you prepared to share the fate of those of our countrymen whom the cold stone is resting upon to-day? Are you prepared to do this (Cries of 'Yes'). Then if the Government does not grant our request this is the proposition I wish to place before you this morning: That all of us on the first day of the New Year should be ready again to suffer battle, again to suffer imprisonment and march out. (Applause.) That is the only process of purification and will be a substantial mourning both inwardly and outwardly which will bear justification before our God. That is the advice we give to our free and indentured countrymen—to strike, even though this may mean death to them, I am sure it will be justified."[1]

The long struggle, which the London "Times" declared, according to Mr. Polak's report, "must live in memory as one of the most remarkable manifestations in history of the spirit of Passive Resistance," was drawing to its close in 1914. Mr. Gandhi, in connection with the discussion in Parliament and elsewhere in England, just prior to the great "March" of 1913, above described, had accepted full responsibility for his advising the Indian community to resist the law. His plan, which he held to be "of educational value, and, in the end to be valuable both to the Indian community and the State," consisted, as he worded it himself, in "actively, persistently, and continuously asking those who are liable to pay the £3 tax to decline to do so and to suffer the penalties for non-

[1] *Ibid.;* p. 67.

payment, and what is more important, in asking those who are now serving indenture and who will, therefore, be liable to pay the £3 tax upon the completion of their indenture, to strike work until the tax is withdrawn."[1]

This, as has been shown, was his plan of procedure at the very opening of 1914, when he proposed the strike of protest for New Year's Day. But the new year opened with a series of conferences with the authorities, a truce was declared, and the principal points in the long dispute were finally settled by the Indian Relief Act, passed in July, 1914, in the Union Houses of Parliament. Two weeks before this date Mr. Gandhi had written a letter to General Smuts in which he said, "The passing of the Indians' Relief Bill and this correspondence (i. e. with General Smuts) finally closed the Passive Resistance struggle which commenced in the September of 1906." He added that some of his countrymen had wished him to go further and resist certain legal disabilities, such as trade licenses, in the different Provinces, but he had counselled them "to exercise patience and by all honourable means at thir disposal educate public opinion so as to enable the Government of the day to go further than the present correspondence does." Finally he expressed the belief that a continuance of the "generous spirit that the Government have applied to the treatment of the problem during the past few months" would make it quite certain that the Indian community would "never be a source of trouble to the Government."[2]

Mr. Polak's contemporaneous account shows the wider Imperial bearings of this struggle, when he mentions, among other incidents, the enormous Indian mass meetings held in Durban, Johannesburg, and other parts of the Union,

[1] *Ibid.*, p. XLVII.
[2] *Ibid.;* p. 72.

the fierce and passionate indignation aroused in India, the large sums of money poured into South Africa from all parts of the Motherland, Lord Hardinge's famous speech at Madras, in which he placed himself at the head of Indian public opinion and his demand for a Commission of Inquiry, the energetic efforts of Lord Ampthill's Committee, the hurried intervention of the Imperial authorities, the appointment over the heads of the Indian community of a Commission whose *personnel* could not satisfy the Indians, the discharge from prison of the leaders whose advice to the Commission was almost universally accepted, the arrival of Messrs. Andrews and Pearson and their wonderful work of reconciliation, the deaths of Harbatsingh and Valiamma, the strained position relieved only by the interruption of the second European strike, when Mr. Gandhi, as on an earlier occasion, undertook not to hamper the Government whilst they had their hands full with the fresh difficulty, and when it had been dealt with, the entirely new spirit of friendliness, trust, and coöperation that was found to have been created by the moderation of the great Indian leader and the loving influence spread around him by Mr. Andrews [a prominent European leader in India] as he proceeded on his great Imperial mission.[1]

And so, to the accompaniment of farewell meetings in South Africa, and welcoming receptions in London and India, Gandhi left the scene of his eight years' experience in the assertion of "soul-force" as non-violent resistance, and returned to his home land, where still greater leadership awaited him, arriving at the very opening of the World War. He was accompanied by Mrs. Gandhi, who had shared, and was destined to share, his struggles and his sufferings.

An adequate array of authenticated facts seems to warrant the conclusion that Gandhi left South Africa victorious, in the sense that he had accomplished his object by

[1] *Ibid.;* p. xvii.

the sole means of non-violent resistance, a method which, as we shall see, formed part and parcel of his deepest religious convictions. Mr. Polak declared that "passive resistance has given for these disfranchised ones far more than the vote could have won, and in a shorter time. But above and beyond all this," he adds, "is the new spirit of conciliation that has resulted from the hardships, the sufferings, the sacrifices of the passive resisters."[1] It was therefore a victory not only without violence, but devoid of bitterness.

We have dwelt upon these events in South Africa, not only because they are important in themselves, but for the further reason that one finds very clearly presented there, in more or less complete form, every element in the famous non-coöperation policy inaugurated and directed by Gandhi upon his return to India. South Africa was his training-ground for perfecting the weapons of non-violence which he has since employed with such astounding boldness and success. To Western readers he seemed to descend full-armed with all the weapons of non-violence from the forehead of some Hindu Jove of pacifistic proclivity, but the student of his earlier career perceives that he is the legitimate child of history and religious philosophy, whether expressed in the ancient life of India or in the particular experiences of his own career. He went to Africa a well-born and highly educated barrister, yet comparatively unknown; he came away after eight years a leader of national importance, and destined to become a world figure of historic significance. Moreover, Gandhi returned from South Africa with a philosophy and a method of procedure both relatively complete. In the preceding narrative this has been kept largely in abeyance in order to

[1] *Ibid.;* p. xliv.

emphasize the outward course of events in an objective way. It is now the intention to notice more carefully this philosophy and method.

GANDHI'S RELIGIOUS PHILOSOPHY

During his student days in London Mr. Gandhi made a careful study of Christianity, as reflected in its living exponents as well as its literature. Along with "quite eighty" other books, he read the Bible from end to end. When he reached the "Sermon on the Mount" he exclaimed, "Surely there is no distinction between Hinduism, as represented in the *Bhagavad Gita,* and this revelation of Christ; both must be from the same source." [1] Many years afterward, in a speech delivered in 1916, he recurs to this thought, saying, "The spirit of the Sermon on the Mount competes almost on equal terms with the Bhagavad-Gita for the domination of my heart." [2] In an interview reported by Doke, Gandhi is even more explicit. "It was the New Testament which really awakened me," he says, "to the rightness and value of Passive Resistance." [3] The same writer declares: "I question whether any system of religion can absolutely hold him. His views are too closely allied to Christianity to be entirely Hindu; and too deeply saturated with Hinduism to be called Christian, while his sympathies are so wide and catholic, that one would imagine he has reached a point where the formulæ of sects are meaningless." [4]

[1] Doke, *op. cit.;* p. 38.

[2] "Speeches and Writings"; p. 243.

[3] Doke, *op. cit.;* p. 38. Gandhi quotes the following lines from the *Gita,* as those which impressed him most deeply when a child at school: "If a man gives you a drink of water and you give him a drink in return, that is nothing. Real beauty consists in doing good against evil." ("Speeches and Writings," p. 129.)

[4] *Ibid.;* p. 93.

Doke's interviews with Gandhi in South Africa led him to the belief that Count Tolstoy had profoundly influenced him, and that Thoreau and Ruskin had helped to form his opinions. He quotes Thoreau's jail utterances in one of his speeches, but it seems that Tolstoy, attracted by Gandhi's noble fight in South Africa, despatched him a personal letter of encouragement in which he said: "Your activity in the Transvaal, as it seems to us at the end of the world, is the most essential work, the most important of all the work now being done in the world, and in which not only the nations of Christians, but of all the world, will undoubtedly take part."[1] This is convincing evidence of a close spiritual kinship, but, according to a writer in the "London Times," in December, 1920, Tolstoy wrote "A Letter to a Hindu" in Russian, under date of December 14, 1908, which was translated in a German periodical at the time. In this letter, as finally rendered into English in the "Times," occur the following remarkable sentences: "Do not fight against evil, but, on the other hand, take no part in it. Refuse all coöperation in the Government administration, in the Law Courts, in the collection of taxes, and, above all, in the Army, and no one in the world will be able to subjugate you." There is no evidence that this is the letter referred to by Mr. Ray, or that Gandhi ever saw it, but it is evident that, assuming its authentic character, the great Russian apostle of non-violence outlined the policy of non-coöperation in astonishing detail ten years before it startled the world in India under that very name, but not before it had been actually begun in practice by Gandhi in South Africa.

The gist of his indebtedness to Christian teaching was apparently summed up by Mr. Gandhi himself when he said that the Sermon on the Mount aroused him and led

[1] Basanta Koomar Ray, in "New York American"; May 8, 1921.

him to recognize more clearly the non-resistance teachings in the Hindu literature, especially the poem known as the "Bhagavad Gita," to which he refers again and again at all the turnings of his career. His philosophical and religious outlook are essentially Oriental in form and substance, although so closely akin to the spirit of Christ's teachings that many Western observers have commented upon the fact. The essentially Indian character of his doctrines will most clearly appear if we allow him to state his principles in his own words.

> By birth I am a Vaishnavite, and was taught *Ahimsa* in my childhood . . . though my views on *Ahimsa* are a result of my study of most of the faiths of the world, they are now no longer dependent upon the authority of these works. . . . Literally speaking, *Ahimsa* means non-killing. But to me it has a world of meaning and takes me into realms much higher, infinitely higher, than the realm to which I would go, if I merely understood by *Ahimsa* non-killing. *Ahimsa* really means that you may not offend anybody. . . . [Nevertheless] It was. . . . most proper for the passive resisters of South Africa to have resisted the evil that the Union Government sought to do to them. They bore no ill-will to it. They showed this by helping the Government whenever it needed their help. *Their resistance consisted of disobedience of the orders of the Government, even to the extent of suffering death at their hands.* *Ahimsa* requires deliberate self-suffering, not a deliberate injuring of the supposed wrong-doer. In its positive form, *Ahimsa* means the largest love, the greatest charity.

We have here combined extracts from an article and an address, both given in 1916.[1] Eight years earlier, in an address delivered before an audience of Europeans at the Germiston (Transvaal) Literary and Debating Society, Mr. Gandhi had explicitly declared that "Passive resis-

[1] "Speeches and Writings"; pp. 251, 287.

tance was a misnomer. . . . The idea was more completely and better expressed by the term 'soul-force.' . . . Active resistance was better expressed by the term 'body force.' Jesus Christ, Daniel and Socrates represented the purest form of passive resistance or soul-force. . . . Tolstoy was the best and brightest (modern) exponent of the doctrine."[1]

In this same South African address Gandhi held also that "no transition was . . . possible from passive resistance to active or physical resistance." At the close of that struggle, in 1914, he wrote that the kind of "passive resistance" used by the Indian community "means truth-force," and he held that it might be used "by individuals as well as by communities," and "as well in political as in domestic affairs." He then enunciates the "immutable maxim that government of the people is possible only so long as they consent either consciously or unconsciously to be governed." In soul-force he saw a power able, if universally adopted, to "revolutionize social ideals and do away with despotisms," but this new kind of revolution operated by suffering the penalties prescribed under the law "long enough to appeal to the sympathetic chord in the governors or the lawmakers."[2]

This soul-force and truth-force, which he later combined in the term *Satyagraha*,[3] contains radical implications of which Mr. Gandhi was clearly aware before he left South Africa. It was during that period that he declared: "I am perfectly aware of the danger to good government, in a country inhabited by many races unequally developed, when an honest citizen advises resistance to a law of the land. But I refuse to believe in the infallibility of legis-

[1] *Ibid.;* p. 132.
[2] *Ibid.;* pp. 154, 155.
[3] June 1917. See *Ibid.;* p. 157.

lators. . . . It is no part of a citizen's duty to pay blind obedience to the laws imposed upon him."[1]

This clearly shows that Gandhi returned to India from his experiences in South Africa with a very definite conception of the ethical foundations and the socio-psychic processes upon which the methods soon to be applied by him really rest. He was well aware that they could be applied effectively in India. He may have held then the intention to use them in part, although events yet to transpire, notably the massacre at Amritsar, were needed to bring him to such a momentous decision. But in any case he did not return in any spirit of disloyalty or defiance, for, as he declared in 1918, at the end of his successful leadership of the laborers in the Kaira district, "A Satyagrahi sometimes appears momentarily to disobey laws and the constituted authority, only to prove in the end his regard for both."[2]

After the occurrence of events in India that made the name of Gandhi one for writers to conjure with, certain correspondents announced the horrifying discovery that the Gandhi revolution was really nothing less at bottom than an impious conspiracy against Western civilization itself! While there is room to differ as to how great a depth of wickedness is involved in such an attitude, particularly on the part of an Oriental patriot, the scandalized reporter was not unsupported by facts if he had only known the history of the man. As far back as the year 1909, Mr. Gandhi, writing to a friend, gave expression to fifteen propositions which are published in his "Speeches and Writings" under the title, "A Confession of Faith." Among other startling assertions he declared that "there is no such thing as Western or European civilization, but

[1] *Ibid.;* pp. 193, 194.
[2] *Ibid.;* p. 188.

there is a modern civilization which is purely material. . . . East and West can only really meet when the West has thrown overboard modern civilization in its entirety." If the general proposition is challenging, the specifications are even more so, for we read that "medical science is the concentrated essence of black magic. Quackery is infinitely preferable to what passes for high medical skill," while "hospitals are the instruments that the Devil has been using for his own purpose, in order to keep his hold on his kingdom." The conclusion is that "India's salvation consists in unlearning what she has learnt during the past fifty years. The railways, telegraphs, hospitals, lawyers, doctors, and such like have to go, and the so-called upper classes have to learn to live consciously and religiously and deliberately the simple peasant life, knowing it to be a life giving true happiness." He then goes on to say, "It is the true spirit of passive resistance that has brought me to the above almost definite conclusions," and he plainly says to his correspondent and friend: "If you agree with me, then it will be your duty to tell the revolutionaries and everybody else that the freedom they want, or they think they want, is not to be obtained by killing people or doing violence, but by setting themselves right and by becoming and remaining truly Indian." The student of his later career will find faithfully applied there the principles here formulated during his South African days.

CHAPTER XX

NON-VIOLENT COERCION AS NON-COÖPERATION

WHEN requested by the Rev. J. J. Doke, in 1906, to send through him as interviewer a message to the young men of India, Gandhi wrote these significant words: "The struggle in the Transvaal is not without its interest for India. . . . Passive Resistance . . . may be a slow remedy, but I regard it as an absolutely sure remedy, not only for our ills in the Transvaal, but for all the political and other troubles from which our people suffer in India."[1] Again, writing for the "Indian Review" in 1909, he suggests that "for the many ills we suffer from in India, passive resistance is an infallible panacea." These words have since proved to be prophetic. In the same connection it is interesting to note that Sir Walter Strickland, Baronet, in a printed address to the people of England and India, in 1913, suggested that an excellent measure "would be as far as possible to boycott English justice by forming interracial arbitration committees and settling your disputes as much as possible out of court." The non-coöperation movement was therefore not without its very definite presages when Gandhi took ship for his native land late in 1914.

Accompanied by Mrs. Gandhi, he arrived in Bombay on January 9, 1915. They were welcomed with a great public reception, presided over by Sir Pherozshah Mehta. In replying to the toast in his honor Mr. Gandhi remarked

[1] *Op. cit.;* p. 93.

"they had also honoured Mrs. Gandhi as the wife of the great Gandhi. He had no knowledge of the great Gandhi but he could say that she could tell them more about the sufferings of women who rushed with babies to the jail and who had now joined the majority, than he could." "In conclusion," runs the report, "Mr. Gandhi appealed to them to accept the services of himself and his wife for, he said, they had come to render such service as God would enable them to do. . . ."[1] At a similar meeting of welcome in Madras he dwelt, with the consummately persuasive skill which marks all his speaking and writing, upon the heroic spirit shown by their humble fellow-countrymen in South Africa. At the same time he stressed the harmonious union of the various Indian religionists, who realized in South Africa "what their destiny was as Indians."

In all this it is apparent that Gandhi reëntered the life of India as a marked man, toward whom the masses of his countrymen looked with admiring expectation. If the Government felt some uneasiness, this did not prevent the king-emperor from bestowing upon him, among the recipients of the New Year's honors of 1915, the Kaisar-i-Hind Gold Medal, in recognition of his unique services in South Africa. However, his beloved statesman-friend, Mr. G. K. Gokhale, took it upon himself to prevent a too precipitate entrance into political affairs at that critical period in the life of the nation. Fearing that Gandhi's long absence might have led him to idealize certain aspects of Indian life and to lose a clear grasp of reality, he won from Gandhi, whom he hoped to see become his own successor in public leadership, the promise to refrain from any utterance on public affairs until at least a year had passed from his return. This was quite in accord with

[1] "Speeches and Writings"; p. 80m.

the general policy of a leader of Gokhale's balance, since this truly great statesman was accustomed to have his disciples study any subject five years before assuming to instruct the people concerning it. But in the present instance this precaution was partly due to the misgivings aroused in the mind of the practical politician and statesman by the very advanced views on Western civilization which Gandhi had recently set forth in a proscribed pamphlet on "Hind Swaraj."[1]

This promise was faithfully kept by Gandhi, who settled at the capital of his own province of Gujarat, where he founded his *Satyagrahashrama,* a boarding-school where the students were instructed in the usual academic studies and trained to the austerities of a self-supporting, ascetic life, in which the public service without hope of gain was held in view as the life career. It might be called "a school for passive resistance."[2]

It does not appear, however, that Gandhi went into complete retirement during that year of suspended judgment on public affairs. The annual gathering known as the Madras law dinner occurred in April, 1915, and Gandhi was specially invited to propose the toast to the British Empire, which he consented to do. The toast-master, no less important a personage than the Hon. Mr. Corbet, advocate-general, introduced Mr. Gandhi as "a very distinguished stranger, a stranger in the sense that they had not known him long, but one whose name they were all familiar with." Mr. Gandhi, he remarked, was a member of their own profession, who "had laboured strenuously, with absolute devotion for many years," for the consolidation of the British Empire, whose toast he had been

[1] See "Speeches and Writings," p. xviii.

[2] *Ibid.;* xviii, and 283-296. *Ashrama* he translates as "institution." Hence *Satyagraha* (passive resistance) *Ashrama* (institution).

asked to propose. In his brief remarks, Gandhi referred to himself as "a determined opponent of modern civilization and an avowed patriot," a combination whose consistency had been often questioned. He therefore found it "the greatest pleasure . . . to re-declare my loyalty to this British Empire." This loyalty, he confessed, was based upon selfish grounds, namely that a passive resister could find the freest scope for his conscience under that Government, which was one of the very best just because it governed least. "Hence my loyalty to the British Empire," he concluded amid loud applause.[1]

The story of the Indian revolution is a long and complicated one. At the time of which we are speaking the movement for self-rule, *Swaraj,* was about thirty years old. The Indian National Congress, an unofficial deliberative gathering, was of some years' standing, and Mrs. Besant was just about to launch the Home Rule League, after the plan had been rejected by the National Congress of 1915.[2] Moreover, Hindu-Moslem unity was on the near horizon, the great Moslem leaders, Mohamet and Shaukat Ali, having been in internment since the opening of the war, the bond of a common hope and suffering thus being provided to bring about that close copartnership which they and Gandhi were destined to share.

As for Gandhi's activities, the reader of his "Speeches" next finds him telling, in May, 1915, of a census of handlooms and weavers which he had recently been taking in the course of his travels. This had to do with the *Swadeshi* movement, already gathering momentum, and having for its object the economic independence of India, especially along the line of the national dress and the related

1 *Ibid.;* pp. 201–202.

2 "Speeches and Writings of Annie Besant," third edition, Madras, September, 1921; pp. 33, 34.

manufacture of cotton materials. This *Swadeshi* movement, started by the Indian National Congress, has been very clearly defined by Gandhi himself, very near the time of which we now speak. In an address before the missionary conference at Madras, in February, 1916, he says: "After much thinking I have arrived at a definition of Swadeshi that perhaps best illustrates my meaning. Swadeshi is that spirit in us which restricts us to the use and service of our immediate surroundings to the exclusion of the more remote. Thus, as for religion, in order to satisfy the requirements of the definition, I must restrict myself to my ancestral religion. That is the use of my immediate religious surrounding. If I find it defective, I should serve it by purging it of its defects. In the domain of politics I should make use of the indigenous institutions and serve them by curing them of their proved defects. In that of economics I should use only things that are produced by my immediate neighbors and serve those industries by making them efficient and complete where they might be found wanting."[1] This makes it very clear that the movement was not conceived negatively as a boycott of foreign goods so much as positively in the form of a revival and promotion of native industries. In a speech of the following year Gandhi referred to this census of his, and declared: "The hand-loom industry is in a dying condition. . . . If we follow the Swadeshi doctrine, it would be your duty and mine to find out neighbors who can supply our wants and to teach them to supply them where they do not know how to proceed. . . . "[2] And this is what was actually done with such vigor that the *charkha,* or spinning-wheel, became the symbol of the whole revolution, being carried in state all bedecked with

[1] "Speeches and Writings"; p. 242.
[2] *Ibid.;* p. 247.

garlands through the thronged streets of Indian cities.[1]

At the close of his year of silence we find Gandhi organizing the ryots of the Kaira district in his own province in a passive resistance movement, i. e., *Satyagraha,* against the payment of taxes which they asserted should have been suspended because of a partial failure of their crops. The struggle continued to 1918, when the passive resisters were released from jail and their contention accepted.

Gandhi's speeches and writings during the years 1917 and 1918 dealt largely with the wrongs suffered by Indians in the colonies of the empire, especially those who went out under the system of indenture. His relations with the Government continued to hold that character of mutual forbearance and respect which had always distinguished them. In September, 1917, he publicly expressed his gratitude to the authorities for their help in his efforts to improve the lot of the weavers. As the World War advanced he was found even actively coöperating with the Government in its effort to mobilize the resources of India. At the Gujarat educational conference, held in October, 1917, he delivered an extended address as president, in the course of which he said: "There is no provision for military training. It is no matter of great grief to me. I have considered it a boon received by chance, but the nation wants to know the use of arms. And those who want to, should have the opportunity." Further on he remarked: "If anything western is worthy of being copied it is certainly the western drill. . . . Nor need it be supposed that drilling is used for military purposes only."

While to some this might look like a compromise of his principles of non-resistance, such an interpretation does not seem to be in accord with the facts. For Gandhi

1 Cf. "Literary Digest"; October 15, 1921.

blends unswerving devotion to basic convictions with surprising freedom in choice of methods. This may admit of a larger self-consistency, since one could hardly expect predictable behavior from such a strange combination of the religious ascetic and the cultivated man of affairs. The careful student of his career, as expressed in action and in his utterances, will probably agree that they indicate a man intent upon the redress of wrongs by the positive assertion of a spirit of resolute good will, called *soul-force* by him, and only incidentally concerned with the literal obedience to any absolute formula, either positive or negative. For himself *Ahimsa,* non-killing, is the one great principle from which there must be no departure, but he neither carries it so far as to make it identical with non-*coercion* nor refuses to make common cause in non-violent ways with men whose code justifies resort to *Himsa* when they face a dilemma in which it seems the lesser of two evils. These remarks are based upon the fact that Gandhi and the "Ali brothers," Moslem adherents of a religion which finds full play for the sword, have worked together with great harmony, and the further fact that he not only acquiesced in military activities during the war but positively advocated the same. His position was stated with the utmost clearness at the Gujarat political conference in November, 1917, over which he presided. In his presidential address Mr. Gandhi said: "A superficial critic . . . is likely to conclude that the views herein expressed are mutually destructive. On the one hand I appeal to the Government to give military training to the people. On the other I put Satyagraha on the pedestal. Surely there can be no room for the use of arms in Satyagraha, nor is there any. But military training is intended for those who do not believe in Satyagraha. That the whole of India will ever accept Satyagraha is beyond my imagination. Not to defend the weak is an entirely effeminate idea, everywhere to be rejected. In order to protect our innocent sister from the brutal designs of a man we ought to offer ourselves a willing sacrifice and by the force of Love conquer the brute in the man. But if we have not attained that power, we would certainly use up all our bodily strength in order to frustrate those designs. The votaries of soul-force and brute-force are both soldiers."[1]

But he was prepared to take even more militaristic ground as the exigencies of the war unfolded. In a letter to the viceroy of India soon after the war conference at Delhi, Mr. Gandhi stated that it was in his desire to "make India offer all her able-bodied sons as a sacrifice to the Empire at its critical moment"; his purpose being to demonstrate India's fitness for full partnership in the empire. In July, 1918, speaking at a meeting of his followers in the district of Kaira, he argued that it "behooves us to learn the use of arms and to acquire the ability to defend ourselves," because "there can be no friendship between the brave and the effeminate. We are regarded as a cowardly people. If we want to become free from that reproach, we should learn the use of arms." At this point he becomes an active recruiting-agent, declaring that "even if the Government desire to obstruct us in enlisting . . . it is incumbent upon us to insist upon joining the army." After explaining the importance of such action for the moral regeneration of the nation, sunk in a sense of its own inferiority, actual or alleged, Gandhi appeals directly to the women in his audience, saying: "To you, my sisters, I request that you will not be startled by this appeal, but will accord it a hearty welcome. It contains the key to your protection and your honor." For just before this he had declared, "to sacrifice sons in the war ought to be

[1] "Speeches and Writings"; p. 364.

a cause not of pain, but of pleasure to brave men. Sacrifice of sons at the crisis will be sacrifice for Swaraja."

But the days of coöperation between Gandhi and the Government were coming near to their end at the very time these utterances were made. In his "Reply to the Commissioners" issued some time before in the Kaira difficulties already referred to, he had declared it "the sacred duty of every loyal citizen to fight unto death against such a spirit of vindictiveness and tyranny" as he believed the commissioner had shown in the taxation dispute. His method of fighting was of course to be that of non-violent resistance, although he was opposed to forcing the use of that method upon others, by even so much coercion as a majority vote adopting it as a program in any assembly or district. At the same time he vigorously protested against the high-handed methods used by Lord Wellingdon as chairman of the war conference held in June, 1918. Gandhi's speech, delivered at a protest meeting in Bombay, was a defense of the Home Rule League, although he confessed himself not a league member, yet a home ruler, like every other patriot in India. This occurred on June 16. The July immediately following found him sounding the first note of non-coöperation. In the course of a speech in the district of Kaira, which seems to have figured as his strategical base, Gandhi complains: "Governments do not give us commissions in the Army; they do not repeal the Arms Act; they do not open schools for military training. How can we then co-operate with them?"[1] Scarcely more than six months after this question was asked he inaugurated the great program of non-coöperation which was to astound the whole world. It came about in consequence of a chain of circumstances of which the following paragraphs present the barest outline.

[1] *Ibid.;* pp. 176, 182, 410.

The general movement for self-rule, *Swaraja,* in India, and its particular expression in the Indian National Congress, an extra-legal, voluntary organization, had been going on, as has been already remarked, for a generation and more. During the World War the magnificent services freely rendered by the princes and people of India brought forth from the press and the statesman of Great Britain expressions indicative of a different attitude toward India and of a more liberal policy in the governance of that dependency. These utterances aroused high hopes among the people of India, and their disappointment was very great when these fair promises tended to fade and be forgotten as the war-clouds passed away. At the same time the policy of the British Government in India began to grow more stringent, partly on account of disturbances in the Punjab, that northwestern region most fully exposed to invasions then threatening from the West, and partly because of some tendencies toward *dacoity*[1] and rioting.

On the other side, the Moslem League, the Home Rule League, and the All-India Congress were actively agitating and organizing, as they long had been doing, for *Swaraja* and *Swadeshi.* But the internment of Mrs. Besant, along with many others of only lesser importance, had greatly strengthened the home rule movement. This, and *Swadeshi,* likewise, was in the vigor of its youth, and Gandhi's movement for passive resistance, or *Satyagraha,* was becoming freely talked about as a movement capable of being expanded into a national program. Such was the situation when the Imperial Government, speaking through the secretary of state for India, declared that responsible government was the goal of British administration in India. It was also announced that the English colonial sec-

1 An Indian word meaning acts of violence by armed bands.

retary, Mr. Montagu, would make a visit to India and conduct a tour of inquiry and consultation.[1]

Mr. Montagu came, the tour was made, and remedial legislation, known as the Montagu-Chelmsford Reforms, was promptly put forward by the Government. The moderate party in India favored these reforms, but they were not satisfactory to the more ardent elements; and when they issued in the form of the Rowlatt Bills a storm of opposition began to break. Mrs. Sarojini Naidu, the eloquent poetess, declared that "the visit of Mr. Montagu to India, his sentimental journey through the length and breadth of the land in the company of Lord Chelmsford, and their expressions of sympathy bore no fruit, for in one hand they held the sword and a cup of poison in the other (Cheers). They seemed to say, 'Here is bread for you, but before you reach out for it you must drink this cup of poison to the dregs.'"[2]

While these bills were under debate in the Imperial Legislative Council, Gandhi had toured the country in opposition to their passage. All the native members of the

[1] *Ibid.;* p. 43.

[2] Naidu, "Speeches and Writings"; pp. 260-262. The following is, in abbreviated form, a digest of an abstract presented by Dr. Sudhindra Bose:

1. The sudden arrest without warrant of any suspected person, detention without trial for an indefinite duration of time.

2. Conduct of proceedings in secret before three judges, who may sit in any place, and who may not make public their proceedings.

3. The accused is kept ignorant of the names of his accusers or witnesses against him.

4-9. No witnesses, counsel, or appeal allowed the accused.

10. Any one associating with ex-political offenders may be arrested.

11. Ex-political offenders must deposit securities.

12. Ex-political offenders may not take part in any political, educational, or religious activities.

(Cf. "Home Rule for India," by Sudhindra Bose, in "The Open Court," August, 1920; p. 459.)

council, to a man, spoke against them, but their protest went unheeded. At this stage, despairing of results from non-official opposition within the council, Gandhi appealed to the people by launching what has since been known as the *Satyagraha* movement, and, still later, as non-coöperation. In a communication to the press on February 28, 1919, Gandhi commended the following "pledge" to the people of India:

Being conscientiously of opinion that the Bills known as the Indian Criminal Law (Amendment) Bill No. 1 of 1919, and the Criminal Law (Emergency Powers) Bill No. 11 of 1919, are unjust, subversive of the principle of liberty and justice, and destructive of the elementary rights of individuals on which the safety of the community as a whole and the State itself is based, we solemnly affirm that in the event of these Bills becoming law and until they are withdrawn, we should refuse civilly to obey these laws and such other laws as a committee to be hereafter appointed may think fit, and further affirm that in this struggle we will faithfully follow truth and refrain from violence to life, person or property.[1]

This is the "civil disobedience" which became a household word at the later stages of the movement. It is explicitly *non*-violent, and implicitly *coercive,* inasmuch as it aimed to cause the Government to withdraw this legislation against its will or judgment. It is, therefore, a clear case of "non-violent coercion," in the meaning of that term as used in this study. The student of Gandhi's earlier career in South Africa and in the Kaira district of India will find nothing new in it. It was, however, a very definite formulation of the principle, which he had already tried and tested, to a new situation of such momentous magnitude as might well have caused a heart less stout to quail. Gandhi, while fearless, is not reckless.

[1] "Speeches and Writings"; p. 419.

He fully understood the significance of the situation. "The step taken," he wrote to the press, "is probably the most momentous in the history of India. I give my assurance that it has not been hastily taken. Personally I have passed many sleepless nights over it. I have endeavored duly to appreciate Government's position, but I have been unable to find any justification for the extraordinary Bills. I have read the Rowlatt Committee's report. I have gone through the narrative with admiration. Its reading has driven me to conclusions just the opposite of the Committee's. I should conclude from the report that secret violence is confined to isolated and very small parts of India, and to a microscopic body of people. . . . They have convinced themselves that the disease is serious enough, and that milder measures have utterly failed. The rest lies in the lap of the gods."[1]

Meanwhile, the adherents of violent methods were making sporadic outbursts in various parts of India, while insurrection by intrigue with hostile powers to the northwest was believed to be brewing, especially among vast millions of Moslems. These were known to be aroused over the humiliation which the war and the treaty were about to heap upon the sultan of Turkey, whom they revered as the khalif, or supreme head, of the Mohammedan world. At this juncture, as is everywhere the case, the advocates of physical force found their opportunity, and, as is so often true, they demonstrated their essential kinship of spirit with their violent opponents by conducting a reign of terror in the name of law and order.

The indignities and punishments inflicted in this endeavor to suppress an essentially spiritual movement, inasmuch as it is profoundly nationalistic in character,

[1] *Ibid.;* pp. 417, 419.

by sheer dependence upon brute force, culminated in the appalling atrocity at Amritsar.

It is no exaggeration to say, with a leading Indian patriot, that General Dyer was being used, though hardly aware of the fact, "as an instrument for burying with full military honours the British Empire *as we have so far known it.*"[1]

That this atrocity sounded the knell of British rule in India seems amply corroborated by the testimony of the Duke of Connaught, who was sent to India, as was the Prince of Wales more recently, for the express purpose of trying to regain, with the pomp of royal processions and related spectacular proceedings, that position of prestige which British power once held in the mind of India. But the duke was frank enough to confess: "Since I landed I have felt around me bitterness and estrangement between those who have been my friends. *The shadow of Amritsar has lengthened over the face of India.*"[2]

Among the millions thus alienated forever from British rule, with all its acknowledged virtues and accomplishments, must be reckoned the central figure in this sketch. We have seen that Gandhi remained a loyal supporter of the empire long after his return to India. The repressive Rowlatt legislation aroused his active opposition, but Amritsar, and kindred doings, completed his defection. In his "Open Letter to Every Englishman in India," published in December, 1920, he said: "So late as last December I pleaded hard for a trustful coöperation. I fully believed that Mr. Lloyd-George would redeem his

1 D. N. Bannerjea in "The Venturer," (London). The present writer received the detached article, "Mr. Gandhi's Policy of Non-Co-operation," from a friend, and is unable to ascertain the date of issue.

2 Quoted by Basanta Koomar Ray, in "New York American"; May 8, 1921. Italics mine.

promise to the Musselmans and that the revelations of the official atrocities in the Punjab would secure full reparation for the Punjabis. But the treachery of Mr. Lloyd-George and its appreciation by you, and the condonation of the Punjab atrocities have completely shattered my faith in the good intentions of the Government and the nation which is supporting it.''[1]

Meanwhile the non-coöperation movement, the strangest revolution in human history, had been launched at a special session of the Indian National Congress, which met in Calcutta in September, 1920. Three months later the program was amended and strengthened in what are known as the Regular Congress Resolution, or the Nagpur Resolutions, of December, 1920. The resolution is based upon the two fundamental propositions, (1) that the British Government in India had forfeited the confidence of the country, and (2) that it should be brought to an end by the non-violent method of simply refusing to coöperate with it longer. The program of non-coöperation was planned to culminate in ''civil disobedience,'' specifically in refusal to pay taxes for governmental support. It was realized, however, that this drastic measure would subject the social order to a terrific and perilous strain. Therefore a more or less extended period of discipline was seen to be necessary by way of preparation for the final stroke.

In the subdivisions of the Resolution, as summarized below, the stages in this movement are clearly perceptible.

It was proposed that, while awaiting the final signal from ''either the Indian National Congress or the All-

[1] In "India, the Organ of the Indian National Congress"; December 10, 1920. A large section of the British Public, and some departments of the Government, did themselves the honor to disavow and condemn the iniquitous outrages of the militarists, but could not secure their official repudiation.

India Congress Committee . . . . effective steps should continue to be taken in that behalf:

(a) by calling upon the parents and guardians of school children, and not the children themselves, under the age of 16 years to make greater efforts for the purpose of withdrawing them from such schools as are owned, aided, or in any way controlled by Government and concurrently to provide for their training in national schools or by such other means as may be within their power in the absence of such schools";

(b) by calling upon students above 16 to withdraw voluntarily from school and either devote themselves to the Non-Coöperation movement or attend national schools;

(c) by calling upon school authorities to aid in nationalizing the schools;

(d) by calling upon lawyers to boycott the courts and favor arbitration of disputes;

(e) by calling upon merchants and traders to sever foreign trade relations by a gradual boycott of foreign goods and the active encouragment of hand-spinning and other native industries;

(f) by calling upon men and women everywhere to organize Committees, upon the village and provincial basis, for the promotion of the movement despite the self-sacrifice required;

(g) by organizing a band of workers to be called the Indian National Service;

(h) by raising the All-India Tilak Memorial Swarajya Fund for financing the whole movement.[1]

[1] The movement was not by any means merely negative, as its critics have asserted. Along educational, as other lines, positive measures were undertaken to offset the negative side of the program. Thus Mr. C. R. Das, of Calcutta, gave his entire fortune to found a National University. The national fund, coming mostly in small subscriptions, had reached three and one-half million dollars in

These Nagpur resolutions, whose adoption by the regular Congress has been reckoned one of Mahatma Gandhi's greatest triumphs, refer to the clear progress of the movement during the three months of its existence and express the confidence thus gained in declaring unequivocably for Swaraj as the goal, which it is proposed to attain, along with the redress of the Khalifat and Punjab wrongs, "within one year."[1]

The scheme of non-coöperation as inaugurated by Gandhi did not include the boycott of foreign goods, but it did emphasize the surrender of titles. The revised resolutions at Nagpur add this special boycott measure, but omit the stress upon relinquishment of titles. Concerning this feature a contributor to the "Democrat" frankly remarked: "With some exceptions, title-holders and placemen are generally possessed of a mentality that cannot comprehend self-sacrifice for a great object. No rousing response was ever expected from their ranks to the Nation's call." But the notable exceptions can be numbered by the hundred at least, and foremost among them, in both time and eminence, stands the famous poet, Rabindra Nath Tagore, who surrendered his title of English knighthood with these noble words: ". . . Knowing that our appeals have been in vain and that the passion of vengeance is blinding the noble vision of statesmanship in our govern-

Bombay alone before midsummer of 1921.—Personal statement of Mr. V. D. Gokhale, a graduate student in the University of Chicago. The writer is also indebted to Mr. T. J. Cornelius, likewise a graduate student in the same university; and especially to Dr. Sudhindra Bose, of the State University of Iowa, whose courtesies have been many and invaluable.

[1] "The Revised Non-Co-Operation Resolution," in *The Democrat*, Jan. 30, 1921. (An Indian newspaper) The actual work of education and organization was carried on by the "National Volunteers," authorized by the Indian National Congress, twenty being elected by the people in each district.

ment which could so easily be magnanimous as befitting its physical strength and moral tradition, the very least that I can do for my country is to take all consequences upon myself in giving voice to the protest of the millions of my countrymen, surprised into a dumb anguish of terror. The time has come when badges of honor make our shame glaring in their incongruous context of humiliation, and I for my part wish to stand, shorn of special distinctions, by the side of those of my countrymen who, for their so-called insignificance, are liable to suffer a degradation not fit for human beings.''[1]

This particular feature of the non-coöperation program is of peculiar interest to the student of social pressure, inasmuch as it was held that this movement among the masses could ''refuse to give any social honour to the title holders . . . [and thereby] reduce absolutely the social value of the Government service.''[2] This indicates a penetrating insight into the psycho-social basis of many institutions, and, along with the refusal to participate in royal processions and other public spectacles, it purposed to lay a very keen ax to the roots of exploitation in some of its most flourishing aspects. The great trouble with this method, however, is that the ax is too heavy for most mortals to wield. Multitudes of men and women are capable of dying nobly for a cause, but very few of them can forbear following the band, or at least from craning their necks at a procession. Nevertheless, this difficult feat of self control was actually performed in India upon an extensive scale, as will appear below, and one reads of the Sikh soldiers returning their war medals in large numbers, as well as of thousands of individuals who re-

[1] Quoted by Bose, *loc. cit.;* p. 463.

[2] "The Bengalee," August 18, 1920, quoting Mr. Bepin Chunder Pal.

linquished their titles.[1] On the other hand, the Madras Government announced in the "Pioneer Mail," in 1920, the statements of certain individuals purporting to show that they had been "compelled" to relinquish their titles by "a process of organized intimidation." There is no doubt a measure of truth in this. If not intimidation it was non-violent *coercion* in part, no doubt. But it was doubtless also, along with the other provisions of the program, "a measure . . . of suffering," voluntarily self-inflicted.[2]

With the adoption of the revised non-coöperation program at Nagpur the battle was on in full force.

It is impossible, within the space of this sketch, even so much as to touch upon the various phases of that great struggle, which, despite the utmost efforts at censorship, has riveted the attention of the world and whose ultimate outcome is even yet undetermined. It will be borne in mind that Gandhi had launched his Satyagraha movement considerably more than a year before the Congress Resolutions of December, 1920, but with that action it became larger than the work of any one man. Opposed by Mrs. Besant and other able and influential patriots, it numbered others equally influential among its supporters. Mr. Achariar, President of the Nagpur Congress, most vehemently opposed the Resolutions, believing that the Non-Coöperation program would plunge the country into chaos. On the other hand, Mohomet Ali contended that the "British Empire was dead and buried," while his brother, Shauket Ali, declared that "the army was ready if any one would lead it." The Non-Coöperators won, as we have seen, and the press despatches of Jan. 1, 1921, announced that

[1] "Westminster Gazette" (London); November 17, 1920. Article by St. Nihal Singh.

[2] "Young India," September 29, 1921.

Gandhi had been given practically dictatorial powers, and that even self-defense had been sanctioned. Whether it went to this length does not appear, but the London "Times" of January 4th, 1921, declared editorially that the Indian National Congress had "now discarded all pretence of being a body based on constitutional principles"; while on January 6, the London "Morning Post," which had condoned and championed "Dyerism," described the Congress session as an orgy of license, threats, and menacing suggestions.

An editorial in the London Daily "Telegraph," Jan. 3, 1921, referred to the Indian National Congress as a gathering of "Indian sedition-mongers," and stated that the delegates were at such odds that they "had it out in the lobby with loaded bamboo sticks." This turmoil may be taken as typical of the situation for all India, for it is evident that subsequent to the Nagpur Congress, if not before, that land has been a seething caldron, the outcome of whose varied agitations no man can foretell. In so far as violence is concerned, we have to note that the Gandhi movement has been haunted at every step by that evil tendency, which has wrecked many a good cause before it. During his earlier *Satyagraha* campaigns which followed his return to India, particularly that of 1919, he had to contend with this folly among his adherents, and had clearly shown his mettle. Thus, in April of that year there was throwing of stones and obstructing of cars in Bombay, whereupon Gandhi protested to his followers, saying, "I . . . suggest that if we cannot conduct this movement without the slightest violence from our side the movement might have to be abandoned. . . . The time may come for me to offer *Satyagraha* against ourselves. . . . As against ourselves. . . . I do not see what penance I can offer excepting that it is for me to fast and if need be by so doing to give up this body and thus prove the truth of *Satyagraha.*''[1]

The disorders continuing, he entered a fast of seventy-two hours, with the warning, ''beware that I may not have to fast myself to death.''[2] A few days later he announced a temporary suspension of the movement, April 18, 1919. In so doing he said: ''I am sorry when I embarked upon a mass movement I underrated the forces of evil and I must now pause and consider how best to meet this situation. . . . I would be untrue to *Satyagraha,* if I allowed it by any action of mine to be used as an occasion for feeding violence, for embittering relations between the English and the Indians. . . . The main and only purpose of this letter is to advise all *Satyagrahis* to temporarily suspend civil disobedience, to give Government effective coöperation in restoring order and by preaching and practice to gain adherence to the fundamental principles mentioned above.''[3]

But since those words the massacre of Amritsar and other unforgettable wrongs had taken place, while his program had been revived and was now no longer his own but that of the Indian National Congress and of the All-India Moslem League as represented in the intrepid ''Ali brothers.'' He was being drawn into the ever-widening currents and cross-currents of a great national uprising, a prophet of non-violence who numbered among his followers not only a multitude who shared from the heart his abhorrence of violence but also a great host who adhered to his program for the time from necessity, but who lacked only the weapons and the occasion to take to deeds of destruc-

[1] "Speeches and Writings," p. 466.
[2] *Ibid.*
[3] *Ibid.;* pp. 470, 471, 474.

tion. His influence seemed nevertheless to grow with the widening circle of his activities. Thus one reads in the periodical, "Hind," for August 22, 1921, this tribute to his personal power: "This frail and solitary figure, travelling bare-footed, with the simplest clothing and way of life, a man who has learnt by suffering to be independent of personal ambition and wholly free from fear, exercises a sway over his people unparalleled in history. He journeys, and at every station the countryside in its thousands waits to see him pass; he addresses a meeting and the place is thronged for hours before his coming; he visits a village, and as he sits cross-legged the people pass before him to gaze on him or touch his garment, or bring their children that he may lay his hand upon them."

In sharpest contrast to this is the cold indifference with which the Duke of Connaught and, later, the Prince of Wales were received upon their ill-timed processions throughout India. Both were decidedly unwelcome on account of the enormous cost of their visitation, and, in the case of the latter, his visit was imposed in face of the protest of every province of India. But such is the weakness of humanity for the trappings of royalty that it was expected that the revolution might in this way be bound with silken fetters and held with gilded chains. But the power of expanded boycott had not been sufficiently appreciated. The gaily caparisoned horses, the magnificently howdahed elephants, and all the rest of that gorgeous paraphernalia which has figured as the resort of class-control in the past, particularly in the Orient, failed dismally to work its magic spell; for the multitudes failed to run out to see it. In other words, they failed to *coöperate.* And what is the use of the most impressive spectacle, when no one is there to be impressed? So we read that "In Madras, when the Duke landed, the British Government built platforms to accommodate 30,000 people, and there were only thirty men to greet the Royal visitor; but in another demonstration in honor of Mahatma Gandhi, the same day, more than 70,000 people took part."[1] And so it was in many of the larger cities, the streets being almost deserted while the duke was passing through. But, on the other hand, we are told: "In Delhi . . . when Gandhi arrived a crowd of 20,000 took possession of the railway station and was permitted by the station officials to superintend the arrival of the train in which the popular leader was traveling. As he drove through the streets of Delhi there were crowds lining every thoroughfare numbering more than 100,000."[2]

As for the visit of the Prince of Wales, conflicting reports concerning his reception have been given. In November, 1921, despatches told of rioting in Bombay, on the occasion of the prince's visit. The account exonerated the non-coöperationists but accused a Parsee faction. Another correspondent blamed the "hooligan" element hanging on to the skirts of the Gandhi movement, but joined in the charge against the Parsees. At the same time he reported the streets deserted, the city in mourning, and the reception ruined. A few days later Calcutta was reported as the scene of disorder, with the authorities accusing the non-coöperationists, while the prince was described as mingling freely with the crowds! On the whole the fact last named is the most significant of all, and warrants the assertion that the safety of the prince on this ill-timed expedition was assured only by the fact that the millions of Indian people really are, as their leaders have declared, among the "gentlest" races on earth. On the other hand,

[1] Basanta Koomar Ray, in "New York American"; May 8, 1921.

[2] W. W. Pearson, in magazine section, "New York Call"; September 18, 1921.

the authorities are within the truth in blaming the non-coöperators if they mean that the frigid reception accorded the prince is the result of their non-violent activities. In fact, their intentions were not only announced but blazoned in huge posters and newspaper broadsides.[1]

It will be recalled that the Non-coöperation Resolutions promised *Swaraj* within one year. But as the tumult tended to increase with the passing months of 1921, it became necessary, time and again, to postpone the most drastic measure, namely civil disobedience or refusal to pay taxes or remain in the government service, in which it was planned to culminate.

After his break with the Government Gandhi made no concealment of his desire to paralyze it in order to wring from it the justice his people demand. He is quoted as saying frankly, "My speeches are intended to create 'disaffection' as such, that people might consider it a shame to

[1] "The Servant," (a newspaper of Bombay) for November 16, 1921, contained a huge advertisement which ran as follows:

"REMEMBER THE LEADERS IN JAIL
BOYCOTT BUREAUCRATIC WELCOME

"His Royal Highness the Prince of Wales lands in Bombay on the 17th. instant to see, so we have been told, the country and to learn things for himself. The loyal duty of every patriot is to help the Prince to learn the true state of things and this duty he will best discharge by thoroughly boycotting the bureaucratic welcome that is being arranged for the Prince." (After some argumentative references to the khalifat wrong and *Swaraj*, the broadside concludes):

"Listen to what Mahatma Gandhi says,

"1. Organize complete boycott of all functions held in the Prince's honour.

"2. Refuse to illuminate or to send your children to see organised illuminations.

"3. Religiously refrain from attending charities, fetes or fire works organized for the purpose.

"4. Publish leaflets by the million and distribute.

"5. See that your city wears the appearance of a deserted city on the day the Prince visits it."

assist or coöperate with a government that had forfeited all title to respect or support."[1] But there could be no greater mistake than to confuse this with a condonement of violence. In his paper, "Young India," for September 22, 1921, Gandhi answers a set of questions put by some sort of anti-non-coöperation committee in Barisal, and among them is one asking if he approved of the doings of persons who had been perpetrating violence while shouting his name. His answer was: "My 'followers,' I hope, are assimilating the spirit of non-violence. But if it ever comes to pass that *they* under cover of non-violence resort to violence, I hope to find myself the first victim of their violence, but if by a stroke of ill-luck or by my own cowardice I find myself alive, the snow-white Himalayas will claim me as their own." Yet in the same paper only one week later he says, in reply to a warning issued by the governor of Bombay, that his Excellency "must know, that sedition has become the creed of the Congress. Every non-coöperator is pledged to preach disaffection towards the Government established by law. Non-coöperation, though a religious and strictly moral movement, deliberately aims at the overthrow of the Government, and is therefore legally seditious in terms of the Indian Penal Code." Yet, despite these politely defiant words, and many others of similar import, not to mention deeds, Gandhi was not apprehended until late in the spring of 1922, although many others, including Mohomet Ali, had been long before arrested, literally at his side. In the autumn of 1921, the All-India Congress met at Delhi, where Gandhi, according to the despatches to London of November 8, declared it necessary to accelerate the movement by using all the measures in the non-coöperation arsenal. "This," he declared, "embraces the policy of civil disobedience, which means civil revolu-

[1] Pearson, *ibid.*

tion. Whenever it is practised it will end Government authority. It means open defiance of the Government and its laws. I will launch this campaign in my own district, in Gujarat, within the next fortnight. The nation must await the result of this example, which should open the eyes of the whole world."

The congress committee pointed out in a resolution that only a little more than a month then remained of the year within which *Swaraj* had been promised. In view of this and the "exemplary self-restraint" observed by the nation in its adherence to non-violence, the committee then authorized "every province on its own responsibility to undertake civil disobedience, including non-payment of taxes," provided they would observe Hindu-Moslem unity and all the other features of the non-coöperation program. So much for the individual provinces, but, as for the nation as a whole, the decision was that it must await Gandhi's signal.

During the next month, December, the despatches showed the Government taking a firmer stand and arresting greater numbers, with the non-coöperators courting arrest and refusing to provide bond, with the intention, presumably of overtaxing the jails. At the same time Gandhi was reported as having postponed *Swaraj* until January 11, 1922.[1]

The situation was then at the breaking-point, with the police combating with armored cars the threatening mobs, whose rioting soon caused the plan of *mass* civil disobedience to be laid aside by Gandhi for the less inflammatory plan of individual and private disobedience. The order was given that non-coöperators were "not to disobey in public, for a crowd might gather and violence ensue."

[1] Correspondence from India of Thomas F. Ryan, in "Chicago Tribune"; December 4 and 12, 1921.

Gandhi's forebodings, hinted at in his speech at Delhi, seemed to be growing as the disorder increased, and so he was no doubt very willing to attend a conference of representatives of all shades of opinion which met at Bombay early in January, 1922. There he said, speaking merely as an informal participant, that he was prepared to persuade his adherents to abstain from hostile activities, provided all political prisoners were released and the round-table conferences came into existence before January 31; with the reservation that the enlistment of volunteers and preparations for civil disobedience should meanwhile continue. And so it came about that at a meeting of the working committee of the All-India Congress on January 19, 1922, with Gandhi presiding, a resolution was adopted postponing civil disobedience until January 31, or pending the final result of the negotiations at the round-table conference then in progress between leaders of all parties as mentioned above.[1]

During an interview with an American correspondent, in February 1922,[1] Mr Gandhi admitted that mass civil disobedience had been abandoned on the very eve of its promised inauguration, because "the country was not ready." "The principles of non-violence," he explained, "had not yet made themselves felt." But he declared it merely a postponement, adding, "We will continue individual disobedience and boycott."

It was only a few days later that the India office in London announced through the press that Gandhi had finally been arrested. This took place near Ahmedabad, at his religious and political institute, described above.

[1] Bombay dispatches to "Chicago Tribune"; January 16 and 19, 1922.

[2] Mr. John Clayton, in the *Chicago Tribune*, Mar. 1st, 1922.

On his way to jail he exhorted his pupils and followers to "work hard, tire not," and to *suffer* steadfastly *without violence.* Along with a leading Nationalist arrested with him, he refused to offer any defense, and was promptly sentenced to six years' imprisonment, *without* hard labor. About the same time it was reported that the leadership of the movement had passed to a Mohammedan, Abdul Kalam Azan.

At the time of this writing, although Mr. Gandhi has begun his prison term, and thousands of his followers are flocking into the jails, it is impossible to estimate the ultimate outcome of non-coöperation, but we may say, entirely without regard to its ultimate fortunes, that we have here presented the most extraordinary manifestation of passive resistance and non-violent coercion in the history of the world. It is worth while to observe that, until these very recent movements in China, Korea, and India began, one had to say that the teachings of those lands on this subject had been entirely negative and individualistic, with no visible tendency toward those organized forms of mass movement which had given them an important place in the moral and social history of the West. But all this is reversed by non-coöperation, whose momentous importance is due primarily to the fact that it is preëminently a *mass* movement, by means of which, through a strange arithmetic, the socially negative effect of individual non-resistance is multiplied into a tremendously powerful and highly positive social force. If Gandhi had failed to arouse the multitudes in simultaneous, concerted, well-aimed protest, his teaching would have been as barren of social results as we found, in an earlier chapter, that of Buddha himself to be.[1] But Gandhi has ap-

1 See Chap. II, above.

plied the principle on a national and historic scale which will give it permanent significance no matter what the particular outcome may be. And so our story of passive resistance and non-violent coercion fitly ends in the ancient Oriental lands where it began.

CHAPTER XXI

SOCIAL SIGNIFICANCE OF NON-VIOLENT CONDUCT

THERE are obviously two or three possible types of response to the activities of other persons as they impinge upon one's own interests. Aside from those in which one actively coöperates, or maintains an attitude of indifferent neutrality, there arise countless situations in which the choice lies between submission and resistance. The last named is the domain of conduct with which we are here concerned, and it also in turn presents two aspects. The first is the case where the subject resists or repels the aggressions of others; the second is that where he seeks to modify the conduct of others for the purpose of promoting his own ideals. While this often tends to merge into some form of coercion, such is not necessarily the case; since for one who resists or seeks actively to control the conduct of others there are three, and if our analysis is correct, only three, methods of procedure. These are persuasion, non-violent coercion, and violence.

PERSUASION

Persuasion is that form of social action which proceeds by means of *convincing* others of the rightness or expediency of a given course of conduct. It may rely upon *argumentation,* which is the recognized procedure to which the name is commonly applied; or it may seek to convince by *suffering*. Persuasion through suffering presents two types. The first is that so abundantly illustrated in passive resistance of the older, orthodox type. Perhaps nothing has stood out more prominently in our account of the great passive resistants than their stress upon capacity and willingness to suffer. This suffering may be passively endured at the hands of others or self-inflicted, as in the modern instances known as the "hunger-strike." In either case the method is to produce in the mind of the one appealed to, i. e., the subject, a change of mental attitude without the use of coercion. In persuasion of the ordinary type he is convinced by a series of ideas or chain of reasoning. In persuasion by suffering it is done through the sight of distress which a word or simple act of desistance or consent on his own part would avert. When the suffering is self-inflicted for the express purpose of producing such a dilemma in the mind of the subject, as in the hünger-strike, this form of persuasion partakes of the nature of non-violent coercion, as explained below. But in the typical situation, where the suffering, while not self-originated, is passively endured, the subject is persuaded and swerved from his course by a rush of admiration, gratitude, compassion, remorse, or other powerful emotion, while sometimes his hostile and threatening attitude is suddenly changed into one of active benevolence. All this has been concretely illustrated and fully explained in our earlier chapters, and the purpose here is simply to bring it under its proper category as essentially a form of persuasion. In a recent sociological treatise the psyschology of such situations is clearly formulated as follows: "A significant feature of sentiments and attitudes is inner tension and consequent tendency to mutation. Love changes into hate, or dislike is transformed into affection, or humility is replaced by self-assertion. This mutability is explained by the fact . . . that the sentiment-attitude is a complex of wishes and desires organized around a person or object. In this complex one motive—love, for example—is for a moment the dominant component. In this case components which tend to excite repulsion, hostility, and disgust are for the moment suppressed. With a change in the situation . . . these suppressed components are released and, gaining control, convert the system into the opposite sentiment, as hate."[1]

In the situation under discussion here, wherein the aggressor and passive-resistant confront each other, the mental movement is in the opposite direction, i. e., from hate to love; but it will be readily perceived that the process described is the same.

In meeting the opposition of hostile social forces the typical passive resistant has always shown himself strong to *suffer*. Therein are seen his "tokens of power," which have helped the laws of crowd psychology to work oftentimes in his favor. The courage and spectacular sufferings of the unresisting martyr impress tremendously the imagination of the crowd, producing "a startling image that fills and besets the mind."[2] In studying the religious persecutions of earlier passive resistants, the further fact must not be overlooked that the infliction of punishment and martyrdom is made a *public* affair by the persecuting authorities, in the very nature of the case. For they not only seek to impress the public mind but even depend upon the multitude to make the affair a success, although the people sometimes play a disappointing part from the point of view of the party of bigotry. Allard shows[3] how it was the practice during the early Christian persecutions to make of the occasion "a spec-

1 Park and Burgess, "Introduction to the Science of Sociology," Chicago, 1921; p. 442.

2 Le Bon, "The Crowd"; p. 58.

3 In his "Dix Leçons sur le Martyre"; pp. 332, 333.

tacle and fête." The crowd gathered around the scene of torture, he finds, were "not only spectators, they were almost actors: the crowd filled then a rôle analogous to that of the chorus in the ancient tragedy; it was heard loudly expressing its sentiments: many times even, as if unconsciously, it fell to it to distinguish the various moral aspects of the drama which was being played before it."[1] A sort of social dialectic is thus set in motion by these "men of ardent conviction" who have always exercised the power to sway the multitude.[2] The spectacle of such suffering for a cause may lead even the persecutor to reëxamine his own dogmas, if for no other purpose than to revel in their correctness. But reëxamination admits new light, this modifies his view, and often the conquered becomes in the end the conqueror; for so effective is this social *indirection* of the passive resistant in forming public opinion that eventually persuasion may become the wiser policy on the part of government.

As a result of his striking devotion to principle, and his peculiarities, the image of the peace sectarian, as the symbol of a certain moral and social integrity, becomes impressed upon the public mind, figures in literature, art, and even in advertising,[3] and is of value to all concerned. It protects its bearers by capitalizing the past history of the sect for integrity and good will, and it inspires, through imitation, the same qualities in others. Thus, in the end, persecution, as "a short-cut to uniformity,"[4] goes down in defeat before the roundabout moral and social indirection of passive resistance.

It should be understood, however, that this applies only

1 *Ibid.*

2 Le Bon, *op. cit.;* p. 114.

3 For example, the various commercial labels exploiting the picturesque images of the Shaker, Puritan, and Quaker.

4 Cf. Ross, "Social Psychology"; Chap. XVII.

to those few instances where a passively suffering individual or group causes, by such means, an assailant to desist from his purpose, or advances an unpopular social policy toward final acceptance by society. It is to the process operating in such situations only that the term persuasion through suffering is herein applied.

The forms of non-violent coercion described in the later chapters of this book constitute the purest, most typical examples of *indirect* action in the field of social behavior. They are the strike, the boycott, and non-coöperation, which last-named is an extension of both the preceding to non-economic relations. One and the same principle underlies all these various manifestations, and that is a strategic recognition of the fundamental and indispensable importance of *coöperation* in every form and phase of associated life. More vital even than this is its recognition that this coöperation is necessarily more or less *voluntary* in every social situation and process, not excepting the grossest forms of exploitation, oppression, and tyranny. In the last analysis the victims always gild their own chains, even where they do not help to forge them. No people on earth ever yet had the dignity and self-control to refrain from gaping at the triumphal processions of its conquerors, or to refuse to validate the master's aggressions by accepting at his own valuation the titles and honors bestowed by his hand. India has come nearest to attaining this high moral level, but even there it is apparently no more than a passing phase. Nevertheless the method has been utilized to a greater or less degree, as witnessed by the fact that the strike and boycott are quite familiar instruments of coercive social pressure.

In all these cases the procedure consists in the concerted withholding of social contacts or relations residing within the control of the agents. The strike, as every one knows, cuts off the employer-workman relation, while the boycott suspends the contact of buyer and seller. In all such situations the subject against whom pressure is being directed is presented a pair of real alternatives, provided the strike (or boycott) is correctly conceived and opportunely carried out. To take a concrete instance, the employer is given the choice between ceasing to purchase raw materials from non-union sources or to suffer the interruption of the productive operations brought about by the withdrawal of his labor supply. Neither of these alternatives appeals to his desires or his judgment, yet he is compelled by the situation to choose between them. In the example assumed no act or threat of physical force or violence is used against him, on the one hand, nor is he persuaded of the excellence of either alternative, on the other. He is utterly opposed to the idea of ceasing to purchase his materials in the accustomed place, but he looks upon the disruption of his productive operations as scarcely a lesser evil. Whichever he accepts of the alternatives, he remains unconvinced, either by the assent of his judgment to facts and reasons given in argument, or by a reversal of his emotional state, his sentiment-attitude,[1] through the contemplation of suffering passively endured. He is coerced, non-violently coerced it is true, but coerced nevertheless.

For many persons, perhaps to most, the word "coercion" has an ominous and odious sound; and this is especially true of those who might otherwise feel a special interest in non-violent procedure apart from coercion. In fact, we have noticed in earlier pages the argument of those who condemn the *strike* in itself, no matter how just or peaceable, for the simple reason that it is a form of coercion. Moreover, even among those who do not lay so much

[1] Cf. Park and Burgess *op. cit.;* pp. 451–490.

stress upon distinctly pacific and conciliatory conduct, there is a tendency to think of all coercion as necessarily involving the application of physical force. Such is not the correct interpretation, even in the common usage recorded in the dictionary. Thus Webster speaks of coercion as "the application to another of such force, *either physical or moral,* as to induce or constrain him to do against his will something that he would not otherwise have done."[1] This in itself disposes of the notion that the justification of coercion carries with it the indorsement of injurious physical force, but other authority, both lay and clerical, is easy to find. Thus De Maeztu contends: "Coercion . . . is bad when it is used for evil purposes, as . . . to punish thought, to put difficulties in the way of the production of wealth, and to impede the development of human values, either cultural or vital. Coercion is a good thing, on the other hand, when it sacrifices individual apathy on the altar of national defence or the progress of thought, hygiene, morality, or national wealth."[2] A clerical writer likewise maintains that that aspect of a strike which consists in "the enforcing of certain demands is by its very nature morally indifferent."[3]

It is beyond dispute that the most righteous means can be used for the wickedest ends, and evil methods are oftentimes practised that good may come. Nevertheless, there is an intrinsic quality about *methods,* apart from the motives and objects of those who use them, and it renders them unequally desirable in themselves. Accordingly it

[1] Italics mine.

[2] "Authority, Liberty, and Function, in the Light of the War," by Ramiro De Maeztu, London and New York, 1916; p. 113.

[3] "The Morality of the Strike," by the Rev. Donald Alexander McLean, M. A., S. T. L., New York, 1921; p. 44. This work relies mainly on the papal letters on social questions and other Roman Catholic authorities; it contains an introduction by the Rev. John A. Ryan, D. D.

is here maintained that some methods, notably violence, i. e., the use of physical force in private hands for personal ends, are essentially and incurably evil. On the other hand, persuasion is essentially good, or at worst non-injurious, in itself. Government, in the political sense, is a combination of both the preceding, and tends toward good or bad according to the relative emphasis placed upon persuasion or violence. Non-violent coercion presents a less simple problem, since it combines the inherent excellence of non-violence with the more questionable element of coercion, so that it, more than any of the other methods named, is good or bad according to the object sought and the spirit in which it is pursued. This makes it of first importance to understand clearly the essential spirit of passive, or non-violent, resistance.

Willingness to suffer is inseparable from all passive resistance of the purest type; and a measure of the same fortitude and self-control must be at their command who would successfully wield the related methods of non-violent coercion. It is eminently right that this should be so, for thus only can the interests of society be secured. True non-violent coercion is, and ought to be, a two-edged sword. In other words, it causes, and it is well that it should cause, inconvenience and suffering to those who wield it, as well as to those against whom it is invoked. In this it is exactly contrary to violent methods; for a principal reason accounting for the appalling growth of terrorism in modern times is the unfortunate fact that the development of firearms and high explosives carries no automatic check and penalty for all who use them, as in the case before us. As for the methods of non-violent coercion, particularly the strike and the boycott, the public usually stands more or less in position to determine which way the blow shall fall, that is, which party to the controversy shall suffer the greater loss. It is well that this should be so, for it is not in the interest of the general good that any group of men should exert irresponsible power. So it constitutes a saving virtue of these methods that in the strike or boycott in their pure form, the voluntary moral, financial, and social coöperation of the public is required for success. When violence or intimidation is resorted to on either side, it constitutes a confession of weakness in the party using it, suggesting a lack of confidence in the ability of one's cause to command the necessary support, or a greater willingness to inflict than to endure pain and loss. For these reasons, we hold that there is a most vital, salutary, and socially necessary connection between the open, truthful, self-denying spirit of passive resistance and the *constructive* use of non-violent coercion in any of its forms. This fairness and willingness to face the consequences are characteristic of passive resistance, whether its opponent be private parties or the state itself.[1]

The unflinching willingness of the passive resistant to bear his just punishment for refusing to obey the commands of the law has been frequently alluded to in earlier chapters. It is safe to say that no true non-violent resistant ever entered into a combination to evade the consequences of civil disobedience, as in certain *clubs for fine paying* reported in an English legal journal.[2] For, as

1 The position taken by the principal actor in the now famous Debs Case was distinctly that of a true passive, i. e., non-violent and moral, resistance. "I had my own views in regard to the war, and I knew in advance that an expression of what was in my heart would invite a prison sentence under the Espionage Law. I took my stand in accordance with the dictates of my conscience, and was prepared to accept the consequences without complaint." Eugene V. Debs, in "The Century Magazine"; July, 1922.

2 "Clubs for Fine Paying," in "The Justice of the Peace, and County, Borough, Poor Law Union, and Parish Law Recorder," London; Vol. LXXXIV, No. 8, February 21, 1920.

the commentator on this phenomenon points out, "the object of the infliction of fines is to deter persons from breaches of the law which would render them liable to such punishment, so that it necessarily follows that when an offender has no longer to suffer the punishment, because the fine need not be paid by him, the object of the law in decreeing the punishment is frustrated." Such agreements are therefore held by jurists to partake of the nature of a conspiracy to defeat the ends of justice. But we have yet to hear of an instance where non-violent resistants have shown the least disposition toward such a purpose.

The truth is that passive resistance and non-violent coercion are methods of social behavior that possess in theory the most extraordinary claims upon the consideration of all men and women who are actuated by a zeal for truth and social justice, unmixed with the spirit of hatred and reprisal. Indeed, it does not seem too much to affirm that here lies at hand, so far as its *theoretical* merits are concerned, the most just and powerful weapon conceivable in human affairs. If resolutely applied, in a spirit of unswerving fairness, by populations or classes able to control themselves and to pay the price in suffering, non-coöperation seems capable of destroying every last program of tyranny and exploitation in the world. But, while the abstract truth of this can hardly be denied, it is valid largely in theory alone. In actual practice the strike, the boycott, non-coöperation, and every other program of non-violence is dogged by two mortal enemies, to either one or the other of which it is almost sure to fall a prey. That is to say, it either ebbs away through discouragement and apathy, or flares forth into self-destructive violence. And the longer the struggle the more sure is its defeat through the one or the other of these betrayals. In short, non-violent coercion demands a stronger self-control, a more enduring solidarity of purpose, a greater capacity for passive suffering, a higher ethical development, than most human beings have thus far attained. It is capable of great achievements at favorable moments, but its victories must be swift, its campaigns not too long drawn out, and its field of operations more or less restricted. In the strike and the boycott, and all other applications of this principle, an unusually heavy draft is made upon human emotions and sentiments, whether of resentment, moral indignation, group-loyalty, class-consciousness, or devotion to a cause, all of which require a nervous tension greater than that required for the ordinary conduct of life. Non-violence, therefore, whether it takes the form of *persuasion* or *coercion*, seems too idealistic and exacting to accomplish the every-day work of the world. Yet both these methods are of greatest value when kept within the bounds set by the emotional limitations of human nature.

In connection with this tendency to rapid exhaustion on the part of mental exaltation, another practical merit of the *political* method appears. It avoids the overstrain on feeling by combining the advantages of intermittency and permanence. In the periodical excitement of the political campaign, the processes of argumentation and persuasion have free play, and emotional tension rises, with safety, to great heights. This, once registered at the polls, permits the feelings to relax, because they have thereby become more or less permanently embodied as the public will expressed in law or legal procedure, which endure by their own momentum until contrary forces accumulate in sufficient volume for their modification or repeal. Thus the purpose of an hour of high feeling, when expressed through the semi-rational processes of political procedure, may be counted on to operate long after the ebbing away of the emotions that attended its origin.

Because of these facts, among others, it may truly be said that the liberties of a people consist largely in its institutions, or at least in its accumulated culture. Of course no stupid and ignoble population could permanently maintain a high and free institutional life. Mr. Herbert Spencer was most finely right when he said that "there is no political alchemy by which you can get golden conduct out of leaden instincts."[1] Nevertheless, a rich social heritage will carry a people a long way, not only because of initial momentum but also because such structures constitute social forces in themselves. While it is not true in the long run, yet, for the time being, the culture, and particularly the political institutions, of a people may be better than those who created it. This is because it embodies in permanent form the experiences of the better moments of the social life. In fact, many of the permanent treasures of liberty, which seem to endure with the uncreated and impersonal stability of Gibraltar, were really the slogans of some particular, local place and hour. For example, the struggle of the American colonials against Great Britain, was, as an earlier chapter has shown, the protest of a very limited, commercially motived class at first, and it was directed against specific measures of trade which it sought merely to have repealed. Even after it was widened both in scope and purpose the struggle was for a long time very much in the nature of a political family quarrel. Yet in the course of events it was said that "taxation without representation is tyranny," and this has been enshrined in American tradition as a universal principle of freedom which moves on a level above the accidents of time and place. So will it be found with the

[1] "Social Statics and The Man vs. the State;" essay on "The Coming Slavery."

earlier principles, i. e., "bills of rights," upon which this one rested in part; and so will it be found with all that have followed it. Struck off from the fire of conflict, and for partisan purposes, in an hour of high feeling, they embody truths and ideals that come to possess an eternal and universal significance, and are so accepted during the more placid times that succeed their stormy origin. Then, suddenly and unexpectedly, as in England and America under the shadow of the World War, they rise up to hamper and plague those who never suspected that their allegiance to those "sacred and immutable principles of freedom" was a mere lip-service. In such a situation, if those bending all their energies to meet an actual crisis in the world of action can hear this voice of the nation's calmer and better reflections and permit it to rule even the passionate purposes of the moment, the traditions and institutions will act as a balance-wheel, and its liberties will be preserved. We repeat, then, that in this systematic blending of the feeling and the remembering aspects of the social experience, this combination of partisan persuasion and impersonal coercion, lies the strongest claim of the political method.

It is plain that, if persuasion and non-violent coercion must fall short of realizing the largest hopes of aroused and eager social crusaders, it is still more clearly demonstrated that the methods of *violence* offer infinitely less of permanent good. But in the processes of democratic and progressive government, the excellencies of all of these, as has been shown, are blended, along with some of their evils which it may be entirely possible to eliminate. Therefore, in so far as the cause of the masses of disinherited men makes lasting headway, we cannot but believe that it will turn of necessity toward the state as the one supreme adjuster of all conflicting interests, and as the only agency wherein the social gains of to-day may be permanently funded for the needs of to-morrow. For this reason those whose sympathies are with the masses in their struggles will look with approval on their all too feeble endeavors to gain control of government by the methods of public discussion and the ballot-box. This is the fruitful plan of constructive reform, by means of methods which no one can deprecate except selfish foes of democracy and of the general welfare. The proletariat have the numbers, if nothing else, to control the course of political action. All they lack is the political sagacity and the leadership to bring their voting power to bear in concert at the right point, and all things are theirs, within the limits of social possibility. The real trouble in the past has been that they have not enjoyed the support, even within the ranks of labor, of an organized public opinion, which is obviously the condition precedent to all effective legislation or other political action. The present rage for "direct action" by violent means is a misleading and fatal cry. The true direct action would be to get control of the state as the supreme agency of social justice, and the agency which is sure to have the last word in the end, because it represents nothing less than the dominant, effective, public will. If the exploited multitudes, every one armed with his ballot, cannot find the wisdom and the patience to capture the state in times of ordered peace, they will never hold it captive long by violence and disorder.

In magnifying the state as the supreme agency of social self-direction we are in no sense concerned with the advocacy of any abstract theory of sovereignty, or the exaltation of political authority for its own sake. "Sovereignty," as Professor Giddings forcibly phrases it, "is never under any circumstances the absolute power to compel obedience babbled of in political metaphysics. It is finite and conditioned."[1] Our concern lies exclusively in the field of practical expediency and social justice. The state, about which there has been such a vast deal of metaphysical dogmatizing from Hegel to the present hour, is simply a state of the collective mind after all. Just as long as the preponderant opinion within a human population is marked by a unity of purpose which leads its members to pursue a common destiny and to maintain a common system of law and order, just so long does the state endure. When the populace abandons that unified state of mind, rebellion, secession, or simply general disorder ensues, and the state is dead. There is at bottom nothing more mysterious or august about this than the maintenance or dissolution of a debating society, except in respect to the spontaneous growth and imposing magnitude of the *political* organization as compared with all minor groupings.

In holding to this non-occult and thoroughly utilitarian view of the state and politics, the present argument is not impaired by the new conception of political authority advanced by pluralistic thinkers.[2] Social reconstruction through the agency of the truly democratic state offers the one method which does not lure men to grasp more than they can hope to hold; consequently, if they reject political methods in the outset they will inevitably return to them in the end. The truth seems to be that with all its injustices, and they are many, even the finite and imperfect state of the present offers the only way to just and enduring benefits to the masses of mankind; and to men and women with ballots in their hands there is no easier

[1] "Studies in the Theory of Human Society," p. 276, New York, 1922.

[2] "Authority in the Modern State," by Harold J. Laski, 1919; "The New State," by Mary Parker Follett, 1920.

road possible than that of learning to use them unitedly and wisely. When a nation has once reached the stage of constitutional liberty and adult suffrage no short cut to social amelioration, through the exercise of physical force in any form whatsoever, can thenceforth be looked for; since beyond the point where real political freedom is reached the road of social progress lies straight, though long perhaps, through moral territory controlled by the state and the appropriate political procedure. Professor Small puts it well when he says: "The modern state is both a political organization and an economic system, but it is much more. The State is a microcosm of the whole human process. The State is the coöperation of the citizens for the furtherance of all the interests of which they are conscious."[1] A state that is more than this partakes of tyranny, but one that is less paves the way to social confusion and loss. It is only for the permanent and paramount *serviceability* of the state in this *responsive* as well as responsible sense that we conclude in these pages.

Yet it must be confessed that, while we argue in theory for social progress by political methods, we witness too often in practice merely a political gesture; while the dynamic economic and social forces, after more or less of disappointment and delay, continue their immemorial way of cutting directly across lots to the destined goal, but always at the expense of enormous suffering, disorder, and waste. One need not, however, embrace Mr. Herbert Spencer's gospel of social despair,[2] but must at least admit that the ultimate and complete success of the legislative and political method will have to wait upon the social and political enlightenment of the voters, and that methods of non-

[1] "General Sociology," by Albion W. Small; p. 226. Chicago, 1905.

[2] *Op. cit.*, particularly the essays on "The Sins of Legislators" and "The Limits of State Duty."

violent coercion seem capable of really constructive social usefulness in the meantime, if used in that open, truth-asserting spirit of fair play and long-suffering fortitude which we have seen to be the hall-mark of non-violent resistance. Perhaps it is only through a working partnership of such seemingly incongruous forms of behavior as non-violence and coercion that the problems of social collision can be permanently solved. For the solution must be twofold in character, avoiding the devastating furies of violence and terrorism on the one hand, and the stagnant and deadening unanimity sought by insipid sentimentalism upon the other. Sociologists too numerous to mention have expounded the permanent and indispensable significance and value of conflict in social life. No normal human being could endure the horrors of perfect and uninterrupted agreement with all other human beings. So the problem is not how all conflict can be annihiliated, but how it can be divorced from brutality and vindictiveness and raised to higher and higher levels, more worthy of men and women who like to think that they have arrived at mental and moral maturity.

To *social coercion*, therefore, the last words are devoted at the end of this investigation. As used in this study it stands between private coercion on the one hand and public, i. e., governmental or political, coercion on the other. It is called *social* because its enforcing sanctions are neither in the personal use of force nor the appeal to formally constituted political authority resting on force, but to the concerted manipulation of the ordinary social relations of daily life. Its treatment in connection with passive resistance is explained by the fact that the writer, in studying that subject, and perceiving that its essence, socially considered, consists at bottom in the rejection of violent means, was brought to inquire how much room remains for the positive effectuation of social purposes and ideals on the part of those who reject the use of physical force. This led to an examination of the strike, the boycott, and non-coöperation, particularly to an effort to understand their exact mode of operation when disentangled from the violent excesses that all too often accompany them. Analyzed in this way these methods disclosed the fact that their effectiveness when successful is really due to a form of collective pressure which is most accurately designated by the term non-violent, or social, coercion.

Its social importance for the future is hard to estimate. The large place such movements have filled in recent and even current affairs, both national and international, has been amply portrayed in the preceding chapters. In actual operation as described, and also in theory, these methods seem capable of producing powerful effects upon economic and political affairs, without entailing the bitter and irremediable after-effects that spring up in the paths of violence. Yet even non-violent methods are capable of being unjustly wielded, and the reckless use of the strike and the boycott may eventually force society to forbid the appeal to this form of coercion. Moreover, while those who are most keen for the exercise of coercion too often find adherence to *non-violence* an unbearable check upon their actions, the convinced apostles of non-violence, on the contrary, are often equally repelled at the thought of *coercion.* In view of all these paradoxes and uncertainties it would be rash to predict the future importance of those principles, methods, and movements centering upon the repudiation of violence, which it has been the attempt to portray in these pages.

INDEX